What a treasure to see how God has used the talents of His people to express their faith and His glory through music, literature, architecture, and more. I loved seeing threads of God's goodness woven throughout each unique story. Thank you, Terry, for your passion to bring these masterpieces to our attention and into our hearts!

Lysa TerKeurst, *New York Times* bestselling author
and president of Proverbs 31 Ministries

Why should the Creator have stopped speaking through art and music with Giotto or Bach? In this beautifully illustrated and conceived book, Terry Glaspey takes us on a comprehensive tour of art, music, and architecture from the ancient world up to the present.

Michael Card, singer/songwriter and bestselling author

Thousands of Christian books are published every year. In the midst of the steady torrent of clamoring voices, there will inevitably stand above the rest a few that make a unique mark. This is one of these books. My friend Terry has penned a gem here, helping us see and appreciate the voice of God's Spirit in the cultural matrix of the now and the past. *75 Masterpieces Every Christian Should Know* is simply magical. Trust me. This stands way out.

A. J. Swoboda, professor at George Fox Evangelical
Seminary and author of *A Glorious Dark*

Terry Glaspey offers a feast of art, film, music, and literature to satisfy the soul. In *75 Masterpieces Every Christian Should Know* he presents enduring works that brilliantly express the faith, exploring their meaning, technique, and significance. An essential for any Christian, this book beautifully celebrates the creative spirit of Christianity.

Judith Couchman, art historian and author of
The Art of Faith and *The Mystery of the Cross*

As a songwriter, I have found it impossible to separate the most important part of my life—my faith—from my music. Thanks to Terry's new book, I now see that I am in good company. Terry masterfully blends his gift of words with his passion for history and the arts, making it inspiringly clear that so many of the greatest works of art in history indeed do bear the fingerprints of our Creator.

Matthew West, award-winning singer/songwriter

This is more than a collection of art; it is a trove of carefully studied treasures. Terry Glaspey's research and insights combine, much like the art he's studied, to create rich and redemptive readings that both engage and inspire. These pages will cause you to wonder at the creative genius resplendent in the people of God and fill you with the pleasure of His presence as it appears in all things skillfully crafted.

Marty Trammell, Humanities Chair, Corban University

I absolutely love this book! Reading *75 Masterpieces Every Christian Should Know* feels like a walk through an art museum, where you relish each creative piece before you. To discover commonality in the creative works of Dante, Hildegard of Bingen, Albrecht Dürer, Michelangelo, Martin Luther, Frederick Buechner, J. R. R. Tolkien, Emily Dickinson, Bob Dylan, and dozens of other artists, musicians, painters, writers, and scholars from various time periods is to find my heartbeat. Terry doesn't just introduce us to these fascinating, breathtakingly beautiful works of art—some of them familiar and some of them new—but also shares the background of each artist's life, faith, historical timeframe, and how they came to craft their particular work. While experiencing this book, you will, as Buechner's Saint Godric, find "the grace of God smack in the middle of a fallen world."

Cornelia Becker Seigneur, author of *WriterMom Tales*
and founding director of the Faith & Culture Writers Conference

Terry Glaspey seems to know a bit about everything and a lot about the things that matter most. I would read anything he wrote, but this unique volume surpassed my great expectations. If you enjoy pondering the connections between faith, art, culture, and daily discipleship, you will adore this. *75 Masterpieces Every Christian Should Know* is itself a masterpiece.

Who else can tell you about a painting by Caravaggio, a novel by Jane Austen, and a live album by Johnny Cash all in the same book? Thanks be to God for Glaspey's clear faith, informed knowledge, and winsome writing that can help us glean spiritual insight in cultural projects from to Dante to Dylan, from Rembrandt to *The Tree of Life*.

Byron Borger, owner and founder of Hearts and Minds Bookstore

Most writers just set the table, but Terry Glaspey has brought the meal. By curating these great works into one book, Terry offers an artful feast of the ages! Come and partake; you will not leave hungry! He reminds us that we have a magnificent "heritage in the arts of which we can be justifiably proud." May this rich album of our artistic inheritance inspire us as we but "stand on the shoulders" of the giants who have come before. Every artist should read this book. Every Christian should too.

Nicole Johnson, author, dramatist for Women of Faith

In *75 Masterpieces Every Christian Should Know*, Terry Glaspey traces the scarlet thread of Christian thought through the ages, following it through the veins of fine art, music, poetry, and architecture. Expounding upon the historical significance of each masterpiece, and including stunning images, Glaspey opens the vault, showing us the treasures of our Christian artistic heritage. A page-turner from the start, *75 Masterpieces Every Christian Should Know* exposes us to the uncommon beauty birthed by the uncommon men and women of faith. Simply put, Glaspey's work is one of the most informative, enjoyable, and artistically inspirational books I've read in some time.

Seth Haines, author of *Coming Clean*

Terry Glaspey has done us all a great favor with his new book, *75 Masterpieces Every Christian Should Know*. He invites us to become his traveling companions on an adventure through two thousand years of Christian expression. These stories will inspire and expand your appreciation for the beauty, glory, majesty, and mystery of God as expressed through art, literature, music, and film.

Jim Thomas, pastor of The Village Chapel, Nashville, Tennessee

Sitting down with *75 Masterpieces Every Christian Should Know* is like enjoying a great meal at a fine restaurant—it's rich, it's fulfilling, and each new piece is wonderful. There is so much to like I'm not even sure where to start. Terry Glaspey has created a great read, with interesting stories about the best art ever created.

Chip MacGregor, MacGregor Literary Agency

New York Times columnist David Brooks has written that when "you experience great art, you widen your repertoire of emotions." If Brooks is right (and I believe he is), then Terry Glaspey has given us a profound resource for expanding our repertoire through the works he introduces and reflects on wisely, deeply, and artfully in this book. Feast on the sights, sounds, and words covered here as Glaspey does what few could with such elegance: dwell on centuries of art, architecture, poetry, books, music, and film created to the glory of God and in doing so, open a well of appreciation—and emotion—in the hearts and minds of his readers.

Jeff Crosby, editor and compiler, *Days of Grace through the Year*

75 Masterpieces Every Christian Should Know is a spectacular affirmation that yes, we are created in God's image. The very God who created the cosmos has placed within us the desire to create as well—no wonder we are so compelled to paint, to write, to sing! This book is a museum unlike any other—one that explores some of the noblest expressions of human creativity that, in one way or another, point back to the majesty and beauty of God. You'll find yourself enriched as you survey the remarkable variety of ways people who profess faith have reflected God's image in the arts.

Steve Miller, author of *C. H. Spurgeon on Spiritual Leadership*

Writing voluminously through lovingly spare words, Terry Glaspey has done a great service to the church and the world. He reminds us of the loamy richness that is the legacy of those who relentlessly "kick at the darkness till it bleeds daylight." There is so much to be grateful for in this book.

Steve Bell, award-winning singer/songwriter

75 Masterpieces

Every Christian Should Know

75 Masterpieces Every Christian Should Know

THE FASCINATING STORIES BEHIND GREAT WORKS OF ART, LITERATURE, MUSIC, AND FILM

TERRY GLASPEY

Moody Publishers
CHICAGO

Moody Publishers Edition 2021
Previously published by Baker Books

Edited by Mackenzie Conway
Interior Design: Erik M. Peterson
Cover Design: Kaylee Lockenour

Library of Congress Cataloging-in-Publication Data

Names: Glaspey, Terry W., author.
Title: 75 masterpieces every Christian should know : the fascinating stories behind great works of art, literature, music, and film / Terry Glaspey.
Other titles: Seventy-five masterpieces every Christian should know
Description: Chicago : Moody Publishers, 2021. | Includes bibliographical references. | Summary: "Art becomes a masterpiece when it stands the test of time and challenges its viewers to see the world from a new perspective. The vast legacy of human expression is therefore a rich resource of introspection and wisdom for Christians today. 75 Masterpieces Every Christian Should Know anthologizes some of humanity's most influential and renowned works of art. Through engaging these masterpieces, Christians today can enrich their own faith with the creativity of history's brilliant artists. Terry Glaspey masterfully analyzes how each piece responds to the reality of the human condition and Christian truth. Glaspey examines architecture, plays, novels, paintings, films, and even albums, evoking how some probe the dark corners of human suffering, while others capture the mystery, beauty, and wonder of life. This book serves as both historian and biographer, as devotional and art criticism. May this book be a modest doorway into a world of deeper appreciation, a guide to the treasures of our tradition that enriches both your faith and understanding of the human experience"-- Provided by publisher.
Identifiers: LCCN 2020034954 (print) | LCCN 2020034955 (ebook) | ISBN 9780802420879 (paperback) | ISBN 9780802499202 (ebook)
Subjects: LCSH: Christianity and the arts. | Artists--Religious life.
Classification: LCC BR115.A8 G55 2020 (print) | LCC BR115.A8 (ebook) | DDC 261.5/7--dc23
LC record available at https://lccn.loc.gov/2020034954
LC ebook record available at https://lccn.loc.gov/2020034955

Originally delivered by fleets of horse-drawn wagons, the affordable paperbacks from D. L. Moody's publishing house resourced the church and served everyday people. Now, after more than 125 years of publishing and ministry, Moody Publishers' mission remains the same—even if our delivery systems have changed a bit. For more information on other books (and resources) created from a biblical perspective, go to: www.moodypublishers.com or write to:

Moody Publishers
820 N. LaSalle Boulevard
Chicago, IL 60610

1 3 5 7 9 10 8 6 4 2

Printed in the United States of America

For all the creatives
who carry on the tradition
of expressing your faith
with skill, artistic integrity, and a sense of wonder.
You are part of the story this book tells . . .

Contents

Introduction

On a sunny, leaf-strewn fall afternoon a couple of years ago I visited the Philadelphia Museum of Art, which is one of the finest art museums in the United States. I was captivated by their fine array of classic and modern masterpieces, lingered over their wonderful collection of Impressionist paintings, and even paused outside the building for a few minutes at the top of their long flight of steps leading up to the entrance, where Rocky Balboa once stood triumphant in the iconic scene from the movie. I barely managed to restrain myself from raising my hands like the fictional prizefighter had done.

One of the areas of the museum where I spent a little extra time that day was in their impressive American Art galleries. I won't soon forget the experience of entering one of the rooms in that area and finding my eyes immediately drawn to a large and powerful painting depicting Mary's visit from the angel Gabriel in which he announced that she would be the mother of Jesus. I hadn't previously known of this painting, but the warm, bright golden tones, the look of shy astonishment on Mary's face, and the unusually creative way the angel had been rendered all combined to take my breath away. This moment of biblical history portrayed in the painting is commonly known as "the annunciation," and as I bent forward to read the information plaque affixed to the wall nearby I discovered that this was the title of the work, and that its creator was Henry Ossawa Tanner.

When I returned to my hotel room, I searched the internet for information about Tanner and found that he was an African-American painter from the late nineteenth and early twentieth centuries who specialized in paintings of biblical subject matter and was himself a committed Christian. The more I researched, the more fascinated I became by the man and his work, and the more I was inspired by his vision of the biblical stories.

It's my hope that this book can have the same effect on you as that moment of discovery in the museum had on me—of introducing you to some of the great artistic achievements of fellow spiritual seekers, from the very beginnings of the church to our present time. I'd love for you to meet some of these fascinating people and experience some of their work so that you might be inspired, entertained, and challenged by their art, music, writing, and films.

It is not possible to do full justice to the works discussed in this book within the constraints imposed by page count. These short introductions are more like trailers for a movie rather than the movie itself. Think of this book, if you will, as a fistful of invitations—invitations to begin your own personal exploration of art, music, literature, and films that you've never experienced before, or as an opportunity to revisit some old favorites. Let this volume be a departure point for your own journey of exploration.

As a culture, we are often enamored with the latest thing. We "consume" art, music, books, and films and then pass on quickly to whatever is the next big thing, often neglecting the rich heritage of the past. I think this is especially true for Christians; many of us are unaware of how many of the great masterpieces—works universally admired—were created by people who share our faith commitment. We have a heritage in the arts of which we can justifiably be proud.

What this book offers is a selection of seventy-five creative expressions of faith that range across time, genres, and nationalities. This is most emphatically not a list of the absolute best or greatest works, nor does it imply any ranking system. Instead, it attempts to represent the breadth and depth of what Christians have accomplished in the arts, and is an intentionally quirky mix of the widely known and the mostly unknown. I could easily offer an alternative collection of seventy-five works that would be just as valid as these. Frankly, it was a painful process to limit myself to the works represented in these pages. Many of my favorites got left out in my desire to express something of the stylistic variety of creative work done by believers.

My guidelines for the selection of the works featured in this volume were pretty simple: (1) they had to be works that are universally esteemed for their craftsmanship and creativity, not only admired by Christians but also by those outside the faith; (2) they had to be works that stand up well to repeated exposure, the kind of art that can be visited again and again, because there is always something new to discover; (3) they had to be works that speak to people across time, cultures, national boundaries, and denominational divides.

The artists whose works are represented here come from a variety of traditions —Protestant, Catholic, Orthodox, and sometimes a little bit *unorthodox*. They didn't always express their beliefs with carefully constructed theology. They were not trained theologians, but through their works they give us fresh insights into Scripture, key teachings, and experiences of faith.

Though the works of these artists deserve the highest regard, their lives were not always so praiseworthy. As you read their stories you'll discover that many of them lived messy and imperfect lives, and didn't always live out their convictions very well. They were fellow strugglers more than role models, and their honesty about their own personal battles makes them that much more accessible to us today.

These artists were not interested in creating propaganda or some sort of advertisement for Christianity but simply in recording the truth as they saw and felt it. Through the years, though, many people have ultimately found their witness to faith more compelling and convincing than even the best of sermons or theological treatises. Art can reach places in the human heart that reasoned argument can never penetrate.

As you begin to explore these works, you'll find that some are pretty easy to access and immediately enjoyable, while others may take a little more time to reveal themselves, especially when they represent an unfamiliar musical or artistic style. Just because you don't "get it" the first time around doesn't mean there is something deficient in the work or in you. For example, I grew up with virtually no exposure to jazz, and when I first started to explore it, it seemed hard to access. But spending a little time with Miles Davis, John Coltrane, and Charles Mingus taught me to love jazz. All it took was a little patience and some exposure.

On the other hand, if you find that some of the works in this book just don't touch your heart and mind, then don't sweat it. We all have different tastes, and different things appeal to different people. Just make sure you have allowed yourself to be challenged a bit before you move on. Remember, great art is the result of hard work on the part of its creator, and therefore it sometimes demands a bit of work on the part of its audience—deeper and more focused attention than we are often used to giving in this fast-paced world of ours.

Whether you are looking to expose yourself to some of the greatest masterpieces ever created by people of faith or are an artist looking for inspiration and motivation, I hope you'll enjoy seeing your faith, the world around you, and maybe even your own self a bit differently than you did before. May this book be a modest doorway into a world of deeper appreciation, a sort of travel guide to the treasures of our tradition.

Introduction to the Moody Edition

I'm so pleased that Moody Publishers is releasing a new paperback edition of *75 Masterpieces Every Christian Should Know*. It's been encouraging to see the way that the original book has been received. Not only was it chosen as a book of the year by *Christianity Today*, but it was also given a best book award for its category by the Evangelical Christian Publishers Association. These awards are especially meaningful because the competition that year was so worthy.

The book also opened up a lot of doors for me to speak all over the United States and around the world, sharing about what the arts can mean for our faith. I've enjoyed meeting many people whose spiritual lives have been enriched by great works of art, music, literature, and film, and who welcomed learning more about how the arts could assist them in their spiritual formation. This journey of sharing my passion for the connections between faith and the arts has been so fulfilling, and I have learned so much from those who have shared their own insights and journeys with me. We've talked about how the arts can energize one's prayer life, help one become more compassionate and empathetic, and give one more creative ways to talk about their faith. I've become so interested in these issues that my next book will be about how anyone can use the arts to enhance their spiritual formation. The arts can literally be life-changing.

The release of a new edition provides an opportunity to reassess the original. One of the practical criticisms of the earlier volume is that there weren't enough pictures of the artwork and that some of them weren't large enough. Moody has graciously allowed close to twenty additional pages, which permits some expansion in that area. Still, there are practical limitations of space remaining—and not everyone will be satisfied. Some will still wish for more and larger images. For this reason, may I suggest keeping your computer, tablet, or phone handy so that you can not only view the pictures in a larger format, but even zoom in closer to look at the details? Often the delight is found in the details!

A number of readers have shared that they have used the book as part of their daily devotions, reading one chapter a day or one a week. They tell me that they have been fascinated to learn about these creative giants and that their stories and their work have inspired, challenged, and blessed them in unexpected ways. If such is the case, well then, mission accomplished! I hope this will be a book you read with both your heart and mind fully engaged.

As I expressed in the introduction to the earlier version, it was a struggle to decide what to include and what to leave out. While I remain content with the decisions I made, it still pains me to consider how many wonderful pieces were not included that I wish could have been. There are, for example, other paintings by Rembrandt that are equal to *The Return of the Prodigal Son* and other pieces by Bach that are as transcendent as *St. Matthew Passion*.

Even more painful are the artists, musicians, writers, filmmakers, and architects who couldn't be included due to the constraints of creating a book that wouldn't be overwhelming in size. I pause to think of those who I wish could have graced these pages. Painters like Masaccio, Fra Angelico, Tintoretto, Matthias Grünewald, John Constable, and He Qi. Writers like Shakespeare, Thomas Traherne, Mary Oliver, Wendell Berry, François Mauriac, and Shusaku Endo. Musicians like Duke Ellington, Arvo Pärt, Mark Heard, and Tomás Luis de Victoria. And filmmakers like Wim Wenders, Alfred Hitchcock, and Paul Schrader. I hope you will look into some of these further masterpieces. And this just scratches the surface of other creative artists whose works could have been included in this book. Hopefully this present volume will be a jumping-off point for your own exploration of other artists whose faith has enriched and inspired their work in various ways.

There is a lifetime's worth of masterpieces just waiting to be discovered!

Terry Glaspey

1

Paintings in the Roman Catacombs

(paintings, c. 300)

The earliest surviving Christian art is not hanging on the walls of a museum or adorning a cathedral but rather can be found in the labyrinth of tombs underneath the city of Rome. At a time when Christianity was not seen as an acceptable religious option, Christian art went underground. Literally. Beneath the streets of the Roman capital and its suburbs, Christians decorated the tombs of their loved ones with simple paintings of biblical scenes or Christian symbols, there in the dimly lit maze of catacombs.

One of the common images in early Christian art, an image that can frequently be seen in the catacombs as well as in mosaics and in the earliest statuary, is the depiction of Christ as the Good Shepherd. His features bear a strong resemblance to traditional depictions of Apollo in classical art—handsome, strong, and dignified—and He is tending to His flock with gentle care, usually with a lamb draped over His shoulders. It is an image that reminds the viewer of Jesus' love for His people and the protection He offers in a world filled with predators—precisely the message most needed by early Christians suffering from marginalization and persecution. In the days of Christian faith's infancy it could be dangerous to be a believer. And because the image of a shepherd with a flock wasn't a blatantly religious image, it was art that could communicate from one Christian to another without drawing unwanted attention from hostile authorities. It was a sort of coded message of reverence for the Savior based upon Jesus' words from John 10:11,"I am the good shepherd."

Finding a way to memorialize their dead was one of the things that inspired the artists who created most of the earliest surviving Christian art, and much of it can be found in these catacombs. These underground burial sites were composed of a network of narrow interconnected passages with niches where the dead could be laid. Developed in the second century, about

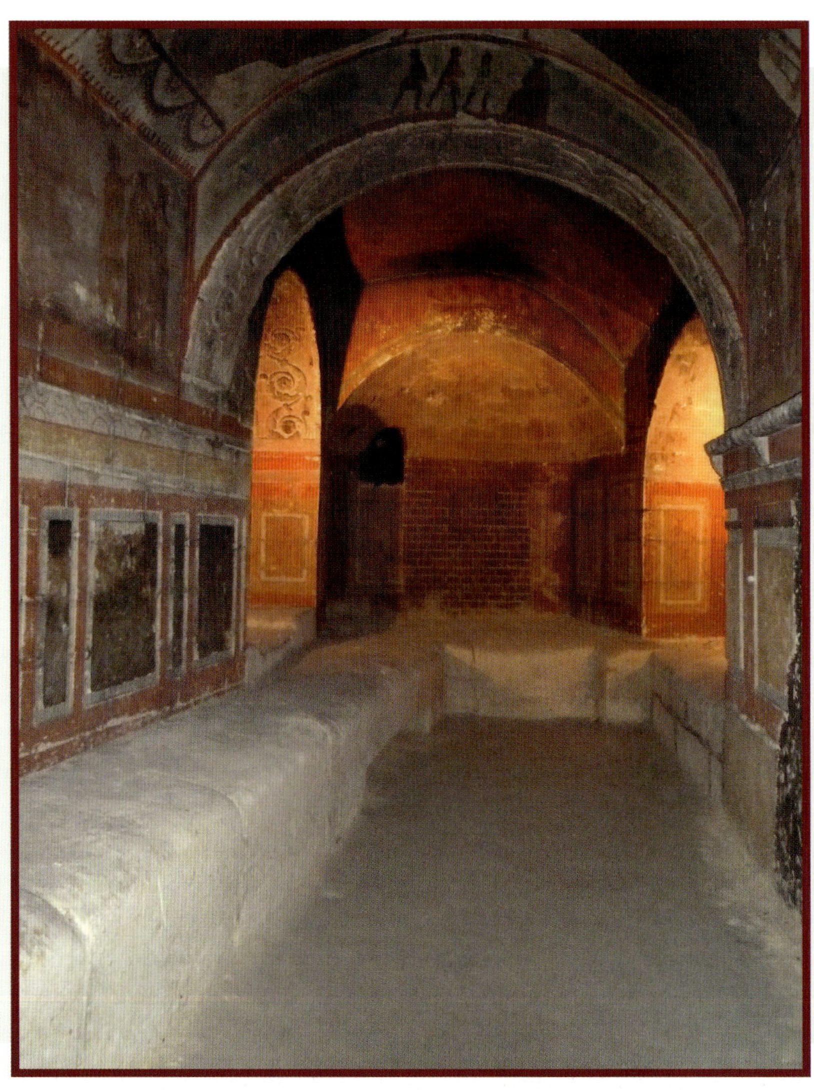

WikiCommons

Roman catacombs, photo by Romaine

the time of the persecution of Christians under the emperor Decius, the catacombs were a common burial ground until the mid-fifth century. There were about 550 miles of catacombs around Rome, and an estimated 4 to 6.5 million people were buried in them. They were a popular option for citizens of Rome who could not afford land in which to bury their dead, as real estate was scarce and expensive in the capital of the Roman Empire. Since the early Christians generally considered cremation to be a pagan practice, burial in the catacombs was a good and reasonably priced alternative. The soft volcanic rock underground was easy to dig and carve but hardened nicely when exposed to air, so these niches in the network of catacombs were an ideal way to lay the bodies of loved ones to rest.

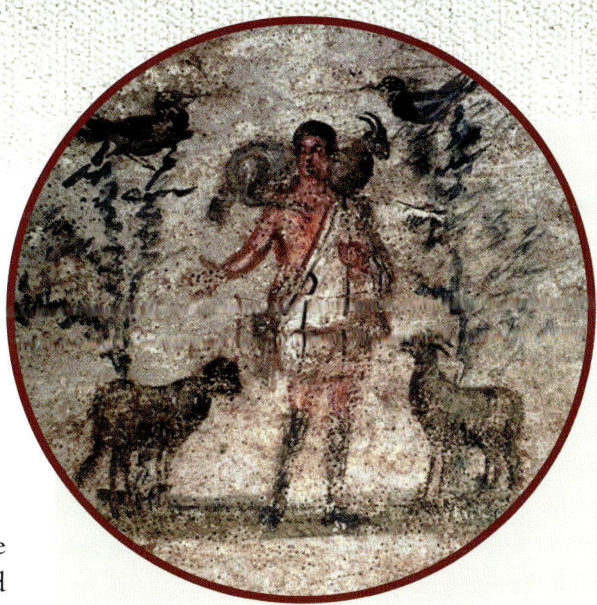

The Good Shepherd, Roman catacombs

Contrary to popular mythology, the catacombs were not generally used either as places to hide from persecution or as places where Christians worshiped. But they were places that were visited with some frequency, where one might celebrate a deceased loved one by having a funerary meal—a kind of "picnic with the dead." And since the early Christians had few other public places to display their art, the catacombs are one of the main places in which it can be found.

The art used to decorate these funereal niches is somewhat crude and naïve in style, pretty much what you would expect from paintings done underground by the light of a torch. We do not know the identity of the artists who created the images for the catacombs or exactly when they were created, but they share a simple beauty and dignity and are the earliest artistic masterpieces of the Christian tradition. Classical Greek and Roman art was their main stylistic source, and the most common subject matter is either stories from the Old Testament or events from the life of Christ.

These early Christian artists drew especially upon the redemptive stories of the Old Testament, stories where God was portrayed as a deliverer, such as the story of Daniel and the lions, the three Hebrew brothers in the fiery furnace, Noah and the ark, or the trials of Jonah (who was considered as a prefiguration of Jesus and His resurrection). Their favorite subjects from the life of Jesus were the miracle stories, especially stories of healing. Interestingly, images of the cross and the crucifixion are very rare in early Christian art, and it seems there was a distinct preference for images and symbols that represented resurrection and immortality—images such as doves, palms, peacocks, the phoenix, and the lamb. Instead of focusing on the sufferings of Christ, as became so common in later Christian art, these early artists seemed more interested in painting pictures that offered hope.

In a time when it was a crime to practice the Christian faith, and where one could be sentenced to death for proclaiming Jesus as Lord instead of Caesar, it should not be surprising that much of this art also shows an interest in venerating the holy martyrs of the faith, those who had surrendered their lives in the cause of Christ. In fact, Christians sometimes jockeyed for a place in the catacombs so they could bury their dead as near as possible to where the martyrs of the faith had been laid.

In ancient Rome, wealthy Christians were fewer in number but they could more easily afford to be buried in the traditional way rather than in the catacombs. They were often laid to rest in a sarcophagus, a stone casket on which decorative art could be carved. One of the most well preserved of the surviving sarcophagi is that of Junius Bassus (c. 350). The front of this sarcophagus is decorated with two rows of sculpted images that are more artistically refined than the paintings in the catacombs. The top level depicts scenes of Abraham, Paul, Christ with Peter and Paul, Christ before Pilate, and Pilate washing his hands of responsibility for Jesus' fate. The bottom level has carvings of Job, Adam and Eve with the serpent wound around the tree of life, Christ's entry into Jerusalem and meeting with Zacchaeus (the wee man in the tree), Daniel flanked by tamed lions, and the apostle Paul being led to his execution. These key biblical stories show both the Old Testament roots of the faith and scenes from Jesus' life. (The scene of Paul's execution is not recorded in Scripture but drawn from extrabiblical studies.)

In the generations that followed, Christian art would begin to become more grand and showy, striving for splendor and a highly aesthetic effect. The earliest Christian art, however, with its greater simplicity and obvious devotion, remains a powerful testimony to the way that art could reflect deep faith and trust in God, even at a time of great persecution. Despite the threat of death, early Christians held fast to a faith in the God who was a deliverer, and who would ultimately snatch them even from the jaws of death. That message echoes out from the Roman catacombs.

2

The Book of Kells

(illuminated manuscript, c. 550)

Christians have long been considered "people of the book" because of the importance they place upon the Bible as the Word of God. In a time when books were rare and very precious, no book was more precious than the Scriptures, and no part of the Scriptures more precious than the Gospels, which tell the story of the One who was Himself the Word. Therefore, it is fitting that one of the most beautiful books ever created was an illuminated copy of the Latin translation of the four gospels, which has come to be known as *The Book of Kells*.

A monastery on a small, lonely island off the western coast of Scotland was the home to a group of monks who created this masterpiece. They were far away from the violence and chaos that spread across Europe in the centuries following the fall of the Roman Empire, and were able to develop the art of copying manuscripts to an unparalleled degree of accuracy. But their peaceful existence on this remote island ended when the Vikings attacked the monastery in 806. Sixty-eight monks were killed, but the rest escaped to the mainland of Ireland, where they established a monastery at Kells, not far from Dublin. It is almost a certainty that they brought the book with them. Hence it has come to be called *The Book of Kells*.

And what a book it is. The monks of Kells adapted Celtic artistic traditions to fit the Christian message. Although we can place no names to the anonymous scribes

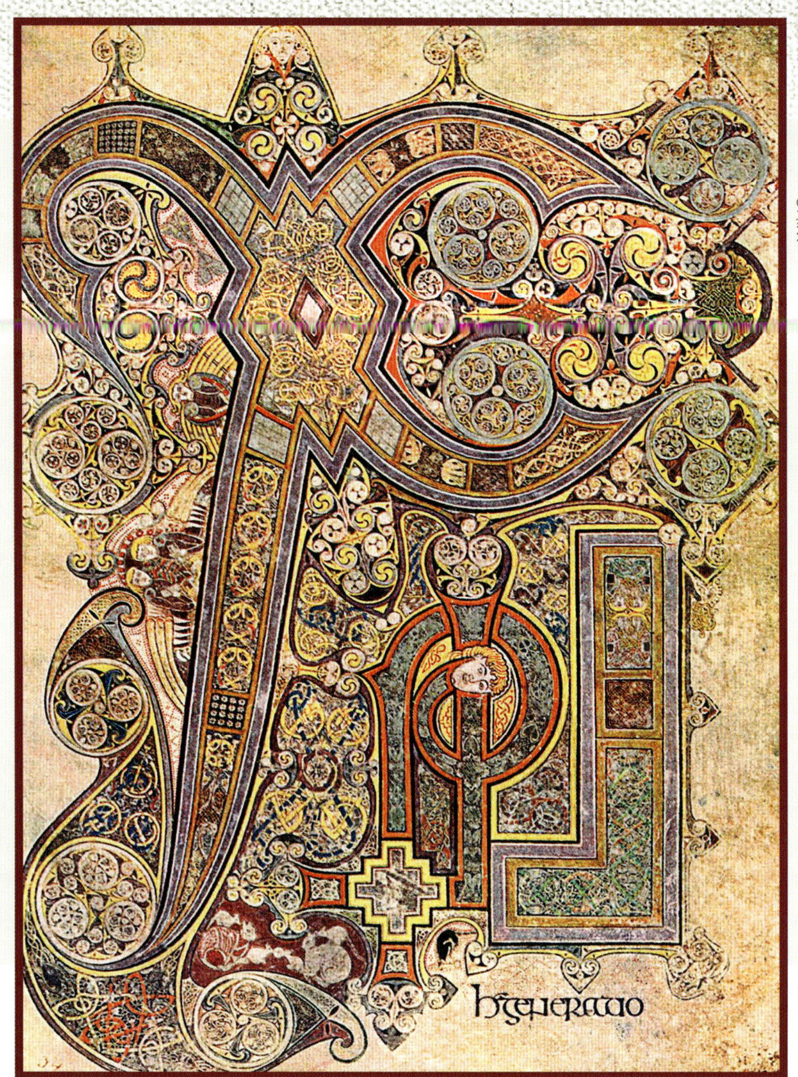

WikiCommons

Chi Ro page from *The Book of Kells*, folio 34r, Trinity College Library, Dublin

who copied out the text and embellished it with imaginative and sometimes playful images, many scholars believe it shows the artistry of at least three distinctive hands. Ultimately, however, it is the product of the entire monastery working together to dry and prepare the animal skins necessary for making the parchment (it is said to have required the skins of 150 calves to provide enough pages for the book), to grind and prepare the colors (the blue, in particular, which is used extravagantly, came from lapis lazuli, a semiprecious stone that in those days was as priceless as gold), to gather and cut and sew the parchments into a codex (book form), and to sit at their desks for hours every day to painstakingly copy and paint and illuminate the manuscript.

The result of their labor is an exuberant work of art—finely detailed, intricate, and imaginative. It evidences a sense of respect for the holiness of the labor of illuminating the Word of God, as well as an undisguised playfulness in creating the interwoven loops and curves and tangled vines and dizzying spirals. Peering out at the reader are a teeming zoological plentitude—birds, snakes, butterflies and moths, cats, dogs, and mice, otters, and many purely fantastical beasts. They share space with portraits of the four gospel writers, tangled and twisted human figures (some likely the images of fellow monks), and angelic beings. It is high and holy art combined with a deep humanity. It contains an abundance of the ornate and beautiful, rich in symbol and meaning, but with little touches that make us smile.

One medieval writer gives witness of how greatly *The Book of Kells* moved him:

> Fine craftsmanship is all about you, but you might not notice it. Look more keenly at it and you will penetrate to the very shrine of art. You will make out intricacies, so delicate and subtle, so exact and compact, so full of knots and links, with colors so fresh and vivid, that you might say that this was the work of an angel, and not of a man. For my part the oftener I see the book, and the more carefully I study it, the more I am lost in ever fresh amazement, and I see more and more wonders in the book.[1]

This quote exemplifies one of the qualities of *The Book of Kells*—it contains layers of detailing that make it unlikely for a viewer to be able to appreciate it all with a single brief look. One can spend hours letting the eyes settle upon a page and explore all the little secrets and mysteries hidden in the beautiful illuminations. It rewards a close look, and it unfolds its beauty, humor, and symbolic profundity slowly to the attentive eye.

Until the fourth century, most writing had been done on scrolls. There were distinct disadvantages to the scroll, however, especially when you wanted to revisit a passage you'd read earlier. You might have to unwind nearly the entire scroll to find what you were looking for. But with the development of the codex, which consisted of individual pages sewn together, we begin to come close to something resembling today's books.

Because of all the effort expended in making a book—the technology to print and reproduce them mechanically didn't exist until around 1450—they were rare and extremely valuable. And monasteries became a place where this work was done. Jakob Louber, a fifteenth-century Carthusian prior, expressed the importance of books: "A monastery without books is like a state without its troops, like a castle without walls, a kitchen without utensils, a table with no dishes upon it, a garden without herbs, a meadow without flowers, a tree without leaves."[2]

Books were viewed as nearly irreplaceable treasures, more valuable than a single human life. In 1237, the library of the monastery of Vorau, in Syria, caught fire. The prior rushed to the library and took his place in the midst of the flames, transporting one book after another to the window, where he tossed them to safety. He kept at the task, rescuing as many books as he could, until he was finally engulfed in flames.

Monasteries were places where these books were stored and copied for posterity in order that the gospel might be spread. Missionary monks would take these books with them when they brought the Christian faith into new lands. Therefore, many early books were small and portable, and often written in miniscule lettering for economic reasons. But the books created for use in worship or at the high altar were another matter. Here no expense was spared. These Scripture portions, prayer books, liturgical aids, and commentaries were turned into works of art. They were also bound in exquisite covers encrusted with jewels and set in gold and silver.

It was not unusual for a monastery to take a year or more to copy out a manuscript of the Bible. It was an arduous task. Sometimes a monk would express his complaints in a personal note appended to the end of a section. One left behind this testament to his frustration: "Thin ink, bad vellum, difficult text. The parchment is hairy. Thank God it will soon be dark."[3] Perhaps a small insight into the human cost involved in creating a beautiful manuscript.

The result of that kind of effort is these luminous pages of text. Our term "illuminated manuscript" comes from the Latin *illūmināre*, "to light up." The effort of these monks truly lit up the pages of the books. Each and every page was an original work of art, created by hand and likely guided by prayer. They copied carefully and added miniature paintings within the text. They sometimes used gold leaf and expensive colors in great profusion. These monks were the first to illustrate the initial letter of the text, on occasion filling a full page with its intricate design. They also created abstract "carpet pages" that look pretty much like they sound—formal repetitive designs of great beauty and detail.

The Book of Kells has its impressive predecessors, among them *The Book of Durrow* and *The Lindisfarne Gospels*, but none can really compare to what the monks created in Kells. Illuminated books are a part of the Christian heritage, and all kinds of such books appeared in the years that followed *The Book of Kells*, including prayer books for the laity (*The Book of Hours*) and breviaries for the clergy, all beautifully adorned with inspiring art. Many times the art overwhelmed the text in these later works, but *The Book of Kells* seems a nearly perfect marriage between text and artistry, and is one of the great masterpieces of the Christian heritage.

3

Gregorian Chant

(choral works, c. 580)

In what can only be described as the most unexpected musical hit in history, a 1993–1994 recording of Gregorian chants by the Spanish Benedictine Monks of Santo Domingo de Silos topped the charts in Europe and the United States. In the United States, the album was number one on the classical music charts but also, more surprisingly, number three on the pop charts. The serene melodic tones of their recording, simply entitled *Chant*, reawakened interest in Gregorian chant and sold millions of copies—over four million units in forty-two countries. It was an overnight hit that was a thousand years in the making! Perhaps it is a sign of our stress-laden modern age that these simple and mysterious musical compositions from the Middle Ages would speak to us in such a fresh way, calling us toward stillness, inner quiet, and peace. They are, in that much-overused term, timeless.

Gregorian chant has demonstrated a peculiar power to help its hearers quiet the mind. The gently rising and falling tones are sung in unison to a simple melody and without any instrumental accompaniment, showcasing the strength of voices joining together in praise. Gregorian chant is spacious, transcendent, and mysterious in its sound, and produces a calming and focusing effect. Perhaps that is why it is even embraced by those who do not readily assent to the truths it proclaims in its biblical texts. It is music that inexplicably arouses spiritual longings, and some have even been set upon the path toward faith by first being drawn to the beauty and mystery of Gregorian chant.

It must always be remembered, though, that however beautiful or relaxing it might be to listen to, Gregorian chant exists for the purpose of proclaiming the sacred texts it illumines. These chants were not created to be artistic masterpieces but rather vehicles for communicating Scripture. The chant is a heightened form of speech, existing in service to the words it expresses. As Bernard of Clairvaux wrote of the ideal chant, "Let it be sweet, but without levity, and whilst it pleases the ear, let it move the heart. . . . It should not contradict the sense of the words, but rather enhance it."[1] Chant gives musical emphasis to each of the words in the text, and expresses their meaning. Those singing must concentrate on every word, and those listening are invited to focus not only on the beauty of what is being sung but also on its message aimed at the heart of the hearer. Through the rising and falling tones, both singer and listener are drawn into prayer, a state of worship, and an experience of the presence of God.

Ultimately, chant is praying with the aid of song. Both singers and listeners are drawn into a unified prayer directed toward God. In its native state in the monasteries, there are no listeners per se, for all are expected to join into these prayers of praise and contemplation. Nor are there soloists in chant, as every singer is an anonymous voice joined together with other voices to create a greater whole. Chant, therefore, requires humility, obedience, and finding one's own small place as part of the choir.

There are fundamentally three different types of chant, each adding a bit more complexity to the structure of the singing. The first is *syllabic*, where there is one note for each syllable. In the *neumatic*, there are groups of notes for each syllable. And in the *melismatic* there can be lengthy passages of music for each syllable, stretching out a word such as "alleluia" by adding drama and flourishes to the singing. But in all cases it is important that the text be clearly understood, no matter how complex the music that carries it.

The origins of chant can be found in the Jewish tradition, where psalms and other Scriptures were chanted aloud, both to emphasize the dignity of the texts and to aid the listener in remembering them. So it was natural that such traditions would carry over into the fledgling Christian movement. In the early churches, lessons were chanted instead of being read so that they could be heard more easily. Otherwise Scripture readings might have been inaudible in larger worship spaces.

As Christianity spread, differing styles of chant began to develop throughout the Christian world. Between the fifth and eighth centuries, chant developed its own regional peculiarities that were characteristic of the musical traditions of the local areas and their own respective pronunciations of the Latin texts. The Roman chant

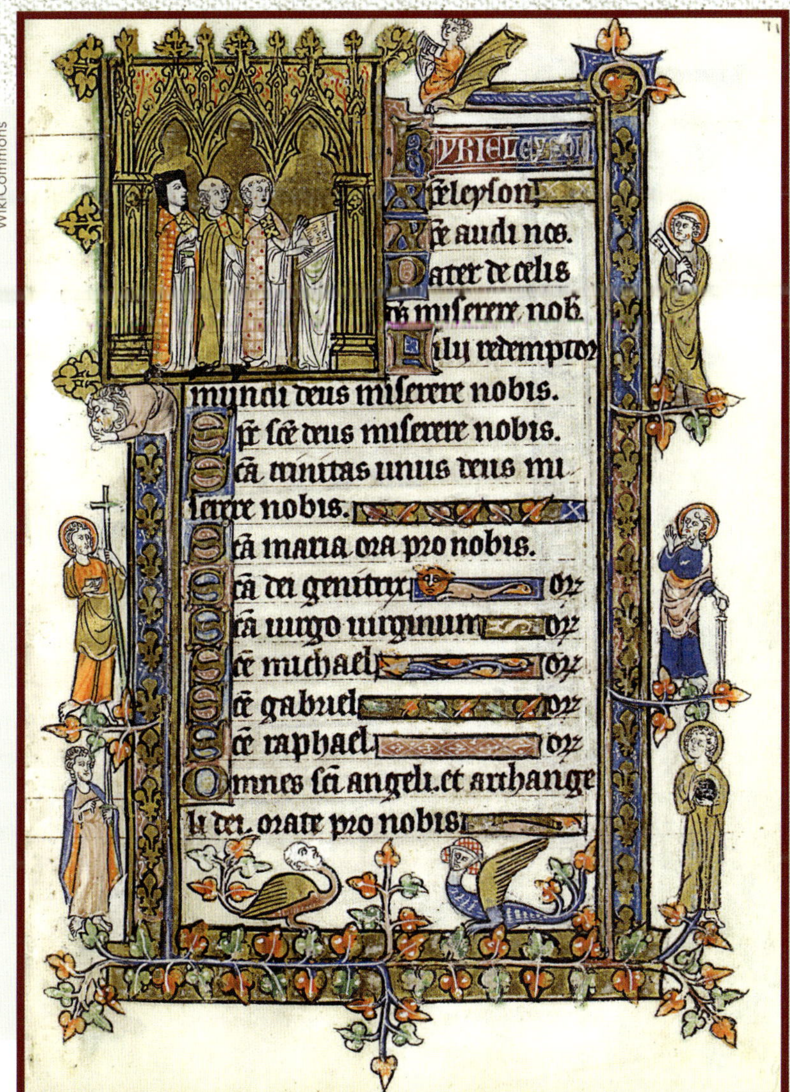

WikiCommons

Three Monks Singing Before a Lectern, c. 1300–25, artist unknown, Walters Art Museum, Baltimore

came to be known as Gregorian chant, named after Pope Gregory the Great, though scholars doubt he actually had any role in the composition of the chants themselves. More likely it is connected with him because he was responsible for important liturgical reforms that had far-reaching influence throughout the medieval church. But legends don't die easily, and during the Middle Ages he was sometimes pictured as receiving chant music directly from the Holy Spirit, who whispered in his ear in the form of a dove perched upon his shoulder. He is famous for calling Gregorian chant "the song of the angels."

When Charlemagne came to power in

the Frankish Empire, he imposed Roman-style Gregorian chant upon the far-flung populations he ruled as part of an attempt to unify the territories over which he held sway. He desired cohesion and stability in his realms, and saw unity in liturgical style as one of the ways to achieve that. He convinced Pope Stephen III to send out cantors to teach the same chants to monasteries throughout his empire. Although other stylistic traditions have lived on, it is Gregorian chant that has remained the standard form. There have been many developments and innovations throughout the centuries, but the basic structure of the chant remains unchanged and continues to be practiced in monasteries throughout the Christian world. Though contemporary chants may be a bit more complex and polyphonic, they are still recognizable to the ear as the kind of singing that has been practiced for so many centuries.

Chant has always been the primary music of the monasteries. When Benedict created his *Rule* for monks, he made the singing of psalms a central part of the life of the monastery. Usually the monks of his order would chant through the entire book of Psalms during the course of every week. Each day was, and still is in most orders, punctuated by voices raised together in unison toward God, speaking His own words back to Him in the form of prayer.

Modern medical experts have done studies on the effect that this ancient form of singing has on the modern listener. They have found it has what they call an *interiorizing* effect. Though it is light and calming, the music of the chant is also passionate and strong. This combination seems to create very positive physiological effects on those who hear it. Dr. Alan Watkins of Imperial College in London has discovered such effects as lowered blood pressure, increased levels of DHEA, and a reduction in anxiety and depression in those who listened to chant. Ruth Stanley, a Benedictine nun who heads up the complementary medicine program at Minnesota's St. Cloud Hospital, has found it useful in easing chronic pain in her patients. Other studies have even suggested that the sound of chant can aid in communication between the right and left hemispheres of the brain by creating new neural pathways.

The gathering of human voices lifted in song toward God, which is the heart of Gregorian chant, is a way of offering praise and worship to God and of contemplating His glory. It is also a sound that is aesthetically beautiful and healing to those who incline their ear toward its soothing cadence. Perhaps that is why the fascination with Gregorian chant continues to this day.

4

Chartres Cathedral

(cathedral, 1134)

One could easily fill a book with seventy-five cathedrals that are worthy of being considered masterpieces of religious architecture. Due to the space limitations of this book, we must limit ourselves to two—Chartres Cathedral, and in a later chapter, La Sagrada Família Cathedral. They will have to suffice as representatives of their respective traditions—one medieval, one modern—each of them awe-inspiring accomplishments of human ingenuity put to the service of honoring God. Both of these cathedrals are immense in size and immense in their emotional impact upon the visitor who encounters them. They are intended to take your breath away, and they do. Mere words cannot really capture their power.

Located about an hour outside Paris, and one of the best preserved examples of early Gothic architecture, Chartres Cathedral is a fitting representative for the entire tradition of Gothic cathedrals. It would certainly be near the top of any list of the greatest and most beautiful cathedrals of the world. Chartres Cathedral had long been a major pilgrimage site and the home to one of the most revered medieval relics: the cloak of the Virgin Mary, which was miraculously preserved when much of the original cathedral was destroyed in a fire in 1134. Most of the earlier building burned and reconstruction was begun almost immediately, this time in the splendid and ornate Gothic style rather than the previous Romanesque.

The reconstructed Chartres is famous

for its use of flying buttresses, which are not only useful—strengthening the structural integrity of the building—but also add to the elegance and style of the building. Chartres is also notable for the grand arrangement of figures representing the Last Judgment that adorns the main portal, and the individual statues of kings and saints (called jamb statues) that decorate the façade. Like the abundant stained glass windows inside, these wonderful sculptures remind us of the heritage of faith.

Chartres Cathedral contains the most extensive collection of stained glass in any cathedral, with 165 windows including three rose windows. One of the most popular windows in Chartres is the Noah window, which beautifully depicts the story of Noah and the ark with delightfully intricate detail. The windows at Chartres not only celebrate the glories of the Christian faith but also commemorate the merchant brotherhoods who donated money for building this spectacular edifice. The careful observer will find small images of wheelwrights, shoemakers, butchers, carpenters, and other skilled laborers pursuing their crafts and trades. It is a good reminder of the unified effort of labor and financing that went into building the cathedral. We will look more closely at the topic of stained glass windows in the next chapter, but surely the main rose window of Chartres is one of the most beautiful of them all, radiating color and harmony as natural light illuminates all the individual sections of colored glass that revolve in various patterns out from the central section, where Christ sits on His throne.

While Chartres Cathedral has many unique characteristics, it also contains many elements that can be seen in every Gothic cathedral. When one experiences the totality of these elements—standing before a cathedral or kneeling inside it—it feels kind of like a miracle, more of a supernatural phenomenon than something manufactured by human hands. But it is a "miracle" with a history.

Early Christians did not have elaborate public places to meet and had to settle for meetings in private homes. In time, as Christianity grew in influence, eventually being embraced as the official state religion of Rome, a need for bigger and more elaborate places to worship developed. The first great church building was the Hagia Sophia in Constantinople, built between 532–537 and constructed around a central dome design. This central dome style of architecture, clearly influenced by the design of the Roman Pantheon, but on a much grander scale, was the chief form of church architecture for the first ten centuries of the church.

The basic style that most commonly comes to mind when people think of a cathedral began at St. Sernin in Toulose, France, about 1080, when a large structure that drew upon the design of Roman public buildings, called basilicas, was designed and built. This early medieval architectural style

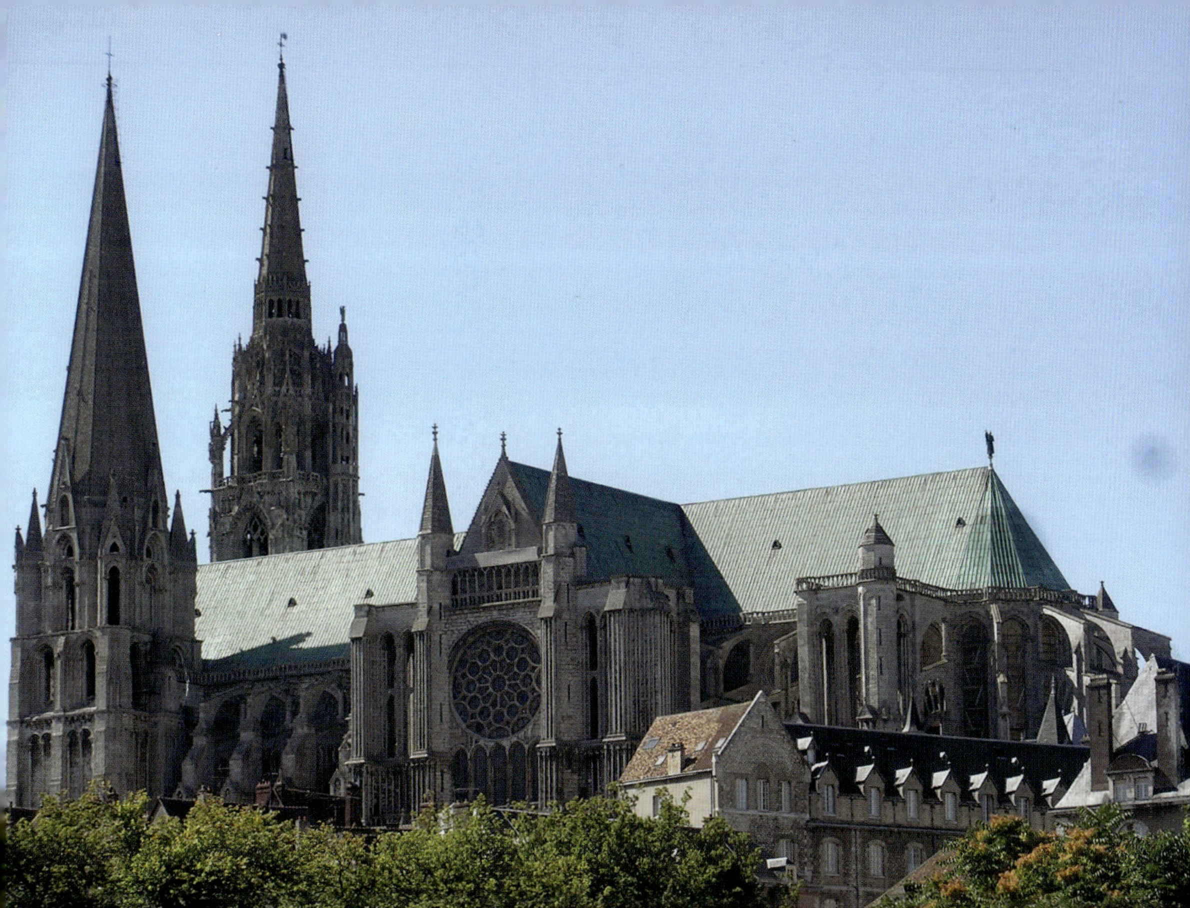

WikiCommons

Exterior of Chartres Cathedral, photographer unknown

has come to be known as Romanesque. It generally features a tower (or towers), a cruciform floor plan (with wings jutting out from both sides in the form of a cross), barrel vaulting, smaller windows, and rounded arches in the windows and interior.

But within a century, the Romanesque had largely been superseded by the Gothic style as the primary architectural style for cathedrals and other religious buildings. When Chartres was reconstructed after the fire, its wooden roof (dangerously susceptible to fire) was replaced with a stone roof. Supporting the greater weight of a stone roof necessitated important innovations, as did the desire for larger and more elaborate windows to let in natural light through stained glass. This led to the invention of flying buttresses, supporting structures attached to the sides of the building that transfer most of the weight of the roof off of the main walls. This allowed for taller, thinner walls and offered the possibility for builders to create structures of dizzying heights. This they did, and at the same time they began to move away from the traditional rounded arches, instead installing elegant pointed arches in the vaulting and windows. These pointed arches helped accentuate the height and openness of the interior of the cathedral, with results that are mesmerizing and breathtaking. Gothic cathedrals are tall and soaring, both inside and out, lifting our eyes and hearts toward heaven. Imagine, in the days before skyscrapers, how dizzyingly tall these buildings must have seemed to those who first saw them.

For a preliterate population, the cathedral was a visual "book" they could read to learn the stories of the Bible and of the saints, as well as the key doctrines of Christianity—a virtual encyclopedia of faith in stone and glass. The cathedrals were decorated with images not only of the supernatural world but also of the natural world, with images illustrating the everyday life of the average person. We see clouds, seas, vines, leaves, trees, insects, birds, sheep, fish, and domestic animals in the windows and statues. We see portraits of people busy at work at their trades, or engaged in some virtue or vice. Alongside these natural images we find portrayals of the biblical miracles, glorious angelic figures, and terrifying demons. And bridging this world and the next are the depictions in glass and stone of departed saints. These blessed dead surround the visitor to a Gothic cathedral. Their figures frame the doorways and radiate from the stained glass, and in many cases their actual bodies lie under the floors and their relics in the altars. In the cathedral their world and ours become one.

Besides its function as an encyclopedia of faith, the cathedral was also a place for communal celebration. Pagan temples had been seen as homes for the gods, and the people would gather around them for worship. The cathedral, on the other hand, was a home for the believing community, a gathering place where people might enter for religious worship, feasts, and even secular gatherings. Often situated on the highest point in town, cathedrals became the central buildings around which everything grew and flourished. They were a communal phenomenon. The process of building them required the efforts of people from every part of the social strata, who joined together to finance the construction, gather the needed materials, and perform the grueling labor required to build them.

Some of the most interesting and unexpected elements of a cathedral are the gargoyles, sculptural embellishments featuring ugly, deformed creatures that combine various natural forms with those of mythical beasts. They are a testament to the strangeness and mystery of life, and also demonstrate the humor, earthiness, and playfulness of the cathedral builders. Plus, they serve a very practical function as well: during a rainstorm they gather the falling precipitation, which gushes from their mouths into the streets below, away from the building.

The Scriptures teach that "God is light" (1 John 1:5); therefore, it is the radiance of light that symbolizes the presence of God in these holy structures. The darkest part of the cathedral is usually the entryway. We stumble out of the darkness of the sinful world with a feeling of disorientation caused by entering the dim interior. But our eyes are drawn toward the light as we make our way into the main part of the edifice. Since the light in a Gothic cathedral comes mostly from its windows, these buildings are characterized by an abundance of windows. In order to have the full experience of any cathedral, it is necessary to visit it at different times of the day, when the play of light creates different effects upon the walls and windows.

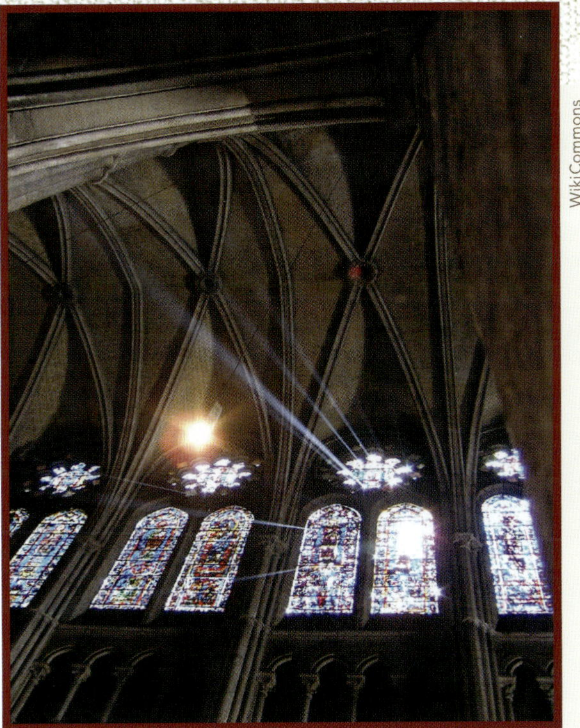

WikiCommons

Interior of Chartres Cathedral, photo by Jörg Bittner Unna

The cathedral was a place of safety and peace in a harsh and dangerous world, a shelter from the storms of life. The central section near the front doors was called the nave, which is probably derived from *navis*, the Latin word for ship or boat. Like a ship, the cathedral is a vessel well suited for taking a voyage—a voyage through the storms to the safe harbor of God's presence.

Above all else, though, the cathedral is a place for worship. It is here that the liturgy is enacted, prayers are offered, and voices are raised in song. It is also a place for silence, for personal communion with God. Each element of a cathedral is ultimately meant to quiet our minds from the distractions of the world and redirect them heavenward.

The great cathedrals can, of course, be appreciated by those who do not believe in what they stand for. They are marvels of ingenuity and intricacy in their design and are breathtaking in their symmetry and elegance. Their almost supernatural beauty, though, may well tempt the unbeliever, at least for a moment, to entertain the possibility of something grander that upholds the universe.

5

Ordo Virtutum

Hildegard of Bingen

(choral work, c. 1151)

We know little about most of the composers of music written during the Middle Ages, a time that is generally shrouded in anonymity. Interestingly, especially considering the lower cultural status of women during this period, Hildegard of Bingen is one of the few composers of the medieval period we can identify by name. Perhaps that is because of her forceful personality and significant accomplishments. Or maybe it is because her music has unique qualities that make it seem so far ahead of its time.

One of her most important works, *Ordo Virtutum* or *The Play of the Virtues*, is the first musical drama in history, an allegorical morality play set to music that explores the power of the virtues (love, chastity, obedience, and so forth) to rescue and transform the lost and struggling human soul. It is one of the earliest examples of a morality play, a genre that would only become common later, in the fourteenth century, and whose best-known example is *Everyman*. In a morality play, each character is a personification of a concept, a virtue, or a vice.

So in Hildegard's drama, a morality play set to music, a lost soul is led to salvation by the work of the virtues, each of whom offers a solo song, and each of whom is praised in turn by a chorus of the other virtues. The devil (the only part designed for a male soloist, whose part is spoken or shouted rather than sung) futilely attempts to woo her back, but in the end he is bound and defeated by the strength of the combined

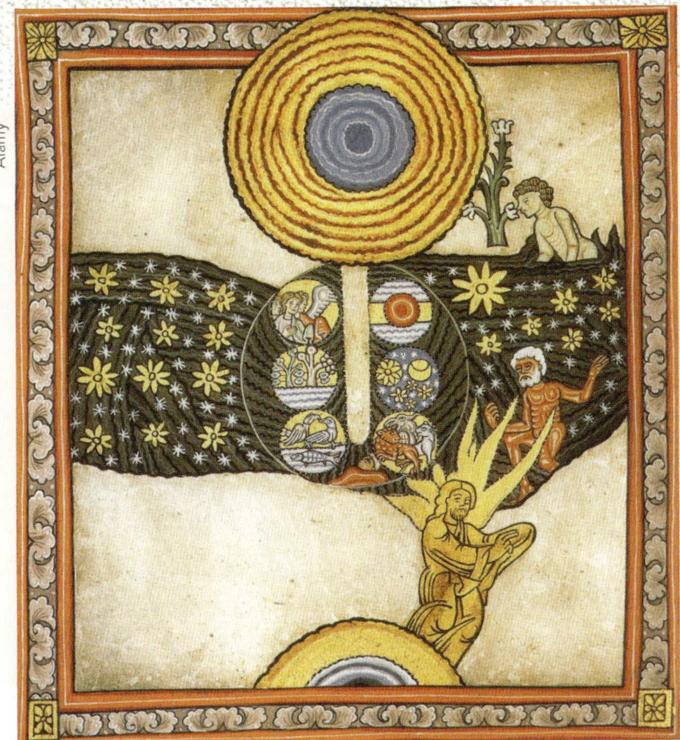
Alamy

The Redeemer. Miniature from Liber Scivias by Hildegard of Bingen, Eibingen Abbey Museum

virtues. At its conclusion, this chorus of virtues joins their voices together in praise to God. Hildegard undoubtedly meant it to be a teaching lesson in song for the nuns under her charge, but it is also a musical composition of great emotional impact.

Hildegard's music is generally much more dramatic than the typical chant of her times, with soaring and leaping and swirling melodies, deeply expressive emotion, and a wide sonic range. It is characterized by both rich sensuousness and purity of sound, as though she were trying to bring heaven and earth together in her music. Melodic phrases are stretched and contracted to create the soaring arches of sound that typify her style and make most other contemporary chant seem mild-mannered and stately when set beside Hildegard's richly expressive compositions. Hildegard's musical expressiveness was also reflective of her personal style. She was a woman who loved beautiful clothing, fragrant scents, and shimmering gemstones. She would, on occasion, even allow the nuns under her care to dress themselves in more extravagant costumes than were normally allowed for cloistered women, or allow them to let their hair grow long and remain uncovered, sometimes even crowned with flowers.

Hildegard of Bingen was born in 1098 to noble parents at Bermersheim in the Rhineland, the youngest of ten children.

As was common at the time, this tenth child was offered as a tithe to the church when she was eight years old and sent to the Benedictine monastery at Disibodenberg. Trained by the small community of nuns there, she joined the religious life and learned how to recite and sing the Latin Psalter. When the abbess died, Hildegard, who had already shown herself to be a natural leader, was chosen as her successor.

Throughout her life, beginning in her youth, Hildegard experienced powerful spiritual visions. She described them as an experience of light: "Heaven was opened and a fiery light of exceeding brilliance came and permeated my whole brain and enflamed my whole heart and my whole breast."[1] Shortly after she became abbess, she was instructed in one of these visions to "tell and write what she saw and heard." She did so with a book entitled *Scivias* or *Know the Ways of the Lord*. The content of these visions was considered orthodox enough that her visions were endorsed by the influential spiritual writer Bernard of Clairvaux and by Pope Eugenius III. Her visions used the language of nature and mysticism to expound upon Christian truths with rich and beautifully adorned imagery, emphasizing gardens, flowers, trees, and other natural phenomena that represented fecundity and growth.

Hildegard saw the processes of nature as an apt metaphor for what needed to happen in every individual human soul—a process she referred to as "greening." She saw the world as the stage for an intense spiritual battle between good and evil, and the "greenness" was a reflection of celestial spiritual light. Humanity existed either in a state of greening and growing or a state of dryness and aridity, and it was only in the light of God that it was possible to find the water to slake our spiritual thirst. Like so many Christian artists, Hildegard was a nature mystic, seeing God at work in His created world. "All living creatures are sparks from the radiation of God's brilliance," she wrote, "and these sparks emerge from God like the rays of the sun. . . . God cannot be seen but is known through the divine creation, just as our body cannot be seen because of our clothing."[2] For Hildegard, both light and the beauty of nature were pointers to the divine reality.

In a time when women were restricted from participating in leadership and teaching roles, sharing her personal visions as a "mouthpiece" of God was the only way Hildegard could get a hearing, and so these visions were a socially sanctioned way to press beyond the normal constraints placed upon medieval women and allow her to be seen as a genuine religious leader.

Hildegard also painted pictures of what she had seen in her visions, which she called "Illuminations." Though the originals were apparently destroyed in WWII, we have faithful copies created by later Germanic nuns. These paintings are complex, mysterious, quite beautiful, and filled with the symbolism of her personal vision of God and His relationship to His creation.

In addition to recording her visions in books and paintings, Hildegard also wrote books in which she related her careful observations of the natural world—books on biology, botany, and herbal medicine. She also wrote numerous letters, many of which survive, offering practical spiritual counsel and sometimes even political advice to secular leaders. In these letters, Hildegard was fearless in speaking of her contempt for religious hypocrisy, and she raised her voice against abuses among the clergy with all the self-assurance of a prophet.

In addition to *Ordo Virtutum*, she also composed seventy-seven songs for use in various parts of the mass and Daily Office, known collectively as the *Symphony of the Harmony of Celestial Revelations* or, more simply, as *Symphonia*. These draw on texts from the Bible, her unique theological ideas, and stories from the lives of the saints. Whether through writing music, penning books, or painting her visions, Hildegard wanted the nuns under her care to better understand their relationship with God, their heavenly Husband and Father. The idea of the "spiritual marriage" between God and the virginal nun was a common theme throughout her writings and music.

Raised in a monastic environment where music (mostly in the form of chant) helped order and structure the day, Hildegard held a deep regard for the power of music to balance and order the human soul. Music was an essential part of the monastic community, as monks and nuns spent literally hours each day singing the Daily Office. Hildegard saw this kind of music as transformative, nothing less than a spiritual discipline, a way to recenter a soul that had fallen out of sync with God. Music, she believed, redirects our attention and focus and brings us back into connection with Him. She used the term *symphonia* to speak of the harmony achieved when voices blended together—an inner harmony mirrored by the unity felt when our voices are lifted with others in song. For Hildegard, music was such an effective metaphor for the deepest transcendent realities that she used musical terminology over three hundred times throughout her writings to illuminate truths about the spiritual life.

Yet with all her accomplishments, Hildegard did not see herself as an exalted person, but only as a humble spokesperson for God. She referred to herself as "a small trumpet" and a "feather on the breath of God."[3] Through her music, her writings, and her paintings, Hildegard called people to find the balance and harmony of a life dedicated to God. She died in 1179 and was largely forgotten until her work was rediscovered and newly translated in the late 1970s, as the modern environmental movement came into full flower. Many readers and listeners today find this medieval nun a fresh and still-relevant voice speaking to the concerns of our modern times.

6

The Windows of Sainte-Chapelle

(stained glass, 1248)

A medieval writer, on seeing the upper chapel of Sainte-Chapelle for the first time, exclaimed that it was "one of Heaven's most beautiful rooms." Perhaps that is an overstatement, but just barely. It is certainly one of the most splendid interiors in the world. Just a short walk from the more famous Notre Dame cathedral, the upper chapel of Sainte-Chapelle is one of the often-overlooked treasures of Paris. Though the chapel is tiny in comparison with the naves of the great cathedrals, its impact is immense. It dazzles like a monumental piece of jewelry, with light slanting through the fourteen stained glass windows that surround the perimeter and sparkling upon the golden stars that are painted against a deep blue in the vaults. Its walls seem weightless and almost nonexistent, surfaces of such translucence they create the illusion that the whole room is enveloped in glass, almost like a heavenly greenhouse built to grow and nurture faith. When night falls and the candelabras are lit, the effect is equally magical.

Sainte-Chapelle was originally commissioned by Louis IX to house his collection of holy relics, most especially the "authentic" crown of thorns and a fragment of the true cross, and was consecrated in April 1248. Although some might dismiss the historical claims of such relics, they were taken very seriously by medieval Christians and were treasured as objects in which the realm of the holy intersected with the earthly. These treasures, so highly valued, were kept out

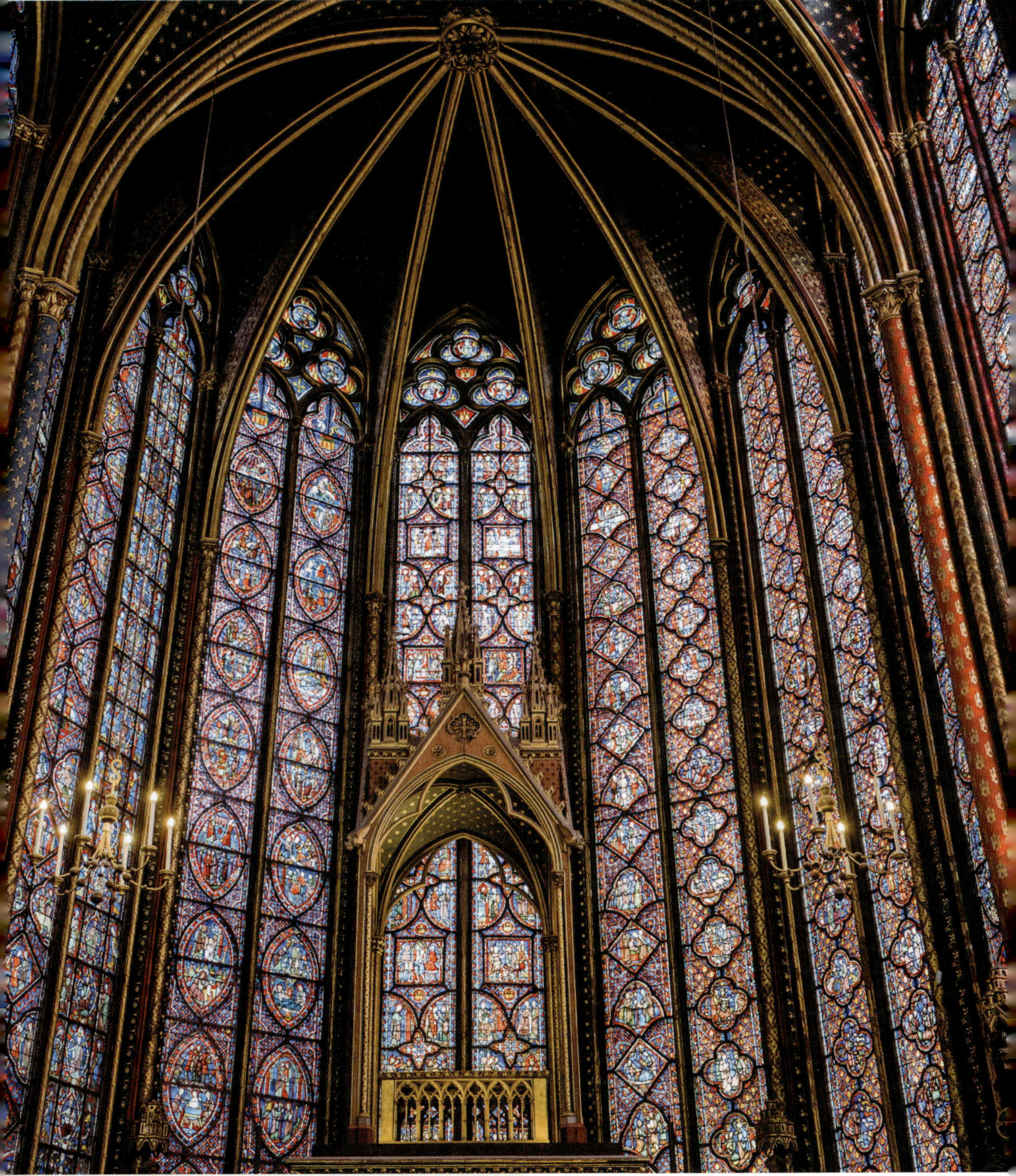

Interior of Sainte Chapelle, photo by Pierre Poschadel

WikiCommons

of general public view in an elaborate reliquary, but what the public could view—the magnificent stained glass windows of the chapel—was a treasure in itself.

The whole story of redemption, from creation to the end of time, unfolds on these windows. Particular emphasis was given to recounting the events of the passion of Christ and to the stories of the great kings of Old Testament history, those ancient Jewish rulers who were seen by the window's designers as precursors to the kings of France. Therefore, the designs often make a nod to French royalty with their heraldic motifs, and one of the windows is particularly occupied with showing the rediscovery and relocation of the sacred relics. The large rose window in Sainte-Chapelle (to the visitor's back as one faces the altar) takes the apocalypse as its theme, perhaps as a warning to those who stand outside this holy history.

Although the individual panes of stained glass in the overall design are not comparable to some of the finest individual panes found in places such as Chartres or Notre Dame, the overall effect created by being enveloped by soaring walls of glass is Sainte-Chapelle's uniquely breathtaking achievement—it is filled with light. Light is a common metaphor for the experience of God's power and glory, one used throughout the Scriptures (see Matt. 4:16; 5:16; John 8:12; 1 John 1:7; Rev. 21:23). It is not surprising, then, that the stained glass window became a common artistic way to express this glory and to reveal the details of God's story.

Stained glass windows are the work of artists and engineers who create them by taking small, shaped pieces of glass in a variety of colors, arranging them in an eye-pleasing design, and painting the finishing details onto their surfaces. These colored panes are held in place by an intricate web of leading that binds them together and incorporates them into the overall design of the window. This leading had to be both strong and pliable to hold the weight of the pieces of glass, yet give the artist freedom to be creative and innovative.

We find a mention of stained glass in churches as early as the fourth century, but the earliest examples were probably just colored glass installed in the windows for beautiful effect. It wasn't until the twelfth century that painting details on the colored glass, and thus stained glass as we know it really came into its own. Around 1120 Theophilus wrote a book, *The Various Arts*, in which he included detailed instruction on how stained glass windows were made, and though there have been innovations, the central process is largely unchanged to this day.

Stained glass windows serve several major purposes in the context of a church or cathedral. First, they provide natural lighting for the interior of the building. Before the advent of electricity, the inside of these towering buildings would have been exceedingly dark and gloomy if it were not for the light streaming in through the many large windows. The technical innovations of cathedral construction in the transition from Romanesque to Gothic style allowed for much larger windows—and more of them. So they quickly became an important element in the overall impact of the cathedrals, which showcase the luminous windows as a major element in their design.

But the windows serve more than a practical purpose. They also heighten the aesthetic experience for worshipers by creating a mystical atmosphere of light. Shafts of light slanting down into the cathedral from the windows produce a play of light as dust motes dance in the shimmering illumination. These windows are a living metaphor for one of the goals of the Christian life—to allow God to shine through our lives and reflect His glory. We may never do so as well as these multicolored windows, but each of us can become a prism for radiating God's light.

Stained glass windows are not only a source of earthly and spiritual light but also an artistic representation of the great stories of the faith. Though sometimes the windows are merely abstract or semiabstract designs, more often they are engaged in telling a story—the biblical stories of the Old and New Testaments, tales of the saints, or important moments from sacred or civic history. In a time when few people were literate, the stained glass windows could be "read" by those who could not get these stories from books. Standing before the windows, one could look up and linger over each important biblical story and be reminded of God's life among His people.

Sainte-Chapelle is just one example of the many extraordinary collections of stained glass that can be found in cathedrals, churches, chapels, and public buildings throughout the world. Other must-see windows might include the stained glass in the cathedrals in Bourges, Strasbourg, Cologne, Sienna, Canterbury, and York Minster.

Nearer our own day, unforgettable designs in stained glass have been created by the likes of Pre-Raphaelite artists Edward Burne-Jones and William Morris, who sparked a nineteenth-century revival of the art form. Other luminaries in this art form include Louis Comfort Tiffany, Christopher Whall, Henri Matisse, and Marc Chagall—the most acclaimed of modern stained glass artists, who brought his own modern style to the creation of incandescent stained glass windows in a synagogue in Jerusalem, at the Art Institute of Chicago, in Union Church in upstate New York, and other locations. The art of light and color found in stained glass lives on in the work of these modern masters of the art.

7

The Scrovegni Chapel Frescoes

Giotto

(paintings, c. 1305)

Nothing about the small and rather plain exterior of the Scrovegni Chapel in Padua can prepare you for what is inside. It is like a simple unadorned jewelry box that contains unexpected and priceless treasures. There, in a small private chapel paid for by Enrico Scrovegni as atonement for his father's usurious and unsavory financial dealings, is a breathtaking series of frescoes by Giotto illustrating the life of Mary and the life of Jesus, as well as a depiction of the last judgment. Nearly every surface is covered in paint, from floor to ceiling, including a bright blue night sky in the curved vault of the roof. There are about forty painted panels, each bursting with creative illustrations of the great sacred stories.

One of the most remarkable of these panels is *The Lamentation of Christ*, which shows the dead Jesus cradled in the arms of His mother, whose face displays her emotional anguish over the death of her son. That anguish is mirrored in the faces of other onlookers, especially in the faces of the angels who hover above the scene, wailing in grief over the slain Christ. This is not a calm and composed religious scene painted for the inspiration of the devout but a fully human moment, and we grasp the monumental tragedy through the expressions of the onlookers. They take us into the narrative and we experience it through them: through Mary's unspeakable sorrow, through the lament of the angelic host, and through the gesture of

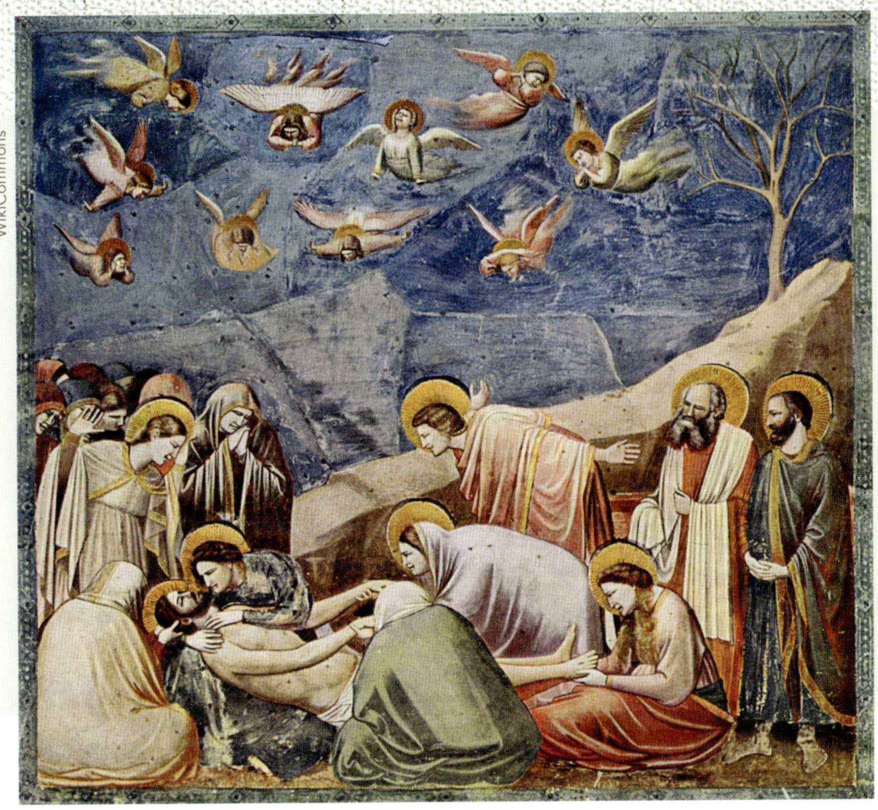

WikiCommons

The Lamentation of Christ by Giotto, The Scrovegni Chapel, Padua

John, whose arms are thrown backward in horror and unutterable grief.

Giotto has created a complex and busy arrangement, and some figures even have their backs to us, adding to the dimension of the work. But everything in the work pulls our eyes toward the face of the dead Christ, who while not at the physical center of the painting is clearly the central focus toward which everything points. Even the rocky ridge in the background descends from the right and toward Jesus. There is no question that something of unbelievable awfulness has taken place. The Son of God has been slain. And Giotto has captured the emotion of the moment.

Giotto di Bondone was born in 1266 near Florence, and spent much of his working life there. In his early days, he was a shepherd. One day, while his sheep were grazing, young Giotto grew restless and decided to pass the time in a way that he had come to enjoy—drawing. He'd never had any lessons, but he had a keen eye. He found a sharp, pointed rock that he thought he could make use of, and a large stone with a relatively smooth surface. His instruments weren't ideal, but he set to work scratching the likeness of one of the sheep onto the stone.

It happened that the most accomplished artist of his time, Cimabue, was taking a walk in the countryside and happened upon the boy. (Cimabue's art was so esteemed that when he completed his altarpiece, *Virgin Enthroned with Angels*, it was carried through the streets of the city in a triumphal procession.) Curious to see what the young man was doing, Cimabue was astonished at the lifelike realism that Giotto managed with his rough tools. According to the story that has come down to us by Renaissance-era art historian Giorgio Vasari, Cimabue decided on the spot to take Giotto on as a student. The rest is art history. The student developed into an artist more talented and innovative than his teacher.

Before Giotto, artists mostly worked from predetermined models and prototypes that had been handed down as part of the artistic tradition. These given rules and paradigms determined that artists would not stray far from the Byzantine heritage—art that was stiff, formal, and highly symbolic. But Giotto took another approach, and with it became the fountainhead of Western painting. When he approached a subject, he asked a simple question: What does it *look* like? And that attempt to paint realistically gave an unusual power to his work. Ignoring normal practices and traditions, he instead painted what he saw and what he felt. He was the first artist in the Western tradition to let his personality and individuality fully shine through. Giotto was not afraid of innovation and experimentation. Some of his experiments, such as in creating a sense of perspective, were not always fully successful. Hence there is a bit of awkwardness in some of his depictions, but somehow that actually adds to their charm and originality.

Giotto's figures have a sense of weight and volume not seen before his time. When you compare his *Madonna and Child* (c. 1310) with that of his teacher, Cimabue, you witness a much greater sense of dimensionality. He has not painted a *symbol* of spirituality and holiness but a *person*. And he surrounds his people with the natural world, which he renders with great care: stones, trees, animals, and the landscapes in which his painted narratives take place.

Perhaps the greatest achievement of Giotto's art is the emotional realism he brings to the traditional biblical and historical stories. His works are full of drama, confrontation, tenderness, overwhelming grief, and humor. He emphasizes the human relationships within the stories he illustrates, and we feel the pain or joy of the events he unfolds with his brush. When, for example, he paints the moment that Judas betrays Jesus with a kiss, we are drawn into the drama through the piercing eyes of Jesus, filled with intensity and sadness that one of His chosen has decided to turn Him over to His enemies. Time stops as we sense the depth of emotion.

In Giotto's day, canvas painting did not yet exist, so most of his work was done as

WikiCommons

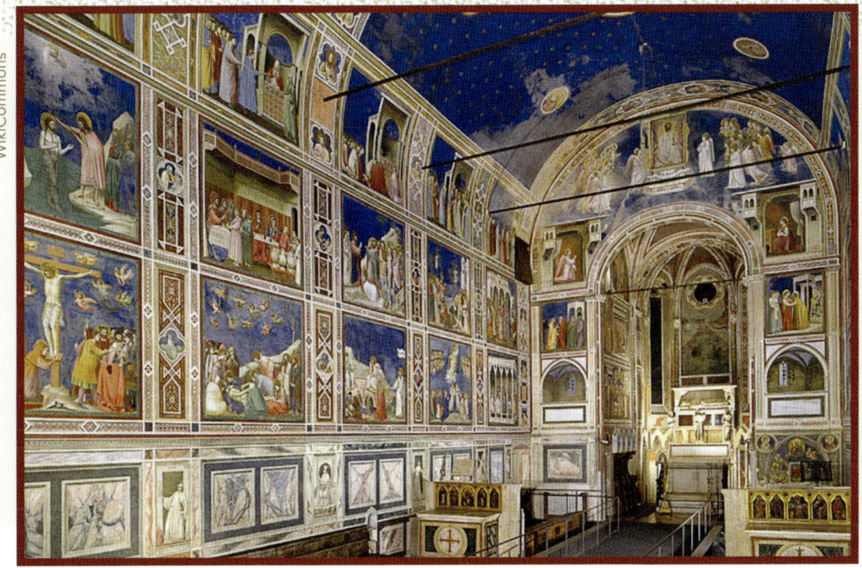

Interior of The Scrovegni Chapel, Padua

fresco painting, a process where paint is applied directly onto the walls while the plaster is still wet. This meant that an artist had to work pretty quickly, but what they created was a work of permanence.

The several series of fresco paintings that Giotto did with his new, more realistic style made him famous in his lifetime. His first great fresco series was done for the Basilica of Saint Francis in Assisi. Here, with some help from assistants, he unfolded the life of the saint with emotion and great charm. When he paints St. Francis preaching to the birds, we cannot help but smile at the simplicity and ingenuity of his characterization and at the menagerie of various kinds of birds that eagerly flock together to hear the saint's message. Another panel, where Francis receives the stigmata, is full of drama and spiritual mystery.

Giotto's greatest achievement, though, is his series of frescoes for the Scrovegni Chapel in Padua. Including *The Lamentation of Christ,* these panels are an inventive and emotionally resonant series of moments from the life of Jesus and the life of His mother. Each deserves study as a great work of art in its own right. But considered as a whole, it is a stunning testament to the faith and talent of the West's first universally admired artist, an artist who brought realism, passion, and drama to the painting of biblical and sacred stories.

Giotto's artistic talent is heightened by his talent as a storyteller. He doesn't just paint. He brings the stories to life with his brush and makes us feel as though we are witnessing an unfolding event. It's all about the little touches that make the personalities of the biblical characters manifest in a way that is convincing and deeply human. We know them. We know their pain. We know their triumph. And we are often moved to a place near to tears.

8

The Divine Comedy

Dante

(poem, c. 1320)

In our present usage, "comedy" usually refers to a work that is humorous and causes us to laugh at ourselves and others. But when Dante used the word to describe his epic poem *The Divine Comedy,* he had a higher definition in mind. For him, a comedy was a work that began with harsh and tragic realities but ended with great joy and the triumph of the good. Such is an accurate description of his poetic journey through the harrowing environs of hell toward the ultimate good—the beatific vision of God. So successful was Dante's telling of this comedy that later commentators applied the modifier "divine" to describe the work. His epic poem was popular in his own time, and he is now universally recognized as one of the very greatest writers of Western civilization. As T. S. Eliot has written, "Dante and Shakespeare divide the modern world between them. There is no third."[1]

The best known and most widely read of the three portions of *The Divine Comedy* is the *Inferno,* which tells the story of Dante's journey through hell. Perhaps its popularity comes from our fascination with the way in which Dante has made eternal punishments fit earthly crimes. Guided by the great poet Virgil, Dante journeys down into the deepest abyss of hell and sees the judgment being meted out to sinners of all stripes, guilty of every kind of sin. Dante's hell is peopled not only by many famous historical personalities but also by his own political enemies, who suffer for their malfeasance and corruption. The judgments are harsh but they fit the crimes. No wonder the inscription that he sees at the gates of hell reads: "Abandon hope all who enter here."

The *Inferno* is the portion that most students are introduced to in college lit surveys, but unfortunately few venture further into the next two portions of *The Divine Comedy* and therefore miss out on many unforgettable moments in both *Purgatorio* and *Paradiso*. In *Purgatorio*, Dante emerges from hell and is guided up the mountain of purgatory, a place where sins are punished but where, unlike hell where the sentence lasts forever, the purpose of this chastisement is not punishment but cleansing and purification in anticipation of the ascent into heaven. Purgatory is the place where believers are perfected, an extrabiblical theological concept very popular in the Middle Ages.

Once Dante has climbed the mountain of purgatory, he is ready to be ushered into the presence of God, but Virgil, being a virtuous pagan but not a Christian, can travel with him no longer. Instead, the saintly Beatrice, with whom Dante had a special spiritual attachment before her untimely death, becomes his guide through the nine spheres of paradise and to ultimate union with God. Dante's grand images of heaven include rapturous light, the music of the spheres, the mystic rose, and a great eternal dance.

Born in 1265 in Florence, Dante Alighieri was broadly educated, as witnessed by his excellent grasp of the medieval Catholic theology of both the Dominicans and the Franciscans and his knowledge of ancient philosophy and science. A major turning point in his life occurred at age nine, when he first met Beatrice. He was immediately attracted to her, but they did not meet again for nine years and then only a handful of times thereafter. They rarely spoke to each other and they both married others. But he loved her from afar throughout his life with a spiritual rather than physical passion. She was his ideal woman, and through loving her Dante believed he had learned how to love God more fully. One of his early works is a collection of poems in her honor, *La Vita Nuova*, or *The New Life* (1295). Even after her death, she continued to act as his muse.

Dante was banished from his hometown of Florence in 1302 because of his involvement with the White Guelphs, the losing side in a drawn-out political and military conflict between two rival factions in the city. Forbidden to return and too proud to later accept a conditional pardon, he spent time wandering around Italy and central Europe and eventually settled in Ravenna, where he lived the rest of his life in exile. The fruit of this exile was *The Divine Comedy*, which he probably began about 1306 and did not finish until shortly before his death in 1321. Upon his death both Florence and Ravenna vied to become the resting place of the now-famous poet. Florence thought it had prevailed when Pope Leo X intervened on their behalf, and Dante's coffin was delivered to them by the city fathers of Ravenna. They later discovered, however, that they had been duped and the coffin contained the remains of someone else!

The Divine Comedy was the first great poem written in Italian, the language of the ordinary person, rather than Latin, the language of the priest and scholar. It gave an aura of dignity to the Italian language and opened the door for others to write serious literary works in their native tongue. Dante's epic poem was an immediate sensation among his contemporaries, and has remained a classic down to our time. In the twentieth century alone, there were more than fifty different translations of *Inferno* into English!

The poem works effectively on a number of levels. First and foremost, *The Divine Comedy* is a creative work of poetic genius and intricate structure. Dante shows great imagination in ordering the afterlife around the seven deadly sins and the virtues that are their positive counterparts. Mirroring the medieval fascination with numbers, and especially with the number three (symbolizing the Trinity), he structures the entire work around it.

There are three major parts: *Inferno* (hell), *Purgatorio* (purgatory), and *Paradiso* (heaven). Each contains thirty-three cantos (*Inferno* has an additional introductory canto). Each stanza in each of the cantos also reflects the trinitarian fascination with the number three, as there are three lines in each one, a rhyme scheme we now call "*terza rima*." (Chaucer borrowed this same technique for *The Canterbury Tales*.) Nine, which is of course the result of multiplying three with itself, is also an important number: the number of circles of hell through which Dante passes on his descent through that dark kingdom and the number of spheres in paradise. Seven, the traditional number of perfection, is used for the seven stages through which he passes on his ascent of the great mountain of purgatory, seeing sinners being cleansed of the seven deadly sins (pride, envy, anger, sloth, covetousness, gluttony, and lust).

But there is much more here than numerological symbolism, for Dante's work, though about the divine realm, is also thoroughly human, filled with both compassion and indignation. Throughout his poetic journey Dante crafts scenes of humor, horror, pathos, and transcendent vision. Even those who cannot accept Dante's theology can revel in this adventure of the human soul in search of ultimate reality.

The poem also functions as a searing critique of the corruption he had seen firsthand in Florentine politics and religion. Dante used his verse as a platform for expressing discontent with the political status quo and taking satirical revenge on his enemies. This can especially be seen in *Inferno,* where he peoples hell with corrupt rulers and popes of the past as well as those who would have been recognized by his contemporaries. He spared no wrath at his enemies, and used his poem as a weapon in his continuing battle against political injustice.

Politics had been in Dante's mind long before he fashioned his comedy. He had been involved in the local politics of Florence, an activist fighting against political and clerical corruption. One of his earlier books, *De Monarchia* (*On World Government*), argues forcibly, in anticipation of later political developments, for the separation of church and state. He clearly saw the dangers of investing secular government with God's blessing and authority or allowing the church to steer the ship of state. When he came to write his comedy, he took aim at those who had misused such power for their own gain. He even placed the current pope, the power-grabbing Boniface VIII, in one of the circles of hell!

Perhaps most profoundly, though, *The Divine Comedy* is a spiritual autobiography and by implication a guidebook of sorts for the reader's own spiritual journey. From the very first verse, Dante announces himself as the main character of his epic poem. It begins, "Midway through the journey of our life I found myself in a dark wood, where the right way was lost." Dante is both himself and everyman, a fallible pilgrim who is as shocked and bewildered and inspired by what he sees and experiences as his readers. As he learns, so do we. Although Dante undoubtedly took the traditional Christian understandings of heaven and hell seriously and, almost certainly, *literally*, he was less interested in trying to create an accurate diagram of the afterlife than he was in pointing toward the vices one should avoid and the virtues one should embrace in their place. *The Divine Comedy* is therefore a profoundly moral tale, intended to be a mirror in which readers might see themselves and be warned of the consequences of a life lived in selfishness, greed, lust, and pride.

In a letter Dante wrote to a contemporary, he explained the purpose of his poem: "to remove those living in this life from the state of misery and to lead them to the state of bliss."[2] Dante wanted to use his creative gifts to remind readers that they had an immortal soul and help them put aside their sin in order to discover the joy that might be found in the union of the soul with God, "the Love that moves the sun and the other stars."[3]

9

The Holy Trinity Icon

ANDREI RUBLEV

(painting, c. 1410)

At first glance this famous icon might be a little puzzling to the modern viewer. Who are these three figures highlighted with golden halos? Their barely sketched-out surroundings give us little clue; then we realize that the tree in the upper-right-hand side of the icon is the Oak of Mamre, from the story in Genesis 18, where three angels visit Abraham and Sarah to deliver news from God. Andrei Rublev, the most famous icon painter, adapted that biblical story to represent one of the most mysterious tenets of the Christian faith: the doctrine of the Trinity. When we look more closely at the three figures, we realize that their faces are identical in appearance, and most experts believe that they represent, from left to right, the Father, the Son, and the Holy Spirit. The three, while distinct, are ultimately One. They cannot easily be distinguished from one another but are each a unique and individual person.

The members of the Trinity are seated around a table, and on that table, in a central position that draws our eyes, is a chalice. That cup is almost certainly intended to put us in mind of the Eucharist and the blood of Christ, who gestures toward it. The three figures are not static; there is a lively communication implied in their eyes, filled with love and blessing. In this icon, we glimpse the truth that the three members of the Trinity are in an intimate relationship with one another. And not only with each other but also with us.

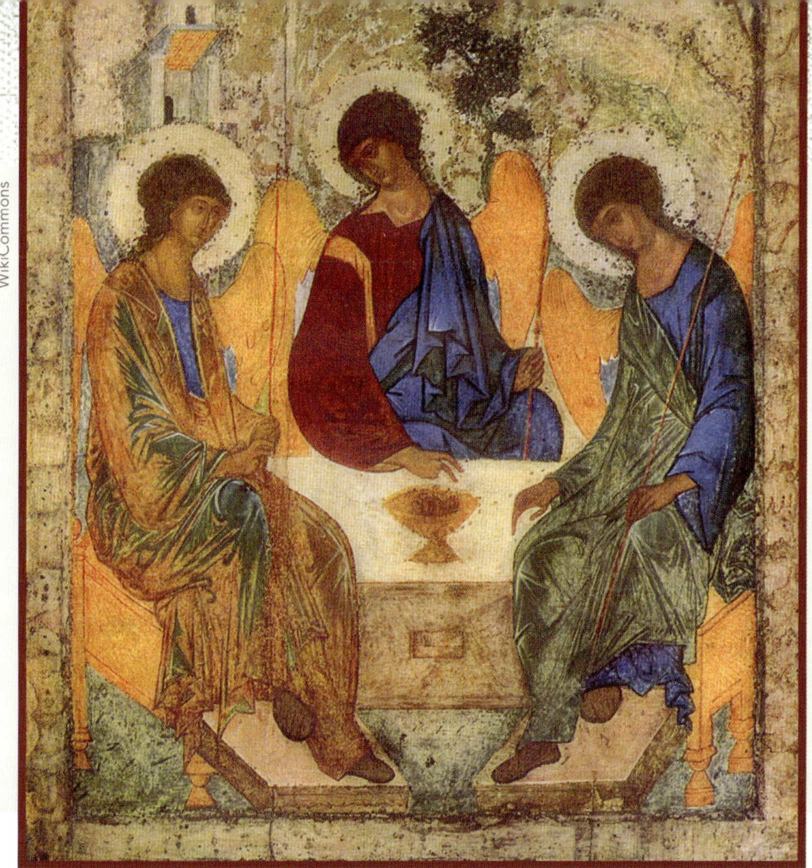

The Holy Trinity by Andrei Rublev, Tretyakov Gallery, Moscow

The icon is a reminder that we are invited into the circle of relationship shared by the divine Trinity, for there is an empty place at the table in the foreground of the image. Perhaps that place has been readied for us, where we may fellowship with the Holy Trinity and partake of the holy cup of salvation.

Very little is known about Andrei Rublev, the artist who created this icon. He was born in the 1360s and died sometime between 1427 and 1430. Rublev was a Russian monk and is considered the greatest of the medieval icon painters; his work is famous for its calm serenity and spirituality. He was canonized by the Russian Orthodox church in 1988.

Our word *icon* comes from a Greek word usually translated as *image* or *likeness*. It is the same word used in Colossians 1:15 in reference to Christ being the image of the invisible God. And that is what icons are attempting to do—make visible the invisible. They are usually painted on a wooden panel, and are normally small enough to be portable. They can be placed on a shelf in the home of an Orthodox believer—unless they are created for use in a church, in which case they are larger and grander. The subject matter of icons is pretty much limited to spiritual subjects: portraits of Christ, the Virgin Mary, angels, saints, or some important spiritual event from Scripture or church history. They are often accented with gold.

According to legend, the first icon was created by the gospel writer Luke, when he painted a likeness of Mary while she was still alive. (There is also a famous icon that shows Luke at an easel painting her.) In the fourth century, Chrysostom wrote of having a portrait of the apostle Paul on his desk to inspire him as he penned his famous sermons. But the earliest surviving icons are from the sixth and seventh centuries, almost all of them preserved at St. Catherine's Monastery in Syria. That remote location saved them from the ravages of the iconoclastic controversy.

In 726, Emperor Leo III, perhaps partially influenced by the Islamic ban on images and concerned that Christians were in danger of the sin of idolatry due to their dedication to icons, banned them from his empire. This ban lasted for over a hundred years, and along with much theological argument, debate, and disputation over the perceived blessing or danger of such images came the destruction of countless icons. They were tracked down, painted over, defaced, hacked to pieces, or burned in an attempt to rid the empire of this particular form of religious expression. Except for those secreted away, most icons were destroyed during these years. Later, though Eastern Church councils finally decided in favor of them, icons were still endangered as the target of thieves due to the gold and gems they contained. But in spite of the difficulties, the traditions of iconography lived on, especially in Eastern traditions of Christianity. Once Christianity was embraced in Russia, icons became a very cherished and important part of spreading the gospel there. In the West, debates over the appropriateness of religious images have long been an ongoing subject of argument, but among Christians of the East, icons are an important expression of faith.

Although Orthodox believers will sometimes speak of *venerating* an icon, that does not mean they conceive of it as an object of worship. It is an image, but not a "graven image" as prohibited in the Ten Commandments. An icon is emphatically *not* an idol.

Neither, however, is it considered to be a work of art in our usual sense of the word. It is not intended for our aesthetic pleasure nor is it open to individual subjective interpretation in the way that much religious art is. Instead, it is meant to be a communication of Christian truths in a visual form. As John of Damascus wrote, "What the written word is to those who know letters, the icon is to the unlettered; what speech is to the ear, the icon is to the eye."[1] In fact, Orthodox believers tend to refer to icons as being "written" rather than "painted." They are meant to be *read*, and the icon is meant to appeal to the mind as much as the emotions. It teaches. And what it teaches is spiritual reality and how we are to relate to it.

The way that the subject matter of the icon is represented, however, does not come from the imagination of the individual painter but from traditions handed down for centuries. Icon painters do not paint freely from their imaginations but instead exercise their creativity within carefully delineated forms and archetypes within the long tradition of icon painting. Individual expression is not the goal of the icon, though it is interesting to see how much difference can exist even when painters are painting the same subject with the exact same formula and parameters.

The icon is understood by Orthodox Christians as a place where God can be experienced. It makes us present to the event or person being portrayed and draws us into a relationship with that person or event. It is, in the words of Linette Martin, a "sacred doorway,"[2] a passage between this world and the spiritual world that lies beyond our senses. Accordingly, when we gaze upon an icon with rapt attention and concentration, another realm opens up to us. Patience and vulnerability will allow an icon to fully reveal itself to the viewer, and that viewer will be drawn into prayer.

An icon is meant to be, above all else, an aid to prayer. One does not pray *to* an icon but rather *through* an icon. Whatever its aesthetic qualities might be, the icon is primarily a stimulus for praying. Since icons rarely portray movement, there is a quiet stillness about them that evokes the same kind of quiet and stillness within the attentive viewer. By helping us quiet our minds, icons prepare us to pray. And through their simplicity, they help us to focus, creating a window through which we might begin to see the eternal. We are invited to join the holy persons who are their subjects, stepping into a place of adoration at the intersection between the human and the divine. God is seen as approachable in that He once dwelt in these holy men and women, but He is also awesome and mysterious, as are the icons themselves. For the heart that is open, the icon becomes a place to meet God, a door to step through into His presence.

Many icons are simply luminous, with a glow that seems to come from within. Perhaps one of the causes of this is that the subject of the icon is not normally lit from either side or from above or from below—or from any light source outside the work, as would be the case in most Western art. Instead, the light comes from behind or within the subject, often aided by a shining gold background, which creates a holy aura about the person portrayed. Also, rarely is there any more than a suggestion of situating the subject within any recognizable location. Instead the icon is timeless, and occupies a holy space that it invites us to enter. As Henri Nouwen has written of icons, "They are created for the sole purpose of offering access, through the gate of the visible, to the mystery of the invisible."[3]

10

The Adoration of the Lamb

Jan van Eyck

(paintings, 1432)

The Adoration of the Lamb, an altarpiece painted for the Cathedral of Saint Bavo in Ghent, is a towering landmark in the history of art. It was the first major masterpiece painted in oil, then a new medium for painting, and its achievement opened the floodgates for other painters to work with oil. This painting is also, in the opinion of many scholars, a fulcrum point in the transition between the style of the Middle Ages and that of Renaissance realism. No previous artist painted with such an eye for the smallest details or attempted to so painstakingly capture reality. It can be argued that Jan van Eyck's *The Adoration of the Lamb* was both the last great medieval painting and the first great modern painting.

It is also a work with a fascinating history, so highly valued that it has been stolen numerous times during its existence—including being carted off to France as one of the spoils of war during the Napoleonic era, then taken again in the First World War. It was also a major target for Hitler's acquisition in the Second World War, and it spent much of that war hidden away in an Austrian salt mine, waiting for the day when Hitler hoped to make it a central exhibit in his planned postwar art museum. It was only due to some heroic intervention that it was not destroyed during the final days of the war, and it is now again where it belongs—in the cathedral in Ghent.

Begun in 1426 by Jan van Eyck's brother Hubert, who died very shortly after work

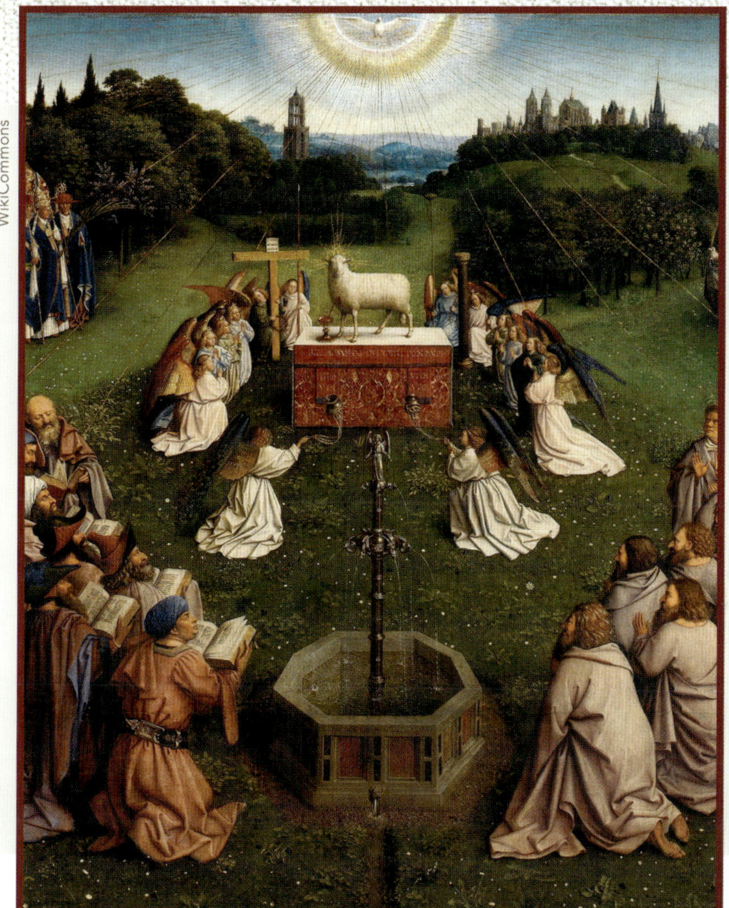

The Adoration of the Lamb (detail of the Ghent Altarpiece) by Jan van Eyck, St. Bavo Cathedral, Ghent

began, the huge altarpiece was not completed until 1432, and is probably almost entirely the work of Jan van Eyck himself. It consists of twenty linked panels: a large central set of images and two large wings that can close over it. These hinged wings are painted on both sides, so that the altarpiece may be viewed either open or closed. When it is opened, which is usually just for religious holidays, the work is a staggering twelve feet high and eighteen feet wide. The altarpiece is crowded with nearly two hundred figures. In the upper middle panel, God the Father sits upon His throne, with a sparkling jeweled crown at His feet, painted with painstaking attention to detail. He is flanked by the Virgin Mary and John the Baptist, angels who sing and play instruments, and Adam and Eve, who are painted with unflattering post-fall realism.

In the lower central panel, we see the image evoked by the book of Revelation that gives the work its name. Christ, represented as a lamb, is in the middle of the painting, standing upon an altar with His sacrificial blood flowing from a wound into a golden

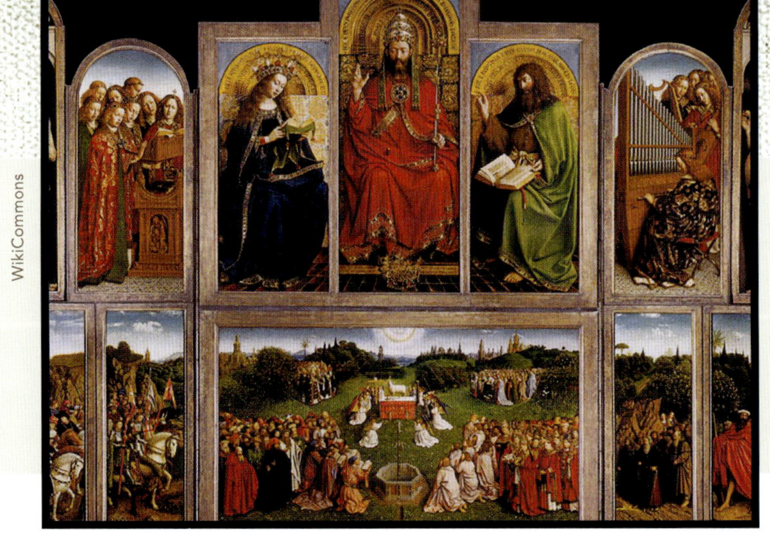
WikiCommons

The Ghent Altarpiece by Jan van Eyck, St. Bavo Cathedral, Ghent

chalice. The Holy Spirit descends as a dove. In front of the altar, a fountain bursts forth with living water, and from every side pilgrims, hermits, religious and political leaders (the "just judges"), and angels converge upon the scene from the four corners of the earth to worship and adore the Lamb of God. Many of these figures are recognizable as historical saints, and others are contemporary figures from van Eyck's day. They have all come to bask in the glory of the Lamb, whose altar is situated in a magical green field bedecked with flowers.

The trees and flowers are painted with such attention to detail that a modern botanist would be able to identify their species. In the distance we see a great city, the New Jerusalem, with its towers and cathedrals, and a lush realistic landscape stretching as far as we can see. Over it all, a heavenly light illuminates the scene. When its wings are closed, the altarpiece reveals an image of the annunciation, the prophets who predicted Jesus' coming, and the figures of John the Baptist and John the apostle, painted with an effect of shadow and spotlighting that replicates the look of statues enclosed in niches.

The level of detail in the painting is without precedent in such a large-scale work. Only illuminated manuscripts had previously gloried in the kind of minute detail that can be seen in every single inch of this masterpiece. As art historian Noah Charney has written, "Viewers can make out tufts of grass, the wrinkles in an old worm-eaten apple, and warts on double chins. But they can also see the reflection of light caught in a perfectly painted ruby, the folds of a gilded garment, and individual silvery hairs amid the chestnut curls of a beard."[1] All these fine ephemera of the visible world are used to make a point about the reality of the invisible spiritual world, now here on display for the viewer. It embraces both this world and the next.

Jan van Eyck was born in what is now Belgium sometime before 1395. We don't know a great deal about his life, but we do know he was a member of two princely courts in Holland. Van Eyck served as the court painter for John of Bavaria until 1425, after which time he joined the court of Philip the Good. Not only did he paint for Duke Philip but he also undertook diplomatic journeys for him, some involving extensive travel and "secret" missions. We don't know the nature of these travels, but they may have helped him to develop the knowledge of landscape that is evidenced in many of his paintings.

We also don't know with whom he studied the art of painting, but his own unique style is without precedent in the history of art. It used to be claimed that van Eyck was the inventor of oil painting, but scholars now believe it is more accurate to recognize him instead as the first artist to take full advantage of what oil painting could offer. Until the fifteenth century, the binding element for pigment was water and egg. But this egg tempera pigment created a flat and fairly uniform color. When oil was discovered as a binding agent, it opened up all kinds of possibilities for artists in terms of subtleties of color, luminosity, and tone. In particular, it allowed artists like van Eyck to render the effects of light with a new shimmering force.

The depth of the symbolism in the Ghent altarpiece would suggest that van Eyck had a strong familiarity with the Scriptures and theology, though it is also possible (as was often the case in paintings of this era) that he was guided in the symbolism by a theologian who helped map out the elements to be included in the work. Whatever the case, there is a profound understanding of the atoning work of Christ evident in this painting. When Albrecht Dürer saw the altarpiece in 1521, he praised it in his diary as a "very splendid, deeply reasoned painting."[2]

The Ghent altarpiece is van Eyck's oldest surviving work, and in the decade that followed it he also painted numerous portraits for private patrons. Only twenty-five paintings now exist that can be definitively attributed to van Eyck, among them the renowned *Arnolfini Wedding Portrait* (1434), a painting filled with finely painted details and rich symbolism. During the last decade of his life he also produced such works as *A Man in a Red Turban* (a 1433 self-portrait), *The Madonna with Chancellor Rolin* (c. 1435), and *Madonna in a Church* (c. 1438), where Mary is enormously tall in relation to the church interior, probably because van Eyck was using Mary as a metaphor for the church.

In each and every one of Jan van Eyck's paintings, the details of architecture, of the natural world, and of the human face are painstakingly rendered and entirely convincing. Again and again, throughout his career, he succeeded in capturing the fine details and minutiae of this world, and he used them to remind us of the reality of the world to come and the Lamb of God who reigns over all.

11

The Four Horsemen of the Apocalypse

ALBRECHT DÜRER

(woodcut, 1498)

As the year 1500 drew near, Europe was grasped by an apocalyptic fever. It was especially fervent in Germany, which had faced so many difficulties during the fifteenth century: ravenous plagues and rampant diseases, grievous social injustices and inequalities, famines, wars, and the imminent threat of the Turkish Muslims who were encamped at the borders of Germanic territory. Surely these were signs of the end of days? In addition to all the social and cultural upheaval, it was a time of questioning the theology and practices of the powerful Roman Catholic Church. Jan Hus, one of the earliest Reformers, preached the need for a return to a simple and pristine gospel unencumbered by all the traditions that obscured it. For his efforts, he became a martyr. But his death did not quiet the growing demand for religious revival and renewal. The Reformation had not yet fully taken root, but the day when Martin Luther would nail his Ninety-Five Theses to the door of the Wittenberg Church was not far off.

With so many wondering if indeed the end was at hand, there was a resurgence of interest in the book of Revelation. Christians looked to it for insight into the dark times they were living in, and for hope that God might intervene in the chaos of their world. It was into this environment that Albrecht Dürer launched his illustrations of the book of Revelation. Dürer was the first artist to make use of the new technology of printing, which had been developed

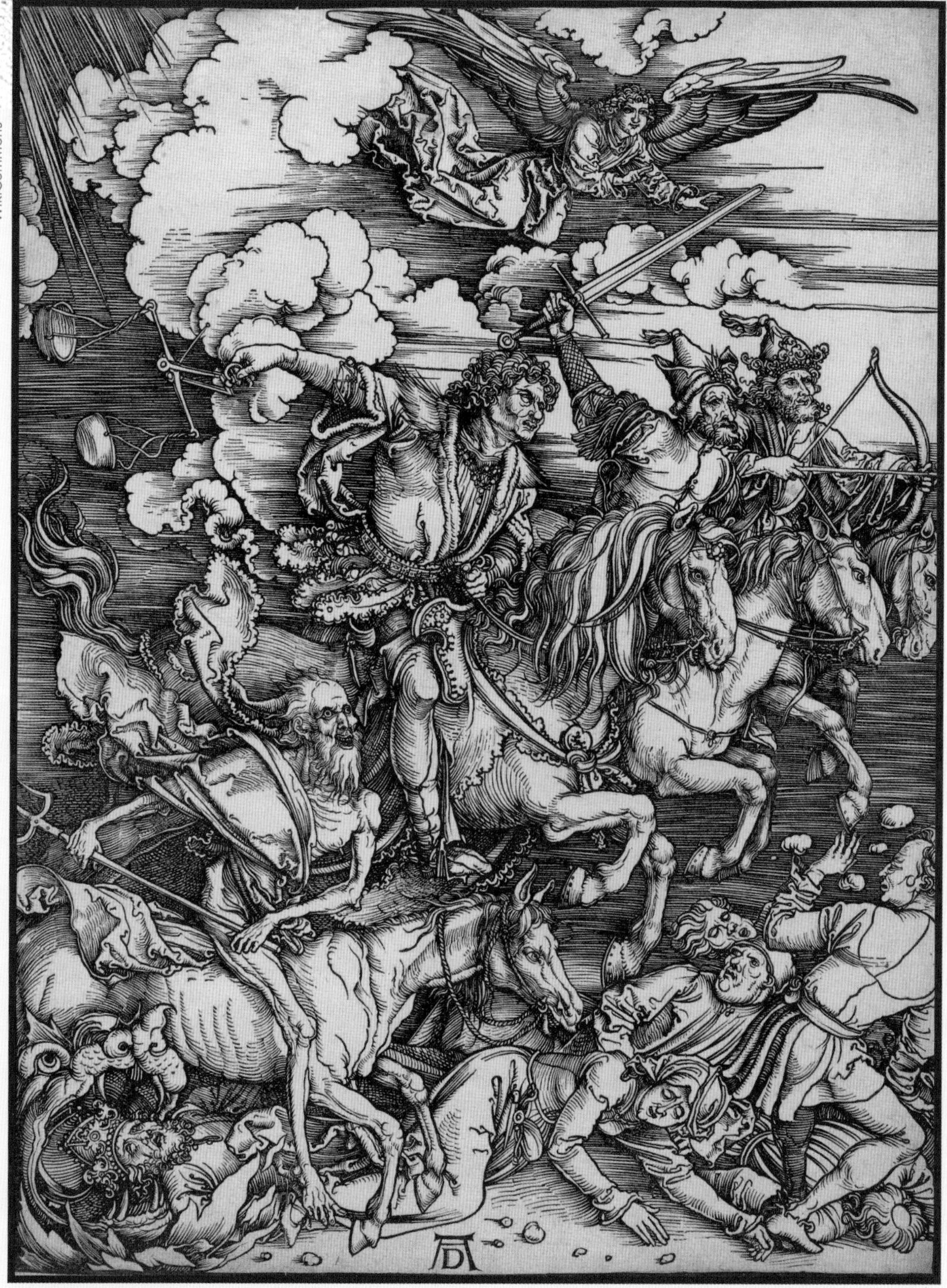
WikiCommons

The Four Horsemen of the Apocalypse by Albrecht Dürer, Metropolitan Museum of Art, New York City

by Gutenberg, to publish his own art book. This book, self-published in 1498, contained the text of Revelation, also known as "the Apocalypse," accompanied by fifteen vivid and detailed woodcuts. It proved of such enduring popularity that it provided Dürer with income for the rest of his life. (In 1511, he created a second version, with Latin text.)

These fifteen striking images rendered the symbolic and the spiritual images of this sometimes rather difficult biblical text with a naturalistic precision and an abundance of fascinating detail. Dürer took the complex imagery of Revelation and made it real, in the process creating mental pictures that still influence contemporary readers of the final book of the New Testament.

One of the most enduring of these images is that of *The Four Horsemen of the Apocalypse*, a nightmare vision of the awful terrors to be faced at the end of time, as predicted in Revelation 6. Dürer shows us Pestilence on a white horse with bow and arrow, War on a red horse with sword in hand, Famine on a black horse carrying empty scales, and Death as a skeletal form riding a pale horse and brandishing a scythe. Humankind is being trampled in their wake as they come sweeping into the scene from out of the shadows. To his contemporaries, Dürer's images were vivid symbolic depictions of realities that they knew all too well. Because he illustrated the horsemen with realistic detail, they took on an even greater resonance.

Albrecht Dürer was born in Nuremberg, Germany, in 1471. His father was a goldsmith and jeweler, and young Albrecht showed an early talent at rendering the kind of fine details demanded by his father's craft. But what really set young Dürer apart was his unusual talent for drawing. His family supported him in this endeavor, and he was given the opportunity to travel throughout Europe, learning the styles and techniques of his most-talented peers. Since he was a diligent student and quick learner, he would eventually outdo most of them.

It is the stunning precision of his paintings, drawings, and etchings that we often think of today whenever Dürer's name is mentioned. His passionate interest in science and mathematics impacted his artistry and enhanced his ability to make things look convincingly real under his brush, pen, or engraving tool. (Such was his knowledge that he even wrote books on geometry, perspective, and proportion.) Because printing had been invented in Germany in the 1440s, Dürer could respond to the need for illustrations for the texts of the volumes that were coming off the new presses. His eye for detail led him to artistic innovations in the woodcuts and engravings that graced the pages of many books. He discovered ways to use the spacing of parallel lines and crosshatching to create different tonalities of dark and light for his compositions, and these are deployed in especially effective ways in works such as the Apocalypse woodcuts; *St. Jerome in His Study* (1514); the much-reproduced *Praying Hands* (c. 1508); *Adam and Eve; Knight, Death, and the Devil* (1507); and the mysterious *Melancholia I* (1514).

Dürer's observational powers are also evident in his many depictions of animals and growing things. He was a keen student of nature, so his lifelike images are utterly convincing—whether of weeds and grasses or of a rabbit whose fur is so finely rendered that you would expect to feel the silky texture were you to touch the paper on which it is drawn.

Dürer used these same powers for depicting people, and was in demand as a portrait painter despite the fact that he tended to take a more "warts and all" approach than other artists who idealized their subjects. His people are real. We feel as if we know them, as if we might have conversed with them in the street. He clearly had a fascination with faces, and no face fascinated him more than his own. He was one of the first artists to make himself the subject of his own painting, and he created numerous self-portraits throughout his artistic career. One of these is a remarkable painting done in 1500, when he was twenty-eight, which is notable for its nearness to the classic depiction of Christ. This "imitation of Christ" self-portrait meant so much to him that it never left his studio. It was a reminder to him that we are all striving to live lives similar to that of our Lord.

A man of deep faith, Dürer was committed to the God who had created all the beautiful minutiae of the world that he so loved to draw, paint, and engrave. Though he was not one given to making grand theological pronouncements, some of the thoughts he shared in his letters and diaries make it clear that he had great sympathy toward the Reformation, which was still in its infancy. In his diary, he referred to Martin Luther as a man "pious and enlightened by the Holy Ghost, a successor of Christ, and a follower of the true Christian faith." One of his great regrets was that he never got to paint Luther, a work that would have served "as a lasting memorial to the Christian man who has helped me out of great anxiety." Dürer was critical of the corruption he saw in the papacy and longed for a purer expression of the gospel. "O Lord," he wrote, "give us hereafter the new beatified Jerusalem which will descend from heaven as told in the Apocalypse; the divinely pure gospel, untarnished by human doctrine."[1]

Albrecht Dürer's art is filled with a love for the rich and teeming wild world that God created as well as a longing for a better world to come. Whether his subject was the book of Revelation, a gentle hare, or a knight in peril on the road to salvation, he illustrated this love and longing with careful detail and great joy.

12

The Garden of Earthly Delights

Hieronymus Bosch

(paintings, c. 1500)

No other artist was as effective as Hieronymus Bosch at depicting the dark creatures that inhabit our nightmares. But he did it with such a sly sense of humor that, while his art sometimes might creep us out a bit, it mostly fascinates us. During his lifetime Bosch painted a number of triptychs (works of art divided into three separate panels), and the most famous of these by far is *The Garden of Earthly Delights*, an altarpiece that was probably never used as such but rather hung in the collection of a nobleman. The left panel depicts a pre-fall paradise peopled by Adam and Eve and a collection of wondrous creatures. The middle and largest panel depicts the delights of earthly existence and is filled with nude figures, oversized fruit (often a symbol for sexuality), and strange exotic birds and animals. The right panel, probably the most famous, graphically depicts the horrors of hell and judgment. When the hinged panels are closed they form another image, that of God creating the earth.

Instead of relying on traditional religious iconography, Bosch employed his own unique vision and an unfamiliar system of symbols in his work. It is a profoundly personal vision—dream and nightmare—rather than an approved ecclesiastical portrayal of heaven and hell. Bosch seemed intent on revealing human nature for what it is—weak, prone to foolishness and sin, and in grave danger of eternal judgment. But he did this with a laugh and wink as

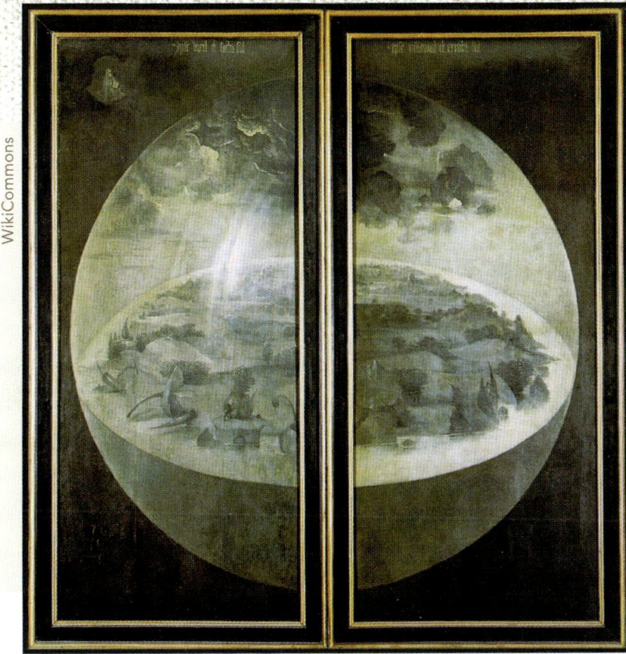

The exterior (or shutters) of *The Garden of Earthly Delights*

he rewrote all the rules about depicting the biblical narrative or the afterlife. Though the triptych is humorous, weird, and continually surprising—sometimes also impenetrable and ambiguous—Bosch was indeed earnest about his message regarding sin and morality.

The Garden of Earthly Delights is not a painting that can be comprehended in a glance but rather a complex chaos of images with few central points of focus. Our eyes wander over the numerous little clusters of activity, pausing over strange and wonderful creatures, writhing human figures, and terrifying beasts. There is a blending of close scientific observation of the natural world with wild, unexpected invention in his people and animals, as well as in the vegetation and landscape. In the left panel, we see God blessing the newly created couple in the pristine first days of the world. In the right panel, *Hell,* we no longer see much of nature as God intended it but instead a world that sinful humanity has made, a world where the things we have created have turned upon us. Human beings are tortured, impaled, eaten, excreted, and variously abused in payment for their sins. Their cities burn and even the musical instruments they have fashioned turn upon them and become instruments of torture. Bosch seems to be clearly saying that we have brought such judgment upon ourselves.

The central panel is the most difficult to interpret. Some suggest that this panel is a warning against unchecked human sensuality and where it leads, an illustration of unbridled lust. Others have postulated that Bosch is depicting an imagined world where the fall never occurred, where humans are free to frolic and enjoy the pleasures of existence without guilt and recrimination. Or perhaps it is his idea of heaven. We'll probably never know exactly what Bosch intended, but it is undoubtedly a depiction of teeming pleasures with large, oversized fruit and birds, and fountains in which people splash and play and couple.

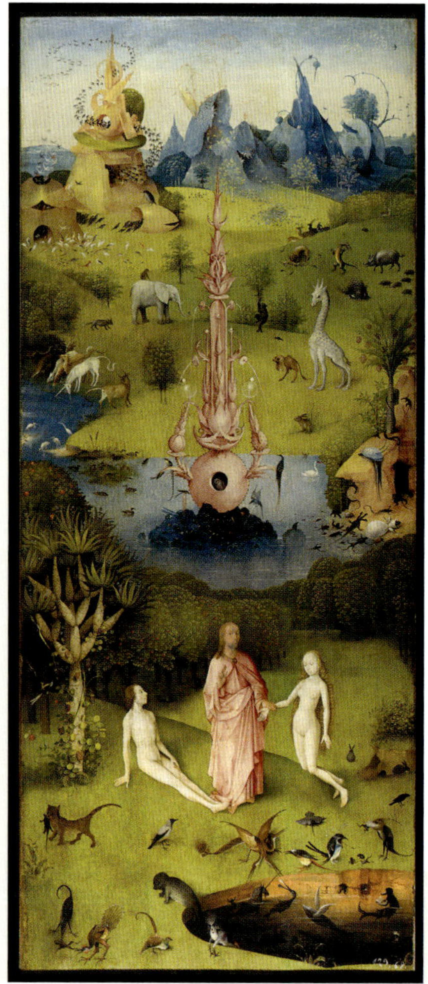

WikiCommons

Garden of Eden (detail from *The Garden of Earthly Delights*) by Hieronymus Bosch, Prado Museum, Madrid

Born Jheronimus van Aken about 1450 in the Netherlands, he derived the name under which he painted from his birthplace, Bosch, hence Hieronymus Bosch. We know very little about the details of his life, but we know he came from a family of painters and belonged to the Illustrious Brotherhood of Our Blessed Lady, a conservative religious group that had a wide influence throughout Europe. His early work is similar to many other artists of his time, but he soon developed a style of painting and a grammar of symbols that were uniquely his own. There really is no one who preceded him to whom he can be compared—a true original. Nor is there anyone who came after him who painted in quite the same manner at which he excelled.

Some interpreters of Bosch's work have explored his strange symbolism and suggested that he was a member of a heretical sect, such as the Cathars or the Adamites, but there is no evidence to suggest that his theology was anything other than orthodox. His paintings of saints and biblical narratives show a deep familiarity with the Bible and the stories of the saints. There is little pious sentimentality in his paintings, and he is not adverse to attacking traditional religious institutions. While there are many caustic attacks on religious hypocrisy within the details of his paintings, including a pig dressed in a nun's habit among the denizens of hell, such a decorative denunciation of the failings of institutional Christianity does not indicate that he was operating outside that belief system. Instead, they reveal him as a passionate critic of the abuse of religious power and the scandalous behavior that he witnessed among members of the clergy, a corruption that clearly did not harmonize with the teachings of the Bible.

Bosch created his art to impart lessons about virtue and vice as well as offer warnings of judgment upon those who persisted in immoral behavior. In addition to imagery drawn from the Bible, there is much in his work that draws its message from contemporary folklore—aphorisms, wise sayings, and humorous parables illustrated from the daily lives of his contemporaries. Through humor and through the shock of recognition, he raised questions about the way people lived their lives and the immediate and eternal consequences of continuing in a life of sin.

Bosch had a mostly pessimistic view of humanity, and saw our various forms of self-indulgence as the cause of our downfall. He is the great painter of the folly of humanity, seeing foolishness as our universal state of being. In fact, one of his most well-known paintings is entitled *The Ship of Fools* (c. 1490–1500), an illustration of our shared journey into perdition. In another, *The Seven Deadly Sins* (c. 1500), he enumerates some of the forms that this folly takes.

Perhaps it is Bosch's rich and vivid sense of humor that saves his work from solemn self-righteousness and moralism. His paintings are spiced with depictions of foolishness being repaid in appropriate coin, and with many subtle puns and not-so-subtle jabs at hypocrisy and corruption. He created rich and unforgettable satire, peopled with the strange and exotic visions that burst forth from his imagination. Sometimes these delight, but sometimes they horrify.

Death was an ever-present reality in late medieval times, with life expectancies much shorter than in our own time, and there were always the specters of famine, pestilence, and disease. After death, Bosch reminds us, comes judgment. He illustrated the hell we create for ourselves on earth, what follows our life on this planet, and how our sinful actions might be repaid in kind in the afterlife. Though Bosch painted other subject matter, he is best known for his depictions of hell, the place where judgments are meted out. For Bosch, the devil is quite literally in the details, the nightmarish elements present in his depictions of hell.

Sometimes the grotesque creatures that inhabit his imaginative visions of judgment are hybrids of humans and beasts, or of humans and trees, or of humans and inanimate objects. The variety of Bosch's invention is stunning. His paintings often work in the same way our nightmares do, merging elements of things that are familiar to us in combinations that make them seem menacing and horrific, playing on our fear of the unknown and unfamiliar. He can often be scatological, as we see demons of hell excreting sinners from their rectums or a man standing over a pit defecating gold coins into the abyss. The later Surrealist painters owe a sizable debt to Bosch's work for showing how the familiar can be made unfamiliar, and even frightening, by combining elements of reality in unexpected ways.

The other great subject for Bosch was the passion and suffering of Jesus. His images of *The Mocking of Christ* (c. 1490–1500), *Christ Crowned with Thorns* (c. 1490–1500), and *Christ Carrying the Cross* (1515–1516) are all memorable for the quiet composure on the face of Christ as He accepts His fate, contrasted with the hideous faces of those who laugh and hurl scorn at Him. Perhaps Bosch is reminding us that in these stories we—sinful humanity—are the real horrors.

Hieronymus Bosch was realistic about the human condition—our tendency to pursue pleasure at the expense of that which is truly good. His paintings are stern warnings against living a life oblivious to the eternal consequences of our actions, and his is a harsh message. But because it is couched with such creativity, endless invention, earthiness, and a bold sense of humor, these paintings have continued to amaze, puzzle, horrify, and delight viewers down to our own time.

13

The Ceiling of the Sistine Chapel

Michelangelo

(painting, 1508–1512)

It is unlikely that any masterpiece in the long history of Western art was undertaken with more trepidation and less enthusiasm than the paintings Michelangelo did for the ceiling of the Sistine Chapel. Michelangelo saw himself as a sculptor, not a painter. It was in the art of sculpture that he had distinguished himself, to the extent that Pope Julius II requested him to sculpt a spectacular tomb by which the pope might be remembered. Michelangelo envisioned an ensemble of forty life-size sculptures arranged around a tomb the size of a small building. He set to work on the task, but before long he found that the pope was losing interest. Perhaps this was due to an uncharacteristic twinge of humility on the part of the proud Julius, but more likely it was due to the mounting costs already expended and the much greater sum still envisioned. When Julius finally canceled the project, Michelangelo left Rome in disgust and disappointment.

But the pope was not done with Michelangelo. He soon summoned him back to Rome and tasked him with painting some figures for the Sistine Chapel. The Sistine Chapel had been built in 1477–1480 on the exact dimensions of Solomon's temple. Its decoration featured the art of many famous painters of the time, and Julius wanted to add Michelangelo to their number. But Michelangelo, though he had some experience as a fresco painter, did not believe that was where his true gifts lay. He begged and pleaded to be excused from the task, even suspecting that the commission was part of a scheme hatched by envious artistic rivals to set him up for failure and make him look bad.

When Michelangelo finally saw that he had no choice, and must reluctantly undertake the task given him, he looked up at the chapel's ceiling, which was painted like a night sky, and envisioned the possibilities of creating something much greater than what was being asked of him. He then spent the next four years completing it. As it was an awkward place to paint, he even designed a special scaffold from which he could work. (The popular image of him lying on his back as he painted is, while romantic, only a popular myth.)

Michelangelo used the extensive canvas of that ceiling to create an unforgettable study of Old Testament stories that foreshadowed the coming of Christ. It contains a total of three hundred figures, and these figures—beautiful, strong, dignified—provide ample evidence of his skill as a sculptor. They look like sculptures chiseled out of paint. The work is centered on biblical episodes that deal with the big issues of life: innocence, sin, judgment, and reconciliation. Three biblical stories, highlighting important episodes from the origin of the universe, the creation and fall of man, and the tale of Noah are each rendered on three "panels." In particular, the image of God creating Adam is so familiar to us that it is in danger of being dismissed as a cliché—until you actually look at it closely and take in all its grandeur and majesty. There is a good reason why it is one of the most popular images in all of art.

Around these three central stories are arrayed seven Old Testament prophets and five Greek sibyls, all of whom are credited with predicting the coming of Christ. The effect of the whole unified work on most viewers is to be awestruck and overwhelmed. But not everyone loved Michelangelo's masterpiece. One later pope referred to it dismissively as a "bathroom of nudes."[1] Most, however, have recognized the genius and skill of its execution and the creativity with which the biblical motifs are revealed. Clearly Michelangelo had great knowledge of the Scriptures, but he read and interpreted them through his own unique lens. He once prayed, "Lord, make me see Thy glory in every place."[2] Michelangelo's art was clearly a vessel through which that glory was revealed.

Born in Italy in 1475, Michelangelo Buonarroti lived his early years among stonecutters. At age twelve he apprenticed in the workshop of the great sculptor Domenico Ghirlandaio. Later he had the opportunity to study classical Greek and Roman models at the sculpture gardens of the rich and powerful Lorenzo de Medici, who took the young artist into his home and treated him like one of the family. After Lorenzo's death, Michelangelo was given important patronage by religious leaders

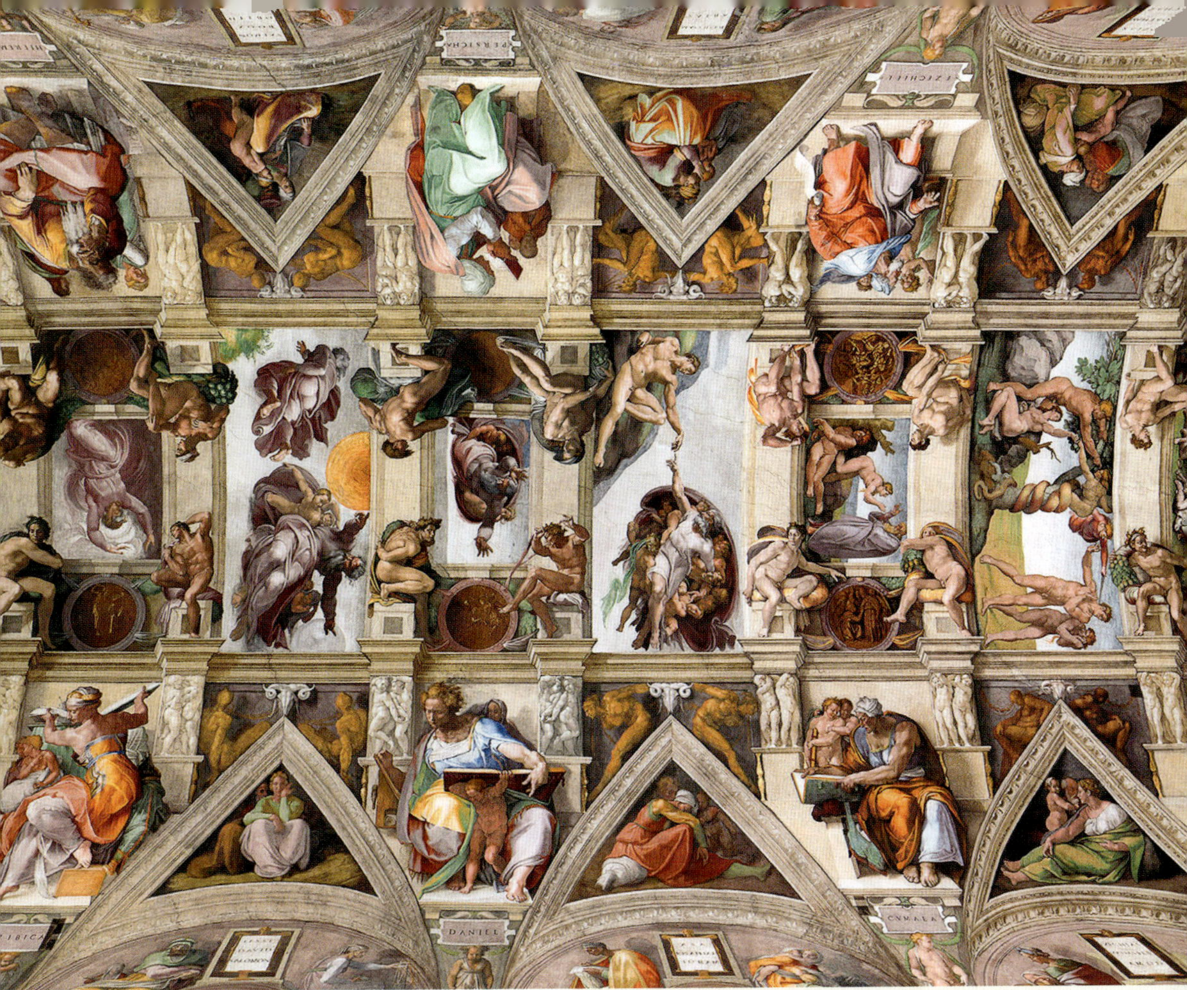

The Ceiling of the Sistine Chapel
by Michelangelo, Vatican City

and eventually a succession of popes.

Michelangelo was a Christian humanist whose perspective was formed by the influences of Renaissance philosophy, Greek Neoplatonism, and especially the Bible. The tension between these traditions can be seen in his work and thought. Classical art, especially the sculptural masterpieces of Greek and Roman heritage he studied under Lorenzo, deeply influenced his depiction of the human figure.

Michelangelo was convinced that his artistic talents were a special gift from God and that he was a chosen instrument of the divine will, with all the attendant responsibilities. He sometimes worried that his unquenchable desire for beauty distracted him from the pursuit of personal holiness, and he was concerned about the danger of making beauty into an idol. Many of his poems (he was an accomplished poet as well as an artist) show the struggle he experienced in trying to understand exactly how

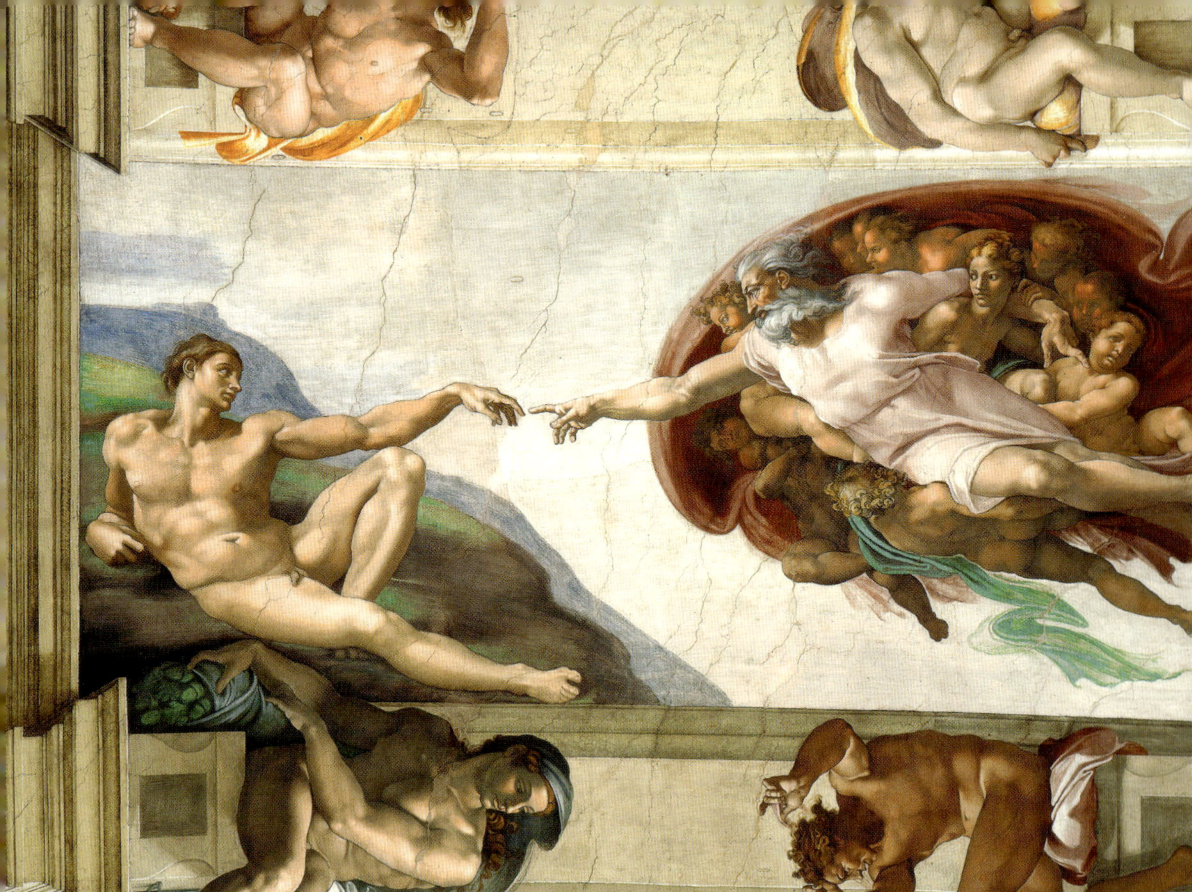

The Creation of Adam (detail from the Ceiling of the Sistine Chapel) by Michelangelo, Vatican City

art and beauty fit into the spiritual life.

But there is no question about the strength of Michelangelo's commitment to his faith. Throughout his life, his many letters to friends and patrons constantly invoke the name of God in a way that is clearly beyond mere convention. "I live and love," he wrote, "in God's peculiar light."[3] Along with the comforts of his faith and his sense of divine calling came a strong sense of his own sinful nature. He had a clear awareness of both the mercy and the judgment of God.

Perhaps this emphasis on judgment, which is especially prominent and powerful in Michelangelo's later works, was the result of the abiding influence of Savonarola, the fiery Dominican monk who was both preacher and reformer. Savonarola warned against God's wrath in the most strident terms, and for a time was very influential in Florence. Many who heard him repented and destroyed art and objects that bespoke wealth in "the bonfire of the vanities." Eventually his criticism of papal corruption could no longer be ignored by the authorities, and Savonarola was burned at the stake. But some of Michelangelo's sense of human sinfulness and the threat of divine judgment makes its way into his art.

The work that first established Michelangelo as a major artist was the beautiful *Pieta,* carved from marble when he was not yet twenty-five years old. The sculpture finds Mary cradling the body of her dead son, Jesus, in a way that is reminiscent of how she cradled him as a child. It is a work of breathtaking beauty and sadness. When the young Michelangelo overheard someone attributing it to another artist, he snuck into the place it was displayed one night and carved his name onto the sash around the Virgin's torso.

This work was followed up by an iconic statue of the biblical king David, which Michelangelo carved from an inferior block of marble that other sculptors had been afraid to use. When he finished the monumental statue, it was immediately embraced as a symbol of the city of Florence and installed in a place of honor. Michelangelo could see in that rejected piece of marble something that no one else could see, and he carved away everything that was *not* David. Michelangelo once described his process of sculpting in these terms: "I saw the angel in the marble and carved until I set him free."[4]

Thirty years after Michelangelo painted the Sistine Chapel ceiling, the pope summoned him again—this time to paint a depiction of the last judgment above the altar in the chapel. The result, probably influenced by his reading of Dante's *Inferno* and possibly by the residual influence of Savonarola, is a harrowing picture of Christ as judge, dealing out retributive justice. The fate of the damned is presented in nightmarish and uncompromising fashion. One interesting note is the depiction of the martyr St. Bartholomew, who had been flayed alive for his Christian witness. He is shown holding up his own skin, which has been freshly peeled from his body. On the skin Michelangelo has painted a world-weary self-portrait! Perhaps this is an indication that he saw the overwhelming task of painting this huge mural as his own personal "martyrdom"?

Over the centuries, the ceiling of the Sistine Chapel became covered in layers of grime and residue from burning candles, so a major project of cleansing and restoration was undertaken. When this effort was finished in 1994, Pope John Paul II celebrated mass there and spoke these words, which so effectively summarize Michelangelo's achievement:

> The Sistine Chapel is precisely—if one may say so—*the sanctuary of the theology of the human body*. In witnessing to the beauty of man created by God as male and female, it also expresses in a certain way the hope of a world transfigured . . . in the context of the light that comes from God, the human body also keeps its splendour and its dignity.[5]

14

"A Mighty Fortress Is Our God"

Martin Luther

(hymn, c. 1529)

One of the best-loved hymns of the Christian church, "A Mighty Fortress Is Our God" is based upon Psalm 46, which speaks of God as "our refuge and strength, an ever-present help in trouble" (v. 1). It may have originally been sung by Martin Luther and his companions at the Diet of Worms (1521), where he was first called to defend himself against charges of heresy, and where he and his followers initially feared for their safety.

Because of its stirring martial tune, it has sometimes been referred to as "The Battle Hymn of the Reformation," though in modern times it is often included in Catholic hymnals as well. It is best known in English through its translation by Frederic Henry Hodge, a very poetic and memorable rendering. In this hymn, Luther expresses unshakable confidence and trust that God will be our protector and source of strength, even "though world with devils filled should threaten to undo us." He highlights the intense struggle of the spiritual battle that is faced by believers but also expresses triumphant assurance that evil will be put to flight and God's Word will ultimately prevail, no matter what the immediate outcome of the struggle: "The body they may kill; God's truth abideth still; His Kingdom is forever." "A Mighty Fortress Is Our God," in both its words and music, echoes the great qualities of the man who wrote it—boldness, confidence, and defiance in the face of opposition.

Martin Luther was born in 1483 in Germany, and attended the university in Erfurt, where he was recognized as a brilliant debater with a keen intellect and biting wit. One day the young Luther was out for a walk when a tremendous storm flared up and he was nearly struck by lightning. Crying for God to rescue him, he promised to become a monk if God would spare him. Despite the impetuous nature of the vow, he made good on it, entering an Augustinian monastery, where his intelligence and his ability with words soon earned him an assignment as a teacher to the younger monks.

The order Luther joined was very strict, and was fastidious about the disciplines of rigorous fasting, long prayers, and regular confession. Though Luther performed all these to perfection in an attempt to please God, he could not escape a deep and abiding sense of guilt. The harder he tried, the guiltier he felt, and the more he examined his heart, the more tormented he became at his own unworthiness. And the more he tried to live an exemplary life, the less likely it seemed to him that there was any hope for his soul. He became angry at God, as well as at himself, and began to suffer from despair, chronic insomnia, and constipation.

One day, while studying the book of Romans, Luther came upon the phrase "the righteousness of God," and suddenly he saw a truth he had never before grasped: it was impossible for him to please God with his own efforts at righteousness, and the only righteousness he could hope for was the righteousness offered by God Himself. God's grace, he discovered, came not as a result of human effort and discipline but as a free gift arising from simple faith. As he meditated on this discovery he felt the burden of guilt lift, and true happiness and peace entered his heart for the first time.

This theological revelation was the spark that set the Reformation ablaze. Armed with the truth that salvation is by grace, not by works, Luther began to write and speak about practices in the church that he felt were contrary to this biblical imperative. He marshaled his passion and his rhetorical skills to question many teachings of the established church, and this eventually led to a split between Roman Catholicism and the various forms of Protestantism. Luther didn't originally envision anything more than reform within the church, but when his teachings were attacked by the church hierarchy and they attempted to silence this sharp-tongued monk, Luther refused to budge from his convictions and his commitment to the teaching of the Bible. "Here I stand," he famously said. "I can do no other."

As incalculably immense as his impact upon theology would prove to be for reshaping the church and Christian thought, it is not this achievement that earns Martin Luther a place in this book. Rather, it is for his talent in turning these truths into unforgettable hymns that Christians still sing today. Luther loved music and had an extremely high view of the musical arts. He once wrote, "Next to the Word of God, the noble art [of music] is the greatest treasure in the world! The riches of music are so excellent and so precious that words fail me whenever I attempt to discuss and describe them."[1] From someone who had written countless sermons, biblical commentaries, and theological treatises, this is an arresting statement.

Though Luther was not a professionally trained musician, he was a skilled lute player and an excellent singer. As an Augustinian monk, he would have been trained in the singing of Gregorian chants, and this experience of singing the psalms with the other monks is likely the root of his deep love for music.

Although Luther did not really consider himself a composer, he sometimes wrote original hymns or created complex choral compositions for four voices that show the depth of his musical knowledge. More commonly, he borrowed music from Catholic composers and adapted or rewrote the lyrics of existing hymns to express his Reformed theology. He even appropriated tunes from the German folk songs commonly sung in the taverns, by workers in the mines, or by children at school, and penned new words that reflected his biblical worldview to accompany these jaunty melodies. He designed his hymns to appeal to the ordinary German: joyful, not overly complex, and easily memorable. He saw them as tools for instructing the young in Christian beliefs and values and reminding the old of what the gospel meant in their lives. Based on his understanding of 1 Corinthians 3:21, "All things are yours," Luther believed that Christians could appropriate the beauty and power of music and use it to worship God and spread His Word. Some have credited Luther with asking the question, "Why should the devil have all the good music?" He understood music's power to move the emotions and saw how this could be pressed into God's service.

On this point—music's emotional power and usefulness for the believer—he differed from John Calvin and other Reformers. These leaders, in trying to distance themselves from the trappings of the Roman Catholic Church, emphasized austerity and attempted to cleanse their churches of every taint of "popish excess." They tore down decorations and images, removed organs from their lofts, did away with elaborate vestments, and drastically simplified the singing, all in an attempt to remove any distractions that might get in the way of the centrality of the preaching of the Word of God. Although Calvin was not opposed to music itself, he was suspicious of music's ability to move the emotions and was wary of the delight and enjoyment it brought, and therefore limited his congregations to unaccompanied unison singing of the psalms in order to maintain a serious focus in the worship service. He did not allow instrumental music in his churches. Zwingli, the Swiss Reformer, banned not only Latin choral singing but even the singing of German psalms and hymns.

Luther had a very different perspective. He saw music as an effective method to communicate the truths of Scripture in a manner that could move and stir the soul of every man and woman. Rather than fearing the emotional power of music, Luther saw it as a useful tool in the war against the devil. Because music had such power to lift the human heart, he recommended passionate heartfelt congregational singing as a way of putting the devil in his place. As he once opined, "The devil does not stay where music is."[2]

Luther wrote at least thirty-six hymns, of which "A Mighty Fortress Is Our God" is the most famous. His hymns were so compelling that they were sung not only during worship services but also in homes, while toiling in the fields, or at social gatherings. They were a way of teaching solid biblical theology to the unlettered and the illiterate.

The ultimate purpose of all Martin Luther's music was in its message: to shine a fresh and unforgettable light upon the texts and teachings of Scripture, and to give a voice to the joy that the gospel brought to the human heart. As he wrote:

> This precious gift has been bestowed on men to remind them that they are created to praise and magnify the Lord. But when natural music is sharpened and polished by art, then one begins to see with amazement the great and perfect wisdom of God in this wonderful work of music, where one voice takes a simple part and around it sing three, four, or five other voices, leaping, springing round about, marvelously gracing the simple part, like a folk dance in heaven with friendly bows, embracing, and hearty swinging of partners. He who does not find this an inexpressible miracle of the Lord is truly a clod.[3]

15

The Procession to Calvary

Pieter Bruegel

(painting, 1564)

In 1987, British illustrator Martin Handford launched the first in a very popular series of children's books called *Where's Waldo?* Its uniqueness lies in the fact that the bespectacled protagonist of the series is on every page of the book, but is hidden from plain view amid all the busyness and chaos around him. The fun, for readers, comes in trying to locate the skinny young man with the striped shirt with all the other stuff going on in each picture. Sometimes it can be quite a challenge to answer the question, "Where's Waldo?"

In his famous painting *The Procession to Calvary*, Pieter Brueghel seems to be asking a similar question: Where's Jesus? Though the title clues us in to the fact that we are looking at a religious painting, at first glance this is anything but obvious. For the figure of Christ, laboring under the effort of carrying His cross, may not immediately be seen by the viewer of the image.

But when you look carefully, you'll find Him at the very center of the canvas. Jesus has fallen under the weight of the cross He is carrying and is struggling to regain His feet. He is wearing a robe that is appropriate to the first century, but all those who surround Him are wearing sixteenth-century garb. And what a mass of figures there are in this painting! Dozens of them are clumped together in little painted vignettes, going about their business, most seemingly oblivious to the Savior's travails. Those who are leading Christ to His execution are dressed in red and mounted on horseback.

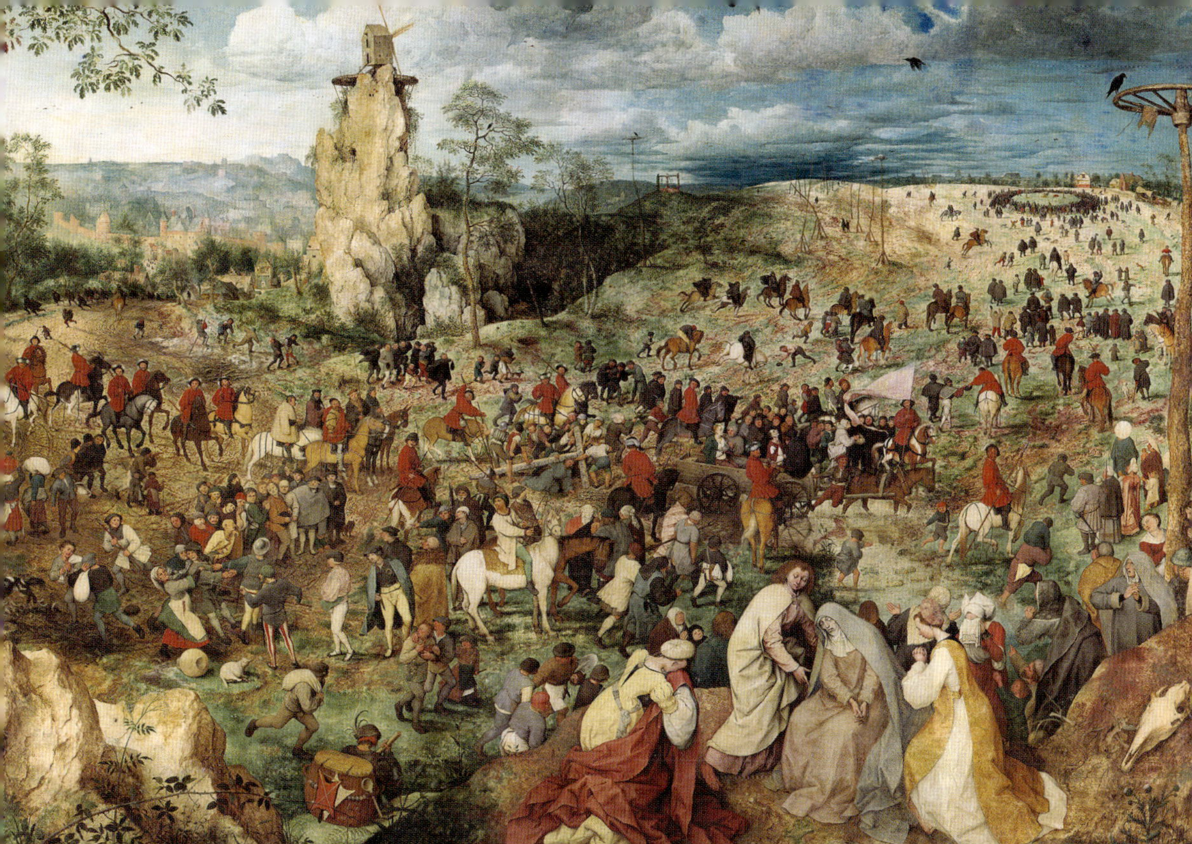

WikiCommons

The Procession to Calvary by Pieter Brueghel, Künsthistoriches Museum, Berlin

This is the costume of the troops who would have been responsible for executions in Brueghel's day, known to be merciless and efficient. Soldiers and bystanders alike all seem unaware of the spiritual import of what is happening right there in their midst.

Above all the flurry of activity a solitary mill stands upon a craggy mountain peak, which is a very unlikely location for such a building but may represent a "God's-eye view" of the unfolding story below. It stands as a quiet sentry over the whole ordeal. In the right foreground of the picture, we find the only figures other than Jesus who are dressed in ancient costume. These include Mary, the mother of Jesus, who is being comforted by John and two women. The solemn mood of deep sorrow implied in their poses contrasts with the people in the rest of the painting, who are either just going about their business or seem excited about the opportunity to witness a public execution.

Perhaps Brueghel is asking us to ponder the fact that the most sacred moments can occur right under our noses. That in the hustle and bustle of our lives we can miss the thing that matters most. That whether in the sixteenth century or our own, Christ walks the Calvary road for our sins, His sacrifice ever-relevant and ever-available. That God is hidden in plain sight, but we must have eyes to see.

Pieter Bruegel is one of those famous artists whose personal life we know very little about except what we might learn from looking at his paintings. Art historians generally place his birth in the late 1520s somewhere in the northern Netherlands, and records indicate he was living in Antwerp by 1551, where he was a member of the guild of painters. We also know he traveled to Switzerland and Italy between 1552 and 1554, as he created a series of dated landscape sketches from that period. These remarkable sketches show an interest in broad, sweeping landscapes that would remain with him throughout his painting career.

Bruegel married the daughter of the man who was likely his artistic mentor, Pieter Coecke van Acist, and had several children, two of whom (Pieter the Younger and Jan) became very accomplished artists themselves, working in a style similar to their father.

Much of Bruegel's earliest work was with prints and engravings based upon his own drawings. One of his most common early themes was illustrating the virtues and vices, often with Bosch-like humor and bizarre figures. Some of these kinds of figures made their way into early paintings that were crowded with people involved in various activities, some strange as in *Battle Between Carnival and Lent* (1559), some playful as in *Children's Games* (1560), a visual encyclopedia of children at play in various games, and some moralizing as in *Flemish Proverbs* (1559), which depicts well over one hundred different traditional wise sayings, many of them quite humorous. A famous biblical proverb is also illustrated in one of his later paintings, *The Parable of the Blind* (1568), which is based on a saying from Jesus about the danger of trusting oneself to corrupt and foolish religious leaders: "Leave them; they are blind guides. If the blind lead the blind, both will fall into a pit" (Matt. 15:14).

Of course, Bruegel is best known for his delightful paintings of peasant life, which are filled with energy and celebration and honor the dignity of the peasant class. The dancing and feasting bring a smile to the most jaded viewer, but it would be a mistake to think that this was his primary subject. While these paintings are wonderful, they do not have the gravity of some of his biblical paintings.

The painters of the northern Renaissance developed a great love for painting the natural world, and artists such as van Eyck took great pains to paint lush and detailed landscapes as backdrops for the human figures who were the primary focus of their paintings. But Bruegel was one of the first to do something different: to place his human figures into vast landscapes almost as if they were an afterthought, as though nature itself was the real subject of the work. In one of his earliest works, *Landscape with the Parable of the Sower* (c. 1557), we have to work a little to find the man sowing seeds in the bottom left of the painting. The landscape, which stretches for miles, seems the main point, and the only suggestion of Jesus as the teacher of this parable is the likelihood that He is among the little mass of figures next to the river far, far below. A similar effect occurs in *Flight Into Egypt* (1563), where the holy family pass by at the very bottom right of the picture and the rest is all majestic scenery. It would have been almost inconceivable to a sixteenth-century artist to paint a landscape for its own beauty, so his contemporaries would have looked to find the meaning of the work in whatever narrative was unfolding, even if on a very small scale compared to the way nature was presented.

The perspective for many of Bruegel's greatest works is a high vantage point that takes in all the teeming activity of human beings in the midst of an immense and lovely landscape. This might suggest God's own exalted viewpoint over His creation and imply His sovereignty over all that happens below. In Bruegel's famous series of paintings of the seasons of the year, we see this perspective and can easily intuit a divine eye overseeing the hunt in the snow or the harvesting of the fields. These are also some of the first paintings in history that effectively evoke a sense of the weather and climate. You can feel the cold snow crunching under the hunter's boots in *The Hunters in the Snow* (1565), or long for a rest on a hot autumn day like the man sprawled under the tree in *The Corn Harvest* (1565).

When Pieter Bruegel painted a biblical narrative, the main story usually receded into the background or was embedded among the usual goings-on of sixteenth-century life in the Netherlands. This can be seen in *The Procession to Calvary* but also in his two famous paintings of *The Tower of Babel* (c. 1563), in *The Massacre of the Innocents* (c. 1565), and in *The Census at Bethlehem* (1566). In a painting like *The Census at Bethlehem,* it would be very easy to miss the important event that is occurring in what appears to be a normal village in the Netherlands on an unremarkable snowy winter day. While the townspeople go about their business, Mary and Joseph ride in to register themselves in their hometown as required by Roman law. As in *The Procession to Calvary,* one must look closely or miss the main point. The unfolding of God's plan is taking place amid all the hustle and bustle of ordinary life. And isn't that how the spiritual world usually interacts with our own? Bruegel reminds us that we must pay attention if we are to see the divine story of redemption hidden in the midst of our own story.

16

The Burial of the Count of Orgaz

El Greco

(painting, c. 1586)

Sometimes art can be an elaborate way of saying thank you. Such is the case for El Greco's famous painting *The Burial of the Count of Orgaz*, created between 1586 and 1588. It honors the memory of a long-dead church benefactor with an image that is more a fevered spiritual vision than a traditional memorial. The count was esteemed for his generosity to the poor and for giving a large gift to adorn the church of Santo Tomé, El Greco's parish church. Legend had it that St. Augustine and St. Stephen had both miraculously appeared at the funeral of this pious man to assist in the burial of his body, so in El Greco's painting, commissioned by the parish priest, he depicts not only this miracle but also the moment at which the count's soul was received into heaven. El Greco also included a number of contemporary nobles from Toledo among the throng that gathers to witness the scene, including a self-portrait and a likeness of his son, Jorge, who kneels at the edge of the picture plane as though invoking the viewer to join him in contemplating this moment.

In this altarpiece, El Greco broke down the boundaries of time and space. Dividing time into zones within the canvas, he includes figures of the long-past, the near-past, and the present, all participating in this one defining moment. And he also gives us a privileged glimpse into the spiritual realm, where the soul of the saintly count, in the form of an infant carried by an angel, is being received by Jesus, the Virgin

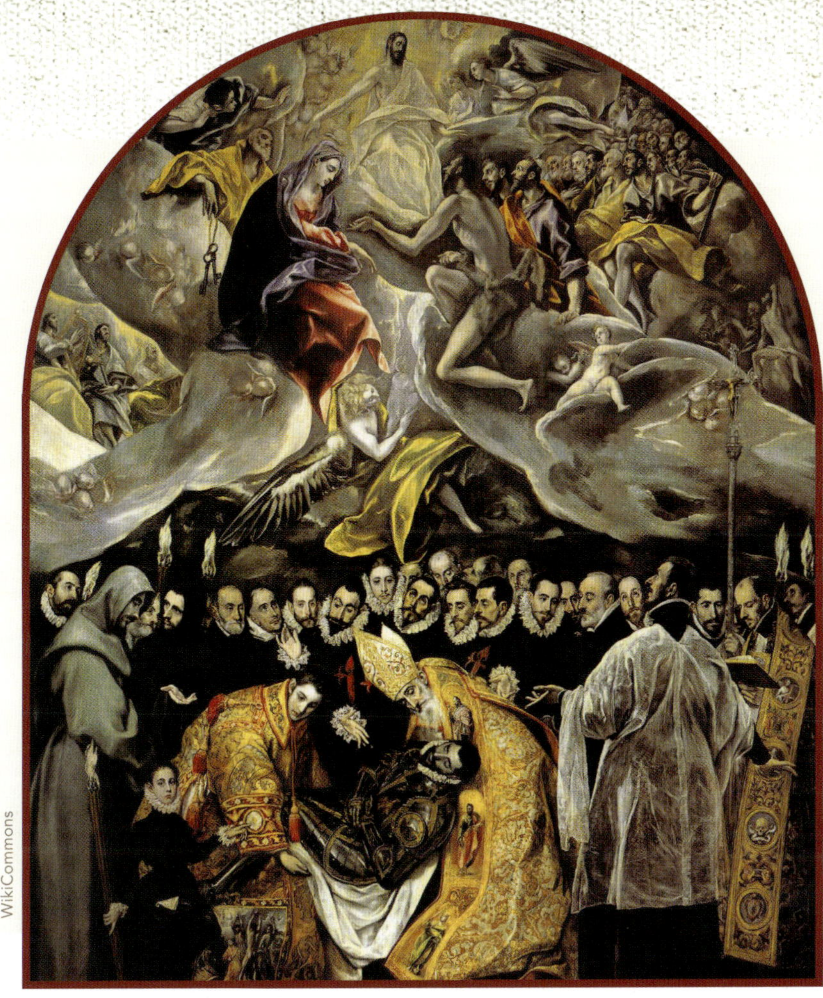

WikiCommons

The Burial of the Count of Orgaz by El Greco, Church of Santo Tomé, Toledo

Mary, and a throng of heavenly witnesses. The lower half of the painting is solemn and realistic, while the upper half is bursting with such vigor and energy that the painting itself seems something of a miracle.

Doménikos Theotokópoulos was born on the island of Crete in 1541, and he was most likely brought up as an Orthodox Christian. Because of the difficulty his friends in Italy and Spain had in pronouncing his name, they simply called him *El Greco*, "the Greek." The name stuck. El Greco was trained as an icon painter and later used some of the techniques he had learned in that tradition as he forged his own direction. In 1567, he moved to Venice, where he fell in among the great painters of the day—Titian, Tintoretto, Veronese, and Jacopo Bassano. From their example he set about mastering the key elements of Renaissance painting: perspective, fully rounded figures, and a dramatic presentation of the narrative. Three years later he moved to Rome, hoping for the opportunity to paint a major altarpiece. But after six years he had still not received even one important commission, perhaps partly because of his ill-advised criticisms of Michelangelo, who had died a few years before and was still held in the highest esteem. His negative opinion about the *Last Judgment* in the Sistine Chapel may well have caused potential patrons to question his taste and abilities.

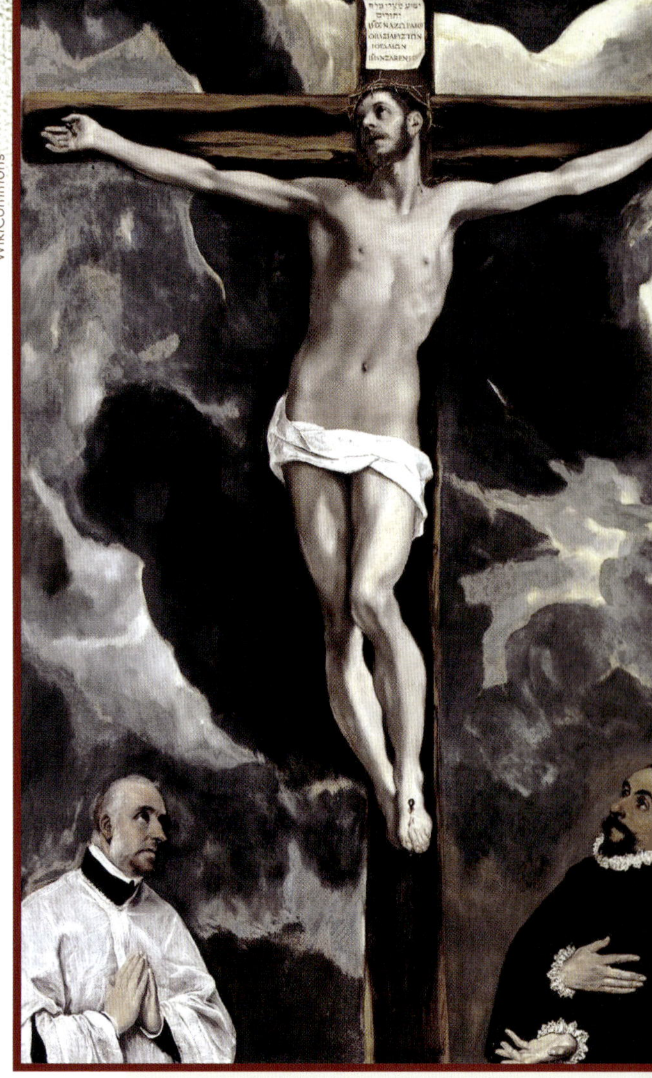

WikiCommons

Christ on the Cross Adored by Two Donors by El Greco

After moving to Madrid in 1576, El Greco sought royal patronage from Philip II, but once again failed to find a patron who would support his work. As he had done in Venice and Rome, El Greco had to eke out an artistic living by painting portraits and small devotional works. It was not until he moved to Toledo that he finally found the support he needed to let his creativity flourish and grow. Diego de Castilla, the dean of Toledo Cathedral, commissioned three altarpieces for the Church of Santo Domingo el Antiguo and helped El Greco find other important commissions.

Up until his move to Toledo, El Greco's work was fairly conventional, clearly showing the influence of the Venetian masters. In Toledo, his style came to fruition with a series of masterpieces that combined the naturalism he had developed as a portrait painter, the representational skill he had picked up from the Venetian painters, and the powerful expressiveness he learned from the later work of Michelangelo (in spite of his criticisms!). The first work he executed in Spain, *The Assumption of the Virgin* (1577), was also his first major large-scale painting. In the years that followed, his own distinct style emerged, a style unlike any artist of his time.

By the time he died in 1614, the intense realism of painters like Caravaggio had become the standard toward which most artists were striving and El Greco's work fell out of favor. He was largely dismissed for generations as an oddity of art history until he was newly championed in the twentieth century by the likes of Picasso, Rothko, and Franz Marc, all of whom saw him as a predecessor to the expressive emotionalism of modern painting.

El Greco's exceptional skill as a portraitist gives ample evidence of his ability to paint in a naturalistic manner when he wanted to, and some of his paintings in that genre are widely considered to be among the greatest portraits ever created: *Giulio Clovio* (1572), *Portrait of a Cardinal* (1600), and especially the unforgettable *Fray Hortensio Félix Paravincino* (c. 1609). Some of his most accomplished works are his portraits of biblical figures or the great saints (he was especially fascinated by Francis of Assisi, whom he painted many times). But instead of placing them in realistic backdrops, El Greco surrounded them with an atmosphere of mystery, using the natural elements of skies, clouds, rocks, and trees to fashion an intensely otherworldly environment. These paintings manifest the great spiritual intensity of their subjects, and he frequently portrayed Mary Magdalene, the apostle Peter, John the Evangelist, or St. Francis with rapt expressions, their moist, emotion-filled eyes turned upward to heaven.

In general, El Greco was not so much interested in the simple, straightforward appearance of things but rather in the way they revealed the spiritual realm. This can be seen in his famous *View of Toledo* (c. 1599), one of the earliest independent landscapes in all of Western art, a painting in which he rearranges the architecture of the city under threatening skies in order to portray the essence of the place rather than its actuality: a spiritual portrait of a new Jerusalem. The cathedral, which could not actually have been seen from this view, is given a painterly nudge into a place of prominence.

In *Christ on the Cross Adored by Two Donors* (c. 1580), a priest and a nobleman, both painted with realistic fidelity, are standing in prayer and contemplation at the foot of the cross, but as the viewer's eye moves upward on the canvas we see Jesus stretched out upon the cross, surrounded by a sky of roiling black clouds. El Greco's Christ comes across as more of a divine and spiritual being than a human and physical one, as there is only a dainty trace of blood coming from his wounds and a look of quiet resignation upon His face. Rather than trying to capture the realism of the crucifixion, El Greco was pointing toward what it accomplished—that the incarnation brought together the earthly and spiritual realms. In his painting, Jesus is suffering, and He is suffering for these two men gathered at the foot of the cross—and for us.

During the time El Greco was active, Spain was undergoing immense religious and theological changes. The Protestant Reformation's powerful influence throughout Europe had unleashed a Counter-Reformation movement that was seeking to address some of the criticisms raised by the Reformers while still embracing Catholic distinctives. This was a time of soul searching throughout Spain, and not surprisingly, a time of spiritual renewal.

Mystical writers such as Teresa of Avila and John of the Cross stressed the need for a more individual and personal experience with God, and although there is no clear evidence that El Greco was influenced by them, there is a definite mystical flavor to much of the painting he did during his years in Spain. His last painting is perhaps his most mystical image: a vision of the apostle John receiving the revelation of the Apocalypse. John's arms are thrust upward in prayer and adoration (and perhaps in surprise) as the figures surrounding him, suspended in the air in a dance-like arrangement amongst crumpled draperies, stretch toward the heavenly realms.

El Greco's distinctive later paintings are peopled with these elongated figures, smoothly curved and flame-like in the way they almost undulate in the foreground of the picture. His flickering brushstrokes add to the effect, as does the way that background elements are simplified and de-emphasized. There is a nervous, energetic quality to these works, a fevered swirl of dissonant colors and almost phosphorescent light.

Drawing upon his heritage as an icon painter, El Greco used light in a much different way than most artists of his time. Instead of the light coming from an implied source somewhere outside the picture itself, El Greco's images seem, like the icons he once painted, to be lit from within, as though the light is emerging out of the painting. It is a silvery light, accented with quick, almost impressionistic brushstrokes. There are few shadows. And as in an icon, these canvases are a place where earth and heaven meet, and where the sacred is made accessible.

El Greco was one of art history's true originals, fusing a variety of influences into a passionate style that was uniquely his own. One of his last paintings, which he created for the altarpiece above his own tomb, is *The Adoration of the Shepherds* (1514), a painting that perhaps sums up his own spiritual convictions. In the middle of the painting the infant Christ radiates an unearthly luminous glow, and He is surrounded by the shepherds and the holy family. Above them, clouds of angels rejoice, inviting the viewer to join El Greco in adoration and worship of the newborn King.

17

The Incredulity of Saint Thomas

Michelangelo Merisi de Caravaggio

(painting, 1601–1602)

The startling painting *The Incredulity of Saint Thomas* is almost shocking in its blunt physicality—a religious painting with nary a hint of sentimentality or devotional piety. In it, Caravaggio explores the moment when Thomas, not present when Jesus appeared to the other disciples and therefore in a state of skepticism regarding the resurrection, finally gets the proof he has required. As two other apostles look on, Jesus guides the probing finger of Thomas into the gaping open wound in His side. The face of Thomas registers disbelief as Jesus steers Thomas's finger (with dirt still under the fingernails) into the place where His side had been pierced. Can we not all identify with Thomas, the man full of doubts and questions, who wants evidence that what he believes is not just wish fulfillment? He is, in a sense, the stand-in cynic for all of us, and Jesus honors the bravery he shows in asking the hard questions.

The answer to the question Thomas has posed is that Jesus indeed has risen, though the resurrection in this painting does not receive its usual treatment by picturing a ghostly, spiritual Christ. Instead, this is a testimony to a physical, bodily resurrection. The risen Savior is real flesh and blood that can be seen, felt, and even probed. Through this picture we see a miracle made real, which was the great talent of Caravaggio.

Born Michelangelo Merisi in Milan in 1517, he and his family later moved to

Caravaggio to escape the plague sweeping across Europe. Later in life he took on the name of the city for his own and became known simply as "Caravaggio." His highly original and unusual style earned him fame and recognition, and the powerful Cardinal del Monte became his patron for a time, even providing him a place to live and work. Caravaggio's paintings were in great demand by many rich collectors and art lovers, but his specialty was painting biblical scenes as altarpieces for churches.

Caravaggio's unique approach to his art often caused him to be misunderstood, and in some cases his paintings were rejected by those who had commissioned them. To paint "holy" moments of the sacred story with all the dirt and grime of real life was seen by some as vulgar and blasphemous. They expected the traditional pieties of sacred art, but instead he gave them depictions of reality that were not idealized or prettified. His innovation was to paint things as they *actually looked*.

Since Caravaggio had little interest in painting an ideal, his early still-life paintings puzzled the art connoisseurs of his time by showing the fruit as imperfect—battered, sometimes rotting, and even worm-ridden. In his biblical paintings, that same striving for realism meant setting aside many of the conventions of religious art and attempting to capture a real moment on canvas. Putting aside religious sentimentality and sweetness, Caravaggio was able to render the world as the dirty, broken, and imperfect place it was, and the people in his compositions were the sort of people one might rub shoulders with on a dusty Italian street.

Indeed, Caravaggio would usually find the models for his paintings on such a street—often among the poor, the destitute, or the prostitutes who worked those streets. He would painstakingly pose them in a tableau, rearranging them until the scene suited his eye. Only then would he proceed to paint. And he painted what he saw, his keenly observant eye capturing the worn and tattered clothing, the ravages of age upon the human face, and the dirt and grit of daily life, transferring these to his canvas. His biblical characters are usually wearing the clothing of his day (Caravaggio didn't seem to worry too much about such anachronisms), and it is clothing that has been worn until it is *worn*. There are small rips in the seams and a generally tattered appearance, and the feet of these holy figures are often unshod, soiled and dirty with grime. The great events Caravaggio depicts seem like events that took place in the real world we all experience, not something that occurred in an idealized spiritual realm.

What Caravaggio so effectively captured in his many biblical scenes was the terror and immediacy of revelation—the frank shock of those moments when the spiritual breaks into our careworn existence. In his work this does not happen with the accompaniment of halos and singing choirs of sweet cherubs, but with violence

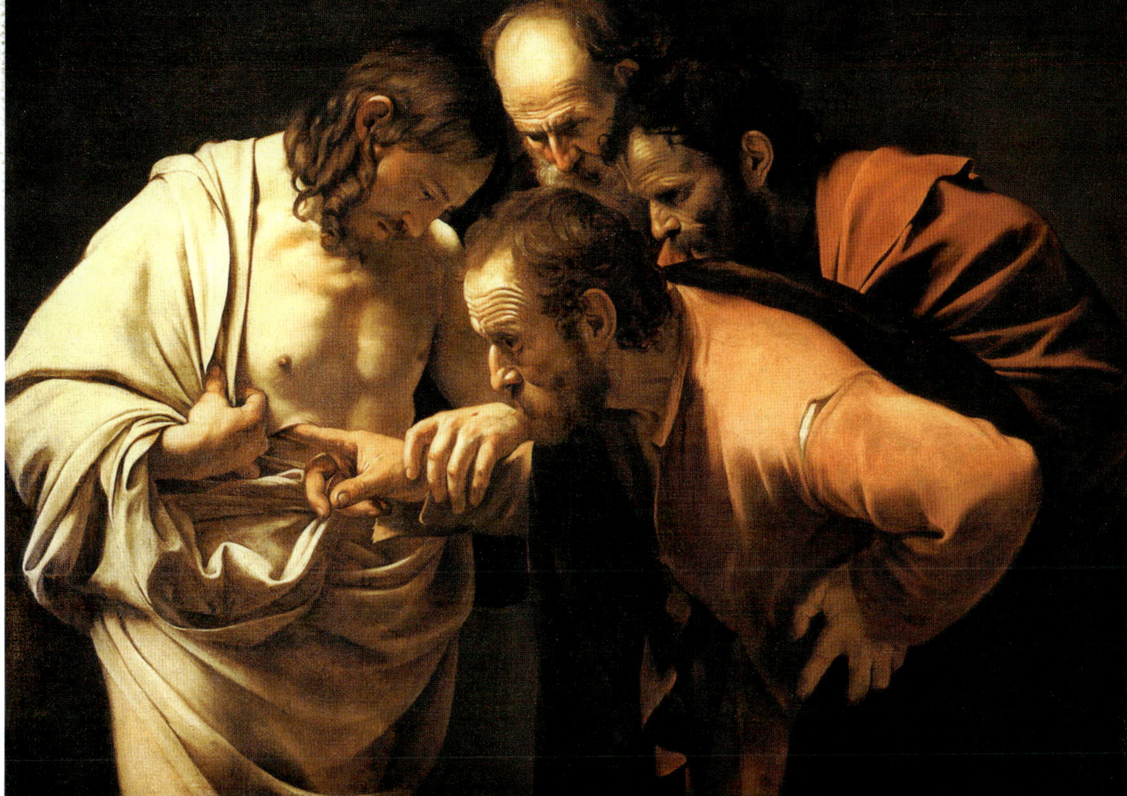

WikiCommons

The Incredulity of Saint Thomas by Caravaggio, Sanssouci Picture Gallery, Potsdam

and surprise, often in the midst of suffering. In Caravaggio's paintings God invades the real world, and it is often a messy and untidy business. It comes with light invading and illuminating the darkness but not eradicating it.

The innovative way Caravaggio used the effects of light has come to be called *chiaroscuro*, and he used these dramatic contrasts to intense dramatic and emotional effects. His use of theatrical lighting was a powerful tool for rendering the psychology of a spiritual drama and a way of making the moment look both true to life as we know it yet somehow full of supernatural import. Though it took some time for the art "experts" of his time to appreciate his unique approach, the common person more readily responded to this new kind of religious painting. As biographer Francine Prose suggests:

> Often ahead of his patrons, the people responded to an art that reminded them that these miracles had transpired neither in primary colors, nor in brilliantly hued paintings of sanitized saints and celestial fireworks, but in dusty streets and dark rooms much like the streets and rooms in which they lived.[1]

If Caravaggio's paintings portray a gritty reality, that might be because he lived a

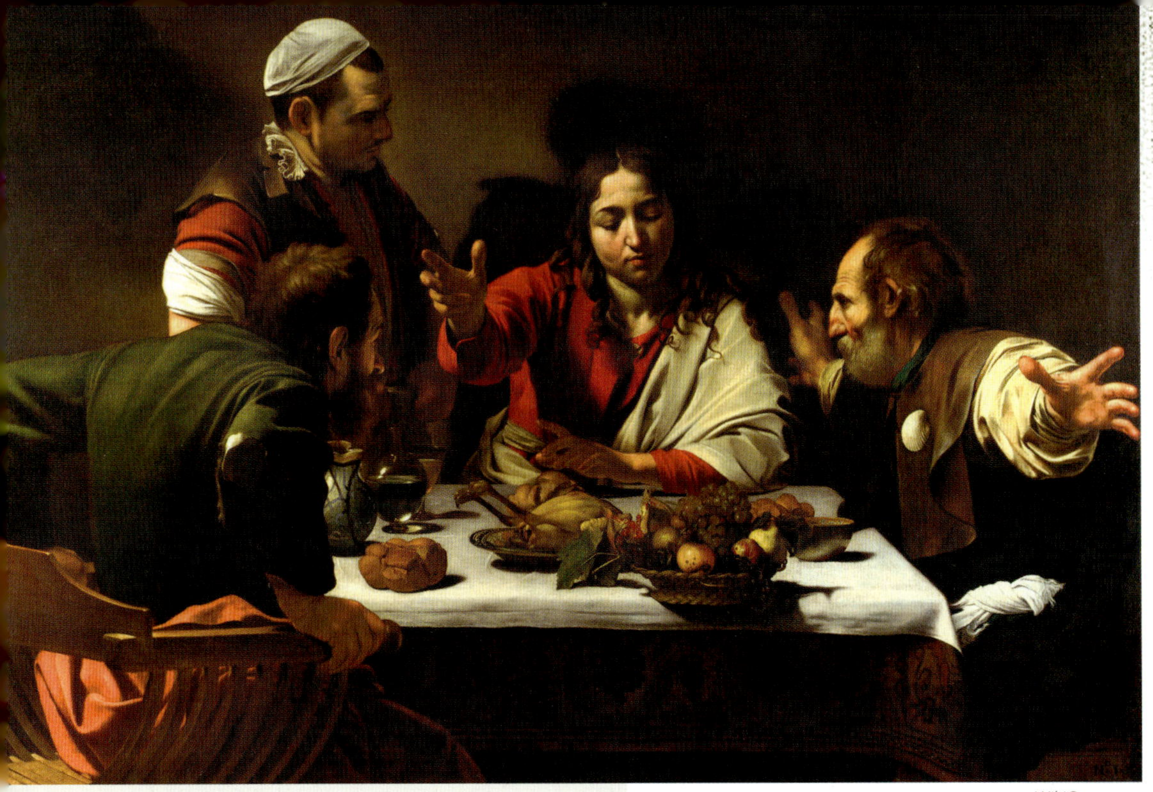

The Supper at Emmaus by Caravaggio

WikiCommons

gritty life. He was no model saint. He loved to gamble, fight, and duel, and he usually carried a sword with him wherever he went. Even some of his biggest supporters knew him to be a swaggering braggart who was fiercely competitive with other painters whom he was convinced had much less talent than he did. He was in and out of the law courts for various reasons, and much of what we know about him today comes from surviving police reports, cross-examinations, and other court records.

Caravaggio's reckless lifestyle finally caught up with him when he killed a man during a street fight and had to go into hiding for several years. The details about this event are sketchy, as are many of the events of his life. After a few years on the run, though, his friends and supporters were able to convince the pope to pardon him. On his way back to Rome in July 1610 to receive his pardon, he died of natural causes, probably as a result of the complications of a long struggle with malaria.

Despite this unconventional and chaotic life, Caravaggio never stopped painting. It is for his great biblical subjects that he is most esteemed today. He so very effectively captures moments of revelation in his paintings, such as when Jesus fully reveals Himself as the risen Christ to the two unsuspecting disciples with whom He had been conversing in *The Supper at Emmaus* (1606). One of the disciples throws his arms out in surprise, and the other grasps the arms of his chair, preparing to rise up in amazement. In *The Calling of St. Matthew* (1599–1600), Caravaggio uses the light coming from an undetermined source at the right of the painting to highlight the faces of the uncomprehending group toward whom Christ points His finger, calling forth the tax collector to follow Him. *The Taking of Christ* (1602), where Judas bestows the betraying kiss as others look on, includes a man who is a dead ringer for Caravaggio himself, obviously intended as a self-portrait.

Sometimes when a moment of revelation comes, it is a horrifying and violent one, and Caravaggio usually shows the instant just before the violence or its immediate aftermath. Examples of this include *The Entombment of Christ* (1603–1604), *The Sacrifice of Isaac* (1603), or *The Conversion of St. Paul* (1600–1601), where Paul has fallen, been struck blind, and is nearly beneath the trampling hooves of his horse). In *The Crucifixion of St. Peter* (1600), impassive laborers prepare to lift the inverted cross onto which Peter (who did not deem himself worthy to be crucified in the same manner as his Lord) has been nailed. Peter's musculature testifies to the intensity of his pain. Caravaggio often depicted such moments of suffering, but there is almost always a redemptive note that shows the suffering is not in vain.

One of Caravaggio's last paintings, *David and Goliath* (c. 1610), captures the moment when David raises the severed head of his vanquished foe. Interestingly, Caravaggio painted his own likeness onto the face of Goliath. Some have suggested that David is also a self-portrait, but of his younger self. If that be the case, perhaps it is a testimony to his awareness that the wild behavior of the young Caravaggio had so affected the life of the mature man he had become. Or perhaps he painted it as an act of reflection and confession. Whatever the case, it is a haunting image.

He left no written record of his religious beliefs and practices, but it is clear that Caravaggio knew his Bible well and was able to reimagine its events in fresh and surprising ways. It is possible that he was influenced by the spirituality exemplified by Ignatius of Loyola's *Spiritual Exercises*, which emphasizes the use of imagination and sensual perception in prayer. Ignatius instructed his readers to imagine themselves into the biblical narratives—to use their five senses to see, hear, smell, taste, and touch what had happened. This is what Caravaggio achieved so well in his paintings. He appealed to the full range of senses as he recorded the untidy reality of life and explored the ways God had broken into human history to make himself known, even in the darkness and violence of a fallen world. With his commitment to capturing reality as it is, Caravaggio showed the everyday ordinariness of even the most miraculous of stories.

18

The Holy Sonnets

John Donne

(poems, 1633)

Written during a time of intense spiritual struggle and crowded with startling and unexpected images, *The Holy Sonnets* is one of the most consistently surprising cycles of poems in the English language. They show a man in the midst of a spiritual crisis who is honest about his doubts, his hesitations, and his inability to always practice what he preached. John Donne, an Anglican priest, had once been known as a witty and passionate ladies' man, but in this series of poems he reveals himself to be God's man, with no less passion for God than he had once shown for the women in his life.

The Holy Sonnets contains nineteen short poems dealing with Donne's interior musings about God's love and his own inability to be worthy of that love. The first sonnet starts with a question, "Thou has made me, and shall Thy work decay?" which sets the tone for what follows: an inquiry into the struggles of the spiritual life. That these struggles are all too amiliar to most believers is likely why the poems have stood the test of time. These are not tidy and pious expressions of praise as much as honest outpourings of his wrestling with God. Sometimes he addresses God directly in these poems, but often he is in conversation with his own soul, posing questions to himself and trying to come to terms with his own failure to love as fully as he is loved.

Throughout the poems, Donne is concerned with the close connection between the physical and the spiritual, for he sees humans as frail and sinful beings who long for the release we will only find in eternity. One of the recurrent themes of these poems is confession and repentance, and in the third sonnet he speaks of "this holy discontent," and chides himself for his sins and pride. He also asks God to wash and cleanse him through his tears, and burn away the sins of lust and envy.

Another important theme in the poems is the imminent specter of death and Donne's embrace of a hope beyond it: "Death be not proud. . . . One short sleepe past, wee wake eternally, / And death shall be no more; death, thou shalt die."[1] With this hope in sight, and in the face of his own unfaithfulness, in "Sonnet XIV" Donne invites God to overwhelm and overcome him:

> Batter my heart, three-person'd
> God; for, you
> As yet but knocke, breathe, shine,
> and seeke to mend;
> That I may rise, and stand, o'er-
> throw me, and bend
> Your force, to break, blowe, burn,
> and make me new. . . .
> I like a usurpt town, to another due,
> Labor to admit you, but Oh, to no
> end,
> Reason your viceroy in me, me
> should defend,
> But is captiv'd, and proves weak or
> untrue.
> Yet dearly I love you, and would be
> loved fain,
> But am betrothed unto your enemy:
> Divorce me, untie, or break that
> knot again;
> Take mee to you, imprison mee, for I
> Except you' enthrall mee, never
> shall be free,
> Nor ever chast, except you ravish
> mee.[2]

God is never a spiritual abstraction in Donne's poetry but One with whom he has a sometimes troubled personal relationship; spiritual victory requires being, in a sense, defeated by God. His desperate desire for God and his hope that one day he will shrug off this body of flesh and all its inconstancies are what make these poems such unforgettable depictions of the reality of the life of faith.

John Donne was born in 1572 in London to a prominent Catholic family at a time of religious discord between Catholics and Anglicans. Thomas More and other persecuted or martyred Catholics were part of his mother's family tree. In 1592, Donne entered into the study of law, and at the same time he began reassessing his own religious leanings. For a time he was skeptical of both his Catholic upbringing and the Anglican alternative, and more interested in frequenting the taverns and pursuing the affections of young women. The young Donne also began writing poetry—poems that were witty, clever, and risqué celebrations of both love and lust. Some, like "The Flea," were frankly erotic. In "The

Bracelet" he even dismissed "that silly old morality" and its demands upon his life. There were few clues that he would blossom into one of the greatest Christian poets.

From the very beginning, Donne's poems were not written for the public at large but for a few select friends who passed them around in manuscript form, and they were not published until after his death. Since his early goals were more concerned with career advancement and receiving the attention of the court and the king, he had little interest in being thought of as a poet. In November 1597, he took a significant step toward recognition by the throne by becoming secretary to a prominent favorite of the court, Sir Thomas Egerton. It appeared that from there Donne would advance quickly to a place of prominence himself; that is, until love intervened.

When Donne met Anne More, he knew he had found the woman he had been looking for. She was not yet of marriageable age and was the daughter of a wealthy and important aristocrat, but she had the qualities he desired. The two fell in love and, because of her father's disapproval, had to marry secretly. When the secret came out, Donne was stripped of his position and had to fall back upon his own meager means for survival. As he quipped about the financial fallout of his romance, "John Donne; Anne Donne; Un-done."

Donne spent the next thirteen years living in near poverty, always hoping to find a way to make a place for himself in the world. He also continued to ponder his religious convictions and wrote books that showed his movement away from Roman Catholicism toward an embrace of the Anglican faith. When the king read these works, he pressured Donne to give up his ambitions of serving at court and instead serve the church by becoming a priest.

Donne could not initially imagine himself taking the Holy Orders. He still yearned for worldly glory and was keenly cognizant of his past sins. But in 1615, he was finally ordained in the Anglican church. Two years later Anne died while giving birth, and Donne was shaken to the core. He would never remarry, and instead found a deepening sense of spiritual vocation. In 1621, he was installed as dean in the prestigious St. Paul's Cathedral in London. From this pulpit he preached some of the sermons whose words still challenge and inspire readers today.

During the last decade of his life, Donne's health began to fail, and he experienced numerous bouts of serious illness. The meditations he wrote on his sickbed, *Devotions Upon Emergent Occasions*, contain some of his most beautiful writing, including the famous line "Ask not for whom the bell tolls . . . it tolls for thee." His last sermon, which he delivered despite the concerns of his friends over the weak state of his health, was entitled "Death's Duel," a celebration of the ultimate triumph of God over the power of death and the hope offered for a world to come. In a sense, as Izaak Walton later suggested, Donne had preached his own funeral. He died in March 1631.

Much is sometimes made of Donne's struggles with doubt in his poetry, but these poems do not reflect the kind of intellectual struggles that question the reality and existence of God. Instead, as Michael Schmidt reminds us, "His religious struggle was due to an uncertainty about the terms, not the fundamentals, of faith. His problem was not in believing, but in believing rightly, and having accepted right belief, to behave accordingly."[3] His poems don't so much make an argument for faith as they show it acted out in a real and honest way, with all the interior wrestling that involves. There is little polite piety to be found in his poems but instead honest human spiritual experience. He wavers sometimes between disgust at himself and spiritual ecstasy but he settles into a reluctant yet hopeful trust in God's love and mercy.

Donne's spiritual journey was a quest to overcome his sin and worldliness and replace it with "holy worldliness." His is not an "other-world" centered spirituality but one that sees the physical life on earth as the arena in which the spiritual life is lived out. "To be spiritual [for Donne] does not require the negation of the earthly, but the cleansing and restoring of it to that condition in which God first created it."[4] This involved honest self-examination, the embrace of God's forgiveness, and the acceptance of his love as the balm that heals all our inner wounds.

The abundance of God's mercy is absolutely central to Donne's theology, as that is the reality upon which all our hope can rest. Our lives will be a constant and unending struggle against the power of the flesh, but the end of all that struggle has already been determined—we will be embraced by the God who loves us passionately. Through his poems and his other writings, Donne is a companion for the trenches of life, the endless battle to live out the grace we have been offered. His impatience with his own failings and his willingness to tear off the veil of piety to express his deepest interior battles and spiritual longings make him the contemporary of every man and woman.

19

The Temple

George Herbert

(poems, 1633)

During his brief life, George Herbert never published a single poem. Shortly before he died, sensing that his time was near, this pastor of a small country church gave a fellow pastor who was visiting him a small volume to put into the hands of his close friend, Nicholas Ferrar.

> Sir, I pray deliver this little book to my dear brother Ferrar, and tell him he shall find in it a picture of the many spiritual conflicts that have passed between God and my soul, before I could subject mine to the will of Jesus my master, in whose service I have now found perfect freedom . . . if he think it may turn to the advantage of any dejected poor soul, let it be made public; if not, let him burn it; for I and it are the least of God's mercies.[1]

The "little book" was a collection of 167 poems chronicling the ups and downs, struggles and triumphs of Herbert's walk with God. Though Ferrar was not himself an expert in poetry, he understood the beauty and value in these poems and saw that they were published in 1633 under the title *The Temple*. These poems have been a treasure for Christians ever since and are some of the most honest and searching poems ever composed on the life of faith. They give evidence of a deep and profound belief as seen through the eyes of an intelligent man who struggled at times with

WikiCommons

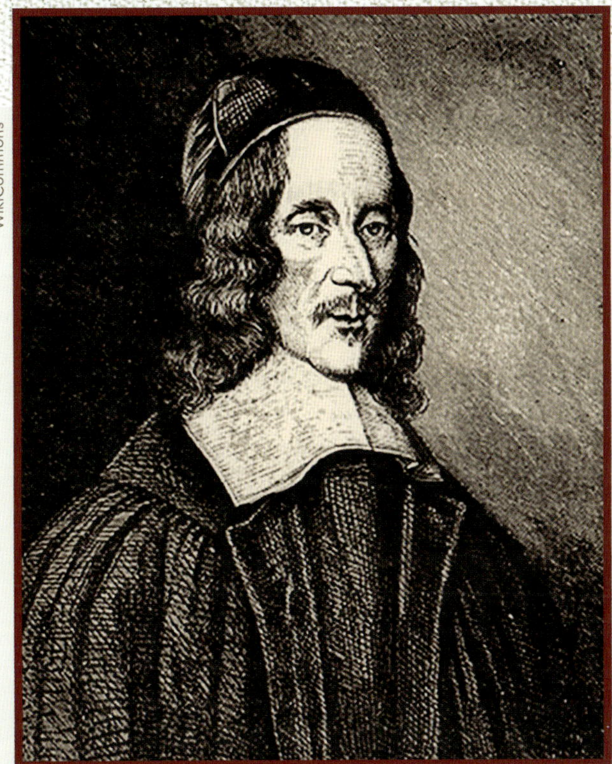

George Herbert, portrait by Robert White (1674) National Portrait Gallery, London.

doubts about his own worthiness and who embraced without reservation the grace of Jesus Christ. Taken as a whole, the collection of poems is a confession in two senses of that word: a confession of sin and a confession of faith. It is an honest accounting of his spiritual weakness and a determined embrace of the theological truths he knew to be true, even when he was not experiencing them.

But these poems are more than just the personal scribblings of a fellow traveler on the journey of faith. They are also extremely artful. Herbert was one of the great experimenters with verse form, so nearly every poem in his collection has its own unique rhyme scheme. He used the length of his lines to control the pace with which each poem unfolds, and a few of them quite literally take on the shape of their subject: in "Easter Wings" the lines are arranged like wings, and in "The Altar" they form the shape of an altar.

Perhaps the best known of these poems is "Love (III)," in which he records an interrogation with God, who invites him to sit down to supper with Him, but Herbert responds to that invitation by drawing back. He is the awkward guest who feels out of place at the table with God, but his Lord is not willing to take no for an answer. The debate continues, with Herbert sure of his own unworthiness and God trying to help him understand that He has borne the sin and shame—and inviting him into intimacy.

> Love bade me welcome. Yet my soul
>   drew back
>   Guilty of dust and sin.
> But quick-eyed Love, observing me
>   grow slack
> From my first entrance in,
> Drew nearer to me, sweetly
>   questioning,
>   If I lacked any thing.
>
> A guest, I answered, worthy to be here:

Love said, You shall be he.
I the unkind, the ungrateful? Ah
my dear,
I cannot look on thee.
Love took my hand, and smiling
did reply,
Who made the eyes but I?

Truth Lord, but I have marred
them: let my shame
Go where it doth deserve.
And know you not, says Love, who
bore the blame?
My dear, then I will serve.
You must sit down, says Love, and
taste my meat:
So I did sit and eat.[2]

Another memorable poem in *The Temple* is "Prayer (I)," essentially a catalog of descriptive phrases that attempt to capture different elements of the mystery of communicating with God. Prayer is, among many other things: "the soul in paraphrase, heart in pilgrimage," "reversed thunder," "heaven in the ordinary," and "church bells beyond the stars heard." Herbert's phrases wed together the wonder, the work, and the mystery of praying with images from Scripture, tradition, and his own fertile imagination.

These poems are just two examples from a collection that can be read and reread over the course of a lifetime. Whatever place one is at in one's own walk with God, there is comfort and wisdom and challenge to be found in these verses.

George Herbert was born April 3, 1593, in Wales, the seventh of ten children. He was an outstanding student at his preparatory school, and he then went on to Cambridge, where he immersed himself in the study of classics. He graduated second in his class, earned a Master of Arts degree, and became a fellow at the university. Three years later, he was elected to the prestigious position of public orator for Cambridge, where he gave official speeches and made friendships for himself among the elite. Then from 1623 to 1624 he served as a member of Parliament. One would imagine that he would have felt he had "arrived," but none of his accomplishments fulfilled the deeper spiritual call that was building within him.

A battle raged within his soul over the direction of his future, which only found its resolution when he was ordained first as a deacon in the Church of England in 1626, and then as a priest in 1630. He purposely did not seek a prestigious parish but rather accepted a call to a small country church in Bemerton. Throughout the time of his ministry there the congregation never numbered more than one hundred people, but those who were the objects of his sermons and pastoral care thought him a humble and saintly man and were impressed by his character, his charity, and his gentle holiness. It is unlikely that many of them even knew he was a poet.

Herbert intended the verses he composed to be for God and for himself, as a way of meditating on the progress of his faith. We are fortunate enough to get to listen in. He had a spiritual purpose in mind for sharing these personal musings, and at the end of his life, when preparing these poems for their final form, he wrote these lines in the introductory poem: "Hearken unto a Verser, who may chance / Rhyme thee to good, and make a bait of pleasure / A verse may find him, who a sermon flies / And turn delight into a sacrifice." He understood that poetry could have a persuasive power quite different from that of a message delivered in a pulpit.

Herbert struggled with his health throughout his adult life, and after three years in the ministry, he died of tuberculosis at age thirty-nine. Not a single one of the sermons he preached has survived, but what has survived are his remarkable poems, generally considered among the greatest religious poems in the English language. He described his own poetic calling as being "a Secretary of Thy Praise."

Herbert referred to his poems as the record of his conflict with God, and they have an intimacy about them deriving from the fact that most of them are directly addressed to God, and as such, he was not shy about expressing the nature of his own struggles. In his poems, we witness firsthand the battle of his will against God's, and his struggle with his sense of unworthiness toward being God's servant. His battle was a losing battle, as he was always bested by God and therefore had to make peace with Him through surrender. Time and again, Herbert found his ultimate victory in being defeated, for the One who defeated him is the God of grace and love.

Although the poems recording his individual journey of faith are intensely personal, they are also deeply rooted in tradition and in a commitment to Christ and His church. Herbert saw the spiritual journey not as a solo excursion but as one undertaken together in community, as members together of the body of Christ, His church. The church, as Herbert saw it, was the proper context for living out the Christian life. Therefore, many of the poems reflect upon the church year, make use of snippets of the Anglican liturgy, or use church architecture as a metaphor.

A great deal of the religious poetry written through the centuries suffers from being overly sentimental and often feels insincere, as though it is expressing what the poet wished to be feeling, or thought he or she *should* be feeling, rather than what he or she was *actually* feeling. The strength of Herbert as a religious poet is that he was not afraid to tell the truth about his struggles and doubts, and about the difficulties of the spiritual path. But he always ended with affirmation and hope. It was hope hard won, but more transformative because of the struggle.

20

Agnus Dei

Francisco de Zurbarán

(painting, c. 1635–1640)

Although Spanish painter Francisco de Zurbarán is best known as a religious artist, one who produced numerous paintings of biblical figures and important saints, it could be argued that his work reached its highest perfection when he turned his brush to subject matter not apparently religious on its surface. One such work is *Agnus Dei*. There is more going on here than meets the eye, as the beautifully rendered lamb is a symbol for Jesus Christ. The other title sometimes given to this painting, *The Lamb of God*, hearkens to the words of John the Baptist, which have been incorporated into the liturgy in the traditional mass, where it is proclaimed: "Look, the Lamb of God, who takes away the sin of the world" (John 1:29).

Behold indeed. It is hard to look away from the combined beauty and horror of the scene before us. Zurbarán's painting is of an ordinary lamb, laid out on a table or altar with its feet bound and trussed in preparation for slaughter. As was common for Zurbarán, he has left the background indistinct, dissipating into darkness, but has lit the main subject (the lamb) with bright illumination. He has painted the scene with such exquisite detail that you feel as though you could reach into the painting and touch the rough softness of the lamb's woolly coat. The lamb does not appear to be struggling but has meekly submitted to its fate without resistance and is prepared to die. One cannot but feel pity for what awaits this helpless victim.

The lamb was, of course, a traditional sacrificial animal in ancient Judaism, offered up to atone for the sins of the people. Isaiah had prophesied that the coming Messiah would be "oppressed and afflicted," and that He would go quietly to His fate "like a lamb to the slaughter, and as a sheep before its shearers is silent, so he did not open his mouth" (Isa. 53:7). So this painting offers us a reminder of the pain and suffering that Jesus took upon Himself on our behalf, a *willing* sacrifice for the sins of us all.

Perhaps this painting should be considered in parallel with Zurbarán's *Christ Crucified* (1629), in which we see Jesus stretched out upon the cross, suffering for the sins of humanity, and painted with such startling reality that He almost seems to spring forth from the canvas, as though He were sharing the same space as the viewer. He is, as in the later *Agnus Dei*, the Lamb of God whose sacrifice has a redemptive power that stretches down through the centuries, embracing all who believe with His atoning work.

Francisco de Zurbarán was born on November 7, 1598, in Fuente de Cantos in southern Spain. He apprenticed as an artist in Seville, where he met and befriended the great Spanish artist Velázquez. For

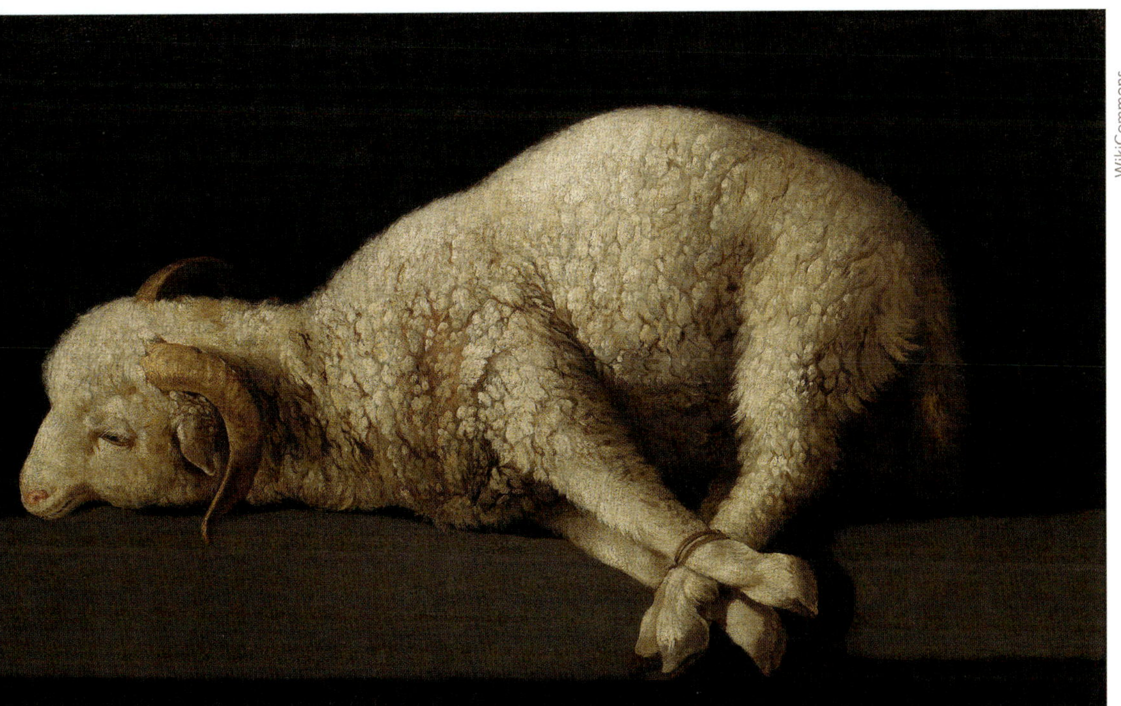

WikiCommons

The Bound Lamb by Francisco Zurbarán, Prado Museum, Madrid his entire career he worked in the shadow of this towering genius, who is universally acknowledged as one of the greatest painters in the history of Western art, and who was considered in his own time to be the greatest Spanish artist. While Velázquez gained fame and recognition painting at the court of Philip IV in Madrid, Zurbarán did most of his painting in Seville, outside the artistic mainstream, working for the monastic orders that flourished there. Though the paintings he created for them are inarguably beautiful, many of them were, quite frankly, workmanlike religious images done to order. But at the same time, without much fanfare, he was also creating some of his most accomplished works.

If the flame-like images of El Greco were visual poetry, the work of Zurbarán is visual prose—solemn, orderly, dignified, and solid. Often depicting moments of great pain and struggle in the lives of Christ or the saints, they reflect a severe asceticism—humble compositions painted with a resigned realism and a focus on the sacrificial nature of faith. Painted during a time of religious conflict in Spain, these are sober and serious meditations about faith and martyrdom in a world filled with suffering and death. The viewer can feel the weary weight that the life of faith exacted upon the saintly figures he has painted.

Some of Zurbarán's best paintings of the saints show the influence of Caravaggio, though any lessons were probably learned secondhand, as there is no record that he ever traveled to Italy. His canvases are typically shrouded in darkness except for the strong light that accents the main figure, creating an almost three-dimensional effect. The mastery he exhibits in lighting figures is almost unparalleled in the history of art. Art critics have sometimes even referred to him as "the Spanish Caravaggio." But in comparison with the vigorous action that usually characterizes a Caravaggio painting, Zurbarán exhibits something different: an inner tension; a coiled-up, austere stillness. He represses the energy, but it is still present and can be sensed. In his composition of these scenes, Zurbarán has pared things down, usually with little in the way of props or backgrounds to distract the viewer from the central figure in the painting, but if there is some sort of accompanying object (such as a book or draperies), it is painted with painstaking detail.

An example of such work is *Saint Serapion* (1628). Serapion was a twelfth-century crusader who became a monk and died a gruesome death at the hands of Scottish pirates. In Zurbarán's painting of the saint, he has placed him against a deep black background, each of his arms tied and suspended (a pose reminiscent of a traditional posture of prayer), and his neck appears to be broken. A bright light rakes over his tortured face and glows on his gleaming white robes. It is a horrific moment painted with pathos and a sense of great serenity, as though pointing toward a transcendent conclusion to the event. This moment of intense pain is not the final word. Though he has fallen victim to his persecutors, Serapion is, in the last estimation, the one who has gained the victory. The painting itself is a perfect fusion of realism with mysticism.

Zurbarán also produced a handful of vibrant still-life paintings, which exhibit the same austerity as his saintly portraits. Set against black backdrops, these serene works highlight the play of light on the objects depicted: cups and utensils, woven baskets, lemons, oranges, and roses. The elements in the paintings are arrayed with all their simplicity and humility, but given great dignity by the manner in which they are lit. Though the subject matter is not obviously or self-consciously religious in nature, they are nonetheless suffused with an austere spirituality. Even the casual viewer senses there is something sacred about these ordinary objects, which is surely what Zurbarán intended. They are serene votive offerings on the humble altar of a polished table and are also pointers toward eternal realities. Some of Zurbarán's best work was done when he brought his spiritual eye to the task of painting subject matter that was not so clearly religious in nature, especially in these still-life paintings or in artistic meditations like *Agnus Dei*. They often give more passionate evidence of his engagement with his faith than most of those containing self-consciously religious subject matter.

When the patronage of the monastic orders began to dwindle due to a changed religious and political climate, a severe plague, and an economic crisis that robbed the monks of their former wealth, Zurbarán had to turn his attention to painting on speculation, and for a time he found a ready market for his works among Spaniards who had settled in the New World. Then, perhaps in response to the emphasis on personal faith that arose with the Protestant Reformation, the fashion among his contemporary Spanish Catholics began to call for a more emotional and accessible kind of art than Zurbarán had been producing. Young upstarts like Bartolomé Esteban Murillo and Francisco Herrera produced canvases that were both sweeter in tone and more energetic in style than the austere manner of Zurbarán. Art historians generally agree that the quality of his work declined when he tried to adapt to the demand for this more popular and sentimental style. He was always at his best when he followed his own artistic muse.

Francisco de Zurbarán later moved to Madrid in search of better commissions, and died there in 1664 in poverty and obscurity at the age of sixty-six. One of his final paintings is a lasting testament to his devotion. *Crucified Christ Contemplated by a Painter* (c. 1660) shows an artist (probably himself) with palette and brushes in hand, gazing reverently at Christ hanging on the cross. This mystical contemplation is the perfect summation of his life and of his status as one of the greatest of religious painters.

21

St. Teresa in Ecstasy

Gian Lorenzo Bernini

(sculpture, 1652)

Perhaps never in the history of art have sensuality and spirituality been so inseparably brought together than in Gian Lorenzo Bernini's statue of the famous Spanish nun St. Teresa of Ávila. It is generally considered to be the greatest work of the man who is probably the finest sculptor of all time. Bernini combined the insights he garnered from his studies of classical Greek and Roman sculpture with the innovations of the great Renaissance artists to create sculptures that almost seem to live and breathe, and none more so than his sensuous carving of the famous saint caught in a moment of mystical ecstasy.

In order to avoid an arranged marriage with a man she didn't love, Teresa of Ávila entered the convent at age nineteen. At first, her new vocation brought her neither happiness nor contentment, and shortly after embarking on her life as a nun she became seriously ill and suffered periods of deep depression. But in time she settled into her new vocation. Then one day, while praying and singing a hymn, she experienced a rapturous sense of God's love coursing through her whole being. It was to be the first of numerous such visitations of God's presence, so real and palpable that she felt consumed by His love and exalted into a state of ecstasy. In her spiritual autobiography, Teresa describes one of these visitations: a vision of an angel carrying a fire-tipped spear with which he repeatedly pierced her heart, an act that induced a state of spiritual rapture. "The pain," she wrote, "was so

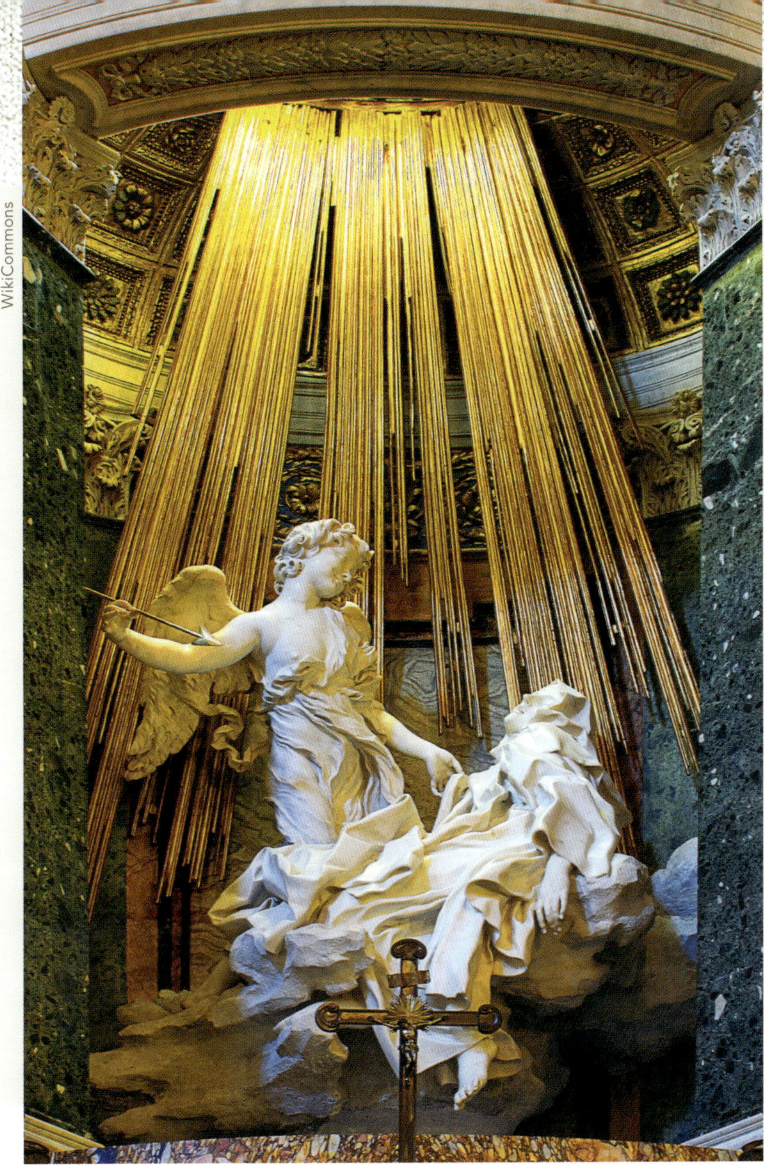

WikiCommons

Detail of *St. Teresa in Ecstasy* by Bernini, Corona Chapel, Rome, photo by Welleschik

severe that it made me utter several moans. The sweetness caused by this intense pain is so extreme that one cannot possibly wish it to cease, nor is one's soul then content with anything but God."[1]

It is this moment that Bernini has fashioned in marble. The cupid-like angel hovers just above her, his gilt bronze arrow poised to plunge again into Teresa's heart. He is a figure of delicacy and grace, but Teresa does not look upon him. Instead, her head is thrown back and her eyes are closed. Her mouth gapes open, and her body seems to collapse backward against the force of love that is so violently thrust upon her and into her heart. Teresa seems lost in the billowing, twisting folds of her heavy robe, as bronze rays rain down divine light upon the scene. Though this highly dramatic tableau is carved of heavy marble, it appears to the viewer to be almost weightless, the saint and the angel floating upon a cloud suspended above the altar of the Cornaro Chapel in Rome.

The statue of Teresa and the angel is the centerpiece of a visual feast in the chapel, an arrangement of sculpture, painting, lighting effects, and architecture, all designed by Bernini to frame this unforgettable masterpiece. He has created not just a sculpture but an entire environment. It is surrounded by dark, patterned marble columns and set in a convex niche that serves to enhance the brightness of the central figures, creating an impression that the very walls of the building have parted to reveal this dramatic moment. Illusionistic windows have been carved on the walls of either side of *St. Teresa in Ecstasy*, through which sculptures of members of the Cornaro family (the patrons of the work) gaze reverently at the unfolding scene. Some of them even lean over the parapet, silent and rapt witnesses to the mystical event.

It is not surprising that the utter ecstasy of Teresa's expression has put some in mind of the ecstasy of a sexual climax. The intense pleasure and pain she feels can only be expressed in ways that mirror one of the most ecstatic experiences most humans can identify with. And that is what Bernini was seeking to do, and what he did so well and so often—create realistic works that show the emotional intensity of an encounter with God. The undeniable eroticism of the work discomforts some viewers, but what Bernini was trying to portray is the eroticism of the soul experiencing the painful pleasure of an intense connection with God. He joined the physical and the spiritual in a way that is unforgettable.

Born in Naples in 1598, Gian Lorenzo Bernini was a child prodigy. His father was his first teacher, and he frequently found it necessary to admonish the young artist when he became so concentrated on his artistic studies that he neglected the childish pastimes that are always an essential part of growing up. Bernini's favorite thing to do was visit the Vatican in order to sketch the classical statues and the paintings of his contemporaries. Here he learned to unite classical and Renaissance styles, studying the work of the ancient Greeks and artists such as Michelangelo and Raphael. Once, when sculpting a statue of St. Lawrence, who had been martyred by being burned alive, he thrust his own leg into a fire so that he could experience what that might have felt like in order to accurately portray the facial expression of the martyr.

Bernini's talents were recognized early and progressed quickly. In short order, he became a favorite of Pope Urban VIII, who appreciated the usefulness of his talents in decorating Rome. His life spanned the

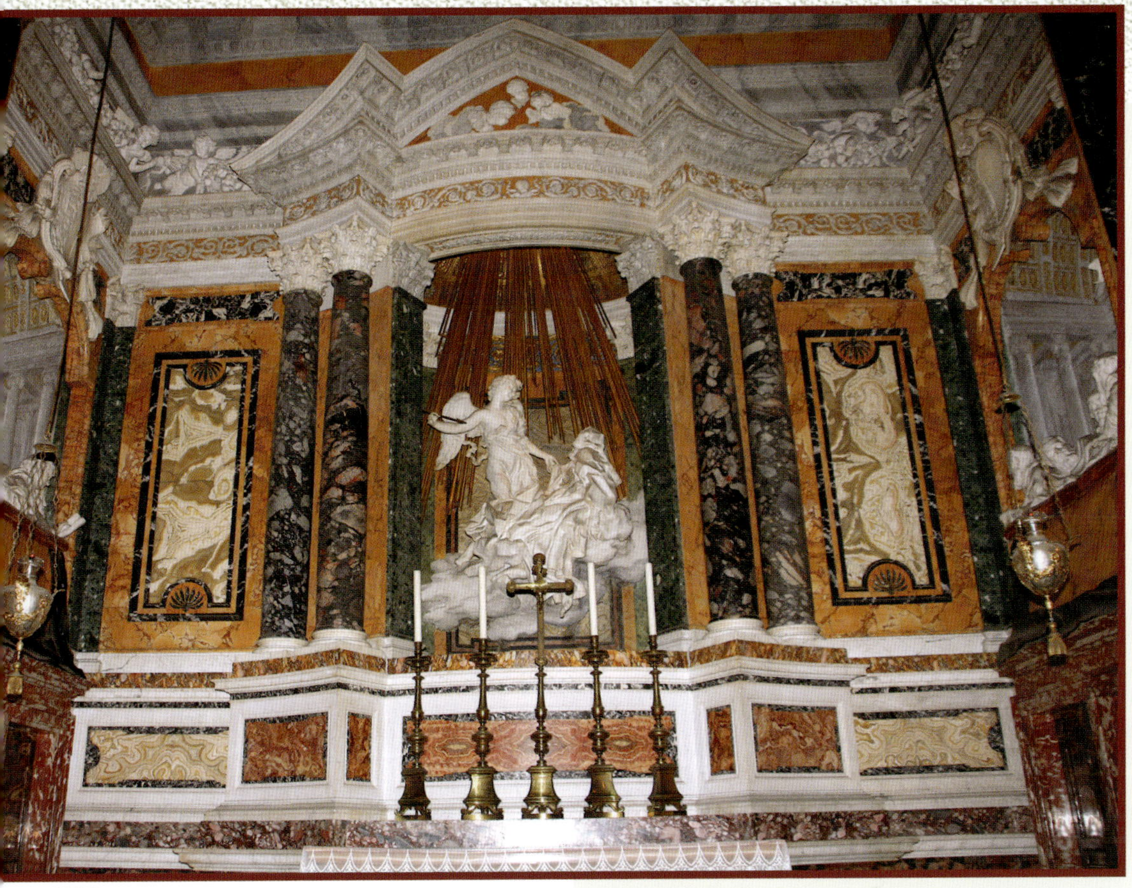

WikiCommons

St. Teresa in Ecstasy by Bernini, Corona Chapel, Rome, photo by Nina Aldin Thune

height of the Italian Baroque period, and his work can be seen as part of a response to the rise of the Protestant Reformation. The Catholic Church launched its own Counter-Reformation to reaffirm its power and attract followers by reformulating their theology and by sponsoring works of art that evoked the emotional power and authority of the Catholic faith. During his lifetime, Bernini was embraced as a genius by his fellow artists and by the many rich patrons who sponsored his work, most especially by a series of popes for whom he created both sensuous sculptures and impressive architectural feats of wonder.

His sculptures are instantly recognizable for their dramatic theatricality and their sense of coiled tension. They appear as if their subjects have been caught mid-movement, with a dynamism wedded to a close observation of the smallest details, which he rendered with convincing naturalism. No other artist could so effectively evoke the softness of skin, the silky curls of hair, or the rustling of crinkling fabric as Bernini did. And as someone who also painted, Bernini knew how to deal with the way light and shadow played upon his subjects, and he carved in such a way as to accentuate those effects. As Joshua Reynolds once wrote, Bernini had the ability to make stone "sport and flutter in the air."[2] He brought this talent to such masterpieces as his own version of *David* (1623) hurling a stone at Goliath, *Apollo and Daphne* (1622–1625), which convincingly captures a metamorphosis in progress, and *St. Longinus* (1638) at the very moment of his conversion as he perceives the divine light.

Bernini was also a genius when it came to architecture, and among other achievements, he was responsible for the great Vatican Colonnade in front of St. Peter's (with its 284 columns arranged in a welcoming pattern, as though the church were opening its arms to receive worshipers into it), decorating the canopy for the throne of St. Peter inside St. Peter's Basilica, and the allegorical *Fountain of Four Rivers* in the middle of the Piazza Navona.

Bernini was a man of deep spiritual devotion who spent a portion of every morning in prayer, and every evening he would attend vespers at a nearby Jesuit church. He saw his artistic work as a channel through which the grace of God might flow to others. Among the books that inspired him were Thomas à Kempis's *Imitation of Christ* and Ignatius of Loyola's *Spiritual Exercises*.

Perhaps a key source of Bernini's ability to create such believable and inspiring moments of spiritual experience in his work was his deep familiarity with the *Spiritual Exercises*. He carried a small copy of this book with him wherever he went, and he would regularly go on Ignatian retreats. The *Spiritual Exercises* teach a form of prayer whereby one imaginatively places oneself into a biblical story, engaging all the senses in prayer. One is encouraged to feel, smell, and fully experience what is happening in the biblical passage upon which one is meditating so that one might personally engage with it at the deepest emotional and spiritual level. Bernini clearly had honed his gift for such sympathetic imagination; with it, he could enter into the emotions of others and convey supreme moments of religious experience.

There is an undeniable theatricality to Bernini's works, which some might find off-putting. But such theatricality was not an accident. Bernini did not want to settle for the calm stoicism of so much of classical statuary. Instead, he wanted to invest his work with emotional power and intense drama. And the drama that he wanted to invoke was the drama that comes with spiritual experience, when the human soul is touched by God. He sought to externalize an interior state. In Bernini's art we are often made witnesses to a mystical miracle, but it is a miracle grounded in realism through Bernini's masterful skill and his penetrating observation of the human figure.

22

The Return of the Prodigal Son

Rembrandt van Rijn

(painting, c. 1669)

Created near the end of his life, during a time of mourning, personal and artistic disappointment, and ongoing financial struggles, Rembrandt's *The Return of the Prodigal Son* is a testament to his security in the love and mercy of God in the face of all these trials. Throughout his artistic career, Rembrandt had revisited scenes from this story several times in drawings, etchings, and paintings. He was clearly moved by Jesus' parable of God's unconditional love, and in this late canvas, he made his culminating statement. It is a painting of great tenderness, capturing the moment when the wayward son returns to his father to beg for forgiveness. The hands of the father rest gently on his kneeling son's shoulders as he leans forward with an expression of absolute acceptance and love. No matter what paths the son has trod, no matter what mistakes and betrayals he has committed, no matter how much he has hurt and disgraced his family, his father has been awaiting his return and welcomes him home.

The emotion in Rembrandt's famous painting is palpable and made even more emotionally resonant by its quiet dignity. It is obvious to the viewer that something important and life changing is taking place among this cluster of family members. But there is clearly more going on here than a simple family reunion. In the face of this loving and merciful father, we glimpse the very face of God.

In his book *The Return of the Prodigal*

Son, acclaimed spiritual writer Henri Nouwen wrote movingly of his own personal encounter with this emotionally engaging painting. He first glimpsed it as a poster pinned to the office door of a colleague at a time in his own life when he was struggling with physical exhaustion, emotional restlessness, and spiritual emptiness. He had just completed a lecture tour on which he had been speaking with great passion about justice and the spiritual life, but his own heart was filled with deep loneliness and a longing for something more. What he discovered as he meditated on Rembrandt's painting was *home*. "The tender embrace of father and son expressed everything I desired at that moment. I was, indeed, the son exhausted from long travels; I wanted to be embraced; I was looking for a home where I could feel safe."[1] The image spoke to his personal yearnings, offering a deeper understanding of the love of God, his heavenly Father.

Months later, Nouwen had the opportunity to sit for several hours in front of the actual painting at the Hermitage Museum in St. Petersburg, Russia. The impact of the time spent in the presence of this masterpiece was life-changing and gave Nouwen a renewed and deepened understanding of God's care for him; he felt almost as though the painting had been created specifically for him.

> I came to see it as, somehow, my personal painting, the painting that contained not only the heart of the story that God wants to tell me, but also the heart of the story that I want to tell to God and God's people. All of the Gospel is there. All of my life is there. All of the lives of my friends is there. The painting has become a mysterious window through which I can step into the Kingdom of God.[2]

One imagines that Rembrandt would have been pleased with such a response.

Rembrandt van Rijn was born in the Netherlands in 1606 to a Dutch Reformed father and a Catholic mother. Both took their faith seriously and taught their children to do the same. Rembrandt's education surely included an immersion in the Bible, upon which he would draw for his art throughout his life. The young man showed artistic promise and was apprenticed first to Jacob Swanenburgh and then to Pieter Lastman, whose own work was influenced by Caravaggio. It is likely under Lastman's influence that Rembrandt began to experiment with the dramatic effects of light, which would be a characteristic of his paintings throughout his career.

In 1631, Rembrandt moved to Amsterdam, the artistic capital of the Dutch Republic. This was the golden age of Dutch art, and the number of painters in the city was said to outnumber the number of bakers! Many of them were painters of the first order, but none was greater than Rembrandt. Three years after settling in

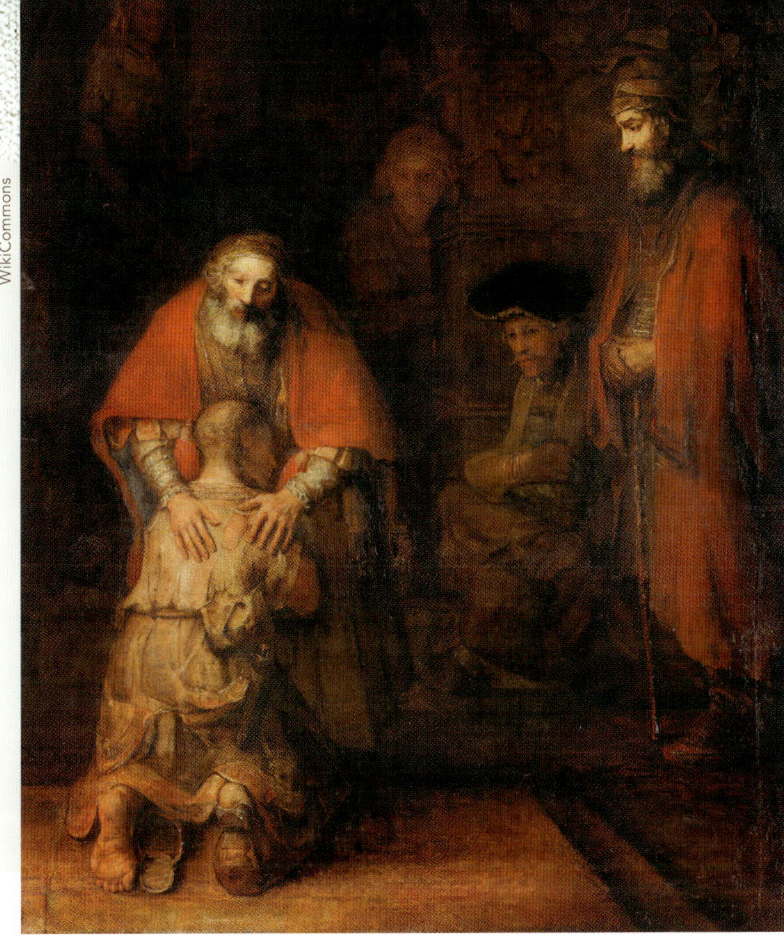

WikiCommons

The Return of the Prodigal Son by Rembrandt van Rijn, Hermitage Museum, St. Petersburg

Amsterdam, he married Saskia van Uylenburgh, whom he had met through a cousin and with whom he had fallen deeply in love. Her family's wealth brought a financial stability and an elevated social status that allowed Rembrandt to focus on his painting. It also allowed him to engage in collecting paintings by other admired artists, as well as various and sundry costumes, hats, weaponry, and miscellaneous exotic items that he used as props for his own works. He soon became known as one of Amsterdam's leading portrait painters and was sought out by discerning collectors throughout Europe. This income allowed him to purchase an expensive home, in which he built a studio where he both painted and trained aspiring artists.

Rembrandt's many portraits of Saskia give evidence of the depth of their relationship, and so it was a great personal tragedy when she died after only eight years of marriage. This marked the beginning of his many personal and financial problems. Saskia's will had a provision that would not allow him to retain any of her family's money if he remarried, so he never did. But in the late 1640s he began a relationship with Hendrickje Stoffels, a maid in his household. This relationship made him a target of criticism for some religious leaders, and also resulted in a suit by another woman who claimed that Rembrandt had earlier promised to marry her and had broken his promise.

Never good with money, Rembrandt would rarely pass up an opportunity to purchase a painting he loved or an exotic prop that might one day make its way into one of his paintings. The result was that in 1658, he lost his beloved home due to unpaid debts, and most of his collections, as well as artifacts, paintings, and household goods, were sold off to pay the debts. By this time his work had begun to fall out of favor with collectors in Amsterdam, he had lost all of his children to premature deaths, and he had little money or property to his name. However, in the very year he was stripped of virtually all he owned (which was put up for auction), he painted one of his most confident and serene self-portraits. Even if nothing else was left, he could still paint. And that was what mattered most. He lived a turbulent life: financial insolvency and debt, relationship struggles, the deaths of all those most dear to him, and a fading reputation. But in all this he remained true to his calling as an artist. He knew what he was created to do.

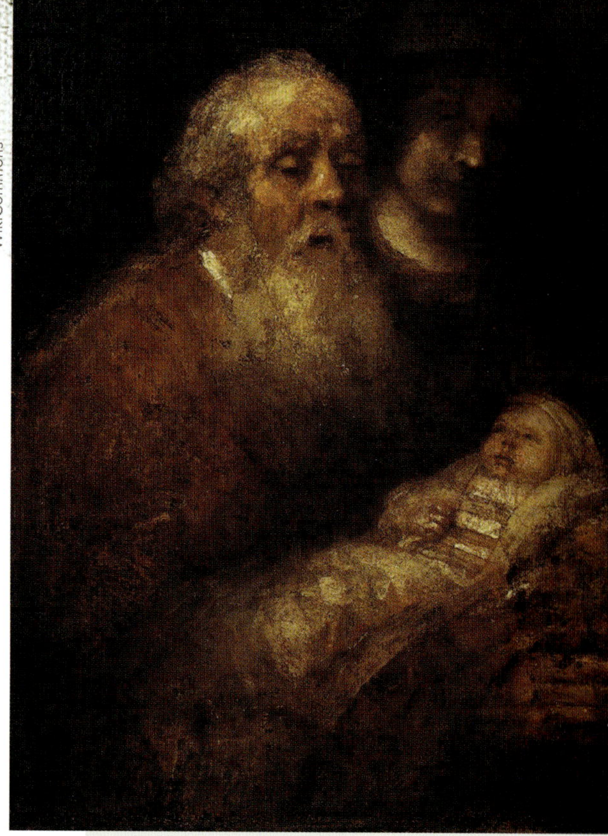

WikiCommons

Simeon's Song of Praise by Rembrandt van Rijn, Nationalmuseum, Stockholm

We know few details of Rembrandt's personal faith. Little writing by him of any kind survives. But his paintings, etchings, and drawings tell the story of what he held to be most important. He invested more energy on biblical themes than any other genre. There are at least 591 drawings, 72 etchings, and 89 paintings that bring scriptural stories to life. His very first major painting was of the story of the stoning of Stephen from the book of Acts, and over the years he added paintings of numerous stories from both the Old and New Testaments. He always sought for biblical realism, building his works from the text of

Scripture (which he obviously knew very well) rather than using the traditional symbols and clichés that were the norm in most religious painting of his time. He studied the work of Jewish historian Josephus and consulted with Jewish rabbis, and he often used Jewish models in his attempt to be authentic. At a time when anti-Semitism was common, Rembrandt was not afraid to call his Jewish acquaintances his friends and use them in his paintings.

In his biblical pictures, Rembrandt wasn't really interested in traditional iconography. He was absorbed in the people in the stories, and he made them come alive for his viewers. He painted them as though they were unaware that they were part of a Bible story; they were just living, breathing human beings. When he read the Bible he also saw himself in its stories, and he sometimes even added a self-portrait to these paintings: himself as a spectator or as a participant in the biblical events. You can see his face as one of those involved in the *Raising of the Cross* (1633). Was he implicating himself as a sinner who was one of those responsible for Jesus' death?

Rembrandt was a great painter of portraits, intrigued by the faces he could bring to life as no one before or since. In these portraits the personalities of his sitters shine through. He didn't just paint the public persona but found the essential human being beneath. His portraits are unflattering but dignified. Rembrandt painted humanity in all its imperfection and glory. And one of the faces that seemed to interest him most was his own. He created a collection of self-portraits that give us a glimpse of him at virtually every stage of his life. In many of his more than seventy-five self-portraits there is an unflattering truthfulness, as he unflinchingly looks straight out at the viewer.

During his career, Rembrandt also painted a number of portraits of Christ, much like the ones he did of himself and other residents of Amsterdam. Departing from traditional ways of portraying Jesus, these images were based on the Jewish models who posed for him and portray a Christ who is serene and introspective, kind and wise. They are not so much demonstrations of his divine power but rather reminders that He was human as well as divine.

In whatever genre he undertook, Rembrandt brought a unique perspective and an amazing painterly touch, applying the paint generously and thickly enough that the brushwork is usually visible. This means that it is essential, if at all possible, to see his artwork in person and not just through reproductions in order to appreciate their tactile effect. And when one stands before one of the great Rembrandt masterpieces, one cannot help but feel something of the magic of what he accomplished. As Vincent van Gogh, another great Dutch painter, was to write of him, "Rembrandt is so deeply mysterious that he says things for which there are no words in any language."[3]

23

The Pilgrim's Progress

John Bunyan

(novel, 1678)

There are those who accuse Christians of embracing a pie-in-the-sky philosophy that promises an avoidance of the harsh realities of life; they declare Christianity is an attempt to wish away all the pain and struggle. While there might be some truth to this in some cases, in John Bunyan's *The Pilgrim's Progress* this is most definitely not true. For the pilgrim in Bunyan's classic book, the life of faith is sometimes less a comfort than a battle—a war against the forces of darkness, against one's own sinful nature, and against a hostile world.

If the influence of a book is measured by the number of copies it has sold, *The Pilgrim's Progress* is second only to the Bible and Mao's *Little Red Book* in this reckoning. Bunyan's allegory about the Christian life was written with such imagination and passion that it has continued to be a formative book in the lives of countless Christians. With its combination of psychological insight, spiritual wisdom, and unforgettable characterizations, it has given believers memorable metaphors for how they can think about their faith. Though it was published in 1678, we still use phrases from the book, even if many of us don't know that they originated in *The Pilgrim's Progress*: "the slough of despond," "vanity fair," "muckraker," and "worldly wise." And because this story probed much deeper than normal allegories, many literary historians consider it to be either the first novel ever written or at least a very important step on the road toward the development of the novel as a literary genre.

While Bunyan was in dead earnest about the message of his book, he leavened his storytelling with gentleness and humor. Purposefully written in his simplest prose, Bunyan sought to create an allegorical parable of the Christian life that could be read, understood, and enjoyed by people from every strata of society—a book that would tell the truth in unpretentious, homey, and straightforward prose. While as an allegory it can be read on a literal level, it also contains layers of deeper meanings just beneath the surface of the tale, making those truths a little more palatable to the hearer. In the introduction, Bunyan invites careful meditation on his book: "Turn up my metaphors, and do not fail: / There if thou seekest them, such things thou'lt find / As will be helpful to an honest mind."

The Pilgrim's Progress tells the story of a man named Christian who awakens to his own sense of sinfulness and guilt before God. He undertakes a dangerous journey through many trials, temptations, and distractions of all sorts as he makes his way toward the Celestial City, his final destination, where God dwells and salvation can be experienced in full. The characters he meets along the way reflect the vices and virtues that they represent, such as Obstinate, Mr. Legality, Mr. Great-Heart, Faithful, Little-Faith, and Ignorance.

Bunyan's book is not primarily a story to teach readers about the way to find salvation, for Christian's encounter with the cross, where his burden of sin rolls away, occurs fairly early in the book. Instead, it is a tale about the spiritual journey, the inner and outer struggles and temptations a believer in Jesus will face as they walk the path of life. When the backpack of sin falls from Pilgrim's shoulders, his journey has just begun. He must make his way past many dangers and distractions and challenges, struggling mightily all the way but empowered by God's grace, until he finally arrives at his ultimate home, the Celestial City. There are many truths to be revealed along the way. For example, in one scene Christian and his companion Hopeful are imprisoned in the bowels of Doubting Castle, until Christian awakens to an important revelation. "What a fool, am I, thus to lie in a stinking dungeon, when I may as well walk at liberty. I have a key in my bosom, called promise, that will open any lock in Doubting Castle." This revelation allows Christian and Hopeful to walk out of the prison and leave despair behind them.

For centuries this book has been cherished by readers as a guide for navigating the challenges of the Christian life. Its topics remain relevant for today's reader: the danger of lusting after riches, the hazards of pride and religious hypocrisy, the struggle with overwhelming despair and depression, the battle with doubt and uncertainty, and the importance of making the right choices in even the smallest of matters. It reminds the reader of how essential it is to listen to wise counselors, and points toward the Bible as the greatest source of wisdom for living. Much of the book's success comes from the fact that readers see themselves and their own internal struggles in the story. For many, *The Pilgrim's Progress* is a mirror in which they can examine their own soul and be instructed in how they can change, which is exactly what Bunyan intended.

Born near Bedford, England, in 1628, John Bunyan received only a limited formal education, probably two to four years, before he settled down to follow his father's trade as a tinker, a repairer of metal household utensils. It was a humble beginning, but when his life got caught in the cross fire of the religious struggles that raged in England in the seventeenth century, he emerged as one of the most popular authors in the English language.

Bunyan enlisted in the Parliamentary army at age sixteen, which represented the Nonconformist party in the civil war that divided England between the Puritan Nonconformists (largely Calvinist) and the Anglicans. The Anglicans had been out of power but came back into their own again when King Charles II, whose own father had been executed by the Nonconformists, was restored to the throne. Bunyan had a very close shave with death during the hostilities, and after the civil war ended, he returned to his life as a tinker, but with a growing sense of spiritual unease. He was tormented by a deep sense of guilt, blasphemous thoughts, and by dreams and visions that rose unbidden in his mind. When he read Martin Luther's commentary on the book of Galatians, he came to the same conclusion that Luther had reached many years before—that his salvation was not based upon his own righteousness and good works but on the saving grace of Christ. This resulted in what he termed a "merciful working of God upon my soul."[1]

Filled with zeal and enthusiasm for this newly embraced understanding of faith, Bunyan joined a Baptist church and began preaching the message of justification by faith alone. This ran afoul of new laws that were intended to keep the Nonconformist faith from spreading too quickly, as Bunyan did not have the required license to preach. He was imprisoned in the Bedford jail for three months in an attempt by the authorities to quiet this firebrand preacher. But as soon as he was released, he went right back to preaching. He was arrested again, and this time served twelve years. When given the opportunity to recant and obey the law, he was frank in his response: "If I were out of prison today, I would preach the gospel again tomorrow, by the help of God."[2] He was finally released when a new proclamation by the king greatly expanded religious rights. But three years later, the king changed his mind and rescinded the proclamation, and Bunyan again found himself in jail, though this time he only served three more months, as his popularity as a writer and preacher had become so great that his adversaries decided it was no longer advisable to hold him.

All told, Bunyan spent almost a third of his adult life in jail, but while serving his several sentences, he made the most of his time. He read books such as *Foxe's Book of Martyrs,* he memorized large portions of Scripture, and he began writing. Taking pen in hand, he produced at least fifty-eight different works, including a great number of theological tracts, devotional meditations, collections of verse, an autobiography entitled *Grace Abounding to the Chief of Sinners* (1666), and allegorical fiction of which *The Pilgrim's Progress* is his most famous. It was followed by a sequel in 1684 that tells the story of how Christian's wife and children tread a similar but different path to the Celestial City. Bunyan's intimate knowledge of the Bible is evident on every page of every book he ever wrote. "I was never out of the Bible," he wrote, "either by reading or meditation."[3]

Bunyan continued as the pastor of the Bedford Church until he died in 1688 after becoming drenched in a rainstorm and contracting a chill. He insisted on preaching despite his ill health, and the chill turned into a fatal fever.

In his works, John Bunyan emphasized the individual nature of salvation, urging that each must choose for themselves to follow the way of Christ—a way that *The Pilgrim's Progress* reminds us is filled with obstacles, temptations, struggles, and great perils. Many of these are the result of the devil's work, but others are the result of the fallenness of humanity that leaves us blind to the truth. Bunyan was not a moralist wagging his finger at the reader, but a fellow struggler who pointed them toward the grace that made all the difference in his own life. He pictured the Christian life as one of intense ongoing struggle, a spiritual combat. Becoming a Christian doesn't mean that your troubles end—it means that you face a different set of troubles, the difference being that you don't face them alone.

24

"When I Survey the Wondrous Cross"

Isaac Watts

(hymn, 1707)

Charles Wesley, himself one of the greatest of hymn writers, reportedly said that he would give up all the hymns he had penned if he could have written "When I Survey the Wondrous Cross." The man who did compose it, Isaac Watts, is widely considered to be the first great English hymn writer, and the headwaters from which the whole tradition of English hymns has flowed. This hymn has had many musical settings throughout the years, but the most widely embraced today is that of Lowell Mason, who in 1824 composed the haunting and stately tune by which is it commonly known today. It has become a staple of hymnbooks from every tradition of the Christian church, combining sensually passionate language with a powerful theological statement.

With imagery that is beautiful yet horrific, Isaac Watts invites us to join him at the foot of the cross and witness the pain and shock of Jesus' death while meditating on what it has accomplished for those who embrace the meaning of His sacrifice. Watts does not spare our mind's eye from the horror of the event, as we are made witness to the blood and the tears of Christ streaming from His crucified body: "See from His head, His hands, His feet, / Sorrow and love flow mingled down." We can imagine the ringing of the hammer on the spikes, the taunting of the crowd, and the wailing cries of those who loved Him.

Yet this is not only a moment of sadness but also of glorious victory: "Did e'er such love and sorrow meet, / Or thorns compose so rich a crown?" In light of this atoning death, Watts reminds us that all our earthly attainments are empty and vain, nothing in comparison to what Jesus attained for us on the cross: "I sacrifice them to His blood." This crucial moment in human history changed everything. Christ's sacrifice reorients what we see as valuable and provides a new perspective on the world and everything in it, calling us to make a sacrifice of our own: giving up our lives for the Savior.

> Were the whole realm of nature
> mine,
> That were a present far too small;
> Love so amazing, so divine,
> Demands my soul, my life, my all.

Originally published in *Hymns and Spiritual Songs* (1707–1709), this hymn was placed within the section of the hymnal called, "Prepared for the Holy Ordinance of the Lord's Supper," which lets us know that Watts's intention is for us to meditate on the sacrificial death of Christ as we partake of His body and blood in the Eucharist. Watts moves our emotions without becoming mawkish, sentimental, or overly subjective about the gracious gift that changes everything.

Isaac Watts was born in England in 1674, the son of a pastor who was a dissenter from the Anglican orthodoxy of the time and who served a couple of stretches in jail for his faith. The younger Watts was a child prodigy, beginning to learn Latin at age four, and by his early teens he had attained expertise in Greek, Hebrew, and French. He also showed a natural faculty for poetry. Rhyming couplets seemed to come easily to him, even from an early age. One day, when he was six, his family was sharing a solemn moment of prayer together when young Isaac began to giggle, fighting back laughter. His father stopped praying and sternly demanded an explanation for his behavior. It seems that the young boy had spotted a mouse running up the bell-rope that hung in the fireplace, and this little couplet has lodged itself in his brain: "There was a mouse for want of stairs / ran up a rope to say his prayers."

At age fourteen, Watts wrote in his diary about a "considerable conviction of sin," and not long thereafter of being "taught to trust in Christ."[1] Because his intellectual gifts showed such promise, a family friend offered to pay for him to attend either Oxford or Cambridge. But because to do so would have required him to renounce the dissenting religious views that had now become his own, he declined the generous offer and attended a less prestigious school. The four years he spent studying at Stoke Newington Academy near London broadened his intellectual horizons even further, and fueled interests in philosophy, astronomy, mathematics, and the ancient classics as well as theology. After graduation, he returned home to search out his vocation.

One Sunday afternoon, while returning from church services with his family, Watts complained aloud of the deplorable quality of the poetry in the hymns that were sung in church, saying that they lacked both beauty and dignity. His father was ready with a challenge: "Try and see if you can write something better." He did. The very next Sunday Watts offered a newly penned hymn, "Behold the Glories of the Lamb." The congregation loved it and wanted more. And so he began to compose new hymns, writing many of his greatest ones during the two years he studied at home as he sought out his calling, which he soon found in becoming an assistant pastor, and eventually head pastor, for the congregation at Mark Lane Independent Church in London. The church thrived and grew under his leadership, and the congregation was treated both to his sermons, which were filled with rich theology, and his hymns, which made that theology come alive in ways that captured their spiritual imagination. No wonder that some have referred to his hymns as "rhymed sermons" that touch both the mind and the heart.

In 1707, Watts published his first collection of hymns, called *Hymns and Spiritual Songs*. Revelation 5:9 ("and they sang a new song") was one of the verses he used to justify the need for fresh songs of faith—ones that were both poetic and spiritually rich—that could be sung by a congregation to affirm their beliefs and celebrate their love for God. John Calvin and his followers had limited congregational singing to the actual words of Scripture—and largely that meant the psalms. Watts saw no reason why Christian songs of praise should be limited in this way, and he could see the effects of the current music clearly: "To see the dull indifference, the negligent and thoughtless air that sits upon the faces of the whole assembly while the psalm is upon lips, might tempt even a charitable observer to suspect the fervor of inward religion."[2] He used plenty of Scripture and its imagery throughout his songs, but to these he added his own unforgettable word pictures to reflect on the meaning and experience of faith. In doing so, he became the first great hymn writer and opened the door for many others to follow, bringing creative expression to congregational singing.

Although Watts was an exceptionally talented poet, he set aside some of his literary gifts to make sure that the songs were easily understood even by the illiterate members of the congregation and that they were easy to sing: hymns for the common man. They were mostly in simple four-line verses and written in common metrical forms that could be sung to familiar tunes. Because of the limitations he set for himself, some of his lyrics and rhyme schemes may seem stilted and awkward to the modern ear, but a great number of them still speak to us with great beauty and clarity. He even created a collection of songs and rhymes on spiritual themes for children called *Divine Songs*.

In all, Watts wrote an astonishing 750 hymns, many of which have their place in nearly every modern hymnbook. He also wrote what has become one of the most popular Christmas songs, "Joy to the World," though he would probably be dismayed to see it relegated to use only during the Christmas season, as it celebrates not only the first coming of Christ but also His second coming as ever-reigning King.

During his pastoral years, Watts also began to work on a new rendering of the psalms. In his time, congregational singing of the psalms was an important element of the worship service, but he found these adaptations of the psalms to be poetically awkward and lacking in relevance for the Christian believer. His poetic reworkings were released as *The Psalms of David Imitated in the Language of the New Testament and Applied to the Christian State and Worship*. This long title summarizes what he hoped to achieve: to Christianize the psalms that were being used in churches, bringing out their relevance for the modern Christian. His goal was to express himself as David would have if he had been alive in the Christian era. Watts said he wanted to see "David converted into a Christian." This project gave us two of his finest hymns: "Jesus Shall Reign Where'er the Sun," based on Psalm 72, and "O God, Our Help in Ages Past," which reworked Psalm 90.

Small in stature and reportedly unbecoming in looks, Watts was also of frail health for most of his life, and eventually had to retire from the pastorate when his health issues became too great to continue with the stresses of clerical life. Watts was invited to stay for a time with a friend and admirer in his rural home while he sought to recover, but this short visit ended up extending for thirty-six years. In these years of poor health, he continued to write hymns that combined wonder at what God had done for humanity with an attitude of humility, gratitude, and praise. By age seventy-five he said he was "waiting God's leave to die."[3] When he did, to quote the title of his own hymns, he entered the "land of pure delight where saints immortal reign."

25

St. Matthew Passion

Johann Sebastian Bach

(oratorio, 1727)

William F. Buckley once remarked that the music of Bach was perhaps the greatest single evidence of the existence of God. Surely the sustained magnificence of Bach's artistry does indeed seem nothing short of miraculous. The robust piety of his music, though, is never mere religious artifice. It is a reflection of Bach's own personal commitment of faith. Perhaps the high-water mark of this artistry is his *St. Matthew Passion*.

Like so much of Bach's work, *St. Matthew Passion* was written to be performed at the church for which he regularly contributed new compositions to use in the weekly worship services. It was not written as a piece for the concert hall but for the Sunday service. Over the course of his life, he wrote music for every season of the church year, but it was in this composition for Holy Week that he particularly outdid himself. *St. Matthew Passion* was first performed on Good Friday 1727, though it underwent numerous revisions as it was performed again and again throughout Bach's life. What an experience it must have been for members of his congregation to spend a portion of Good Friday in such a manner, meditating on this majestic combination of words and music. And its power to move the listener to the deepest spiritual contemplation remains just as great today.

Marshaling all his compositional skills, and putting them at the service of not one but two orchestras and choirs, Bach was

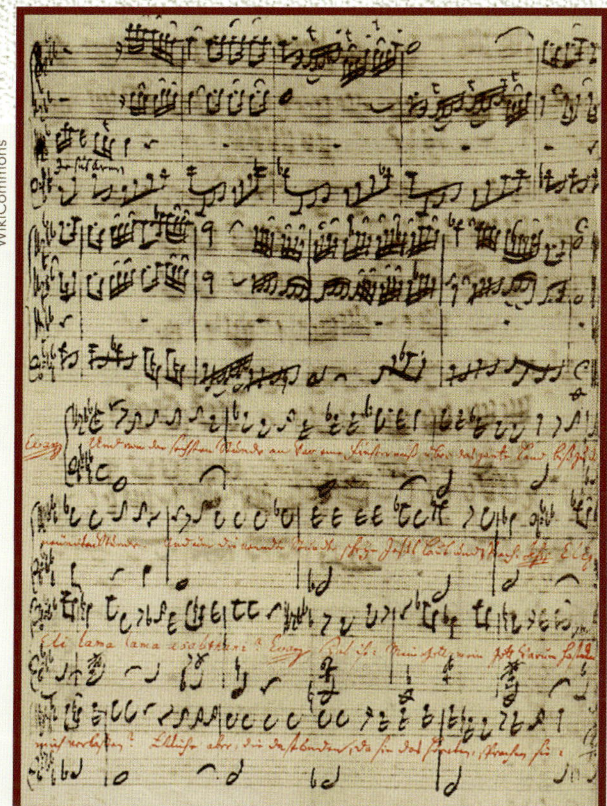

WikiCommons

Portion of Bach's original score (Bible words in red)

able to fashion a piece of great musical complexity and spiritual depth, one that went far beyond the standard Baroque passion settings with which the audiences of his day would have been familiar. The text was created by Christian Henrici, who wrote under the pen name Picander. Like Bach, he lived in Leipzig, and there is little doubt that the two men collaborated on this sublime combination of the actual text from the latter chapters of Matthew's gospel, already extant hymns and chorales (which would have been familiar to their audience), and original poetry of great beauty and emotional weight.

The passion opens with a chorus that sets the tone for the entire piece: "Come you daughters, share my mourning." What follows is a sustained meditation on the atoning death of Christ. Unlike the more celebratory *Messiah* by Handel, the concentration of Bach's work is upon Christ's agony, suffering, abandonment, and death. In fact, the resurrection is only mentioned in passing. The emphasis is upon the pain and anguish that Jesus took upon Himself in our stead: scourged, mocked, beaten, spat upon, tortured, then crucified. Hence there is a stately, elevated, brooding sadness that marks both the words and the music, and the listener is left to contemplate the great exchange—the innocent Lamb of God dying for the guilty.

To listen intently to this masterpiece is to be reminded of the immensity of what Jesus Christ accomplished as "the Lamb of God, who takes away the sin of the world" (John 1:29). Bach does not allow us to simply contemplate this sacrifice as a theological abstraction. Instead, we *feel* it. The deeply emotive music lets us experience again the redemptive sacrifice that arises from the boundless depths of God's grace and mercy. Bach reminds us that our salvation comes at a very high price. Therefore, our proper response is not only wonder at what God has wrought on the cross but also heartfelt introspection and repentance.

Johann Sebastian Bach was born in Germany in 1685 to a family with a rich musical heritage. In the span of seven generations, the family produced fifty-three prominent musicians. But what this particular Bach was able to accomplish outstripped anyone else in his lineage. Schooled in Eisenach, the same school Martin Luther had attended, he received his earliest musical education from his father. But by age ten he had lost both parents, and the young orphan went to live with his elder brother Johann Christoph. It was not long before his immense gifts began to manifest themselves.

He was first a singer and then a violinist in the chamber orchestra of Prince Johann Ernst of Weimar. Then he became the organist in Arnstadt. Always hungering to learn more, in October 1705, he undertook a two-hundred-mile journey on foot to study with renowned organist Dietrich Buxtehude. He had received permission to be gone for four weeks, but was so enthralled that he stayed for four months. On returning to his post in Arnstadt he was severely criticized for his breach of contract in being gone so long and also for employing the new methods and the stylistic flourishes he had picked up from Buxtehude. Never one to abide criticism very well, Bach soon moved—with his new bride—to Mulhausen to take another position. This was the first of several short appointments before he finally settled in Leipzig, where he remained for the rest of his life.

Bach never saw his work merely as some sort of musical diversion for the worship service. He saw his cantatas as an important element in the service, a means of preaching the Word, glorifying God, and pointing the listener toward a deeper understanding of the message of the gospel. As Leonard Bernstein has noted, "For Bach, all music is religious; writing it was an act of worship. Every note was dedicated to God and to nothing else."[1] He frequently annotated his manuscripts with the acronym JJ (*Jesu Juva*, "Help me, Jesus") or SDG (*Soli Deo Gloria*, "To God alone, the glory").

In reality, Bach was nothing less than a theologian who worked with a keyboard. Always a voracious student of the Scriptures, he marked up his Bible with underlined passages, corrections of errors in the translation, and notations in the margins. Near 2 Corinthians 5:13–14 he penned, "In devotional music, God with His grace is always present." His extensive library was equally divided between works on music and theological works. The fruit of his study was to invest his cantatas with a rich theological understanding.

Much of Bach's music was quite literally an exegesis of Scripture. He used music to make biblical texts come alive, to open them to his listeners by the use of music that captured the interior drama of the passage around which he composed. He wanted to reveal the feelings and emotions of the text so that his hearers might experience the truths of the gospel for themselves. Such was his effectiveness that Swedish theologian Nathan Soderblom once referred to Bach's music as "the fifth gospel."

Bach was also a master at word painting, or finding musical equivalents for verbal and written ideas. He could conjure such effects as an undulating melody to represent the sea, or on a more serious note could construct the music around the text in such a way as to maximize its impact. In *St. Matthew Passion,* for example, he used a distinctive accompaniment from the string section, with long, sustained notes, to create a sort of aural "halo" around the words of Christ (sort of like a musical "red letter edition"). Then, as Jesus is dying, this accompaniment drops out altogether for the first time as the question, "My God, my God, why have you forsaken me?" is sung. It is a moment of incredibly powerful emotional effect.

Sometimes Bach's methods were more playful. He was fascinated with numbers and hid numerical clues throughout his works. In one work, there are exactly ten repetitions of the phrase "These are the ten holy commandments," and in other places he uses patterns of five to represent the five wounds Jesus suffered on the cross, patterns of three for the Trinity, or four for the four gospels.

Ultimately, Bach wanted his music to illuminate the Word of God, to throw light upon it. After all, as he once said, "The aim and final reason for all music should be none else but the glory of God and refreshing the soul."[2] Bach was a confessional Lutheran in his theology, staunchly orthodox and traditional in his beliefs, but he was also deeply influenced by the actively devotional faith of the Pietists and the idea of spiritual oneness with God that was taught by the German mystics. Bach was also open-minded enough in his theology to structure one of his greatest works (*Mass in B Minor*) largely around the Catholic mass.

When he began to lose his eyesight he sought the help of a quack doctor whose surgery brought about blindness. (In fact, this same surgeon worked on Handel, with the same result.) Bach's very last work was dictated from his deathbed, a chorale entitled, "Before Thy Throne I Come." Having finished it, he left this earth in search of that throne and his everlasting rest.

In 1977, when scientists were planning to send a probe with artifacts from earth into space in the hope that they might be discovered by unknown civilizations in other galaxies, there was much debate over what to send that would best represent the human race. Lewis Thomas was confident in his suggestion that it be "the complete works of J. S. Bach." Then he hesitated. "But that would be boasting."[3]

26

Messiah

George Frideric Handel

(oratorio, 1741)

In a small house on Brook Street in London in 1741, George Frideric Handel had sequestered himself away to finish his latest oratorio, *Messiah*. After a career of great successes, he now found his work had largely fallen out of favor. His compositions used to pack the house, but lately the turnout for the performance of his pieces had proven unpredictable. A string of failures had left him in dire circumstances. Needing a popular hit to restore his fortunes, he pondered his next project and settled upon a biblical subject—not necessarily the safest choice for drawing a crowd. But he immersed himself in this new work, an oratorio celebrating the life of Christ as prophesied in the Old Testament and fulfilled in the New. For the libretto, he chose a setting of scriptural passages put together by Charles Jennings from the King James Bible and the Psalter of the *Book of Common Prayer*.

For twenty-four days he rarely left the house, all his attention focused on the completion of the work at hand. When his servant brought him a tray of food, he would often find the previous meal untouched. Handel, a man known for his insatiable appetite, was so caught up in composing this music that he sometimes neglected to feed himself. The work came to him, he later testified, almost miraculously, and was fueled by the intense spiritual experience of writing it.

There was something unique for Handel about this particular piece. A friend

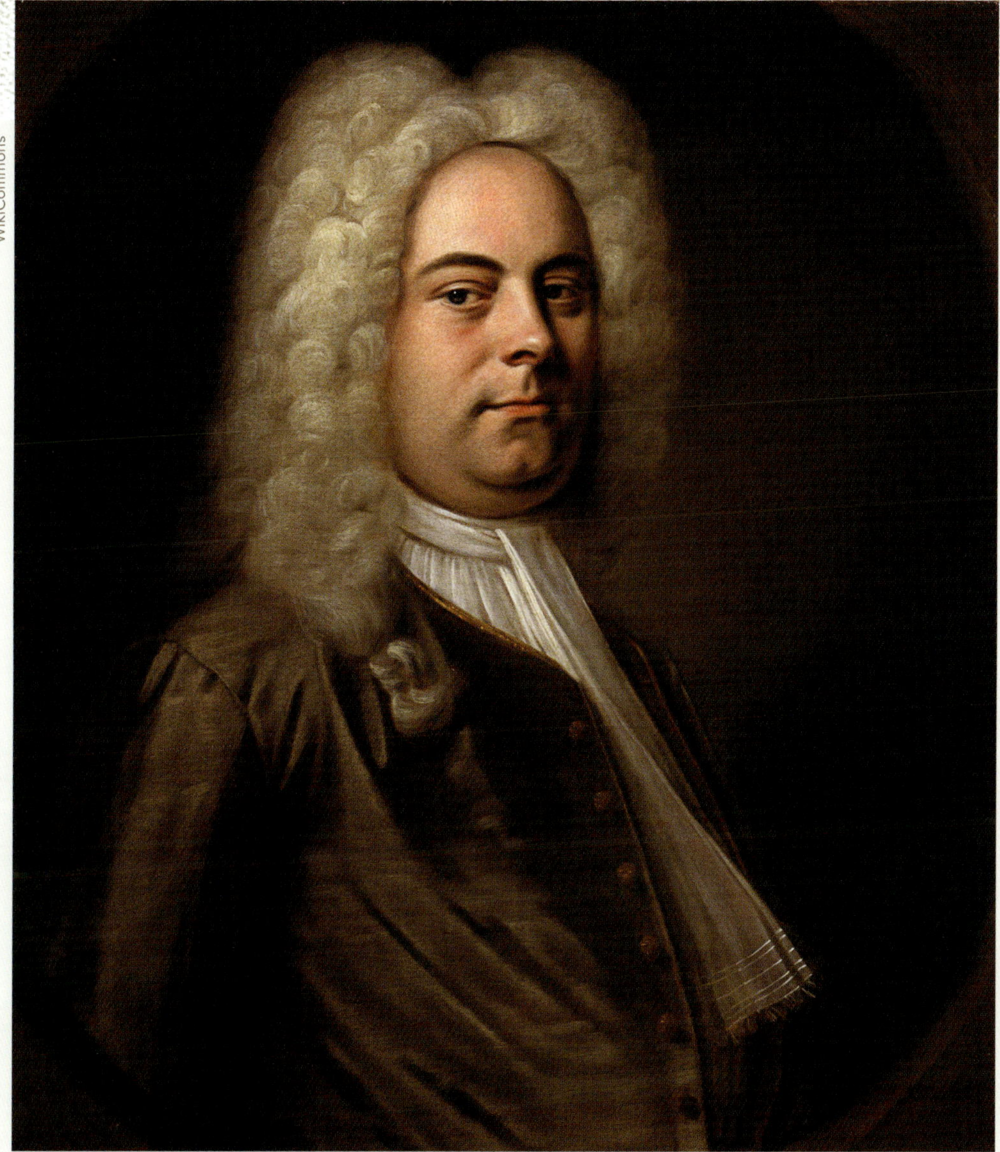
WikiCommons

Portrait of George Frideric Handel by Balthasar Denner (c. 1727)

who visited him during the throes of composition found him sobbing with intense emotion. All his heart, his faith, and his passion were being poured into the creative process. At times he could barely stand the pathos he felt, the overwhelming sense of human limitation in trying to express what he wanted to say through his music. At other moments he was overcome with exhilaration and wonder at God's majesty.

To his servant, who found him alone and weeping after completing the transcendent "Hallelujah" chorus, he could only murmur, "I did think I did see all Heaven before me, and the great God himself."[1]

Audiences throughout the years have testified to a similar experience on hearing *Messiah* performed. Handel's musical settings bring the scriptural passages alive and provide a clear message about the One whose long-expected appearance changed the world forever. *Messiah* was acclaimed from its first performance in 1742, and the proceeds went to three charitable organizations, raising enough money to free 142 men from debtor's prison.

During his life, Handel personally conducted more than thirty performances of his majestic oratorio, and many of them were, like the first performance, staged to raise money for charitable causes. As one biographer has written, "*Messiah* has fed the hungry, clothed the naked, fostered the orphan."[2] It has also probably convinced more hearts of the reality of God than a library's worth of theological volumes. Following its London premier, Lord Kinnoull complimented Handel on how entertaining the performance had been. Handel responded, "I should be sorry, my Lord, if I have only succeeded in entertaining them; I wished to make them better."[3]

George Frideric Handel was born in Saxony in 1685. Unlike Bach, who had been raised in a musical family, Handel's family had little interest in music, and his father wanted him to become a lawyer. But his musical genius exerted itself early and was undeniable. He developed proficiency with a number of instruments and began to compose for the Hamburg opera house. After studying for a time in Italy, where he became proficient with the Italian operatic style, he settled in London and became a naturalized citizen and eventually an icon of English music. Though born in Germany, he was embraced by the British as an English composer.

Handel became known for music with bright and joyful melodies and a grand sense of drama. Although he created wonderful instrumental pieces such as *Water Music* (1717) and *Music for the Royal Fireworks* (1749), he is probably best known for his choral music: operas such as *Xerxes* and oratorios such as *Saul* (1738), *Israel in Egypt* (1738), *Samson* (1742), and, of course, *Messiah*.

An oratorio is essentially an opera performed without the staging. Most of Handel's oratorios dealt with biblical stories and themes, set to music that delighted audiences. *Messiah* was unlike his other biblical oratorios, however, in that it had no plot as such. Instead it was a collection of texts gathered from various parts of the Bible, and it had no named characters, only solos for different voices. Many religious people of his day disapproved of Handel's oratorios, believing it improper to perform biblical texts in the impious atmosphere of a theater, a milieu they viewed with grave distrust. They were also shocked that sacred themes would be used for musical entertainment, as they believed there should be a very clear demarcation between the sacred and the secular. Handel seemed intent on ignoring these seemingly important distinctions. Some self-righteous women even went so far as to plan large teas or theatrical events to coincide with the days when Handel's work was being performed in an attempt to decrease the size of his audience. But Handel believed that the sacred and the secular could not be so easily separated, and his compositions brought the Word of God into environments where it needed to be heard. He believed that entertainment and edification could make good bedfellows.

To his friends, Handel was known to be humorous, generous, honest, and determined. But he also could be intemperate. A man of huge appetites, he once sent word to a local pub, ordering dinner for two to be brought to his lodging. Upon its arrival, he sat down and asked for his dinner to be served. The landlord, looking very confused, apologized, saying that he had expected Mr. Handel would have company for dinner and therefore had prepared two meals. "I am the company," Handel responded, and duly ate his way through both dinners. He could also display a fiery temper, and when moved to wrath, usually by singers who refused to obey his directions, he could swear in several languages. Once, when a truculent singer refused to cooperate with his vision for a performance, he picked her up and dangled her from a balcony until she agreed to do it his way.

Handel's passion and fervor also carried over into the practice of his faith. A good friend, Sir John Hawkins, recorded that "throughout his life [he] manifested a deep sense of religion. In conversation he would frequently declare the pleasure he felt in setting the Scriptures to music, and how contemplating the many sublime passages in the Psalms had contributed to his edification."[4] Handel told friends that he wanted to "die on Good Friday in the hope of rejoining the good God, my sweet Lord and Savior, on the day of his resurrection."[5] In actuality, he died on the Saturday following Good Friday.

Throughout his career, Handel wanted to produce music that would both entertain and inspire the listener. "What the English like," he once said, "is something they can beat time to, something that hits them straight on the drum of the ear."[6] That is what he accomplished with many of his compositions but especially with *Messiah* —a work so accessible that concert halls offer sing-alongs for the general public and yet so profound that theologians ponder its epic celebration of redemption.

27

"Amazing Grace"

John Newton

(hymn, 1779)

John Newton's famous hymn is essentially spiritual autobiography. Written in first person, it rings true with the authenticity of his personal experience. His life's path had been strewn with "many dangers, toils, and snares" as he sought to escape from the watchful eye of God. He had been one who rejected and blasphemed against God, and he'd lived a wild and dissolute lifestyle that had led only to pain and despair. It was a life filled with enough unexpected twists and turns, unforeseen coincidences, and divine deliverances to almost pass for a work of fiction in its telling. But his story is true, and in the end he found grace, *amazing grace*, and it finally brought an end to all his running.

When, later in life, Newton discovered a nascent gift for verse, he was able to share the essence of his own spiritual journey in a hymn that has universal appeal, for we all have, at one point or another, made foolish decisions, taken false turns, and avoided turning to God for mercy. We have all felt ourselves to be a "wretch" at times, we have all needed "amazing grace," and most of us have probably felt the lifting of some of the burden of our imperfect lives when we have raised our voices to sing this hymn.

When he became a curate at Olney in Buckinghamshire, England, John Newton began to write hymns along with his friend and esteemed poet William Cowper. He developed a habit of writing a hymn to accompany and illustrate the sermons he preached each Sunday, and so, on New

Year's Day 1773, he offered "Amazing Grace" to his congregation along with a sermon based on 1 Chronicles 17:16–17. Like his other hymns, "Amazing Grace" was rich with the language of both Scripture and personal experience. A phrase such as "I once was lost, but now am found," for example, echoes the words of the prodigal son in the famous parable. Newton did not let such concepts remain theological abstractions but made specific connections to his own experiences of these truths.

"Amazing Grace" debuted in print in 1779 in Newton and Cowper's collection *Olney Hymns*, along with 347 other hymns that one or the other of them had penned. At the time, "Amazing Grace" did not distinguish itself as more significant than any of the others, and for a time it lapsed into obscurity. It was only in the United States, during the Second Great Awakening (c. 1780–1840), that the song was rediscovered and used extensively among the revivalists, who saw it as an effective way to communicate their emphasis upon human sinfulness and the necessity of reaching out for God's grace. It fit with their passionate preaching and calls for a personal experience of salvation through repentance and an embrace of God's grace.

It is not clear what melody was used when the hymn debuted, and it has been associated with more than twenty tunes over the years. But in 1835, when it was joined to a traditional tune by William Walker called "New Britain," it had found its perfect pairing. This is the version of "Amazing Grace" by which it is most commonly known today, arguably the most popular and famous of all hymns. One Newton biographer estimates that it is performed about ten million times worldwide each year.

In the 1960s, "Amazing Grace" was taken up as an anthem by civil rights marchers and folksingers, and Judy Collins's performance was a surprise popular hit. Despite its clearly Christian message, it has been loved and sung lustily even by those who would not fully embrace its theological message because of its realism about the human condition, the joy of finding mercy and hope, and the longing for a better life in the world to come.

In 1725, John Newton was born in London to a father who was a merchant shipper and a devout mother who died when he was only six years old. She had tried to instill faith in her young son, but it faded once his seafaring father took him on as an apprentice on his ship. Influenced by the coarse habits of the sailors and a shipmate who introduced him to agnosticism, Newton renounced his faith.

Because of his early experiences at sea, Newton was able to secure a position as a sailor on a slave ship that transported its human cargo from Africa to other parts of the world. The captain of the ship, it turned out, was a cruel tyrant, and when the stubborn Newton rebelled, he was imprisoned at sea, put in chains like the slaves they were transporting, and nearly starved to death. Then, on landing at their destination, he was enslaved outright and put to work on a plantation in Sierra Leone. Starving and ill from depravation, he would secretly dig up roots and eat them in order to keep himself alive when there was no food to be had.

Newton was eventually able to write a letter to his father, explaining the dire circumstances under which he was living, and a ship sent by his father was miraculously able to find him on the small island where he was being held. In spite of all his suffering, the hardened and cynical Newton was unsure about whether he wanted to return to his native land and had to be tricked by the captain into boarding the ship bound for England. On the long journey home, Newton distinguished himself among the crew of hardened sailors for his exceptional debauchery and profanity. When a violent storm arose in the North Atlantic, the seas became unbearably rough and threatened to tear the ship to pieces. A man standing next to him was swept overboard and never seen again. Newton joined with the other sailors to bail water and repair the damage, but not before mouthing a quick prayer for God's mercy.

By the time the ship limped into harbor, miraculously spared, Newton was on his way to becoming a new man. He had been reading an abridgment of the classic book *The Imitation of Christ*, which he had discovered on board, and had been pondering the fact that God had apparently answered his prayer. Although he had long been one to turn aside any belief in God's mercy, he now saw himself as a recipient of it. It was not a dramatic overnight conversion, for he continued to struggle with many of the same behaviors that had created problems for him before, but as he reached out for God's grace, he began to change.

Newton continued to work in the slave trade for many years, until health issues necessitated that he give up the life at sea and settle down. Some years later, his conscience began to bother him in regard to his former vocation, and he began to see the great evil he had perpetrated against other human beings. He became an ardent and outspoken opponent of the slave trade and began to work with the young William Wilberforce and other abolitionists. His voice of authentic experience was a valuable help in bringing the evils of slavery to the attention of the populace of England and exposing its inhuman cruelties. It is not unlikely that in the composition of his great hymn, Newton had in mind his own wretchedness when he pondered his earlier blindness toward the evils of slavery.

After working a couple years as a customs agent and immersing himself in the church community, Newton experienced a call to the ministry and became a priest of the Church of England in the small village of Olney. Most of his congregation was poor and illiterate, and he seemed to be the perfect person to communicate the gospel to them. Whereas most clergymen of his day were in the habit of delivering ponderous theological sermons to their churches, Newton was almost unique in his tendency to share his own personal experiences with sin and temptation with his congregation. His passionate, if unpolished, sermons were much loved by his listeners, who also sang with great passion the hymns that he wrote in order to reinforce the lessons from his simple, straightforward preaching.

When John Newton died in 1807, he left behind an autobiography (usually now published under the title *Out of the Depths*) and hundreds of heartfelt hymns such as "Glorious Things of Thee Are Spoken," "Let Us Love and Sing and Wonder," and "How Sweet the Name of Jesus Sounds." In writing them, he generally avoided flights of poetic language in order to make his hymns accessible to all, and he wrote of his own personal experiences with God in such a way as to make them universally relevant to all who followed the same Savior. He composed his own epitaph, which reads: "John Newton, clerk. Once an infidel and libertine, a servant of slaves in Africa, was by the rich mercy of our Lord and Savior Jesus Christ, preserved, restored, pardoned, and appointed to preach the faith he had long labored to destroy."

28

Songs of Innocence and Experience

William Blake

(poems, 1789–1794)

Sometimes profundity comes packaged in childlike simplicity. Such is the case with William Blake, an odd, visionary poet who was anything but a traditional Christian but whose work is suffused with a spiritual fire that comes from his love and trust in God. *Songs of Innocence* was published in 1789, and its companion, *Songs of Experience*, was added in 1794. These two small collections of poetry each combined Blake's poetry with his own distinctive artistic images, which had been engraved on copper plates, and were printed in small print runs. When he gathered the two collections together into one volume, he subtitled it, "The Two Contrary States of the Human Soul."

In *Songs of Innocence*, Blake shows us the world through the eyes of a child. Using seemingly effortless language and rhyme, Blake celebrates the joys of life, the love of God, and the brotherhood of all human beings. There is a wild imagination, a gentleness and childlike wonder at work in these poems, a promise that even when life is agonizing and difficult there is a heaven awaiting us where pain will be forgotten. It is the message of comfort in these poems that probably accounts for much of their popularity.

> Little Lamb who made thee
> Dost thou know who made thee
> Gave thee life & bid thee feed.
> By the stream & o'er the mead;
> Gave thee clothing of delight,

Softest clothing wooly bright;
Gave thee such a tender voice,
Making all the vales rejoice!
    Little Lamb who made thee
    Dost thou know who made thee

    Little Lamb I'll tell thee,
    Little Lamb I'll tell thee!
He is called by thy name,
For he calls himself a Lamb:
He is meek & he is mild,
He became a little child:
I a child & thou a lamb,
We are called by his name.
    Little Lamb God bless thee.
    Little Lamb God bless thee.

The simple joys celebrated in *Songs of Innocence* are balanced out in *Songs of Experience*, written five years later as a complementary text. Many of its poems seem to be answering the views espoused by the childlike narrator of the earlier poems. In our souls, Blake says, we are innocents and children, but this world is often a dark and mysterious place, filled with pain and cruelty. While "The Chimney Sweeper" in *Songs of Innocence* offers a hope in the next life, its similarly titled partner in *Songs of Experience* focuses on the cruel injustice of this life and the guilt of those who "make up a heaven of our misery." To make it worse, this injustice is perpetrated under the protective cloak of piety: "They think they have done me no injury / And are gone to praise God & his Priest & King."

What we see when these *Songs* are taken together is a tension between opposites: good and evil, flesh and spirit, and even seemingly two faces of God Himself—the meek and mild God of forgiveness ("The Lamb") and the God of fearsome power and judgment ("The Tyger"). How can one reconcile the forgiver of sins with the punisher of sins? Of the fearsome "Tyger" Blake enquires, "Did he who made the Lamb make thee?" It is his way of asking the age-old question about where evil comes from. Is it possible that the same God who created the good also created the evil? As Blake's poetry developed, he "resolved" this tension by breaking the paradox and rejecting some aspects of the traditional view of God.

Another of the themes that runs throughout *Songs of Innocence and Experience* is Blake's reaction to the intense changes being experienced in British society due to the influence of the French and American revolutions and the new technologies that gave birth to the Industrial Revolution. Though the Industrial Revolution was still in its infancy when he wrote, Blake already saw the dire consequences its new technology would have, especially on the poor. Blake was one of the most urgent voices raised against the injustices that arose as the greedy barons of industry benefited from these changes while bringing crippling poverty to the working classes, whose sweat and labor made the whole machine of industry run. He saw these new factories where people labored for subsistence wages

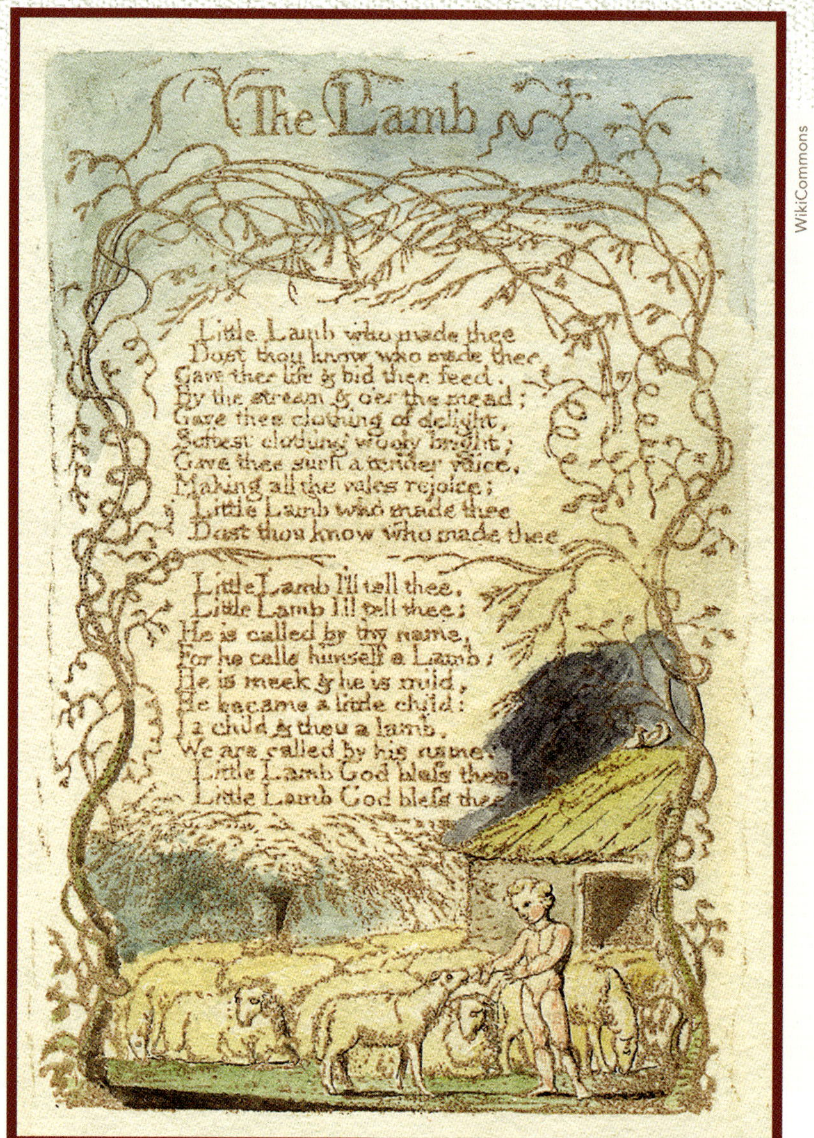

WikiCommons

The Lamb, from *Songs of Innocence*, by William Blake, The Library of Congress, Washington, D.C.

in terrible working conditions as "dark Satanic mills" and longed for a return to the simplicity of rural life.

William Blake was born in London in 1757 and died there seventy years later, spending almost his entire life in that city. From his earliest days he professed that he saw visions, once claiming that he saw a tree filled with angels. This otherworldliness was to characterize him throughout his life, alienating many but enchanting those who momentarily recaptured a sense of their own lost childhood in the immediacy of his childlike poetry. Later in life, he would even claim that much of his work was inspired and encouraged through communication with archangels.

As a child, Blake learned to read by reading the Bible, and its images are prevalent throughout his poems and writings. His parents were dissenters who rejected the prevailing concepts of the Anglican Church, so it is not entirely surprising that he later even dissented from the dissenters, for his mind was formed within a context of the rejection of accepted religious ideas.

As a young man he was apprenticed to a master engraver. In that job, and in a stint at the Royal Academy, he had the opportunity to hone his skills. The paintings and engravings that accompany many of his poems are small masterpieces themselves, art that inhabits an unseen world. Blake did not paint the world that he saw but rather the world of his vibrant imagination. Those who knew him spoke of him as a man of spontaneity and a sweet spirit, whose mind seemed to mostly dwell in a vivid inner world where his imagination took him. "I have very little of Mr. Blake's company," his wife once said. "He is always in Paradise."[1]

Blake saw himself as a prophetic poet with a mission of calling the world away from a simplistic dualism to a vision of a world interpenetrated by the Spirit. He rejected the philosophical materialism of Enlightenment thinkers such as Voltaire, Rousseau, and Bacon, convinced that there was more to life than their reductionist philosophies, and offered his readers a vision of life on a deeper spiritual level. "We ever must believe a lie," he warned, "when we see with, not through, the eye." His outlook was deeply spiritual, though it did not fit neatly into traditional religious categories.

Blake's theology was a concoction of his own making, a mixture of traditional Christian belief with some elements freely cribbed from various less traditional sources and a large dollop of his own unique and idiosyncratic mystical insights. The details and symbolism in his more complex poems are so arcane that few can honestly claim to grasp the entire system and its attendant mythology. How *literally* he took all his own imaginative musings about divinity and humanity is probably an open question. He did not believe that the Bible should be read literally, and one cannot help but wonder what he would have thought of those who try to read his own religious musings too literally. But he did have a central concern with pointing readers away from traditional religious conceptions and toward a faith emphasizing freedom and the primacy of the heart. Rejecting the idea of original sin, Blake embraced what might be called "original innocence." He saw in children a natural goodness and purity of heart that was usually lost by the time most people reached adulthood.

In Blake's system of thought, religion itself is one of the culprits in our loss of original innocence, for religion has too often focused on rules, regulations, and restrictions. It is often more about the attempt to prevent or suppress certain kinds of behaviors through conventional morality rather than celebrating the earthly (and sometimes earthy) joys of human life. In his poem "The Garden of Love," he writes that "the gates of this chapel were shut / And 'Thou Shalt Not' writ over the gate." Instead of people enjoying the freedom of experiencing God, "Priests in black gowns were walking their rounds / And binding with briars my joys and desires." He saw very clearly the hypocrisy within the church and was unblinking in his disdain for its repressive nature. He questioned the need for an intermediary and thought that ordinary people could reach God through prayer, good deeds, and their own imaginations.

Blake took evil very seriously, but suggested that the way of dealing with it was less through rules and commandments than through embracing the God "within man's breast." He made a distinction between the God of the Old Testament (whom he referred to as "Urizen") and the God of the New Testament. The paradoxes about God that were held in creative tension in his early poems are unfortunately resolved in later works with a simplistic rejection of the Old Testament God, which fails to do justice to the complexity of the Hebrew vision of the divine. Blake saw that God as terrifying and tyrannical, a corruption of the truth about the divine. The true God, he believed, could be found in our heart and our imagination as we "cleanse the doors of perception." He hoped his poems would assist in that process.

We can leave it to the scholars to unravel all the complex mythology in Blake's poetry, especially in his latter poems that feel weighted down by the freight of their ideas and rarely soar in the way his earlier poems do. In fighting against religious dogmatism Blake falls into a dogmatism of his own. While few would embrace all the intricacies of his religious system, his central vision is still powerful and compelling: a vision of forgiveness and love that has the potential to bind us all together under the watchful eye of a loving God. Blake believed that the best way to worship God was to love all beings, both human and nonhuman, for he saw a spark or remnant of the divine in every person and every created thing. That is why Blake could exclaim, "Every thing that lives is Holy."[2] He saw a spiritual radiance around everything and wanted to impart to his readers a new way of seeing:

> To see a World in a Grain of Sand
> And Heaven in a Wild Flower,
> Hold Infinity in the palm of your
>   hand
> And eternity in an hour.[3]

Behind all our religion, our morality, and our social systems there is, asserted Blake, a spiritual reality, and at the center of that reality is a God who loves all and who can be glimpsed in all things.

29

The Creation

Franz Joseph Haydn

(oratorio, 1798)

By the time he first heard a performance of Handel's *Messiah,* Franz Joseph Haydn was already considered one of the greatest of all composers and had created countless unforgettable symphonies and string quartets. But when he heard the masterpiece by Handel, he felt that nothing he had created would ever move an audience the way that he saw them moved by *Messiah.* As he listened to the performance, Haydn felt a sense of awe at Handel's wedding of music and lyrics, and at the way the audience exploded in wild applause at its conclusion. There and then he determined that he would create something of the same order—something that would be an expression not only of his musical gifts but also of his faith in God.

Written in his midsixties while at the height of his powers, *The Creation* is a meditation on the seven days of creation as they unfold in the biblical account of Genesis, accented with elements from John Milton's epic poem *Paradise Lost* and the book of Psalms. Devised as a three-part oratorio, the first two parts trace the first six days of creation while the third part takes place on the seventh day, when God rested. The main characters, whose recitatives and arias drive the narrative, include three archangels, Adam, and Eve. These are joined by the glorious choruses, which sing God's praise and celebrate the wonder of His work.

Baron von Swieten originally wrote the text in the hope that Handel would set it to music, but for some reason he never did, so

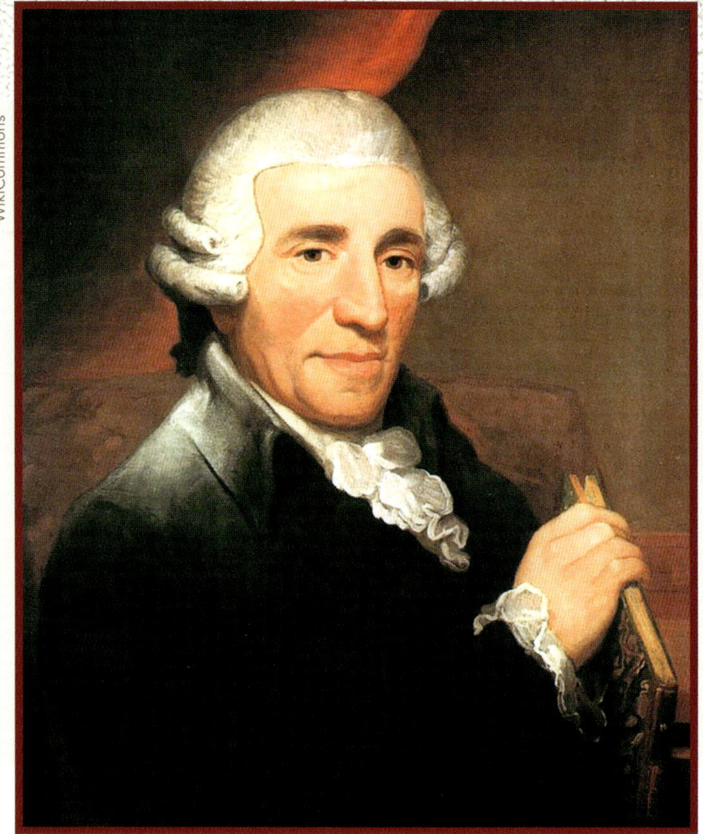
WikiCommons

Portrait of Joseph Haydn by Thomas Hardy (1791)

when Haydn discovered the libretto (originally written in English), he knew he had found words he could bring alive through his music. He asked a friend to translate it into German and entitled it *Die Schöpfung*, or *The Creation*. It is most commonly performed today in German, though sometimes will be offered in English.

Composed, Haydn said, to inspire "the worship and adoration of the Creator," the oratorio is vivid and powerful in its depiction of the unfolding creation story, using Haydn's musical textures to paint the procession of God's creative acts. The first several minutes are a bleak and dissonant musical evocation of the chaos that existed before God began His creative work. That is soon left behind when the chorus breaks into a breathless celebration of the creation of light, a moment designed to lift the audience out of their seats. The coming of light is announced by a soft pizzicato on the strings, which is followed by a shattering C-major chord that crashes upon the scene, and continues with a mighty chorus of voices singing, "Let there be light!" The premiere audience was so surprised and electrified that the orchestra could not proceed for several minutes, as they had to wait for the enthusiasm to subside.

About an hour into the work, Haydn's uniqueness really manifests itself in the section portraying the creation of the animals, each of whom is given a "tone poem" to introduce them: the roar of a lion, the pastoral gentleness of cattle and sheep, and the bounding flourish of a stag. Even the insects and worms get their own musical introduction. *The Creation* concludes with another show-stopping chorus, which leaves the listeners with the exultant praise of God ringing in their ears: "Sing to the Lord, ye voices all!"

Haydn reported to a contemporary biographer about the prayerful attitude he had assumed in composing this work: "Daily I fell on my knees and asked God for strength."[1] He spent more time on *The Creation* than on any other work he ever composed, and the result of the arduous task is an enthralling musical masterpiece that deserves to stand alongside the more well-known *Messiah*. From its first performance, it was recognized as a major achievement from the industrious Haydn.

In the last year of his life, Haydn was very ill and not able to get around, so he was brought on a stretcher to the last performance he would ever hear of his famous oratorio. He listened with satisfaction, but at the moment when the chorus burst into "And There Was Light," and the audience burst into spontaneous applause, he lifted up his hands and said, "Not from me. It all comes from above."

Born in 1732 in Austria, Franz Joseph Haydn was raised in a family that loved music and took their faith seriously. He left home at age six to be trained in music, and by eight he had become a choirboy in Vienna, where he served for nine years. The playful sense of humor that he would later bring to so many of his compositions as an adult did not always serve him well as a child. When, for one of his pranks, he took scissors to the pigtail of another choirboy, he was dismissed from the choir.

After losing his place in the choir, he still wanted to make a living through music, but for a number of years he could only scrape together a meager existence by giving private lessons or singing impromptu serenades along Vienna's boulevards as a street musician. In time, his talents came to the attention of one of the city's premier teachers, who took Haydn under his wing and began to instruct him in counterpoint and other fundamentals necessary for composition. Writing music never came as easily for Haydn as it did for his contemporary, Mozart, from whom great music seemed to pour effortlessly. Ever industrious, Haydn had to work hard throughout his life, disciplining himself to keep regular hours for composing every day. When inspiration failed to come, he would pray for God's help.

The result of his hard work and his prayers is an almost bewilderingly large number of pieces of various kinds, which sustain a very high level of consistency in their quality. Haydn was one of the most productive composers in history because he was one of the hardest working. His output includes 104 symphonies, more than sixty-eight string quartets (these two forms he brought to a perfection never before heard), more than one hundred piano pieces, a dozen masses, and two dozen operas. His renown grew to the point where he was in demand throughout Europe, and he even spent a number of very productive years in England, where some of his most accomplished symphonies were written.

Those who knew Haydn were always struck by his geniality and kind nature, joyous embrace of life, and love of good food, good music, and good company. He loved to joke and play pranks on his friends, and this mischievousness shows itself in many of his compositions. He seemed to enjoy making audiences smile, and surprising them with the playfulness that he worked into the pieces. For his famous *Surprise* symphony (no. 94, 1791), he inserted a jarring chord meant to awaken any listeners who had been lulled to sleep. His *Clock* symphony (no. 101, 1793–1794) has the stately beat of a pendulum clock, and *La Poule* (no. 83, 1785) imitates the sound of a clucking hen. When some church leaders criticized his music for not being serious enough, he replied, "God gave me a cheerful heart, so he will surely forgive me if I serve him cheerfully."[2] Mozart, with whom he shared a deep and lasting friendship, referred to him as "Papa Haydn," and the name caught on with his admirers. When the younger Mozart died, Haydn grieved the loss deeply and spoke with unstinting praise of his talent. Theirs was a relationship of respect and admiration rather than competition.

His cheerfulness was not the result of his circumstances, for Haydn did not have an easy life. He experienced extreme poverty while trying to establish his musical career; he was married for forty years to a woman who showed no interest or appreciation for his music and was even known to roll up his written musical scores in order to use them to curl her hair; and he sometimes worked for patrons who treated him more like a slave than a man of genius. But through it all, the music he composed was a reflection of his personality: beautiful and orderly but also cheerful, joyous, and with a good bit of wit and humor.

Franz Joseph Haydn kept that humor until the very end of his life. When it was falsely rumored that he had died, and a special requiem in Paris was planned by fellow musicians, he wrote a letter thanking them for their good intentions and remarking that "if I had only known of it in time, I could have traveled to Paris to conduct the *Requiem* myself."[3] Just before his death he told a friend, "I have only to wait like a child for the time when God calls me to himself."[4] Haydn joined the chorus of heaven in 1809.

30

Pride and Prejudice

Jane Austen

(novel, 1813)

Who would ever have expected that a quiet and unassuming novelist from the early nineteenth century would become one of the most popular writers of our own time? Jane Austen, who wrote insightful and gently humorous books about the romantic misadventures of unmarried women, has become a cultural icon, and her novels have been made into wildly popular films and miniseries. Imitators have written shelves full of books about the continued adventures of her beloved characters, or tried their hands at writing that could be labeled "Austenesque." But none has been able to match her wit and her probing insight into human nature and human relationships.

Pride and Prejudice is probably the best known of her novels, though you will find partisans among her many fans for each and every one of them. Her initial title for the book was *First Impressions*, which so well captures the main theme of the book—that first impressions are often disastrously wrong. When Elizabeth Bennett, the protagonist, first meets the rich and eligible bachelor Mr. Darcy, she finds him pompous and arrogant. Thinking herself perceptive and a great judge of character, she brusquely dismisses his interest in her. That Elizabeth would reject one of the most eligible of bachelors when she herself has no money, no position, and no prospects is a remarkable assertion of her commitment to true love. Because of her initial perception of Darcy's character, she feels that she would be marrying beneath herself—not socially, but morally. In the course of the novel both Elizabeth and Darcy realize that they have made seriously faulty judgments about the other, and both must humble themselves before they can find true love in each other's arms.

In most of Austen's novels, there is a key turning point that occurs when one of the characters comes to realize that they have not been realistic or correct in their notions of the world or of themselves. The protagonist comes, after many false steps, to the realization that they have seriously misjudged another or treated them unfairly. When this realization comes, it is a moment of genuine spiritual awakening, a kind of repentance that arises from recognizing their tendency to be judgmental and admitting their own proud arrogance. In *Pride and Prejudice*, for example, Elizabeth Bennett comes to realize that she has been blind to the faults of her family, the qualities of her would-be suitor Mr. Darcy, and the superiority and empty pride within herself:

> "How despicably I have acted!" she cried. "I, who have prided myself on my discernment! . . . How humiliating is this discovery! . . . I have courted prepossession and ignorance, and driven reason away. . . . Till this moment I never knew myself."[1]

Such a moment of self-knowledge serves to instigate a process of interior growth in her heroine's personality and the attainment of the virtue that Austen calls "constancy." To be constant is to be grounded and rooted in values that persist beyond the present moment—lasting values. To constancy Austen contrasts that highly valued trait, charm. Charm is the ability to attract the attention of others without necessarily having the qualities one appears to possess. The charming person can simulate the virtues of good character by mere outward polish. Being charming is all about social acceptance rather than actually possessing admirable traits. It is concerned with how things look on the outside—how they seem, rather than what they truly are.

So often in Austen's novels we discover that the person who has great charm is a person we later learn has poor or deficient character. And sometimes the person who may win few "style points" is eventually revealed to be a person of strong personality and depth of character, as is Darcy in *Pride and Prejudice*. But you would never mistake one of Austen's books for a moral tract, for she never preaches. She observes, and she lets us draw our own conclusions. Along the way to making such discoveries, we are treated to a novel that is amusing, insightful, and well stocked with fascinating and flawed characters. She entertains us with her close observation of the human personality and she leaves us with greater wisdom about our own selves.

WikiCommons

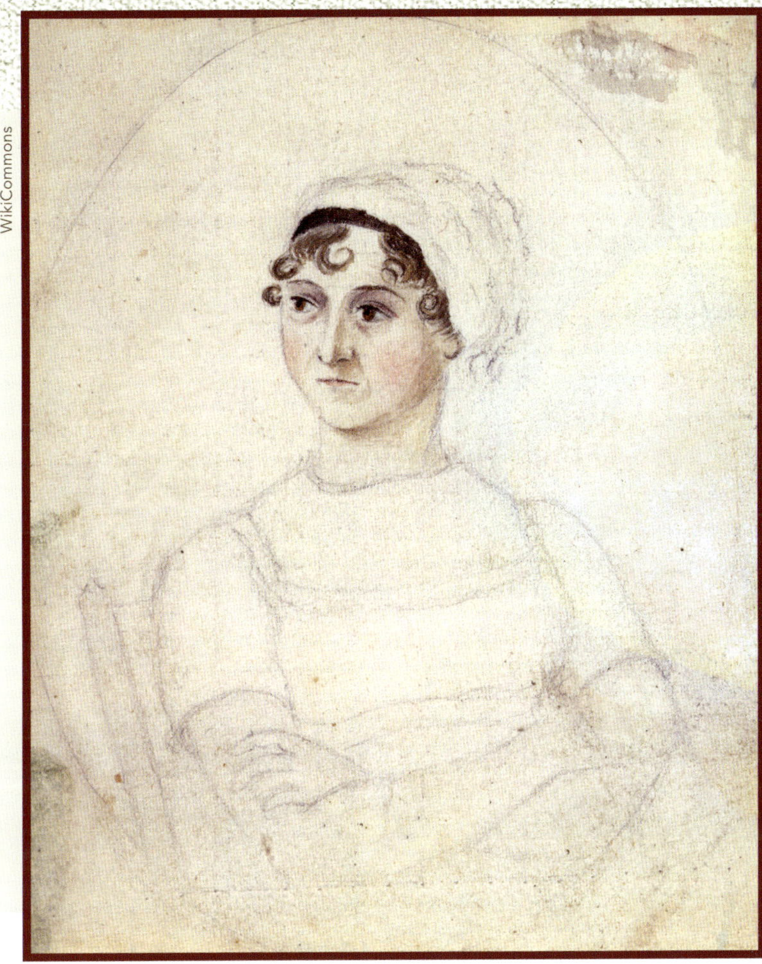

Portrait of Jane Austen in watercolor and pencil by Cassandra Austen (c.1810)

Jane Austen was born in 1775, the daughter of the rector of a small English parish. Unlike her books, her day-to-day existence would not have provided much fodder for a television miniseries, for she lived an outwardly uneventful life and never married. Instead she spent her time writing and caring for her family, including her nieces and nephews, with whom she was a great favorite. She wrote her books mainly for the sheer pleasure of it, concealing her work under the cover of anonymity. Until late in her writing career, no one outside her family knew her as the author of these remarkable novels. Even with her own family she was reticent about drawing attention to her creative work. When someone entered the room while she was writing, she would gently slip her manuscript in progress underneath other papers on the writing desk. It seems she had little desire for fame and recognition, and was

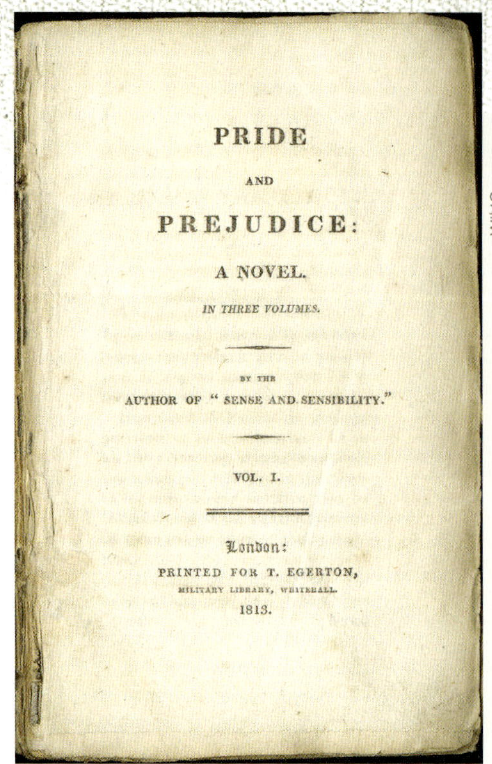
PRIDE

AND

PREJUDICE:

A NOVEL.

IN THREE VOLUMES.

BY THE

AUTHOR OF "SENSE AND SENSIBILITY."

VOL. I.

London:

PRINTED FOR T. EGERTON,

MILITARY LIBRARY, WHITEHALL.

1813.

WikiCommons

Title page from the first edition of *Pride and Prejudice*

content with her quiet domestic life.

Austen began writing when she was very young, and her surviving juvenilia shows that her natural abilities blossomed quickly, though it took her quite some time to get published. In the meantime she worked and reworked her manuscripts. Beginning with the publication of *Sense and Sensibility* in 1811, she produced a string of novels that exquisitely demonstrate that the ordinary human life is the great battleground upon which we all struggle to develop true moral character. After *Sense and Sensibility*, her novels, some of which she had been working on for years, were published in fairly rapid succession: *Pride and Prejudice* (1813), *Mansfield Park* (1814), *Emma* (1815), *Persuasion* (1818), and *Northanger Abbey* (1818). In the entire history of literature, there are few comparable stretches of such fertile literary accomplishment.

When Austen's health began to fail in early 1816, her output declined, but she was still working on books when she died in 1817. Several of her unfinished manuscripts and juvenilia have been published since her death, and her books have remained in print without interruption. Numbered among her countless fans have been such eminent writers as Sir Walter Scott, Henry James, E. M. Forster, Anthony Trollope, G. K. Chesterton, and C. S. Lewis.

Austen's great skill as an author was in uncovering the drama that lies just below the surface niceties of our daily lives, drama that emerges from romantic longings and entanglements, unspoken emotions, strained relationships, and the struggle between societal expectations and the desires of the individual person. Her novels are not epic in scope or filled with adventure. Instead, she chose a small world to write about, a world she knew well. She studied it carefully and reproduced it flawlessly. It is a world that stresses the values of virtue, reason, and moderation rather than high-flown sentiment and emotion.

Compared to those of her great French and Russian contemporaries, the moral range of Austen's characters seems limited. Her books contain bad people, but they are not monsters—just deluded, selfish, and self-absorbed. And the virtuous characters are good people with their attendant faults—they are not saints. Austen does not see duty and morality as complicated concepts. They are not stifling and restrictive but rather essential components in the education of our passions. They are based on commonsense rules for behavior that any ten-year-old should know: honesty, respect for parents, loyalty to friends, proper gratitude to those who have been kind, and the necessity that emotions must be balanced by reason. The oft-repeated theme of her books revolves around the search for a suitable marriage partner who has these qualities and the moral lessons learned in the pursuit of that goal.

Pointing to the lack of attention to religion in the novels, and the fact that she often creates clerical characters who are amusing buffoons, some have suggested that Austen didn't take her faith all that seriously. Perhaps this is evidence of their own bias more than anything else, for there is plenty of confirmation that this clergyman's daughter was a woman of quiet but deep faith. While never one to join in with the religious enthusiasts (who made her rather uncomfortable), she was certainly a devout middle-of-the-road Anglican, raised on the spiritual beauty of the *Book of Common Prayer*.

Among the various writings Austen left behind when she died is a small collection of prayers she wrote for use with her family in evening worship. Couched in a beautiful formality reminiscent of the *Book of Common Prayer*, they give ample evidence of a woman whose heart and mind were touched by faith. In them, she expressed great faith and thankfulness to God and also prayed humbly for God to reveal and forgive her for her own sinful attitudes and actions. She recognized "the importance of every day, and every hour as it passes" and asked for God's help to "earnestly strive to make a better use of what Thy goodness may yet bestow on us, than we have done of the time past."[2]

Austen attended church services regularly throughout her life, and found great enjoyment in reading sermons. On her death, her nephew James Edward Austen-Leigh described her as one who "had lived the life of a good Christian" and said that "piety ruled her in life, and supported her in death."[3] He said that she was someone who was more concerned with living out her faith than talking about it.

For Jane Austen, all the little events of a life could be used as teachable moments to educate us in how to live better lives, free of self-delusion and arrogance. With her novels, she cast a light upon human relationships and, strengthened by the perceptions of her faith, offered her readers gentle lessons in how to become a better human being. And she knew how to make us laugh at ourselves in the face of all our follies.

31

The Wanderer above the Sea of Fog

Caspar David Friedrich

(painting, 1818)

This simple image, so often reproduced, has become an icon of Romanticism, a visual representation of a philosophical and artistic movement that questioned the primacy of rationalism and emphasized the need for imagination, sensation, and feeling. Romanticism called for a fresh way of looking at nature, and saw it as the receptacle of values higher than those trumpeted by the "geniuses" of human civilization. It emphasized the idea that each individual must find their own path to truth through connecting with their feelings, their longings, and their yearnings toward the unattainable. So Caspar David Friedrich's *The Wanderer above the Sea of Fog* would seem a perfect image for such a philosophy. In the painting, a lonely traveler stands at the peak of a rocky mountain and looks out over the forbidding landscape that stretches out before his gaze. Mist and fog swirl around the jutting mountains, concealing the terrain below. Almost beyond sight, a mountain range stretches into the barely visible distance. What path, one wonders, did the wanderer travel to bring him to this breathtaking vista?

The wanderer stands with his back toward us, right in the center of the painting. His placement makes him a stand-in for the viewer, a proxy. The German word used to describe such a man is *rückenfigur*. We can imagine ourselves standing in his place, seeing what he is seeing. But is the Romantic perspective of life all he is experiencing? Or

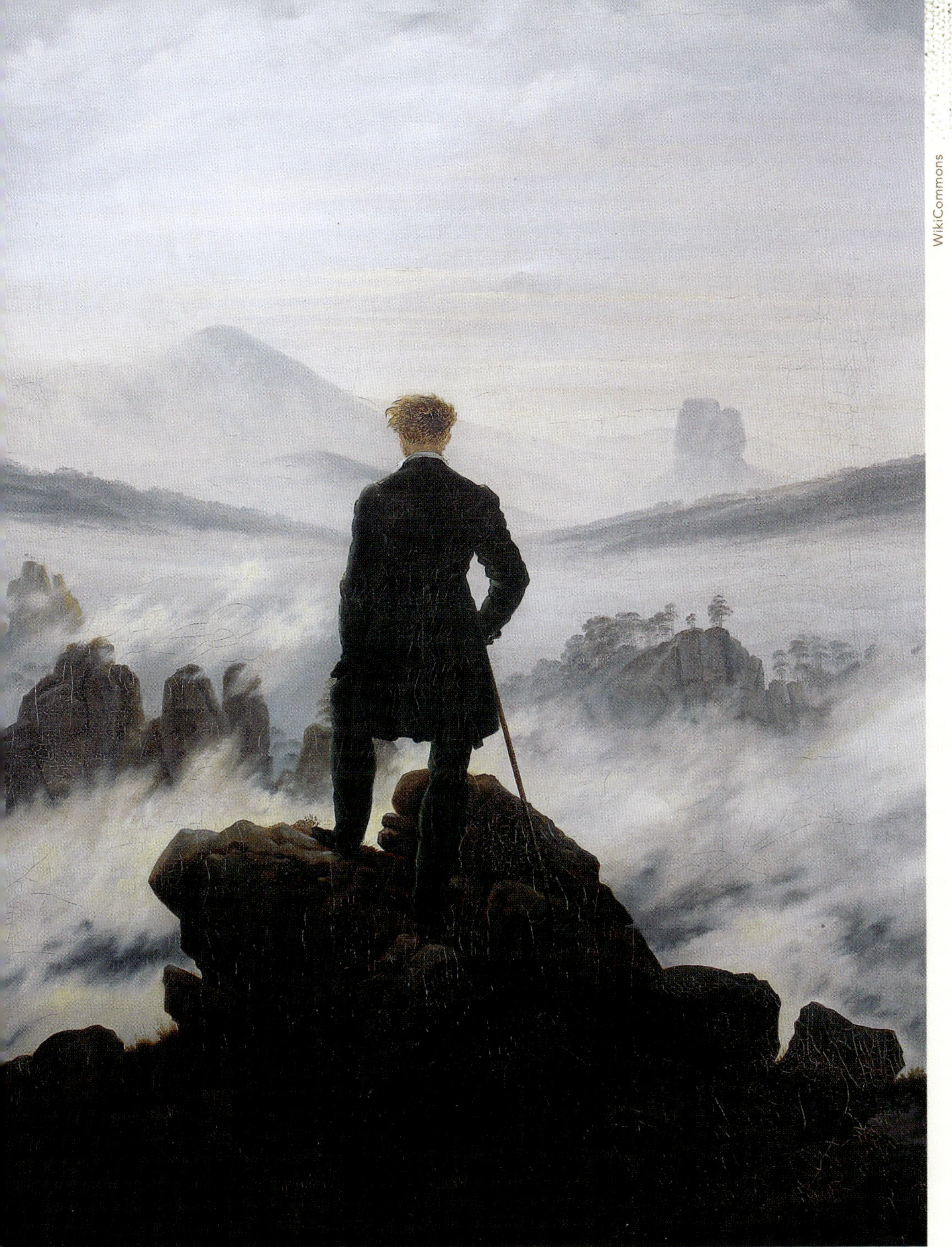

WikiCommons

Wanderer above the Sea of Fog by Caspar David Friedrich, Künsthalle, Hamburg

is this painting also reflective of Friedrich's Christian faith, and is what we are seeing a man standing in solitary contemplation of the mystery of existence, a man in awe of the sublimity of nature, and ultimately a man standing before God?

Born in 1774, Caspar David Friedrich was brought up in a devout and traditional Lutheran home, but as he grew up his family was frequently visited by tragedy. His mother died when he was only seven years old, and his sister died a year later. At age thirteen, he witnessed his brother fall through the ice of a frozen lake and drown. Such traumas probably played their part in his tendency toward melancholy and depression, as well as his lifelong fascination with death and what came after it.

Friedrich studied art under Johann Gottfried Quistorp, who introduced him to theologian Ludwig Gotthard Kosegarten, whose teaching about nature as a revelation of God was very important for Friedrich's development. Also influential was the theology of Friedrich Schleiermacher, who championed the need for a personal existential experience of God beyond mere doctrines and dogmas.

For much of his career, Friedrich's work was in great demand, but in his later years his style fell out of favor. The once popular painter's work came to be seen as old-fashioned, eccentric, and out of touch with newer artistic fashions. The last fifteen years of his life were difficult. He was increasingly isolated and solitary and at times struggled with poverty when he failed to find buyers for his paintings. A series of debilitating strokes limited his output and played havoc with his mental state. By the time of his death he was largely forgotten. It wasn't until the mid-twentieth century that the gradual rehabilitation of his reputation began, and now he has a secure place in art history as an innovative painter of spiritual landscapes.

Among his other accomplishments, Friedrich introduced an entirely new kind of religious painting, one where landscape is not the background for the main image but rather takes center stage—the focus of the work. Through his sublime landscapes, usually peopled only by solitary individuals or small groups of tiny figures, and through his creative explorations of the effects of light, Friedrich sought to find the supernatural aura hidden in the natural world. For Friedrich, nature was a guide toward the spiritual and eternal. He saw the eternal prefigured and revealed by signs in the earthly natural world—if one had eyes to see. The mystical presence of God, though, could not only be seen but also felt in nature. And feeling was the whole point of his art. As he wrote, "A picture must not be invented, but rather felt."[1]

Friedrich's landscapes were not so much intended to be beautiful as they were to be sublime. That which is sublime is awe-inspiring rather than just pretty. Friedrich's

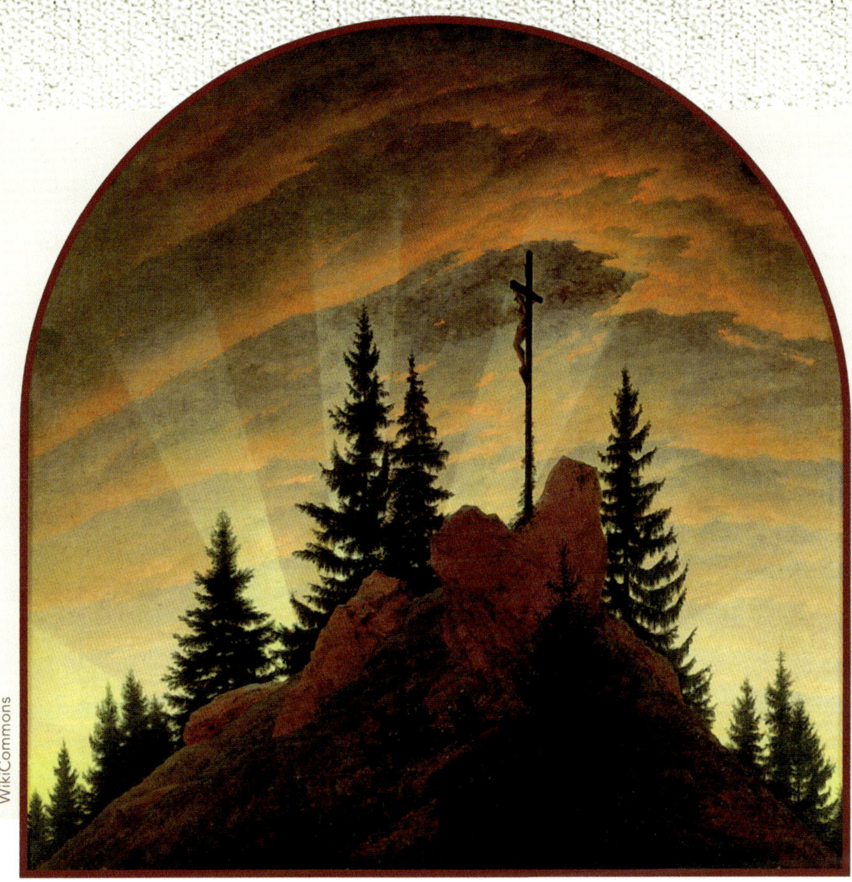

Cross in the Mountains (Tetschen Altar) (1807/1808)

landscapes tend toward the dramatic, capturing the wild and untamed aspect of nature, and sometimes its menacing gloom. They create a mood: melancholy, reverence, longing, or some combination of these. His best work captures the overwhelming immensity of the created world, and, by comparison, the smallness of the human being who experiences it. And the generally small human figures we find in his work are not saints, as in older religious art, but just ordinary people experiencing the extraordinary mystery of the natural world and the God who created it.

Friedrich's canvases are intended to promote a meditative state, arising out of the vision and spirit of the artist and communicated to the viewer as an object for contemplation. "The artist," he wrote, "should not only paint what he sees before him, but also what he sees within him." Thus he gave these directions to would-be artists, "Close your bodily eye so that you see your picture first with your spiritual eye. Then bring what you saw in the dark into the light, so that it may have an effect on others, shining inwards from outside."[2]

Friedrich's first major work, a controversial piece that made him famous, was an altarpiece he painted in 1807 entitled *The*

Cross in the Mountains. It is almost certainly the first altarpiece ever created to depict a landscape as the main element of the painting. The arch-shaped image reveals a cross placed at the pinnacle of a rocky mountain in the midst of evergreen trees. The crucified Savior is hanging on the cross and the sun is either rising or setting behind Him, as three intense shafts of light emanate from a source other than the sun. Here Friedrich has portrayed the central event of the Christian story, but it is being enacted in the midst of the natural world. As he wrote of it, in one of the rare times he ever explained one of his paintings, "The cross stands erected on a rock, unshakably firm like our faith in Jesus Christ. The firs stand around the evergreen, enduring through all ages, like the hopes of man in him, the crucified."[3]

The Cross in the Mountains captures the hope of God's triumph over death, but other Friedrich paintings focus more on the transitory nature of life, with barren trees symbolizing death and ruined churches showing the fate of religion in the modern world in *Abbey in the Oakwood* (1810) and *Monastery Graveyard in the Snow* (1819), a lone monk on a deserted beach in *Monk on the Seashore* (c. 1808), or a crippled man resting before a cross in *Winter Landscape* (1811). At times Friedrich's figures seem alienated from the world around them, solitaries in an unwelcoming environment, while in other images there is an embrace of the beauty and wonder of the natural world—a mystical epiphany, as in *Woman Before the Setting Sun* (c. 1818).

To some religious observers Friedrich's paintings skated dangerously near to pantheism, and to rationalist viewers they seemed far too subjective and mystical instead of accurately reporting the natural world. In many ways, he was an artist ahead of his time. But he refused to compromise his vision. "I am not so weak as to submit to the demands of the age when they go against my convictions. . . . I shall leave it to time to show what will come of it: a brilliant butterfly or a maggot."[4]

For many years it seemed like Caspar David Friedrich's legacy might be the latter, a forgotten footnote to German art. But in these modern times, when alienation and loneliness and existential despair are so deeply felt, his work has once again been embraced. Writers such as Samuel Beckett (*Waiting for Godot*) have seen the primal human condition expressed in his paintings, and artists such as Edward Hopper and Andrew Wyeth have found kinship in capturing the loneliness so many experience. But such artists and writers only see half of the story, for Friedrich was pointing steadfastly to truths beyond the loneliness and alienation, to the God whose presence can be seen in the world He created, and who calls out to His children both in the gathering darkness and in the rising of the light.

32

Symphony no. 5, *The Reformation*

Felix Mendelssohn

(classical music, 1830)

One of the elements in the standard mythology about artists is the idea that their art is born out of the struggles and difficulties of their life; without pain and deprivation it is not possible to produce great creative work. While that may be true for many of the great artists, every rule has exceptions, and Felix Mendelssohn is one of the exceptions to this one. Born into a wealthy family, provided with everything he needed to excel in his prodigious musical gifts, happily married, and with a highly successful career, Mendelssohn made great music in spite of all his good fortune. Throughout his musical career, he produced works that impressed critics and won plaudits from audiences who enjoyed his lively, cheerful compositions.

Mendelssohn's Fifth Symphony, known as *The Reformation,* was composed to honor the three-hundredth anniversary of the presentation of the Augsburg Confession, a key event in the Protestant Reformation. As a devout Lutheran, Mendelssohn wanted to celebrate this important historical moment with a full-scale work. It was the second symphony he wrote, though it was not formally published until after his death and therefore it is numbered fifth of his five symphonic works. Because of issues with his health, he could not complete it on time and it could not be performed as part of the festivities in Augsburg. In fact, it was not performed very often during his lifetime, many finding it either "too learned" or "too Protestant" for popular tastes.

The symphony draws upon Mendelssohn's knowledge of the traditions of sacred music as well as his understanding of church history. It makes use of "The Dresden Amen" in its first movement, a sequence of six notes sung by choirs during German church services, and it ends with a majestic version of Martin Luther's "A Mighty Fortress Is Our God" in which the whole of the orchestra joins together in a blazing musical finale. Mendelssohn didn't consider it one of his best works and was somewhat dismissive about it, so it was not published during his lifetime. But later audiences have found the piece to be a triumphant celebration of faith and recommitment to God and to His Word.

Felix Mendelssohn was born in Germany in 1809 to a well-to-do and culturally influential family. A childhood prodigy, he displayed astonishing gifts from a very early age, which his parents did everything possible to encourage. They went so far as to hire an orchestra to try out some of his youthful compositions. At age twelve, he was even taken to visit the poet Goethe, a living cultural icon, who sat for hours, entranced by the musical skill of this young man. Mendelssohn's sister Fanny was also an exceptional musician, and in a less sexist age might have become a famous composer in her own right. A companion in musical performance, she also remained the best of his friends throughout his life.

When one considers musical prodigies, one cannot but think of Mozart, who is always celebrated for his youthful gifts, but Mendelssohn's compositions at age sixteen show even more musical maturity than those of Mozart at a similar age. The string octet he composed at that young age is considered one of the masterpieces of chamber music. And his stirring *Overture to a Midsummer Night's Dream* (1826), written just a year later, is a piece that still brings a smile to audiences who hear it performed, a veritable bubbling cauldron of joyousness.

Among Mendelssohn's gifts as a composer was his ability to bring a youthful exuberance to almost every piece he wrote, works filled with energy, invention, and lovely melodies. He was a student of the great composers who had preceded him—Handel, Mozart, Beethoven, and especially Bach. He was responsible for a great revival of interest in Bach's music after he arranged and conducted a performance of *St. Matthew Passion,* a work that had not been performed in public since Bach's death in 1750. Mendelssohn knew the piece so well that when he mounted the podium to conduct and found that the wrong music had been placed there, he was able to conduct the entire piece from memory, turning the pages of the incorrect score so as not to raise concern among his musicians! But along with his knowledge and devotion to the classical heritage, he also felt the influence of the budding Romantic movement and injected its lush sensibility into the classic forms forged by his heroes, which makes him a sort of bridge between the two musical eras.

There is a lightness, sweetness, and joy to Mendelssohn's work that reflects the pleasure and serenity he found in his life. This has caused many to wonder if he would have produced even greater music if his life had involved more struggles. But isn't there a place in music for the expression of happiness and contentment? Do we not need the sunny, cheerful joys of Mendelssohn's melodies to counterbalance the angst of Beethoven and Mahler? Surely music need not be grave to be serious.

In 1830, Mendelssohn embarked on a grand tour of Europe, during which he visited six countries. His favorite stop was Italy, which inspired his *Italian Symphony*. For a time Mendelssohn was generally regarded as "the greatest living composer." He directed the orchestra in Leipzig (which he crafted into the best in Europe) and founded a conservatory of music with Robert and Clara Schumann.

His *Italian Symphony* (1833), the gorgeous *Violin Concerto* (1844), and his piano works such as *Songs Without Words* (1829–1845) have all entered the canon of essential pieces in the classical repertoire, but some of his tuneful music is also known (if not recognized as such) by almost everybody. His "Wedding March" from the *Incidental Music to a Midsummer Night's Dream* (1842) is the celebratory music to which countless couples have walked down the aisle at the conclusion of their ceremony, and the tune of one of the most popular Christmas carols, "Hark, the Herald Angels Sing," is also from Mendelssohn's pen.

Mendelssohn traveled to Britain several times during his career and became immensely popular there, counting Queen Victoria and Prince Albert among his biggest fans. His religious works, especially his oratorios, were particular favorites in Britain, including an oratorio based on the life of the apostle Paul (1836), for which he did much preparatory research and study, as he felt he "must not make any mistakes." Perhaps, as a converted Jew himself, he identified in many ways with the apostle. His oratorio *Elijah* (1840) is probably his greatest sacred choral work, based upon the life of the great Old Testament prophet. It has dramatic urgency, and the majestic choruses are not unlike those of Handel, whom he admired, but it also has some spectacular touches all its own, such as the "sound pictures" created to represent earthquakes, fire, and the pounding of the ocean.

Mendelssohn composed furiously throughout his career, driven by a fierce work ethic and the sheer joy he found in musical composition. He wrote, "Even the smallest task in music is so absorbing, and carries us so far away from town, country, earth, and all worldly things, that it is truly a blessed gift of God."[1] Even while he took great pleasure in all his hard work, it may have affected his health and caught up with him in the end, leading to his premature death at age thirty-eight. When he was informed in May 1847 of the unexpected death of his sister, he fainted and a blood vessel burst in his brain. Inconsolable with grief, he suffered debilitating pain and depression, leading to a steady decline and his own passing in November of that same year.

Though Mendelssohn was born into a Jewish family (his grandfather was the famous Jewish philosopher Moses Mendelssohn), his parents converted to Christianity when the children were small and had them baptized into the Lutheran faith. Some skeptics have suggested that his parents' conversion was more about opening doors of cultural advancement than due to any strong religious conviction, but even if that was the case, Felix Mendelssohn took his faith seriously throughout his life. He was a man of prayer, and not hesitant to ask others to pray for him. In a letter to one of his friends, he wrote, echoing Psalm 51:10, "Pray to God that He might create in us a clean heart and renew a right spirit within us."[2]

When Mendelssohn composed, he sometimes imitated Bach's habit of scribbling exclamations and prayers into the margins of his scores, jotting down such things as "Let it succeed, God!" and "Help along." He saw his skills as a gift from God, and felt a personal responsibility to use them, saying, "I know perfectly well that no musician can make his thoughts or talents different to what Heaven has made them; but I also know that if Heaven has given him good ones, he must also be able to develop them properly."[3] Shortly before his death, which he anticipated to be imminent, he wrote, "A great chapter has now ended, and neither the title nor even the first word of the next is yet written. But God will make it all right one day; this suits the beginning and end of all chapters."[4]

33

The Voyage of Life

Thomas Cole

(paintings, 1842)

Sometimes when we stand quietly before a breathtaking natural vista we somehow feel more alive, we sense the pulse of the created world, and all the glory before us causes us to think a little more deeply about the meaning of our lives. Thomas Cole made a career of painting such visions, and he was never shy about the idea that painting could be a way of manifesting the deepest truths. His canvases are gentle sermons, rooted in his appreciation for the wonders of the natural world, which "declare the glory of God" and "proclaim the work of his hands" (Ps. 19:1).

Sometimes Cole let nature speak for itself, but at other times he wed his depictions of the natural world with allegorical ruminations about human nature and destiny, as in his four-painting series, *The Voyage of Life*. *The Voyage of Life* is an allegory for the four stages of human life, filled with both warning and promise about what lies ahead for each of us as we journey through our lives. The same elements are repeated in each of the four paintings: a voyager, an angel, a river, a boat in which the voyager travels, and the landscape, which transforms throughout the series from sublime to forbidding and then back to sublime as it points to the world beyond this one.

In the first painting of the series, *Childhood*, the young traveler launches out from a cave (birth) onto a placid stream. The sun is rising in the distance, and a guardian angel stands watch in the little boat. In *Youth*, the second painting in the series, the view of the landscape widens, as the youth holds the tiller and the angel watches from the shore. Part of growing up is learning responsibility and setting goals for life. The boat is headed down the river toward a ghostly castle that looms before the youth, representing his dreams and ambitions, which Cole referred to as "the romantic beauty of youthful imaginings."[1]

All is peaceful, but not for long, as the third painting, *Manhood*, reminds us of the troubles and travails of existence. The little boat is entering menacing rapids, which threaten to capsize the already-damaged vessel that the traveler is now trying to navigate without its tiller. There are rocks, whirlpools, and other dangers ahead, and nature itself seems arrayed against him. The landscape is dark, the skies are stormy, and the rain is falling in torrents. The angel has not forsaken him, though, still watching him from a distance, high in the sky. Ahead of him the passage is narrow and frightening, but he has no choice, he must journey on. So he folds his hands in prayer. The final painting is *Old Age*. Our traveler has survived the trials of life and now draws near to the end of his journey: death. The guardian angel draws close to him, and angels are descending from above as the river flows into eternity. As Cole describes this scene, "The chains of corporeal existence are falling away; and already the mind has glimpses of Immortal Life."[2]

With this series, Cole shows how faith can sustain a person throughout the whole of life and into the heavenly home. Seen individually, these paintings could come across as sentimental and pious, but taken together they make a realistic statement about the struggles of life and the fact that hope is often hard-won and usually comes on the heels of hardship.

Thomas Cole was born in 1801 in England and immigrated with his family to the United States as a young man. He worked in Pennsylvania and Ohio before settling in New York State, where he spent most of his working life. Cole found early success when his paintings were admired and purchased by three prominent US artists, who later became the younger artist's disciples. His fresh approach to the art of landscape painting, which others soon embraced as their own, gave a new dignity and importance to what had been formerly considered a minor genre for painters.

Cole was a poet as well as a painter, and he left behind a collection of hymnlike celebrations of beauty and the One who created it. "To walk with nature as a poet," he wrote, "is the necessary condition of the artist."[3] One of his poems reads:

> Let us give thanks to God that in
> his love
> He grants such glimpses of the
> world above
> That we poor pilgrims on this
> darkling sphere

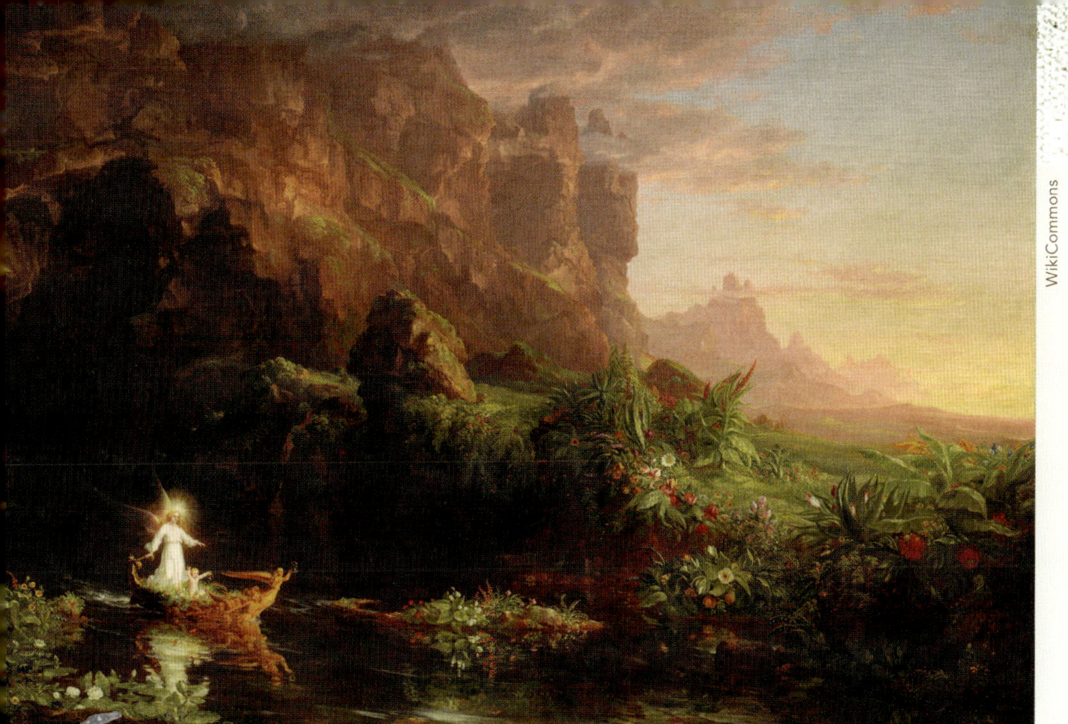
WikiCommons

The Voyage of Life: Childhood by Thomas Cole, National Gallery of Art, Washington, D.C.

Beyond its shadows can our
hopes uprear.[4]

Cole was a poet with a paintbrush, and he sang the glory of God with pen and brush as he perceived it in the awesome expanses of the American wilderness.

One of his greatest early paintings is *View from Mt. Holyoke: The Oxbow* (1836), which shows the wilderness giving way to cultivation, and re-creates the drama of a passing storm as an artist (a tiny figure in the bottom right of the painting, probably a self-portrait) records the majestic scene. An interesting little detail are the Hebrew letters hidden in the hillside of the distant mountains. They are upside down and spell *Shaddai*: the Almighty. Another early work is his reimagining of the *Garden of Eden* (1828), which combines all sorts of flora and fauna that would normally never be seen together in one place, and its corresponding painting, *Expulsion from the Garden of Eden* (1828), where we see, ever so tiny, our first parents being cast out of paradise into a rocky and forbidding landscape.

Cole was the founding father of a school of like-minded American landscape painters, who flourished between about 1825 and 1880, called the Hudson River School because its founders lived and painted in the Hudson River Valley in upstate New York. These painters celebrated the unspoiled and undeveloped landscape of the young

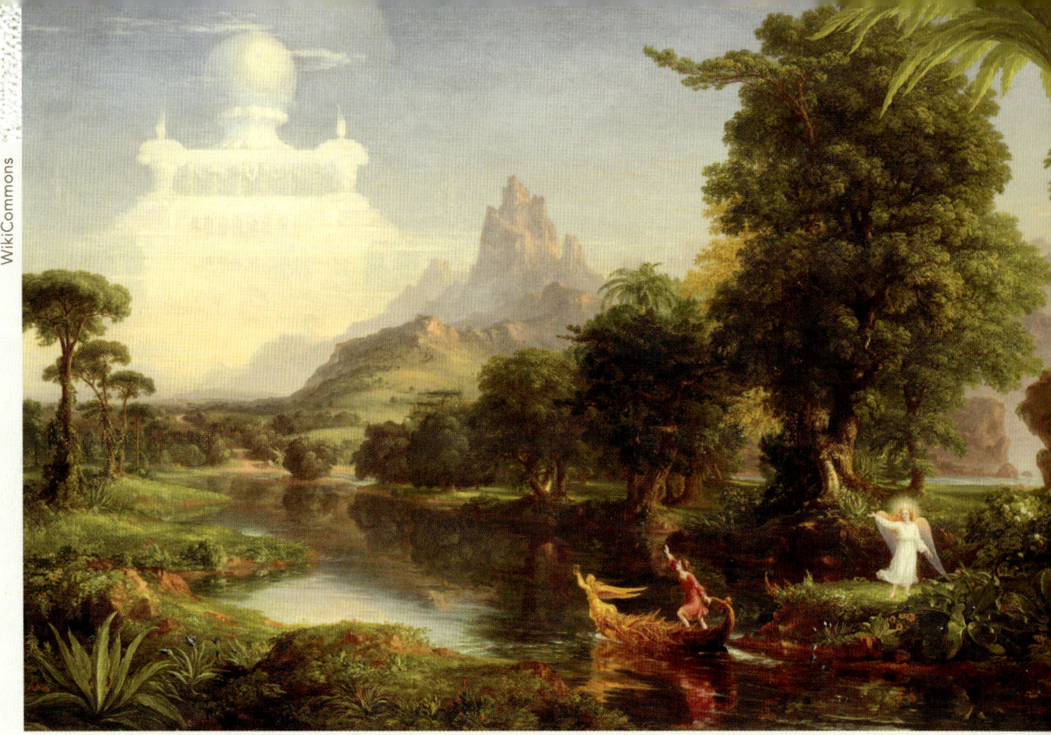
WikiCommons

The Voyage of Life: Youth by Thomas Cole, National Gallery of Art, Washington, D.C.

nation, seeing it as the "new Eden." They were concerned about the high cost of progress and the advance of civilization, and the corrupting influence this had on the country, and were also concerned that the wilderness was slowly being destroyed to make way for humans. For them, nature was a refuge from a materialistic culture that was even then in the ascendency. Cole's *The Course of Empire* (1836) is an extended meditation on how human civilizations rise and decline, but nature will eventually reassert herself. It offers a caution against the prevalent nineteenth-century belief in ever-expanding human progress—and also against materialism, commercialism, and the destruction of nature, calling viewers to a remembrance of our proper place of humility in the order of things.

Nature was not only a refuge for the Hudson River painters but also a source of illumination, revelation, consolation, and wisdom. Theirs was a spirituality founded upon the belief that God's character was revealed in the glories of nature, and so they painted it in all its sublimity. Thomas Cole and his comrades believed that the souls of human beings could be transformed by meditating on the beauties of nature, that the beautiful and the good were closely related to each other. And so the artist is performing a spiritual act in creating art, art that can be a source of moral and spiritual transformation, and a "sweet foretaste of heaven."[5]

These artists composed rather than merely recorded the glories of nature. Instead of trying to simply reproduce what they saw as it existed in nature itself, they hiked through forests and to the tops of mountains, making sketches of the beauties they saw—a majestic mountain, a tree blasted by the weather, a tumbling waterfall—and then returned to the studio to recombine the various elements into a painting that would suggest the Edenic world that existed before the intrusion of humankind.

Cole and the other Hudson River painters saw natural phenomena as not only beautiful in themselves but also as symbolic of deeper spiritual truths, and they were especially interested in the effects of light and how it illuminated the scene they were creating. They saw the contemplation of beauty in nature as a way of preparing the heart and mind for the contemplation of spiritual realities, and their work as a way of manifesting the glory of God. They believed that one was called to art as one might be called to the ministry; the purpose

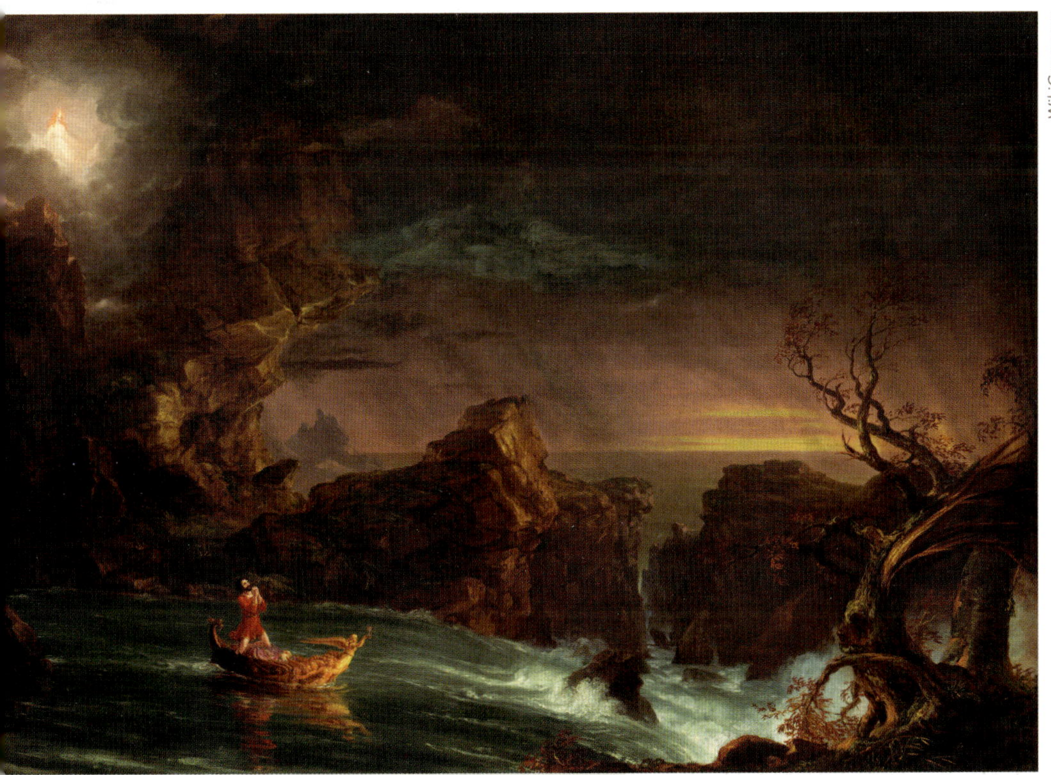

WikiCommons

The Voyage of Life: Manhood by Thomas Cole, National Gallery of Art, Washington, D.C.

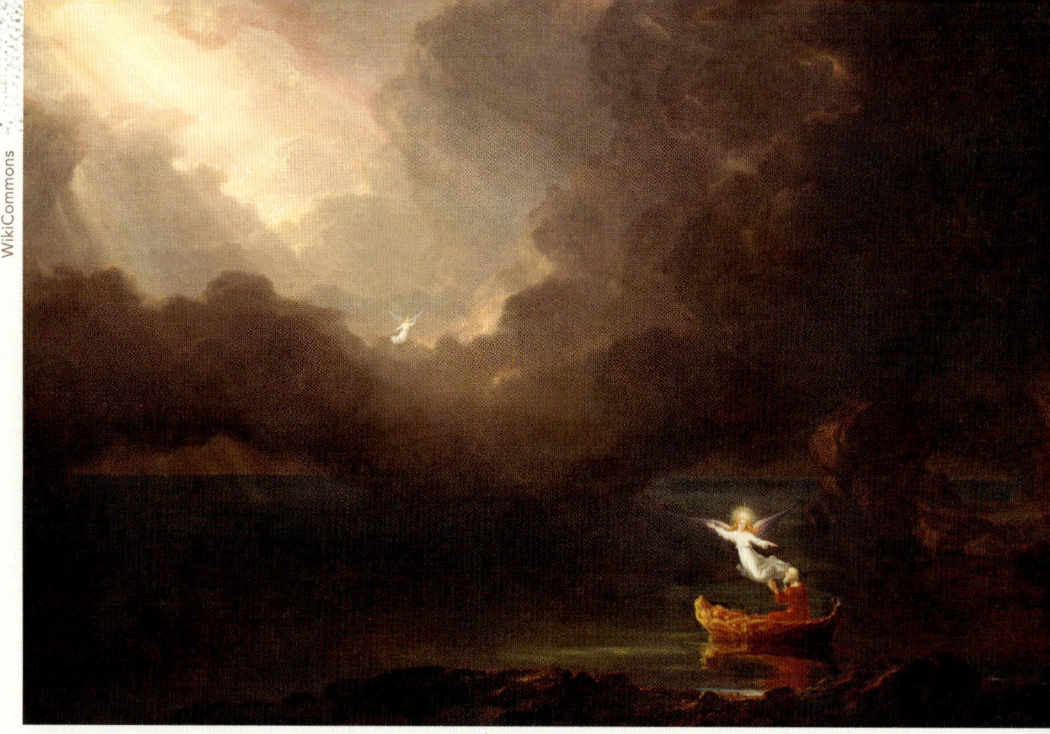
WikiCommons

The Voyage of Life: Old Age by Thomas Cole, National Gallery of Art, Washington, D.C.

of that vocation was to help people to see. The landscape was a grand natural cathedral, or a book that could be "read" to learn of the One who "wrote" it. "There are spots on this earth," wrote Cole, "where the sublime and the beautiful are united—where the heart of man feels its own nothingness or rises with the most ecstatic emotions—when the lips are sealed in reverence, but the soul feels unutterably."[6]

Cole feared that as nature was neglected and forgotten by his contemporaries, so would God be forgotten and neglected, for nature testified to His reality. Cole's paintings, so often painted from a God's-eye view of the world, showed humans to be small and insignificant in the larger scheme of things and offered the spectacle of the wonders of the world God had made. Until his premature death at the age of forty-eight, he stayed true to his mission of depicting glimpses of God's glory as seen in His creation, and reminders of the tragedy of human ignorance of that vision.

34

The Light of the World

William Holman Hunt

(painting, 1854)

Many readers will find *The Light of the World* vaguely familiar, as a version of it created by Warner Sallman has adorned countless Sunday school rooms. But this familiarity should not cause us to overlook the ingenuity and mysterious force of the original painting by English Pre-Raphaelite painter William Holman Hunt. The famous critic John Ruskin, a contemporary of Hunt, called it "one of the noblest works of sacred art,"[1] and its illustration of Revelation 3:20 ("Here I am! I stand at the door and knock") continues to inspire those who see it, right down to our own time.

For his depiction of this famous passage, Hunt did not draw on the kind of complex theological symbolism typical of many religious paintings but used straightforward images drawn from nature and ordinary life. Some critics at the time thought this improper and undignified, but it is likely the reason the painting was so warmly embraced by the general public. A larger version of the picture, which Hunt created late in his life, was sold to entrepreneur philanthropist Charles Booth, who took it on tour around the world, where it was seen live by an estimated seven million people. After that it was placed in St. Paul's Cathedral in London so that it could be readily accessible to the public. The immense popularity of this print and the many alternative versions created by other artists testify to its almost iconic status.

The painting depicts Christ, the Light of

the World, knocking upon a wooden door. The setting is a dark night, and the mood is just a little forbidding. Hunt painted most of this work in his studio during the late-night hours so that he could mimic the effect of an environment lit by a lamp. That lamp, which Christ carries in His hand, provides the main source of light for the scene. Christ wears clothing that combines kingly and priestly dress, representing His two roles, and He has two crowns upon His head, which is illuminated by a halo, the only other source of light in the picture. One of these two crowns is the crown of thorns, reminding us of His sacrifice.

Christ is portrayed as a strong, sturdy figure, which was one of Hunt's intentions. "In England," he wrote, "spiritual figures are painted as if in a vapor. I had a further reason for making the figure more solid than I should have otherwise done," as "it is Christ alive for ever more."[2] In other words, this is not a depiction of the earthly man, Jesus, but the risen Christ. There are clumps of weeds at his feet, partly obstructing the door, which represent the temptations and distractions of life that keep us locked away inside ourselves and can separate us from God. The door itself is shut tight, illustrating that our hearts and minds are closed to Him. And the door has no latch, no doorknob, and no keyhole. This is a door that can only be opened from the *inside*. To add to the urgency of the message, Hunt shows the feet of Jesus turned sideways, as if He is preparing to leave because entry has been denied Him.

The Light of the World was a special painting to its creator, who directly attributed it to an inspiration from God: "I painted the picture with what I thought, unworthy though I was, to be by divine command, and not simply as a good subject."[3] Because it has been so widely disseminated, some version of this iconic image is what often settles into our minds when we encounter the Scripture verse about the One who stands at the door and knocks.

William Holman Hunt was born in 1827 in London, and grew up in a middle-class home where his talents were not encouraged. To be an artist was not seen by his parents as a viable career, though he knew from very early on that this was what he wanted to be. He worked hard at developing his abilities. A crucial influence in his artistic development came from John Ruskin's seminal book *Modern Painters*, which an artist friend loaned him. Since Hunt was only able to borrow it for twenty-four hours, he went without sleep in order to read through the night to finish it. In its pages, he found the encouragement he needed to paint in a way that was "true to nature," which ever after became his goal. Success, however, did not come quickly. By the time he finally sold his first major painting, he was so poor that most of his possessions were in the hands of pawnbrokers.

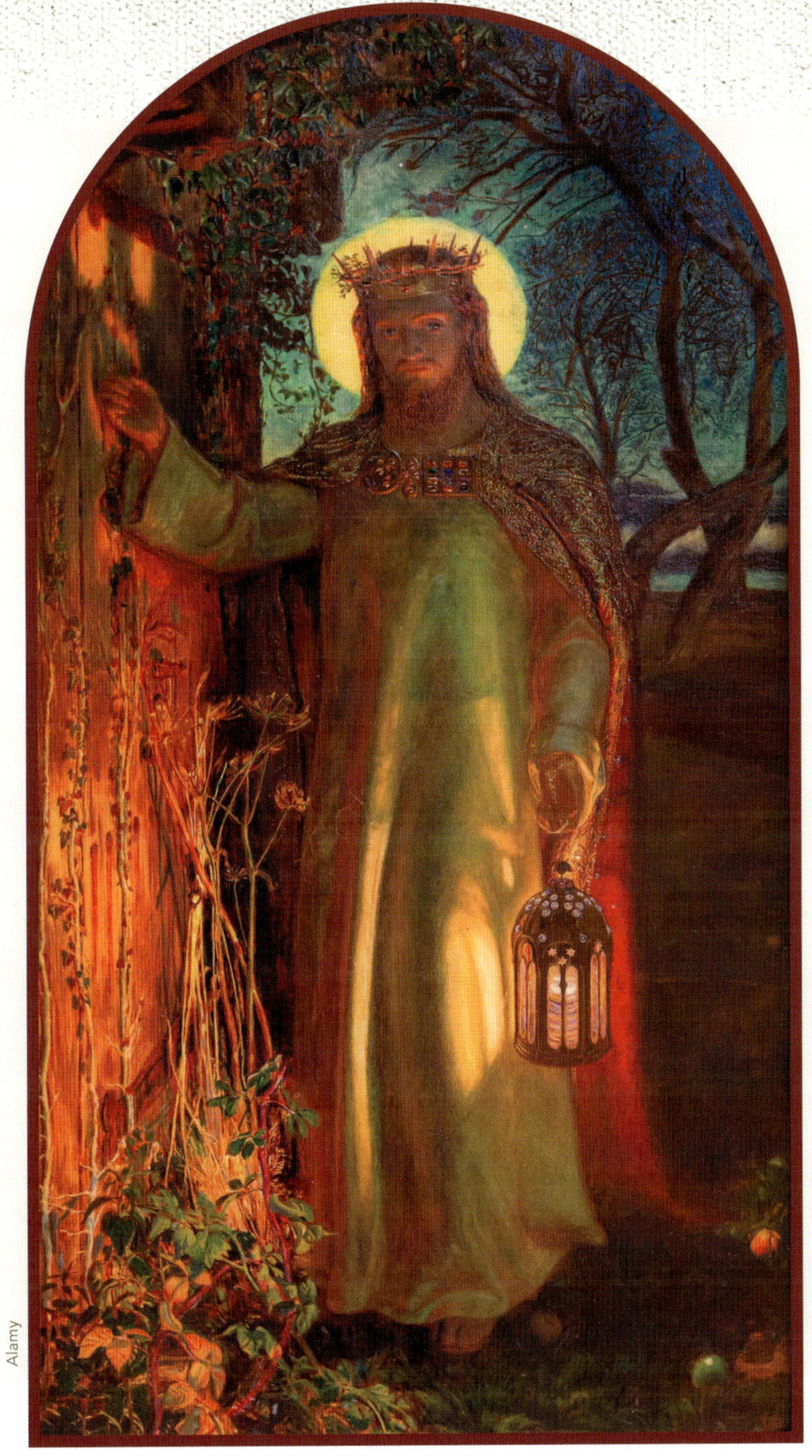

Alamy

The Light of the World by William Holman Hunt, Keble College, Oxford

A turning point in his career came when he met John Everett Millais and Dante Rossetti, two artists with whom he shared similar passions and vision. Together, in 1848, they formed what they called "The Pre-Raphaelite Brotherhood." They were a wild, flamboyant, and rebellious trio, bent upon overturning the artistic standards of their day. They dismissed the general direction that art had taken since Raphael, and disliked the stiff academic style of painters such as Joshua Reynolds and Peter Paul Rubens, who were popular at the time. In fact, in a book of prints that he owned, Rossetti jotted the phrase "spit here" under each reproduction of a Rubens picture. The Pre-Raphaelites did not immediately catch on as an artistic movement and received a great deal of criticism, which meant that few paintings were sold until they were discovered and promoted by John Ruskin, the most important art critic of the day. Because they had little money, they used themselves, their wives, and their girlfriends as models. They are well known for their paintings of these mysterious, attractive women, whom they referred to as "stunners." Their subject matter also showed their fascination with the medieval world, stories from Shakespeare and Arthurian legends, and biblical subjects.

Their style, which Hunt helped to develop, was distinguished by vibrant colors that strike the eye with intensity, by meticulous attention to detail rendered with great painterly skill, and by a polished finish. They sought to be realistic in their work, but it was a magical sort of realism, deeply Romantic and often hearkening back to earlier times.

The rowdy escapades of the Pre-Raphaelites, especially Rossetti, drew almost as much notice as their art, as they fueled their creative endeavors with alcohol and sexual promiscuity. But this kind of lifestyle did not have a long-term appeal to Hunt, who had begun painting religious subjects even before he met the other artists, and whose own struggles with his conscience may have been reflected in paintings such as *The Awakening Conscience* (1853), where he explained that his intention "was to show how the still small voice speaks to a human soul in the turmoil of life."[4]

While painting *The Light of the World*, Hunt underwent a life-changing deepening of his spiritual commitment. He became an enthusiastic student of the Bible, and in late 1854, he traveled to the Holy Land so that he could experience the world in which the scriptural stories had taken place. This was to be the first of three extended trips, and he ended up spending six and a half years of his life in the land where Jesus once walked. Hunt reveled in the experience but was disgusted by the corruption he saw among many of the missionaries as well as the hypocrisy of some who claimed the Christian faith.

Hunt's religious paintings give ample evidence of his creativity and originality. He found unexpected ways to present religious ideas and rarely settled for traditional sacred subject matter. He sought to teach moral lessons through his painted parables, such as *The Hireling Shepherd* (1851–1852), a picture based on John 10:10–14 that features a shepherd being distracted by the wiles of a beautiful maiden while his sheep have wandered into the cornfield and become bloated—a commentary on how he saw church leaders failing their flocks. Similarly, *Our English Coasts* (1852) portrays a flock of sheep that have gone astray and wandered into a precarious spot on the rim of a seaside cliff.

The Scapegoat (1854–1855), one of his most famous paintings, is a canvas based upon Leviticus 16:22, which speaks of the goat upon whom the sins of the people are cast before he is driven from the community. Hunt went to great lengths to create an authentic rendition of this Old Testament "parable" of Christ's sacrifice. He purchased a goat and trekked into the Israeli desert to paint so that he could accurately capture the landscape of the southern shores of the Dead Sea. He subjected himself to blistering heat, violent winds, sickness, and fever, as well as risking the possibility of attack by violent desert dwellers, but emerged with a strangely compelling picture that draws a strong emotional response from viewers. A similar response is created by *The Shadow of Death* (1870–1873), in which Jesus lifts His hands in joyful prayer while the shadow that is cast by them prefigures His death upon the cross.

William Holman Hunt had a gift for capturing moments of spiritual illumination on canvas. The way he recorded them in paint was unusual and unexpected but emotionally stirring. Never one interested in painting ethereal religious visions, his strong, earthy depictions of spiritual realities memorably brought alive the intervention of the divine realm into the earthly one. In one way or another throughout his career, he drew attention to the ways that the Light of the World illuminates the darkness of our human experience.

35

The Heart of the Andes

Frederic Edwin Church

(painting, 1859)

There was a time when a major new painting could attract the kind of interest and publicity that a new film does today, drawing large and enthusiastic crowds to pay to see a single work of art. One such painting was Frederic Church's *The Heart of the Andes*, which he had created following an extensive trip to South America, where he trekked through jungles and up mountain peaks in search of exotic beauty. Traveling where few North Americans had ever gone, Church experienced a journey through Colombia and Ecuador that was filled with much hardship and several brushes with danger, but it produced one of his most awe-inspiring canvases.

The Heart of the Andes is not a literal representation of any one particular viewpoint that one might see hiking the heights of these legendary mountains but rather an idealized view composed from various sketches he made during his journey—the natural world rearranged for maximum dramatic effect. It is a huge painting, without any one central focus, which must be taken in slowly and leisurely, letting the eye wander over the gorgeous expanse that includes a snowcapped mountain range in the far distance, verdant mountains in the middle ground, and a waterfall with lush tropical vegetation in the foreground. Light rakes across the painting, illuminating the plunging waterfall and its surrounding trees and throwing a spotlight upon a solitary cross in the middle left of the canvas.

The cross, for Church, is perhaps the *true* heart of the Andes, a reminder of the God who created these mountains. In his painting, Church sought not only to capture the beauty he had seen but also to impart the same sort of spiritual elevation he had felt when his eyes originally scanned the unfolding splendor. The resulting picture is a grand and sublime vista, infused with Church's vision of the mystery and majesty of creation.

Church was not only a great painter but also an entrepreneur and showman who figured out how to exhibit this painting to greatest effect by installing it in a gallery along a busy street in New York City. The canvas was over five feet high and almost ten feet wide, and it was the sole point of focus for a three-week-long exhibition for which he charged a twenty-five-cent admission. Church wanted the viewing of his painting to be an immersive experience, so he surrounded the giant canvas with potted palm trees and put up curtains around the perimeter to create the illusion that the viewer was looking through a window,

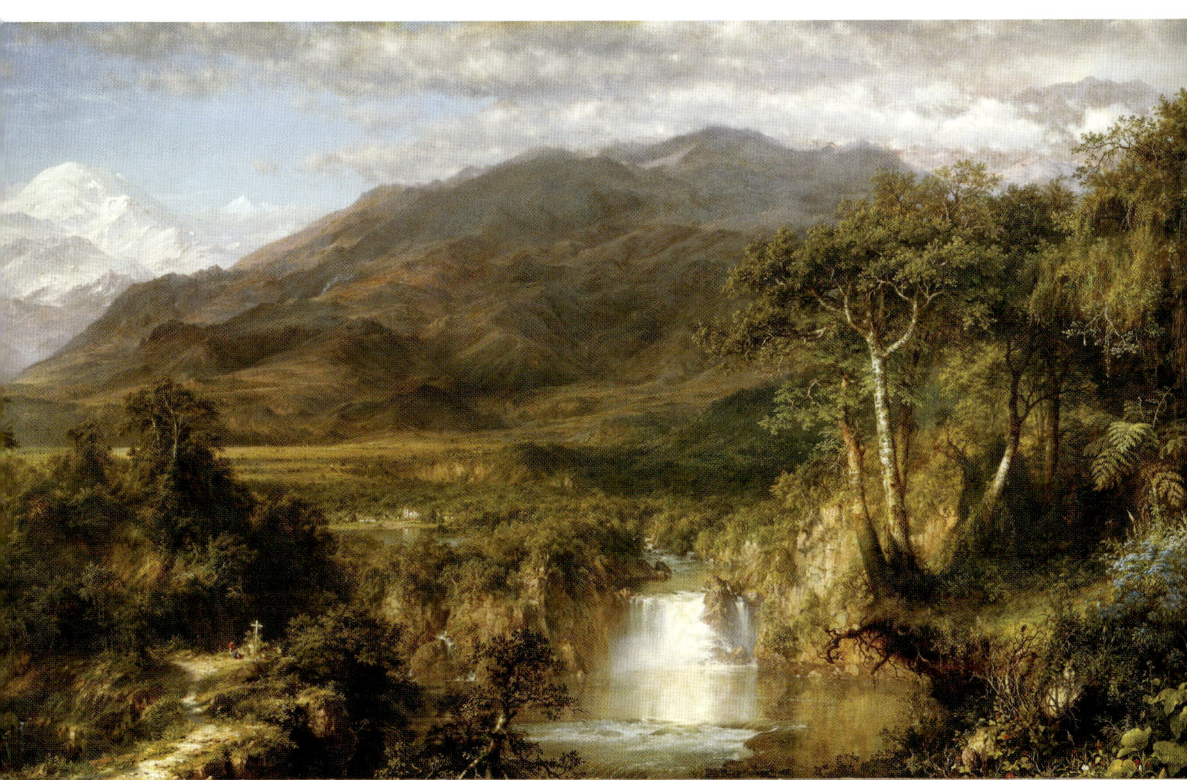

The Heart of the Andes by Frederic Church, Metropolitan Museum of Art, New York City

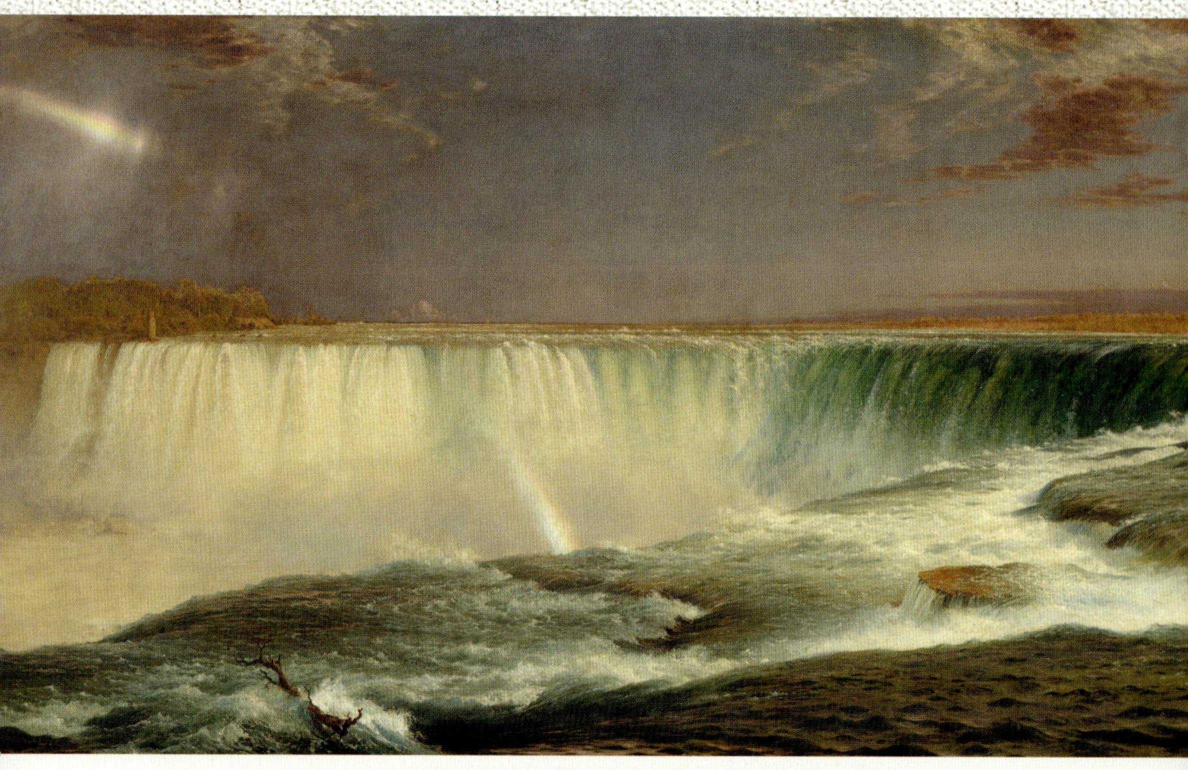

Niagara by Frederick Church (1857), National Gallery of Art, Washington, D.C.

gazing into the far distance. The room was darkened, allowing the painting to be specially lit for maximum effect, and benches were provided so that its viewers might sit and study it, peruse its intricate details, and meditate on its meanings. He even provided opera glasses for closer inspection of his enormous canvas. During its time of exhibition more than twelve thousand people lined up to see it. On the final day of the exhibition the crowds were so large that they blocked the street and the police had to be called in to manage the traffic.

After its successful showing in New York, *The Heart of the Andes* was exhibited in other major US cities and in London, where it was also much admired. Eventually the painting was sold for ten thousand dollars, at that time the highest price ever paid for a work by a living American artist. It has now taken its place as a highlight in the American collection at the Metropolitan Museum of Art.

Frederic Edwin Church was born in 1826. When his artistic talents were recognized, his supportive parents sent him to live and study with painter Thomas Cole. Church was to be Thomas Cole's only student and became, at the peak of his career, the most famous of the Hudson

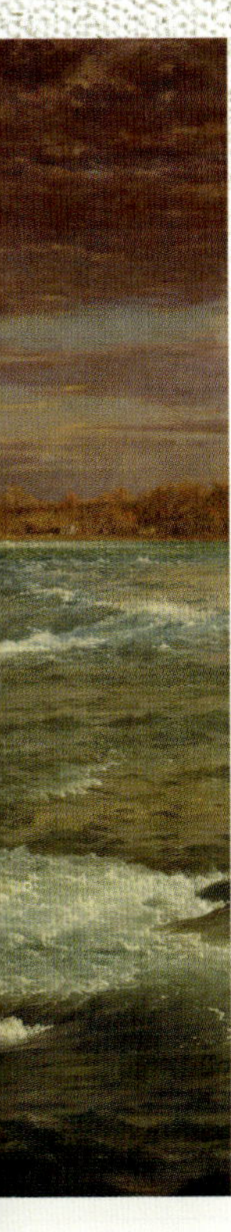
WikiCommons

River School of landscape painters. Where Cole was interested in the allegories he found in nature, Church was more interested in apprehending the beauty of the natural world and letting it speak for itself. He focused solely on landscapes, and perfected a style that combined closely observed realism with a Romantic flourish. Like Cole, Church believed that nature would speak of the Creator to those with ears to hear. His pastor, Horace Bushnell, once wrote, "The whole world is a 'hieroglyph' whose solution is the being of God."[1] It was this mysterious presence of God that Church sought to unveil in his majestic landscapes, and he brought a sense of mystery and wonder to every landscape he painted.

Church's paintings are crowded with intricate detail and rendered with painstaking care; every brushstroke counts. Sometimes his landscapes captured a moment of restful serenity, but more often they reflected the awesome power of nature, especially in paintings like *Cotopaxi* (1862), which shows an erupting volcanic mountain as the sun burns through the haze of its smoke; *The Icebergs* (1861) with its towering mountains of ice, mist, and a threatening sky; or *Niagara* (1857), which portrays the ferocious dizzying power of the famous falls. While Niagara Falls had long been a favorite subject for painters, Church chose to paint it from a unique perspective. In his painting there is no foreground. The viewer is not viewing the falls from a safe distance, but is visually thrust into the very place where the water plunges over the rocks. Given the massive size of the painting, the viewer cannot but feel something akin to vertigo—as though they are about to be swept over the rim and pulled directly into the drama of the torrential fall of the water.

One of the reasons that Church was so successful in his depiction of nature was his status as an amateur naturalist himself. He was intrigued by the inner workings of the natural world and especially fascinated by the sciences of botany and geology. He was an avid reader of the work of German scientist Alexander von Humboldt, and retraced some of von Humboldt's travels in his own journeys. During his lifetime, Church traveled all over the world, seeking fresh natural glories to affix to canvas, including trips to South America, the Arctic, the tropics, mountainous locations in Europe, and the Middle East. Then he rendered what he saw with precision and a feeling for the mystery inherent in the beauty. While he always painted nature in all its fine detail, one cannot help but feel that the physical objects are not in themselves the true focus of the paintings. The mountains, valleys, skies, clouds, trees, and foliage are themselves the canvas on which he paints a deeper reality, and the clue to that deeper reality is his obsession with painting the effects of light.

Church was fascinated with light, and painted the many varieties of its drama—the array of vivid color seen at the rising or setting of the sun, blowsy clouds scudding across the sky or billowing in the distance, rays of light slanting down through a parting of dark clouds, hazy light on a far horizon, mirror-like reflections off still water, fractured light sparkling and dancing upon moving water, rainbows arching across the heavens, the strangeness of the aurora borealis, shimmering light on the leaves of trees, or spotlighting a meadow amid the threat of a coming storm. For Church, light was not just a physical reality but the spiritual aura that surrounded the created world. Beyond nature there was something ineffable that he sought to capture with his brushstrokes. Because Church was a committed Christian of the Dutch Reformed variety, there was always a spiritual dimension to his paintings. His was an essentially sacramental vision, where the presence of God cast a glow over the natural world.

Although Church very rarely placed any human beings in his paintings, and if he did they were the merest specks on the landscape, he sometimes included a cross in the middle of the expansive vistas he composed, as he did in *To the Memory of Thomas Cole* (1848), *Cross in the Wilderness* (1857), and *The Heart of the Andes*. At other times blasted trees or the mast of a ship echo the form of this central Christian symbol. Including a cross was about as far as he would go in making his paintings explicitly religious, though in a very real sense every brushstroke he made was in service to his vision of God's presence in nature.

At the height of his fame, Church was the most famous artist in the United States. But before the end of his career, people's tastes began to change, and his work, and that of the other Hudson River painters, largely fell out of favor. Such are the vicissitudes of the art world. Even so, he continued to paint until arthritis crippled his hands and made it nearly impossible for him to handle a brush. His last great work of art was not a painting, but a building—Olana, the home he had constructed according to his own design on the top of a hill overlooking the Hudson River. Its architecture was inspired by his travels, and especially by the Persian style he so admired. Constructed to look like a combination of a castle and an ancient fortress, it was accented with pointed arches, multicolored brickwork designs, and various other embellishments. From its porch he could look out upon the winding Hudson River that he had painted so many times and be reminded of the sublime beauty that came from the hand of his God.

36

Fairy Tales

George MacDonald

(stories, c. 1871)

Perhaps no other author regularly managed to evoke as much childlike wonder in their writing as George MacDonald did. Throughout his more than fifty published volumes he continually emphasized the reality of the spiritual world and the importance of our relationship with it—and ultimately with God. Few have written stories with the kind of playful seriousness we find in his best work, especially in his fairy tales.

These stories include *The Princess and the Goblin* (1872), *The Princess and Curdie* (1883), and *At the Back of the North Wind* (1871), as well as various shorter tales such as "The Golden Key," "The Light Princess," and "The Wise Woman." As is appropriate for children's stories, they are simply told, but they are also so vividly imagined and highly inventive that they appeal to the child in all of us. Each of his fairy tales features elements that are strange and haunting, as well as moments where the numinous reality of another realm breaks through. In *The Princess and the Goblin*, for example, the princess finds her way to a tower, where a wise old woman sits spinning as she oversees a mysterious burning fire of red and white roses. Later in the story, the princess is only able to find her way through a dark and forbidding mine by keeping one hand on the thread that the old woman has spun. In the story the thread is real but it is also metaphorical and spiritual, for the princess cannot see the thread, only feel it—and she dare not let go or she will be lost in the

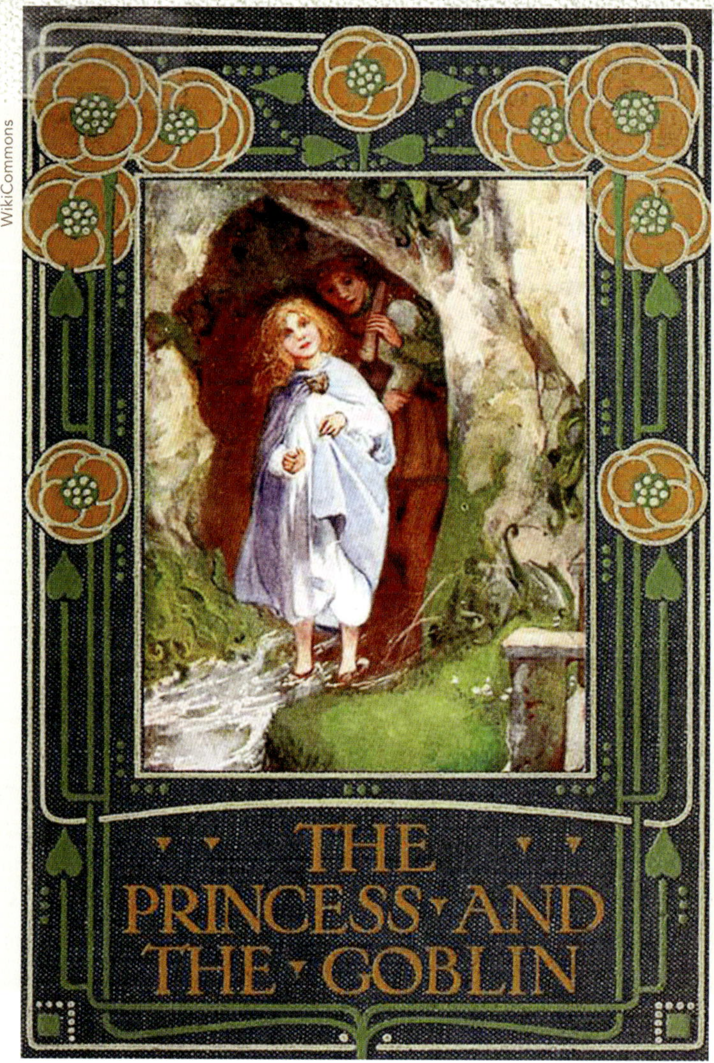

Cover for *The Princess and the Goblin* (c. 1911)

dark. It is perhaps a perfect illustration of the nature of faith.

We should, however, be careful about working too hard at any exact interpretation of these stories. MacDonald himself resisted giving any explanations, and when asked what one of them meant, he tersely replied, "So long as I think my dog can bark, I will not sit up and bark for him."[1] He left the stories to speak for themselves. And they do not speak to us as allegories or intellectual puzzles aimed at the mind but rather as mythic tales aimed at the heart. They are meant to show us truths that do not easily reduce to rational explanations and provoke a more intuitive response from the reader. There are layers of meanings at work here, all of them valid: physical, spiritual, mythical, and psychological. Each of these layers interpenetrate and illuminate each other, which is why these stories are not so much meant to illustrate theological truths as to help us find our way into a different way of experiencing these truths.

MacDonald projected his own inner life into his stories to make them feel universal—a reflection of our own personal stories. His words arouse our dormant longings for truth and goodness as we journey with his young protagonists on their paths through danger and discovery and miracle. Alongside these young heroes and heroines, we meet supernatural beings and find familiarity and friendship with these residents of a realm beyond our own. MacDonald's tales are not unlike dreams, mixing all their disparate elements together into something that creates an impression and a feeling rather than simply communicating an idea.

There are three common elements to most of these fairy tales: first, the existence of a wise, loving guide who gently helps the young protagonist along the journey, as the wise old woman does in *The Princess and the Goblin*. This is MacDonald's reminder that we do not walk the spiritual path alone, but God reveals Himself in various and sundry ways along our journey.

Second, MacDonald shows how his heroes and heroines come to see death in a different way—not as a fearsome enemy but as a friend who ushers us through the doorway into eternity. *At the Back of the North Wind* revolves around the relationship of a young boy, Diamond, with death itself, personified as the North Wind. One need not fear death, the story reminds us, but one can embrace it when its proper time comes.

Third, MacDonald illustrates that the purpose of our lives is to undergo a transformation—to be changed from what we are into what God intends us to be. God wants to impart His "divine life" into our souls, a process that is critical for discovering who we *really* are. And the new self each of us becomes in the process is a more childlike self, for it is only the child whose trusting heart is open enough to see things as they really are. The path to transformation, MacDonald shows us, will not always be an easy one. Images such as the aforementioned "fire of roses" remind us that the cleansing fire of purgation is one of the painful steps along the path. Our ongoing purification prepares us for the presence of the holy in our lives.

George MacDonald was born in Scotland in 1824 and grew up around the beauties of the Scottish Highlands and the preachments of a stern Calvinism. Throughout his life he would look to nature for spiritual sustenance and do battle with the image of God imparted to him by his childhood religion. After earning a master's degree in the sciences, he attended seminary to prepare for ministry and then was called to a church in Arundel. But his career in the pulpit was brief due to what the elders of the congregation considered to be his unorthodox views.

MacDonald had little patience for theological abstractions and viewed the truth as relational rather than judicial, pointing to the central importance of a personal experience of God's love. "To know a primrose," he wrote, "is a higher thing than to know all the botany of it—just as to know Christ is an infinitely higher thing than to know all theology, all that is said about His person, or babbled about His work."[2] His congregation could not accept the conclusions he had reached regarding the idea of penal substitutionary atonement, which he did not think squared with God's character. MacDonald believed that Christ came to save us from sin, not from the punishment for sin, and therefore saw the work of Jesus as not a matter of appeasing the wrath of God but of dealing with the disease of sin itself. Other major points of contention were his rejection of the traditional doctrine of hell and his unapologetic embrace of universalism, the conviction that the love of God would, in the end, mean forgiveness for everyone.

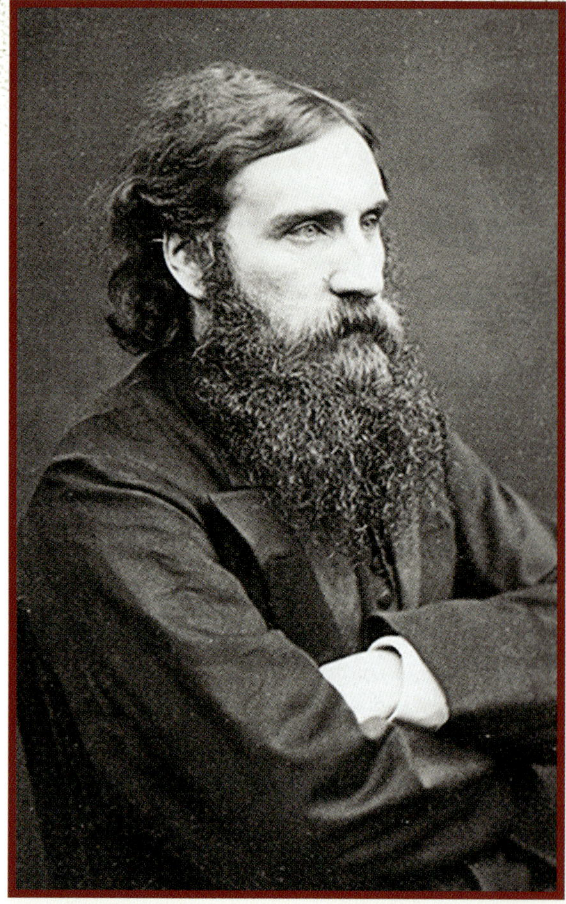
George MacDonald, photo by William Jeffrey (c.1860s)

When MacDonald's two-year pastorate ended in conflict and it became clear that it would not be easy to find another church to pastor, he fell back on what had, up to that time, been only a pastime—writing. If he could not preach in a pulpit, he would preach through his books.

His first major book, an adult fantasy novel called *Phantastes*, was published to little notice in 1858, and he also wrote some children's stories, which were better received. But none of this work brought in very much money, and his financial condition became desperate. One of his friends, a publisher, suggested that the only way to make money as a writer was to write realistic novels, so MacDonald decided this could be an effective way of communicating the ideas about the character of God that were so important to him. In 1863, he published his first such novel, *David Elginbrod*, which was an immediate success. Throughout the rest of his life he churned out a steady flow of these novels that dealt with the spiritual awakenings of his various characters. They became popular enough to provide him a good income, and allowed him to indulge himself with an occasional fantasy story (which sold poorly in comparison) for the sheer joy of it. He continued to write and publish at a steady pace until health issues made it impossible. He had a stroke in 1900 that robbed him of speech, and he died five years later after a slow decline in health.

MacDonald's novels were a laboratory in which his theological ideas could be explored and demonstrated to "work" in real life. He never saw them primarily as entertainment but as a way of communicating his vision of the immensity of God's love. Rarely has a novelist so unapologetically envisioned himself as a teacher, which points toward what is both the strength and weakness of the novels themselves—MacDonald tended to preach a little too much. The novels are full of digressions and digressions from digressions, bulking up their page count but detracting from the unfolding of the story. However, sometimes these digressions are actually the most interesting and enlightening parts of the book, and a chance for MacDonald to offer practical pastoral wisdom and spiritual insight to his congregation of readers.

One of MacDonald's biggest fans was C. S. Lewis, who said that he didn't think he had ever written a book in which he did not quote from MacDonald. In fact, Lewis gathered up some of his favorite MacDonald quotes and published them as *George MacDonald: An Anthology*. But it was not only the insights he gleaned from the great Scottish writer that attracted Lewis; it was also the deep spirituality of the man himself that radiated from the writing. "I dare not say he is never in error," Lewis wrote in the introduction to the *Anthology*, "but to speak plainly I know hardly any other writer who seems to be closer, or more continually close, to the Spirit of Christ himself."[3]

Throughout his literary output, George MacDonald excelled at two things. First, he offered gem-like nuggets of practical wisdom about how to live in the light of God's love and grace. Each of his books has moments where a little unexpected truth flickers into focus as we read, and by its light we see our lives a little differently. Second, he regularly manages to evoke a sense of wonder in the reader, reminding us that there is more to the world than meets the eye. MacDonald shows us a world where the boundary between the seen and the unseen is very thin indeed. Across that boundary, God reaches with His relentless and untamable love, and for a moment, we are all children once again, in awe of our heavenly Father.

37

The Brothers Karamazov

Fyodor Dostoyevsky

(novel, 1879)

Great novelists often draw extensively from their own lives. Perhaps that was never more the case than in Fyodor Dostoyevsky's *The Brothers Karamazov*, widely considered one of the very best novels ever written. The patricide at the center of the novel draws upon the events surrounding the real-life murder of Dostoyevsky's cruel and tyrannical father by the family's servants, a crime that went unpunished. But this is not the only parallel. The very different philosophies of life of the three Karamazov sons directly echo the stages of Dostoyevsky's own personal journey through sensuality and skepticism toward an embrace of faith.

The Brothers Karamazov is a polyphonic novel, written so that the contrasting voices of the three Karamazov siblings are allowed to speak for themselves. These voices play off each other as their perspectives are tested against each other in a search for truths that often feel just out of reach. The effectiveness of such dialogues in the novel comes from their authenticity. It never feels as though the novel is a "set up" for pushing through Dostoyevsky's own philosophy, and the arguments do not feel doctored so as to arrive at any tidy resolutions. Each major character is invested with the integrity of an individual voice, and their arguments are put forward with conviction. Dostoyevsky isn't so much making a point as honestly portraying the reality of a world where questions about God and humanity are many and concrete answers seem few.

Each of the three brothers is a psychologically complex creation, and they represent three radically different approaches to life. Dimitri is a sensualist who lives mostly for pleasure—wine, women, and adventure. Like his father, whom he is accused of killing, he is seemingly unable to say no to his physical urges, even when he wants to. Ivan is an intellectual and a skeptic, a tense and unhappy man who lives in a state of mutiny against God. The horrible suffering he sees in the world—and specifically the torture of children—leads him to a conviction that the God he is rebelling against is a God who simply isn't there. The famous "Grand Inquisitor" chapter in the novel is a story Ivan tells in an attempt to expose faith as a delusion. The youngest brother, Alyosha, is a gentle, spiritual man of great kindness and simple faith, whose closest companions are the monks of the local monastery. From his perspective, forgiveness and long-suffering love are the only hope for humanity.

In the course of this long and complex novel, we hear each of these characters espouse their beliefs about life, and we see these beliefs tried and tested in circumstances of great pain and suffering. Like his character Alyosha, Dostoyevsky had come to believe that there is a redemptive power in suffering that cleanses and purifies the soul. The only rebuttal he provides against Ivan's philosophical arguments can be found not in words but in the simple power of love in action, as exhibited in the life of Alyosha. And near the conclusion of *The Brothers Karamazov* he even affirms the reality of an eternal life beyond this vale of tears. Leaving the funeral of his deceased young friend, Alyosha is asked, "Can it be true what's taught us in religion, that we shall all rise again from the dead and shall live and see each other again, all, Ilyusha [the deceased boy] too?" Alyosha's simple answer, "Certainly," echoes one of Dostoyevsky's own utterances: "If you believe in Christ, then you believe you will live eternally."[1]

Fyodor Dostoyevsky was born in Russia in 1821 to a harsh, tyrannical father and a gentle, saintly mother. In various guises they appear throughout Dostoyevsky's novels. His father's severity was such that he was eventually murdered by his own servants, though the crime was never thoroughly investigated and no one was arrested for it.

Dostoyevsky's first book, written in 1846, was *Poor Folk*, a novel challenging the social injustices of the day. It was an immediate critical success. In time, some of the same discontent about the unfair social conditions in Russia that fueled his novel led him to join a radical group of revolutionaries. That might sound like a major step, but in truth they were not a very dangerous bunch, mostly made up of writers and journalists. They had a secret printing press with which they planned to produce antigovernment propaganda. But the police sniffed them out and they were arrested, tried and convicted of treason, and sentenced to die.

On the morning of December 22, 1849, Dostoyevsky and twenty of his compatriots were carted to the town square, had their hands bound behind them, and were made to stand in front of a firing squad as their death sentence was read aloud. The order was given, the rifles were raised, and at the very last moment a rider from the czar came galloping in, announcing that their sentence had been commuted. The czar had not intended that they die but rather wanted to frighten them enough to make a point about the gravity of their crimes. Instead of death, they were sentenced to serve four years of hard labor in a Siberian prison camp.

The conditions in the prison camp were unimaginably harsh, and the inmates dealt daily with intense cold, lice, stench, and filth. Perhaps it is an indication of the terrible conditions of the prison that when he later wrote a book about his experiences there, he titled it *The House of the Dead*. Amid such squalor, Dostoyevsky lived among people who were flesh-and-blood illustrations of the human capacity for evil; these would later serve as models for some of his alienated characters. But despite the terrible situation into which he had been thrust, Dostoyevsky refused to descend to such a state himself. Instead, since he had the opportunity to stare death directly in the eye and lived to tell of it, he believed he had been given a second chance at life.

As he wrote to his brother, "Never has there seethed in me such an abundant and healthy kind of spiritual life as now. . . . Now my life will change, I shall be born again in a new form."[2] There in the prison camp he was permitted only one book—a copy of the Gospels he had been given by a compassionate woman during the long transport to Siberia. He read and reread the little book, embracing its message as the only hope for himself and for his country, and he kept the volume within reach for the rest of his life. To the woman who had given it to him he wrote of the intensity of his newfound convictions, "Nothing is more beautiful, profound, sympathetic, reasonable, manly, and more perfect than Christ. . . . If someone proved to me that Christ is outside the truth, then I would prefer to remain with Christ rather than with the truth."[3]

After four years in prison, plus another six in exile, Dostoyevsky was finally able to return to his former life and he did so with great relish, beginning to write in earnest. Many of his stories would revolve around the question of whether it was possible for humans to live a good and meaningful life in a world where there was no God. Nietzsche's philosophy of nihilism had taken root with many Russian intellectuals, who asserted that God did not exist and that the only real morality was that which would arise from superior thinkers who were not tied to traditional moral standards but rather could pursue a completely rational ethical system. Dostoyevsky could not embrace such an optimistic view of human nature and its neglect of the human propensity for selfishness, self-delusion, and violence. Subsequent events in Russia were to show the horrific results of a social experiment that tried to create an earthly paradise without reference to God. Dostoyevsky was always plagued by his own questions and doubts, as well as his personal failings (which included compulsive gambling and alcoholism), but he could not imagine living in a world where God did not exist.

But since this world can sometimes feel like a world where God is absent or hidden, Dostoyevsky's novels honestly explore the predicaments and struggles of life in such a world. The stubborn reality of sin winds its way throughout his novels, and he demonstrates that grace must be embraced if his characters are to find inner peace. For example, his novel *Crime and Punishment* (1866) tells the story of one of the aforementioned "superior men" who commits what he considers a justified crime, the brutal murder of his landlady. But he discovers that he cannot live with what he has done. His conscience torments him until he finally confesses the crime and seeks God's forgiveness. Throughout Dostoyevsky's work we witness this kind of struggle, one that takes place in every human soul. "God and the devil," he wrote, "are fighting there and the battlefield is the heart of men."[4]

Dostoyevsky's writing style was not polished and refined but passionate, intensely dramatic, somewhat disheveled, and profoundly emotional. His specialty was in unfolding the dark and complex territory of the human heart—all its petty fears and grand dreams, its agonizing obsessions and fondest delusions, its brutal hatreds—and conversely, its most startling acts of unexpected compassion. In surveying the underside of the human conscience, he never left the reader without the hope that there is a God whose love will one day redeem all the sin and suffering of the human race.

Ultimately Fyodor Dostoyevsky's message is one of grace and forgiveness—not just as abstract theological or philosophical concepts but as lived realities. We can hear his ultimate message of hope for humankind in the words he placed in the mouth of Father Zossima, in *The Brothers Karamazov*:

> Brothers, be not afraid of men's sins. Love man even in his sin, for that already bears the semblance of divine love and is the highest love on earth. Love all God's creation, the whole of it and every grain of sand. Love every leaf, every ray of God's light! Love the animals, love the plants, love everything. If you love everything you will perceive the divine mystery in things.[5]

38

La Sagrada Família Cathedral

Antoni Gaudí

(cathedral, begun 1882)

Towering over the city of Barcelona and still unfinished after over 130 years, La Sagrada Família ("The Holy Family") Cathedral is the jaw-dropping brainchild of one of the most eccentric architects of modern times, Antoni Gaudí. Though he was one of the most influential modern architects, Gaudí was also a diligent student of earlier styles—so much so that one of his fellow architects said that if Chartres Cathedral were to be completely destroyed, Gaudí could, from memory, rebuild it exactly as it had been.

The cathedral he designed himself, however, was very different from the Gothic cathedrals he knew so well. He avoided the usual straight lines and right angles of the Gothic style and created a cathedral that feels organic, more like something that grew up out of the earth rather than being constructed upon it. The building is like an eruption in stone, melting and dissolving into a fluidity of form that is not meant to achieve some abstract ideal of beauty but to reflect the lines and shapes found in nature. "The straight line is the line of Man, the curve is the line of God," he once said.[1] Gaudí found a way to reach the dizzying heights of the Gothic without the use of flying buttresses, which he felt were artificial. Instead, he designed arches that would carry the weight and still allow the multiple spires to soar.

Whereas much of the statuary on a traditional cathedral seems to be an accessory to the building, here the abundant carvings

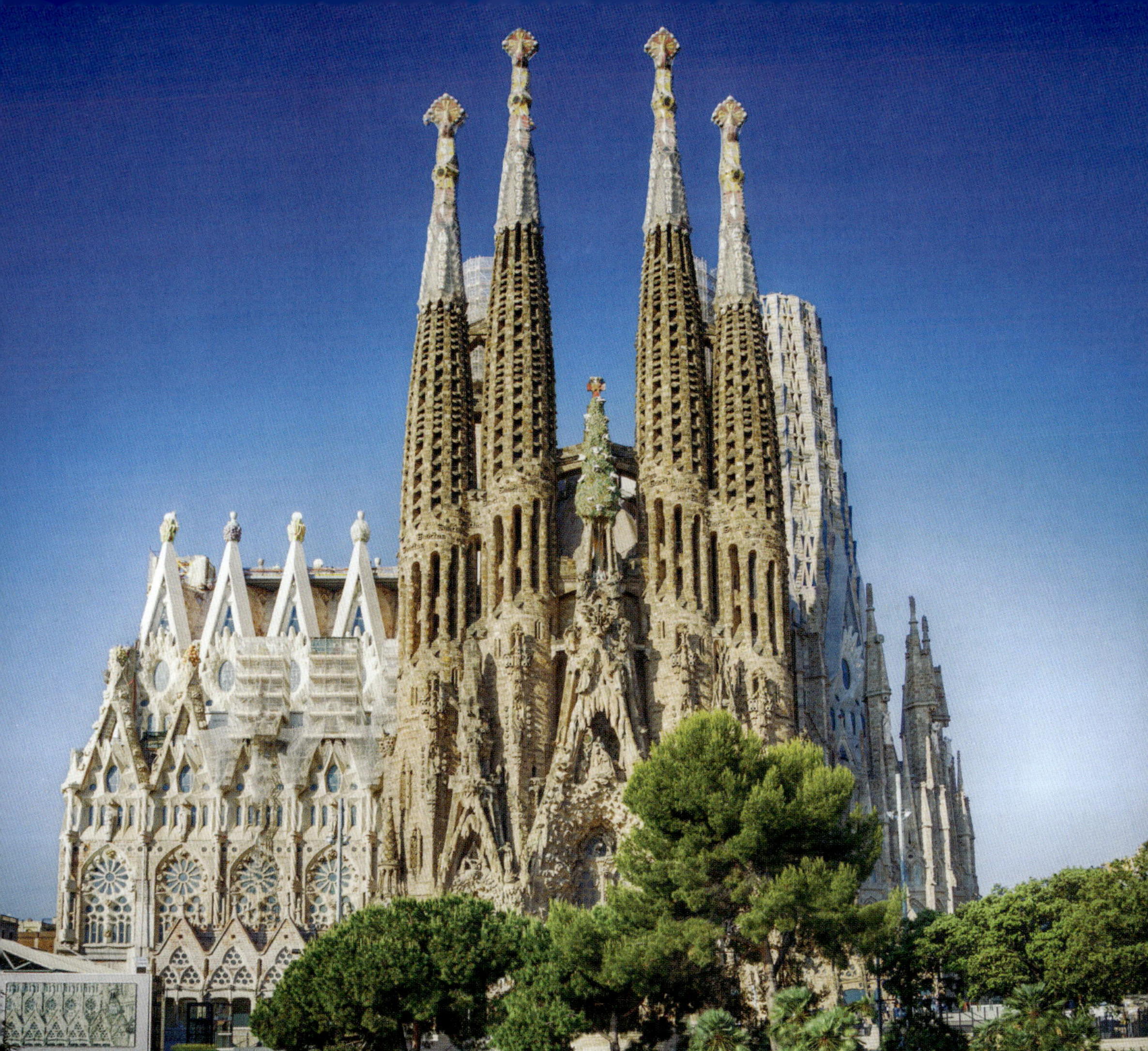

Shutterstock

Exterior of La Sagrada Família Cathedral, "Nativity Facade," Barcelona

swarm over the whole structure in such a way that they seem to *be* the building. These designs are peopled with the usual saints and biblical stories but also with arcane symbolism and with the bounty of the natural world: seashells, birds, flowers, fruit, and foliage. Gaudí was attempting to condense the entirety of the Catholic doctrine he embraced in this one single project, and in doing so the building overflows with an overwhelming profusion of images.

The interior echoes the sense that the building is an organic being, its tree-like columns rising from the ground and branching into the heavens, as though one were standing in a magical spiritual forest or on the inside of a living organism. Gaudí was concerned about every detail, striving so vigorously for realism that he made plaster casts of temporarily anesthetized turkeys and chickens to use as models for the fowl in the statuary on the façade and sides of the cathedral. He even made casts of stillborn babies to be used as models for his portrayal of the massacre of the innocents and had a donkey hoisted up the façade to see how it would look in a nativity scene he was fashioning.

Gaudí's creation is not universally beloved. Some critics find its disparate elements, its strange combination of Gothic and Art Deco design, to be a monstrosity—kitschy and tasteless. One could argue, though, that Gaudí included the ugly elements in order to make it a complete reflection of every element of life and faith—both the lovely and the unpleasant—that he could squeeze into his conception. Gaudí's work might be *gaudy*, but his cathedral is inarguably complex and spectacular—a spectacle of the strength of faith in the face of an unbelieving modern world, which during his lifetime was beginning to chip away at the authority of the church.

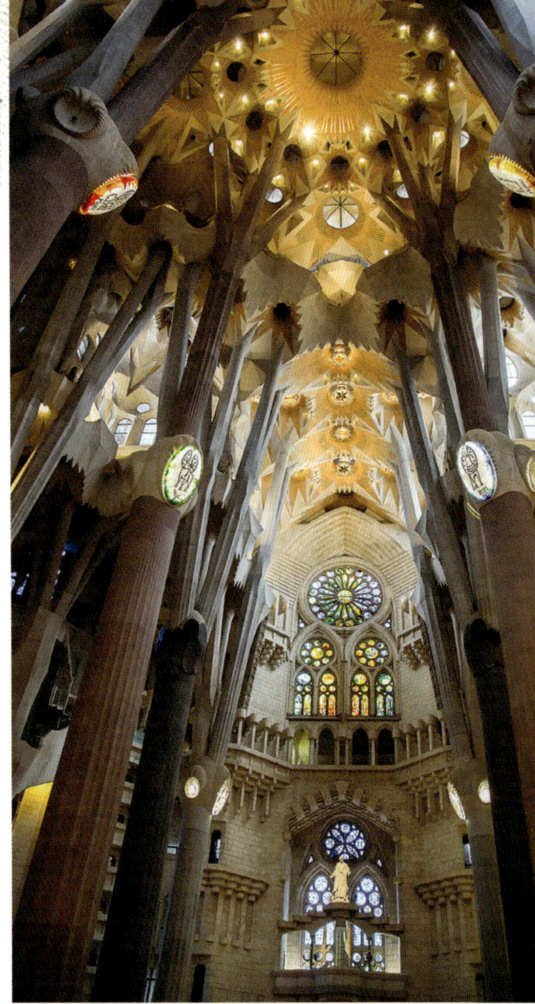
Shutterstock

Interior of La Sagrada Família Cathedral, Barcelona

The great cathedral was first conceived by Josep Maria Bocabella, a devout bookseller who argued that Barcelona needed a magnificent building to stand as an affirmation of the church in the face of the threat arising from an increasingly secularized society. The cathedral would be dedicated to the Holy Family and would represent the strength of faith, family, and tradition. The earliest photos of the building site, located on the outskirts of Barcelona, show a flock of sheep grazing in the spot where the cathedral was being built. In time, the city came to surround it.

When Bocabella found the early efforts of his first architect unsuitable, he had a dream that he would meet an architect with piercing blue eyes who would be the man to finish the job. He found those piercing blue eyes in Antoni Gaudí, a young architect just beginning to establish his reputation. When Gaudí took over the task, he completely rethought the design and incorporated his startlingly unique vision into the conception of the traditional Gothic cathedral.

Begun in 1882, the building still remains unfinished, a project that seemed to grow bigger in conception the further along it went in the process. Gaudí would not be rushed. As he said, "My client [meaning God] is not in a hurry." After his death the building was only about one-fourth complete, but over the years work has continued as funds have been raised. In recent years the cathedral is finally far enough along to be useable for services, and the end of construction might finally be in sight. Throughout the process subsequent architects have tried to stay close to the original designs that Gaudí worked out in great detail. It is an open question whether Gaudí would have adjusted the design as he went along, had he lived longer. He was famous for modifying details in response to the discovery of unusual stones that appealed to him, which he would incorporate into the plan of his buildings. As he said, "In the Sagrada Família, everything is providential."[2] Gaudí knew that the cathedral would not be finished in his lifetime, and was content with the fact that later architects would interpret his ideas in their own way, but in order that the general geometrical and structural rules he established would be followed, he left behind numerous models and drawings.

Antoni Gaudí was born in Catalonia, in southern Spain, in June 1852, and studied architecture in Barcelona, the city where he would create his greatest architectural triumphs. By the time he was in his thirties, Gaudí was the most sought-after architect in Spain, hired by wealthy patrons to design some of the most eccentric and remarkable residences ever constructed. Many of them are now Barcelona landmarks: the Park Güell (with its long, colorful, serpentine bench), the Casa Batlló, and the Casa Milá. Gaudí's designs were largely organic, created to reflect the forms of nature, and therefore are unlike almost anything else in the history of architecture.

Inside the buildings, his columns are tree-like and seem to defy gravity, his surfaces flow like rivers of lava, and his walls swell and bulge. The exteriors of the buildings are adorned with vine-like twisted grilles or inlaid with colorful broken tiles. The beauty he sought to achieve was a beauty based on God's own creation. "Those who seek out the laws of nature as support for their new work collaborate with the Creator," he said. "Originality consists in returning to the origin."[3] He saw nature as sacred and sacramental, a book of symbols that revealed the presence of God through their transcendent beauty, and he wished his cathedral to do the same.

After his offer of marriage was spurned by a woman with whom he had become infatuated, Gaudí was crushed. Shortly thereafter he began to remake his life around an intense devotion to God. He began to attend mass and make confession on a daily basis, a practice he continued for the rest of his life. He fasted for forty days during Lent as an act of repentance and preparation for the work of building the cathedral. He had once been something of a dandy, arriving at worksites with his blueprints clutched in gloved hands, but now he determined to live simply, shedding his wealth and subsisting on breakfasts of burnt toast and lunches of lettuce leaves dipped in milk. His well-worn suits became tinged with mold, his hair was usually disheveled, and his pants were held together with safety pins.

By 1914, Gaudí's life was solely dedicated to the construction of La Sagrada Família, and would remain so until the end. He saw the building of the cathedral as a spiritual vocation; he lived like a monk at the building site and worked with a small group of stone cutters to get everything exactly as he envisioned it. While he lived, he supervised every aspect of the project, even doing some of the carvings himself. As he was a perfectionist, the process was very slow, especially since the cathedral was built exclusively by donations rather than through a central rich benefactor. Most of Gaudí's own earnings were sunk back into the project.

In June 1926, just before he stepped out the door to walk home, he said to one of his workers, "Come early tomorrow, Vincente, so we can make beautiful things." As he made his way home he was struck by a tramcar while crossing the street. Due to the appearance of his worn-out clothes, he was mistaken for a tramp and taken to a nearby hospital for paupers. There, the attendants found a copy of the Gospels in his pocket and discovered that his underwear was held together by safety pins. He died clutching a crucifix and muttering a prayer to Jesus, and was buried a few days later in the crypt of La Sagrada Família.

The cathedral Antoni Gaudí left behind at his death is a reflection of the intensity of his faith, fulfilling his vision of a place where all—rich or poor—could come to experience the transcendent truths of the Christian faith. When the 1992 Olympics were held in Barcelona, where so much of his finest work can be found, a renewed interest in Gaudí and in his awe-inspiring "sermon in stone" was ignited. As the cathedral nears completion, it continues to be both a place of pilgrimage for the faithful and a fascinating spectacle for unbelievers. "Seeing," Gaudí said, "is the sense of Glory, because Glory is the vision of God."[4] This cathedral, built to the glory of God, is Gaudí's testament to the power of that vision.

39

Starry Night

Vincent van Gogh

(painting, 1889)

Starry Night is one of those paintings so iconic—we've all seen it reproduced so many times—that it is difficult to really *see*. We have to step back and take a careful second look for it to begin to divulge all its wonder. This image of a small town seen from a vantage point on a hill is not so much concerned with the town as it is with the night sky overhead—a night sky that swirls and swells and spins above us. The painting itself feels strangely alive, as though it were itself an object in motion. The moon and the stars shine and shimmer in the midst of this pulsating vision of the sky, and one cannot help but wonder if, as he contemplated this scene, Vincent van Gogh experienced some sort of mystical vision of the eternal realities behind the earthly beauty. For van Gogh, a believing man deeply frustrated with religious institutions, it was in such visions that he discovered his connection with God. As he once wrote, "When I have a terrible need of—shall I say the word—religion, then I go out and paint the stars."[1] And that is precisely what he has done in this modern masterpiece.

The viewpoint in the painting from which the landscape is seen was the view from van Gogh's bedroom window. He painted no less than twenty-one canvases of this particular landscape, though *Starry Night* is the most evocative of them all. The village seen in the painting is his invention, not something he could actually see from his window but rather added to the composition. When van Gogh sent several paintings to his brother so that he could try to sell them, he initially didn't send *Starry Night*, evidently considering it less marketable than his others. In fact, he considered it a failure. Time, of course, has proven him wrong, as it has become one of his most popular works.

Some critics have wondered if the vision that produced *Starry Night* might have been something like a hallucination, with its violently expressive character and its paint applied in thick, churning, agitated strokes. But perhaps a better way to interpret the painting is to see it as the fruit of a dynamic spiritual vision, a moment when van Gogh, and by extension the viewer, felt almost absorbed into the swirling cosmos. It is as though we stand at the very threshold of the place where the temporal and eternal join together in a great swirling dance. Though the only traditional religious element in the painting is the inclusion of a chapel (with its light extinguished!), this is an unquestionably spiritual painting.

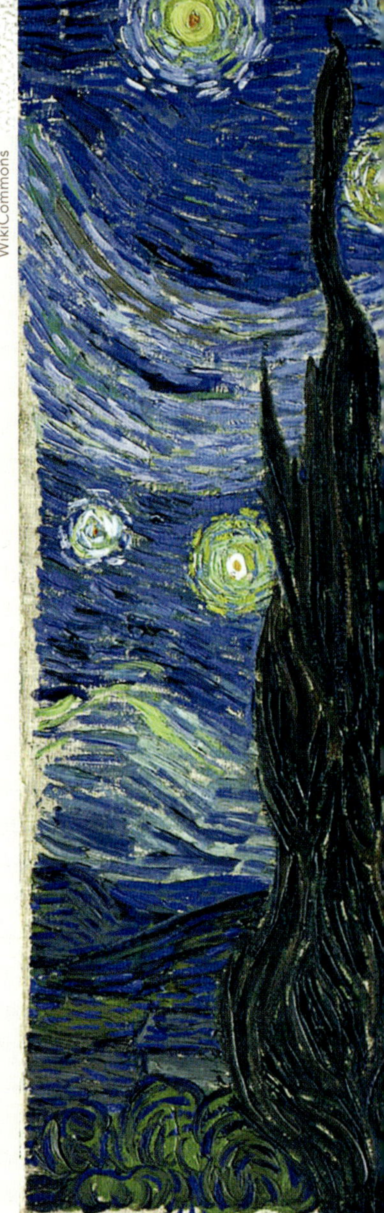
WikiCommons

Vincent van Gogh was born in 1853 in the Netherlands, the eldest son of a Protestant pastor. Both his father and grandfather served as pastors in the Dutch Reformed church. As a child he was quiet, reflective, and a great lover of nature. At age sixteen he was apprenticed to the Hague branch of the art dealers Goupil and Co., where one of his uncles was a partner. This experience helped him to grow in his love and appreciation for fine art, though he did little more than the occasional sketch himself.

From 1873 to 1876, he worked in London

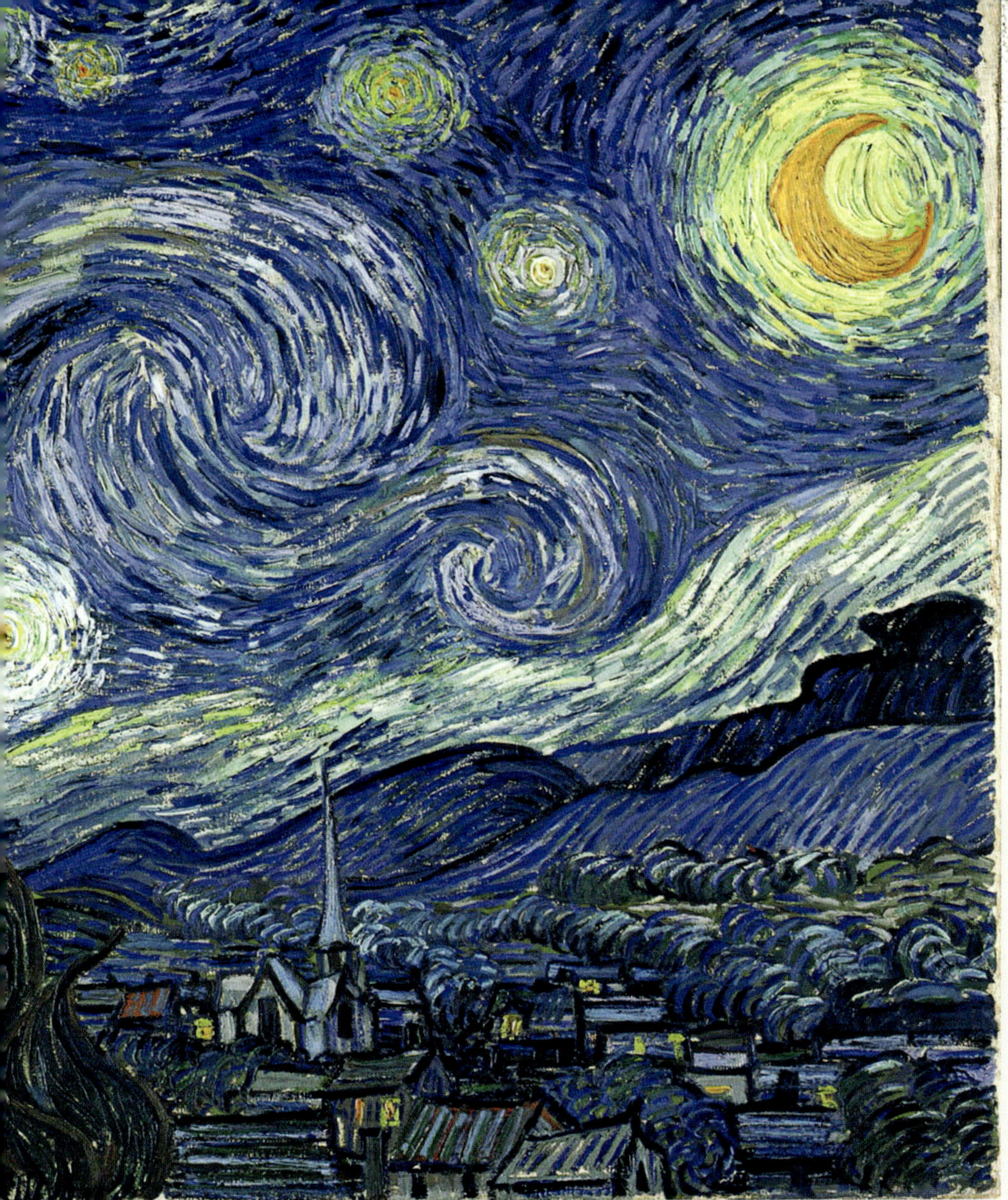

Starry Night by Vincent van Gogh, Museum of Modern Art, New York City

and Paris, where two important things happened. First, he gained an ever-widening exposure to art through the museums in these cities. Second, he experienced a personal spiritual awakening. Beginning in September 1875, his letters were filled with quotations from the Bible and other spiritual writings he was voraciously digesting.

(Much of what we know about van Gogh's life and thought comes from the voluminous correspondence he kept up with his brother Theo, who, as well as being a sounding board for his thoughts, was also a constant financial support and encourager.)

As a young man, van Gogh had embraced his father's brand of liberal Protestantism, but now he became more evangelical in his approach, with a concern for the authority of the Bible, the preaching of the gospel, and personal salvation. His key influences other than the Bible were *The Pilgrim's Progress*, *The Imitation of Christ*, and the writings of famous London preacher Charles Spurgeon. Vincent offered his time to assist the pastor of the congregation he attended and preached his first sermon in November 1876. About the experience, he wrote, "I felt like someone who has risen from a dark vault underground into the kind light of day when I stood at the pulpit, and it is a glorious thought that from now on wherever I go, I shall preach the gospel."[2]

Van Gogh undertook a training program for missionaries and was assigned a temporary position with an organization that sent him to preach to the coal miners in the Borinage area of Belgium. There his goal was, as he told an acquaintance, to be "a friend to the poor like Jesus was."[3] He took this calling very seriously, living in the same squalid conditions as the poorest of the miners rather than in more comfortable lodgings as most missionaries of the time tended to do. He gave away his money and clothes, refused the lodgings of a more prosperous mining family, and instead slept in a bare hovel. He even refused the luxury of soap, and tended to be disheveled, soot-faced, and emaciated.

Fiercely embracing the asceticism of *The Imitation of Christ*, he denied himself physical pleasures and even the simplest comforts. He wanted to model his life on the suffering servanthood of Jesus, and, like John Bunyan, he saw life as an arduous pilgrimage to a heavenly home. He preached and visited the sick and was much loved by the miners for his gentleness, love, humility, and compassion. Taking the Sermon on the Mount literally, he used it as a model for his lifestyle. "Oh that I may be shown the way to devote my life more fully to the service of God and the Gospel," he wrote. "I keep praying for it and in all humility I think I shall be heard."[4] He was, by all accounts, not a talented preacher, but he converted many of the hardened coal miners—less by his words than by his sacrificial love and care for them.

When his six months were up, the organization that had given him the appointment decided not to renew it, citing his lack of eloquence in the pulpit. But the more likely cause of his dismissal was the radical way he chose to live out his faith. "They think I am a madman because I wanted to be a true Christian,"[5] he wrote to Theo. He tried to stay on through the rest of the year, doing without any regular financial means of support, until abject poverty and a growing disillusionment with the church caused him to abandon this ministry. His father also withdrew his support for his son's pastoral ambitions and even sought to have him placed in an asylum for his "excessive behavior."

All this conspired to cause van Gogh to turn his back permanently on institutional religion. He never again set foot in church. Some biographers suggest that he abandoned his faith, but it seems clear, upon more careful reflection, that instead of abandoning it he simply rechanneled his spiritual passion into his art. His break with the church was not over theology but due to deeply personal disappointment, anger, and hurt. He quoted approvingly the dictum, "Religions pass, but God remains." He left the institution behind but continued a personal pursuit of God. "That God of the clergymen, He is for me as dead as a doornail. But am I an atheist for all that? . . . To believe in God for me is to feel that there is a God, not a dead one, or a stuffed one, but a living one."[6]

As his ministerial dreams were collapsing, van Gogh was beginning to take his interest in drawing more seriously and began to produce a prodigious number of sketches, drawings, and then paintings. Much of his early work is focused on recording the squalid life of the underprivileged, while at the same time showing their dignity. This can be seen in such works as *At Eternity's Gate* (1882) and *The Potato Eaters* (1885). Paintings such as *A Pair of Shoes* (1885) reveal his belief in the luminous holiness of simple ordinary objects. A painting he did of an open Bible next to a paperback novel by Zola seems to suggest that the Bible (open to Isaiah 53) and the Zola novel are both preaching the same message about suffering and the call to serve humanity. Throughout his life van Gogh lived out his own personal interpretation of the "suffering servant" passage of Scripture. He saw himself as a wounded healer who could use his own sufferings to bring new hope to others.

In 1886, van Gogh moved to Paris, where he met other important artists of the time and began to develop his own unique style of brushwork and his emphasis on vivid colors. It was a style that was vigorous, passionate, spontaneous, and instinctive. The paintings were highly textured, mirroring the plowing and the weaving of the peasants he so admired. A couple years later he moved to southeast France and made an aborted attempt to found a new working community of artists with Gauguin. But by this time he had begun to suffer from fainting spells and seizures, and the contrast of temperaments between the two artists soon led to a falling out, culminating in the infamous incident during which van Gogh cut off a piece of his own ear.

Van Gogh was hospitalized and then checked himself into an asylum in Saint-Remy. There are numerous theories about what caused his rapid deterioration and frequent bouts of near insanity—

schizophrenia, epilepsy, syphilis, or some combination of these. We shall likely never know, but in the last years of his life he was haunted by recurrent attacks. He would work intermittently when he could free himself from these bouts of intense sadness and despair, and he became afraid that he might eventually completely lose touch with reality. It was his art, essentially, that kept him sane, and his output during his stay at the asylum was unbelievably prodigious. In the last seventy days of his life, he produced seventy paintings. Among his later works there is even a series of three paintings of biblical stories, showing that his interest in such matters had not waned despite the struggles of his life.

The popular image of van Gogh as a creative madman is one of the myths that keep us from properly understanding his work. His battle against his physical and psychological problems—and we'll probably never know exactly what they were—did not enhance his art but more often kept him from working for periods at a time. His paintings were not the fruit of "madness." It was when he was feeling well that he produced paintings of such incredible beauty and powerful original vision.

Another of the elements of the van Gogh myth has to do with the way he died. For years the popular conception was that he committed suicide because of his despair of ever being cured and his suffering from severe loneliness. But biographers Steven Naifeh and Gregory White Smith have recently called that interpretation into question. Their reconstruction of the events and forensic evidence argues persuasively that van Gogh was more likely the victim of an accidental shooting than a suicide. The nature of the wounds and evidence of van Gogh's upbeat frame of mind in the days before the shooting render the suicide hypothesis suspect. So we should be careful about reading his late paintings in light of theories about how he died. One of van Gogh's last paintings, *Wheatfield With Crows* (1890), is often seen as a dark painting with a sense of suicidal despair and foreboding, but it can alternatively be understood as a hopeful vision. The crows taking flight might be an emblem of the eventual human triumph over death and the ultimate promise of eternity.

Vincent van Gogh was never content with just painting what he saw. He painted the sacred presence of the eternal as he saw it in our world. "If one feels the need of something grand, something infinite, something that makes one feel aware of God, one need not go far to find it,"[7] he wrote. For van Gogh, all the simplest beauties that he loved so much were pointers that aimed the heart toward God: "I always think that the best way to know God is to love many things."[8]

40

The Complete Poems

Emily Dickinson

(poems, 1890)

At nineteen, Emily Dickinson was a cheerful and optimistic young woman and an active participant in the polite, sometimes uptight, New England community in which she had been raised. She attended local dinners and dances, and traveled with her congressman father on trips to Philadelphia, Washington, Boston, and New York. But by the time of her death, this once rather conventional young lady had become an almost mythical recluse who dressed almost exclusively in white, rarely left her second-story bedroom, and spent much of her time at her desk, writing poetry and letters to friends.

What had caused the dramatic shift in her life? Some suggest that a devastating disappointment in a relationship drove her inward. Others postulate that she may have suffered from a psychological malady such as agoraphobia. Or perhaps she just discovered that the place where she really found joy was in the confines of her own creative mind and soul. We'll likely never know for certain, for though her poems and letters might provide hints, they generally obscure as much as they reveal about this wonderful but puzzling poet.

Dickinson embraced her seclusion, finding in her solitude a place where she could be spiritually transported. How she saw the world and what she experienced in her inner life provided the subject matter for her poems. She was extremely prolific during her short life, penning over 1,700 poems and writing enough letters to fill three stout volumes. These letters and poems reveal the woman she had become: a careful observer of the world and of her own self, someone cynical about easy answers to life's hard questions, a wrestler with God, and a poet who found her own entirely unique way of communicating about life and death, time and eternity, faith and doubt, the simple beauties she saw in nature, and the exquisite sufferings she felt within her innermost self.

In her poems, she uses language and grammar with a startling freshness, her word choices often unexpected and layered with levels of meaning. Dickinson constantly surprises with her insights, her observations, and her honesty. It is her inquisitive nature and her highly observant eye that give wings to her words, causing them to soar with such simplicity and ease. We see her watchful eye at work in poems such as "A bird comes down the walk" and "There's a certain slant of slight," and we see her playful images and metaphors in poems such as "Hope is the thing with feathers" and "Bring me the sunset in a cup." These poems are crisply and tightly structured, without the waste of extra words, and therefore are usually quite short, which aids their memorability. Underlying her poetic vision is a childlike joy joined with a deep compassion:

> If I can stop one Heart from
> breaking
> I shall not live in vain
> If I can ease one Life the Aching
> Or cool one Pain
> Or help one fainting Robin
> Unto his Nest again
> I shall not live in Vain.[1]

Born in Amherst, Massachusetts, in 1830, Emily Dickinson lived a life that was outwardly uneventful. She died in the same home in which she had been born. She was well educated, attending Amherst Academy and Mount Holyoke Female Seminary, where she found herself resistant to the wave of revivalism and religious fervor that was sweeping through the vicinity, even though it had an impact on her family and friends. Letters written during this period of her life show her drawn toward a dramatic conversion like the others were experiencing but feeling a great caution about being swept into an emotional decision. So while all around her were embracing a Calvinist creed, she held back. And she would hold back throughout her life. Though she attended church with her family for many years, she eventually ceased going at all. But then again, by that time she was rarely leaving the environs of her home for any reason whatsoever.

She kept up most of her relationships via the mail, and one of her frequent correspondents was Thomas Wentworth Higginson, the editor of *Atlantic Monthly*, to whom she sent a handful of her poems. He was not initially an enthusiastic supporter, as her poems were unlike anything else being produced at the time, though some ten poems eventually did make their way into publication.

Upon her death, the extent of Dickinson's literary production became clear. Her sister found sixty little books (sewn together by Emily herself) tied together with twine and tucked away in a box. These little books contained the poems that constituted her life's work. Higginson and another editor eventually published the poems posthumously, but not before tidying up the grammatical "mistakes" that we now treasure as a characteristic of Dickinson's style—the abrupt rhythms, the unconventional punctuation, the unexpected word choices, and the frequent use of dashes for dramatic pauses. These "corrected" versions still circulate widely in the public domain. It was not until 1955 that a complete version of all her poems was issued by Thomas Johnson that allowed her uniqueness to finally be given voice. To fully appreciate Emily Dickinson, one needs to read her poems as they were originally conceived.

While Dickinson never really felt at ease with the religion of her family and friends, her poetry reveals her to be very much concerned with her questions about God and eternity. She had to find her own path, though; her own way to "tell all the Truth, but tell it slant."[2] She was forever puzzling over life's mysteries, asking hard questions, distrusting easy answers, and interrogating herself about her own motives. She could not accept all the tenets of the religion in which she had been raised, nor could she settle for a materialistic philosophy that failed to understand the mysteries she sensed just below the surface of things.

Her poems are a record of her unsettledness and her constant wrestling with God. Sometimes they seem full of faith and assurance. At other times—and sometimes even in the very same poem—they are skeptical, defiant, irreverent, or angry about the injustice of things. There are poems of doubt, and poems of doubt about doubt. Reading her poetry is like eavesdropping on her whispered conversations and angry arguments with God. As she wrote in a letter, "I am one of the lingering bad ones, and so do I slink away, and pause, and ponder, and ponder, and pause, and do work without knowing why—not surely for this brief world, and more sure it is not for heaven—and I ask what this message of Christ means."[3] In the depths of times of loneliness, we hear the expression of her ache for intimacy with Him:

> Savior! I've no one else to tell—
> And so I trouble thee. . . .
> I brought thee the imperial Heart
> I had not strength to hold—
> The Heart I carried in my own—
> Till mine too heavy grew—
> Yet—strangest—heavier since it
>   went—
> Is it too large for you?[4]

Dickinson was a pilgrim who perhaps never quite arrived but was always faithful to the truth as she found it along the path of her journey. She knew that the end of that journey for all of us is death, and so questions about mortality, immortality, and eternity haunt many of her poems. Trying to comprehend and make sense of the death of beloved friends and family members was often the instigation of her musings. She seems to be asking, *What is one to make of life in view of the imminence of death?* "Behind Me—dips Eternity / Before Me—Immortality / Myself—the Term between." The window of her upstairs bedroom overlooked the cemetery, which perhaps kept such matters ever in her sight, and death was never far from her mind: "The Only News I Know / Is bulletins all day / From Immortality." Though Dickinson was a constant questioner, the reality of a life after death seems to be one of the things about which she expressed a great confidence and hope. In a poem about dying she enthused, "Goodbye to the Life I used to live— / and the World I used to know— / And kiss the Hills, for me, just once— / Then—I am ready to go!"[5]

In puzzling out her questions about God, Dickinson was not interested in the received answers of doctrine and dogma. She felt uncomfortable around those who thought they had everything figured out and preferred to commune with God in a garden rather than a church service. In one poem she described her ideal worship experience: "It was a short procession, / The Bobolink was there— / An aged Bee addressed us— / And then we knelt in prayer."[6] Dickinson gave her full and loving gaze of attention to the world around her, embracing it in all its wonder and interrogating it for answers about ultimate things. Her love for God was expressed best through her love for the world He created —a world imperfect, but glorious. "This is my letter to the world / That never wrote to me,— / The simple news that Nature told, / With tender majesty."[7] Emily Dickinson was not waiting for heaven to experience God's presence but looking to find it every day:

> Some keep the Sabbath going
>   to church;
> I keep it by staying at home,
> With a bobolink for a chorister,
> And an orchard for a dome.
> Some keep the Sabbath in
>   surplice;
> I just wear my wings,
> And instead of tolling the bell
>   for church,
> Our little sexton sings.
> God preaches,—a noted clergy-
>   man—,
> And the sermon is never long;
> So instead of getting to heaven
>   at last,
> I'm going all along![8]

Few of Emily Dickinson's contemporaries even took note of this quiet, reclusive woman who found her joys in the things that surrounded her in her small, self-enclosed world. "They shut me up in prose," she wrote; but she sprang free. Today her song still rings out to those who find something of a fellow traveler in the poet who never felt fully at home in this world but tried to embrace it with all her heart and offered up all her doubts along with her deep sense of awe. As she famously teased, "I'm Nobody! Who are you? / Are you nobody, too? / Then there is a pair of us—don't tell / They'll banish us, you know."[9] And so this most reclusive of poets invited us into her most private places—her own heart, mind, and soul.

41

The Life of Our Lord Jesus Christ

JAMES TISSOT

(paintings, 1896)

Though extremely popular in his day, in our time James Tissot has been largely relegated to a footnote in nineteenth-century art history. But when his carefully researched collection of 350 watercolors depicting the life of Jesus was first published as a book in 1896, it found a large and enthusiastic audience. No one who had followed his previous career could have anticipated that this painter of urban life in Paris and London would undertake the project of painting virtually every event in the Gospels.

The Life of Our Lord Jesus Christ project took nearly ten years to complete. When it was done, it chronicled the entire life of Jesus as recorded in the New Testament in a series of 350 watercolors. To research the project Tissot traveled to Egypt, Syria, and Palestine in 1886–1887, and again in 1890. While in the Holy Land, he closely observed the landscape, the vegetation, the architecture, and the manner of dress, and filled sketchbooks with what he saw. He talked with rabbis and studied Talmudic literature as well as theological and historical volumes. He believed that there was still a remaining "aura" in the places where the Gospel events took place, and he spoke of having mystical experiences that added to his careful research. What he wanted to create was something as close as possible to an eyewitness account of the life of Jesus.

Once widely known as something of a playboy, Tissot lived an almost ascetic existence as he worked on the project—

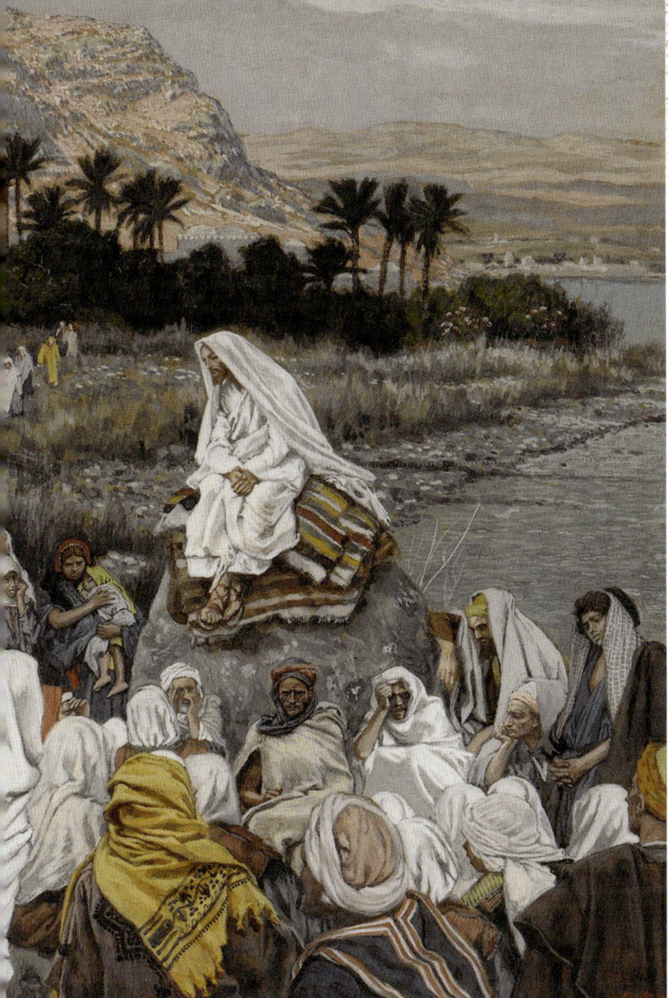

Alamy

Jesus Sits by the Seashore and Teaches by James Tissot, Brooklyn Museum

studying, sketching, and painting. There were even rumors at the time (unfounded) that he had become a monk. He described his effort as "not labor, but prayer." The resulting images covered virtually every event in the Gospels, from the birth of Jesus to His teaching and preaching, His miracles and healings, His parables, and the events of the Passion Week, culminating in the crucifixion and resurrection. All were created with an attempt at "you are there" realism. Some of the events of the last week are horrific in their accurate and careful detail, such as the scourging of Christ. Others are innovative, especially the image of the crucifixion entitled *What Our Lord Saw from the Cross*, which presents that familiar event from an unfamiliar vantage point—how it looked from the perspective of the One who died there for humanity.

In 1894, the finished paintings were exhibited to great acclaim in Paris, London, New York, Chicago, and other locations. They unfailingly drew large audiences, including many who were not normally accustomed to going to a museum or art gallery These paintings had their critics—some saw their realism as cold and vulgar, not at all what one was used to seeing in religious works of art. But most embraced the works and found them deeply moving. There are even reports that the strong emotional responses from viewers included hushed reverence, weeping, and kneeling before the images. Tissot had indeed accomplished what he set out to do: give the viewer a powerful personal experience of the historical events that had changed the world.

These paintings proved to be so popular that they were issued as a multivolume set titled *The Life of Our Lord Jesus Christ* that, in addition to the images, included a harmony of the Gospels, commentary by Tissot himself on the customs of biblical times, stories of his experiences while researching, and quotations from important historical and religious texts. Though an expensive set, it became an international bestseller. The final painting in the book is a self-portrait in which, surrounded by Catholic symbols, Tissot raises his hand in blessing. It is accompanied by a request that the reader pray for him.

James Tissot was born in France in 1836 to parents who were involved in the clothing industry. It is probably not surprising, then, that elaborate costumes and fashionable dresses were a common element of his early paintings. Brought up as a strict Catholic, he ceased attending church as an adult. Instead, he dedicated himself to a life of painting and the pursuit of pleasure. His paintings displayed his love for the finer things of life, for high society, and for beautiful women. A contemporary gossip columnist described him as "a high liver of extraordinary proficiency!" He had a reputation as a flirtatious man, and his paintings were largely of society women dressed in their finery, painted with care for detail and a sense of romance. What they lacked in gravitas, they made up for in sheer loveliness.

Tissot lived in the age of Impressionism and Post-Impressionism, but he was not really a part of either movement, though he was good friends with Degas, Manet, and Whistler. He was invited to take part in the first Impressionist exhibition, but declined. Instead, he blazed his own path, working in a highly finished style and becoming known for his paintings of fashionable ladies, usually in urban settings. He had a keen sense for composition and the arrangement of figures in his work, and for use of space, especially in a painting like *The Ball on Shipboard* (c. 1874), with its carefully arranged groupings of revelers. He also painted a series of four important paintings that recast the story of the prodigal son in a convincing contemporary setting, but Tissot really made his reputation as a painter who recorded modern life. His works are actually a great source of information about what fashions were popular at that time. Such cosmopolitan art proved very popular, and he made a successful career with such paintings.

In 1871, Tissot moved to London, where he continued to build his growing reputation and found a ready audience for his work. Not only were these highly productive years but they also included his introduction to Kathleen Newton, who became his model and the great love of his life. By all accounts, it was a deep and committed relationship. They did not marry, but she moved in with him about 1876. Kathleen was a woman of fragile health, though, and she died of consumption a mere six years later. Heartbroken, Tissot returned to Paris.

Setting to work on a new series of images that depicted Parisian women in a variety of settings, he researched locations for each of the paintings. One of the places he visited was the Church of Saint-Sulpice. Long a Catholic more by custom than conviction, he had a profound experience in the church that day. When the priest raised the host during mass, Tissot experienced a vision that changed his life and his artistic priorities. He was so affected that he went without sleep for several nights to record that vision in *Inward Voices* (*The Ruins*) (1885). This painting showed a bloodied but still luminous Jesus comforting two poor and tattered souls in the rubble of a crumbling building. Jesus displays His bloodstained hands to prove that He is with them in their suffering and that He has died as a sacrifice for their redemption. It is a work of deep compassion and hope, and a sign of what was to come in Tissot's art.

The paintings in *The Life of Our Lord Jesus Christ* series were the major undertaking of his life after his conversion experience, but they would not be the end of his interest in biblical subject matter. In the latter years of his life, he began a series of Old Testament paintings and drawings but died before he could complete the project. These include ninety-five images from the book of Genesis as well as many other paintings of important Old Testament stories.

When Tissot surveyed the long history of biblical art, he was disturbed by the anachronisms of earlier artists, who seemed to care little for historical accuracy in their work. He wanted to create something new—a carefully researched and accurate picture of the events as they would have actually looked if one had been there to observe them. "For a long time," he wrote, "the imagination of the Christian world has been led astray by the fancies of artists; there is a whole army of delusions to be overturned."[1] He wanted to present an authentically Jewish Jesus, strong and charismatic, one who was truly man as well as truly God, and his hope was that viewers would personally identify with the story of Jesus through looking at his paintings.

What Tissot tried to do in his paintings was make the biblical stories come alive while striving for an almost journalistic level of accuracy. The expansiveness of the project, and the piety and care with which it was executed, make it deserving of more attention than it has received in our time. Once a large draw to the Brooklyn Museum, which raised the money to buy the complete *The Life of Our Lord Jesus Christ* series through enthusiastic public donations, the works are now rarely exhibited and are stored in their archives. But they remain one of the most unique treasures in the history of Christian art.

42

The Annunciation

Henry Ossawa Tanner

(painting, 1898)

No matter what the artistic medium, it is always a challenge to portray a moment when the supernatural breaks into our world, and make such a moment believable rather than kitschy or sentimental. Throughout art history, the annunciation—that instant when the angel appeared to the Virgin Mary to tell her that she would be the mother of the Messiah—has been a popular theme in religious painting. Many of these paintings are beautiful, but also tend to be stiff and reverential rather than alive and convincing. Others are cloyingly sweet, flowing over with schmaltzy religiosity, and are not very believable in human terms. But Henry Ossawa Tanner's *The Annunciation* manages to be both lovely and emotionally resonant and at the same time feel utterly convincing.

Mary is portrayed as a young Jewish peasant sitting on the edge of her bed amid crumpled bedclothes, wearing a striped costume that would have been common for a young woman of the poorer class. She has no halo, nor is there anything immediately recognizable as special about her. She is not, as is often the case, surrounded by symbols of her purity. Nor is there anything grandiose about the simple setting. The angel who has appeared to her is not the conventional celestial-winged messenger of religious art, but rather a burst of overpowering golden light that permeates the room with its warm glow. Mary seems a bit frightened, as any ordinary person might be if she had just been addressed by an angelic being.

By the sheer ordinariness of this depiction of the intersection between the divine and human, we are reminded that God communicates to perfectly ordinary human beings in perfectly ordinary circumstances. And the holiness that infuses the picture is less in the flood of golden light and more in the look on Mary's face, captured in the moment when fear is beginning to give way to contemplation and then acceptance. Her hands are folded in her lap, her head tilted upward, and her eyes focused. There is receptivity in her body language, an openness to God's will.

Because the angel is presented in such an abstract form, all the focus of the painting is upon Mary. She is a reflection of the light, and it is through her posture and attitude that we experience the calm, the peace, and the holiness that fills the room. She is our clue to how we are to read this moment of revelation. As in many of Tanner's paintings, it is through his focus on the figure who is receiving the light of revelation that we begin to understand something supernatural is taking place before our eyes.

Henry Ossawa Tanner was born in 1859 in Pittsburgh, on the eve of the Civil War, to a father who was a free black and who later became a minister, then a bishop, in the African Methodist Episcopal Church. His mother had been a slave but was rescued by the Underground Railroad. His father always stressed the importance of an intelligent faith and also instilled a deep sense of dignity in his children in the face of widespread racial prejudice. Tanner would never forget the time that his mother was ejected from a streetcar in a snowstorm when the driver noticed she was black. His father, Benjamin Tanner, was frequently subject to beatings and verbal abuse because he had the temerity to expect to be treated with the same rights as any other American citizen. Benjamin was heavily involved not only in the AME church but also in work for civil rights and the abolition of slavery.

When the young Tanner first saw an artist at work in a park, he knew that he had found the vocation for his life, and he was supported in this by his parents, even though at the time it was highly unusual for a black person to make a career out of art, much less to study it in the academy. But Tanner did just that, studying under Thomas Eakins and other luminaries of American art at the prestigious Pennsylvania Academy of Fine Arts, where he was the only black student. His very earliest work is largely landscape and shows the influence of the Hudson River School of painters, who saw the divine in nature.

As Tanner's own style emerged, he created works like *The Banjo Lesson* (1893) and *The Thankful Poor* (1894), through which he provided a window into the life of African Americans. These paintings subvert racial stereotypes and treat their subjects with dignity and affection. Some critics and supporters wished he would create more works in this vein, but he did not want to be thought of as a "negro artist." Tanner believed, instead, that his true artistic calling was found in painting works that reflected his deep Christian faith:

> I have no doubt an inheritance of religious feeling, and for this I am glad, but I have also a decided and I hope an intelligent religious faith not due to inheritance but to my own convictions. I believe my religion. I have chosen the character of my art because it conveys my message and tells what I want to tell my own generation and leave to the future.[1]

To pursue this calling, Tanner found it necessary to leave the United States, where racial discrimination was so deeply imbedded, and study in France, where he found the acceptance as an artist and as a man that he had not found in the States. In France he did not have to struggle against the kind of prejudice that believed it impossible for a black man to be a great painter. Tanner wanted to be an artist who happened to be an African American, not to be pigeonholed as an African-American artist. It was only after being embraced by the French as an internationally significant painter that he finally gained full recognition in his home country. But except for a handful of visits to the United States, he would make France his home for the rest of his life.

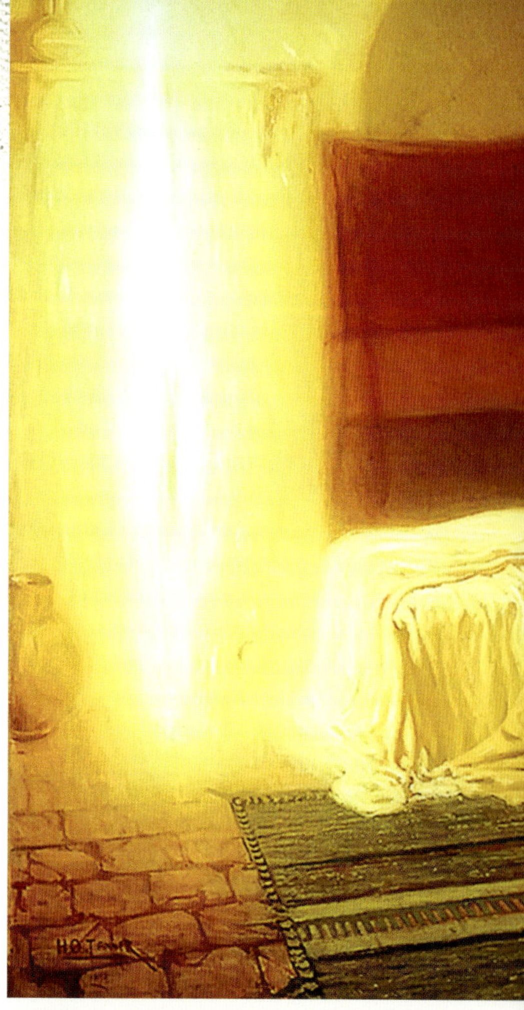

The Annunciation by Henry Ossawa Tanner, Philadelphia Museum of Art, Philadelphia

Rather than becoming a peddler of sacred anecdotes captured in paint, Tanner wanted his paintings to touch something deeper inside those who viewed them. He wanted them to be a place of intersection, where communication could happen between humanity and God. To do this,

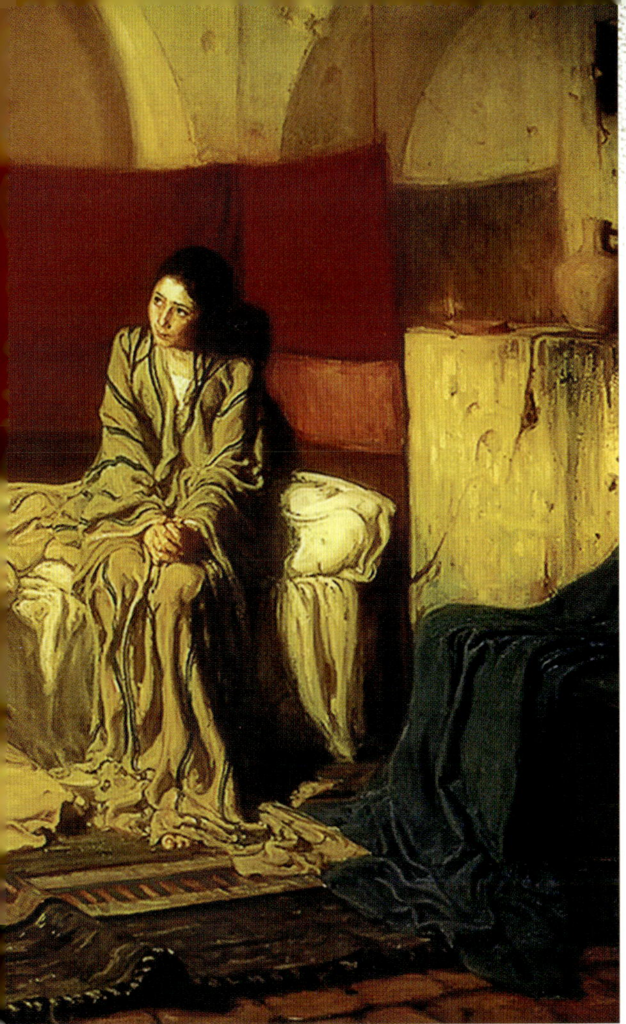

WikiCommons

supernatural presence one could sense in his paintings was available to every human being.

Throughout his work, Tanner used light as the symbol for the arrival of something divine, which infused the scene with meaning; a reflection of God's welcoming presence. He used light not for its dramatic effect but for illumination—in both the physical and spiritual senses of the word. For example, in one of his great early masterpieces, *Daniel and the Lion's Den* (1896), we see Daniel in the shadows, among the lions that pace around him but do not harm him. There is a shaft of light falling upon him that signals to the viewer that God has intervened on Daniel's behalf. Daniel was a figure with whom Tanner, often the target of misunderstanding and racism, could identify, and a man whose lonely faith and courage in the face of persecution he wished to emulate. And like Daniel, he tried to stay pure and true to his values, even when consorting with other Parisian artists who did not share his convictions against drinking alcohol and carousing.

We also see his creative use of light in his painting of Nicodemus meeting Jesus by night. There is a subtle light illuminating Jesus' eyes, though the rest of His face is in shadow, but we cannot see the eyes

Tanner specialized in painting biblical scenes reflective of his deep knowledge and love of the Scriptures. He prayed daily, read the Bible regularly, and even made two visits to the Holy Land in order to drink up the atmosphere and help get the details right when he portrayed biblical events. But it wasn't enough for him to strive for a realism that rooted the biblical incidents in their original settings; he also wanted to convince the viewer that the same

of Nicodemus at all; perhaps Tanner is making reference to Nicodemus's spiritual blindness, which can only be overcome by the words of Jesus, the One whose eyes penetrate the darkness. Nicodemus is clearly the learner, and Jesus is the master teacher.

Tanner developed a style that was singularly his own—a sort of visual mysticism. His expressive brushwork, unusual lighting, and unexpected use of colors reflected the introspection of the figures in his paintings. He hoped thereby to engage the viewers in personal introspection and invite them to an encounter with the living God. Perhaps it is his son, Jesse Tanner, who has best summarized the desired impact of his father's art:

> A Tanner can do more than give you enjoyment, it can come to your rescue, it can reaffirm your confidence in man and his destiny, it can help you surmount your difficulties or console you in your distress. A picture by Tanner is really part of the artist himself, a mystic whose visions are deeply personal yet universal in significance.[2]

43

The Innocence of Father Brown

G. K. Chesterton

(short stories, 1911)

In the 1840s, Edgar Allan Poe created a new literary genre with a handful of stories that each pose a seemingly insoluble mystery that is finally solved by the intellectual brilliance of his detective, C. Auguste Dupin. Some fifty years later, Arthur Conan Doyle brought the mystery genre to an even higher level with his novels and short stories featuring Sherlock Holmes, an eccentric detective who used the science of deduction and his powers of observation to solve the crimes set before him. Gilbert Keith Chesterton was a great fan of the Holmes stories and wrote highly entertaining essays about the mystery genre. He set down his thoughts about what made for a good "whodunit," and put his theories to the test by writing some stories of his own.

Chesterton modeled his detective, the genial Father Brown, on his friend Father John O'Connor, a priest whose intellectual capacities and wit he much enjoyed. The first twelve short stories were first published in *The Saturday Evening Post*, and then collected in a book as *The Innocence of Father Brown*. By the time of his death, Chesterton had produced fifty-one stories about the mystery-solving clergyman. The stories were an immediate hit and became the most popular and successful of his many books. Their format is predictable, but the solutions to the crimes are not. As in any good mystery, a puzzle is set forth in each story that defies logic and seems impossible to untangle. But the quiet little priest, Father

Brown, succeeds where everyone else fails because of the insight he has attained about the darker shades of human motivation from hearing confessions. Father Brown is an easy man to overlook—a short, stubby, unimposing figure, shabbily dressed and with a round, expressionless face that renders him almost invisible. The police investigating the crimes generally fail to pay him much attention until Father Brown gently and relentlessly unravels the hidden truth.

Because Chesterton was a man of ideas, he used his detective stories to explore the effects of mistaken ideologies about human nature and to demonstrate the consequences of wrong thinking. The stories also lay bare the sinful tendencies of the human heart; how and why we do the things we do. While thoroughly engaging as entertainment, they are also meditations on the psychology of humankind and the theology that makes sense of that psychology.

G. K. Chesterton was born in London in 1874 to a family with only a passing interest in religion. When they attended services, it was usually at a Unitarian church. As a child, Chesterton was quiet, clumsy, and reticent. But when his brother Cecil was born, he is said to have proclaimed, "Now I shall always have an audience!" This was something of a prophetic statement, for his brother was his lifelong best friend and sparring partner. Through his arguments with his brother—one of which reportedly lasted eighteen consecutive hours—he learned how to think logically and express himself with rhetorical flourish.

Chesterton got his start in journalism by writing book reviews, essays, and articles. He was quickly recognized as an entertaining and thought-provoking writer, and during the course of his life he churned out hundreds of articles for newspapers and magazines. He soon became a prolific fiction and nonfiction writer as well, and by the time he died in 1936 he had produced several bookshelves full of volumes.

Chesterton has been called "the Shakespeare of the aphorism," due to his ability to pack so many profound insights into a single witty sentence. He had the ability to smuggle more paradox and more truth into a phrase or two than perhaps anyone else in history. Here are a few examples:

> Merely having an open mind is nothing. The object of opening the mind, as of opening the mouth, is to shut it again on something solid.[1]

> The Bible tells us to love our neighbors, and also to love our enemies, probably because they are generally the same people.[2]

> Tradition means giving votes to the most obscure of all classes, our ancestors. It is the democracy of the dead. Tradition refuses to submit to the small and arrogant oligarchy of those who merely happen to be walking about.[3]

WikiCommons

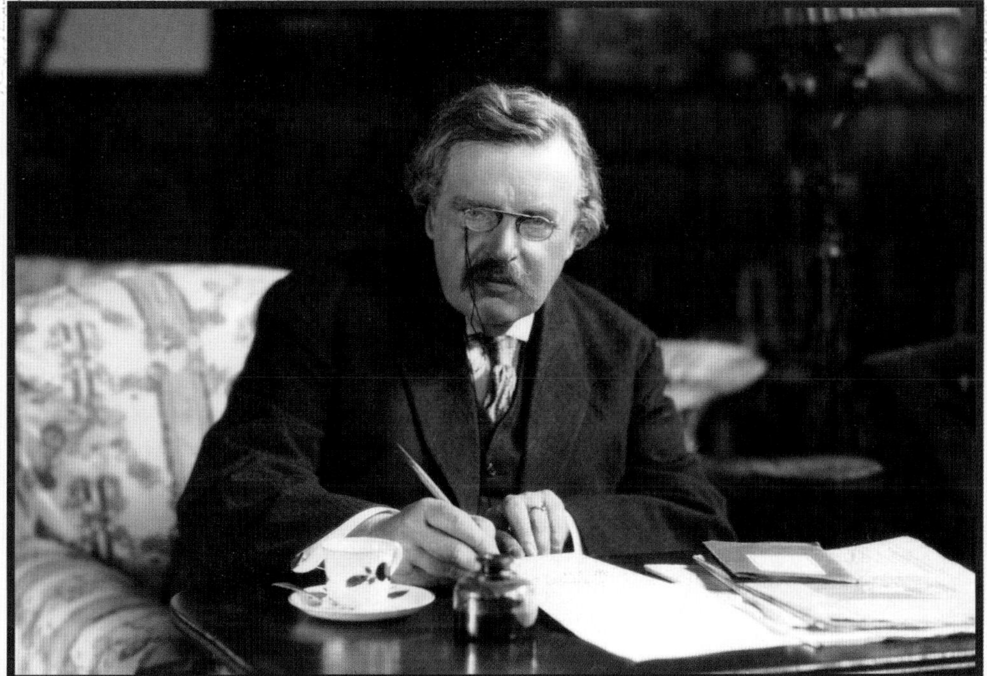

G. K. Chesterton at work (photographer unknown)

As one reads his books, one cannot help but marvel at his ability to load one such insight upon another, creating writing that is entertaining, insightful, and an infectious joy to read, all in the service of a swashbuckling faith.

Chesterton has been esteemed in our day as a defender of the faith, calling his readers to attend to his mixture of playful argument, ruthless logic, and good plain common sense. In his book *Orthodoxy*, he tells of how, as he came to his own logical conclusions about the nature of humanity and the meaning of life, he was astonished to find that these same conclusions had already been reached nearly two thousand years ago. He embraced Christianity because he found it to be the one philosophy that most accurately made sense of the world, and then he spent the rest of his life, and buckets of ink, defending it. In the midst of making his case for the superiority of the Christian philosophy of life against all comers, he was relentless in his search for answers that make sense of life as we know it.

Because he was an eminent journalist, Chesterton was once asked to participate in a series of written responses to the question, "What's wrong with the world?" Most of the distinguished persons who responded waxed eloquently about the various philosophical or cultural problems that kept people from experiencing the good life. But

Chesterton's answer to that question was simple and forceful: "Dear Sirs," he wrote, "I am."

Chesterton believed that the problem of universal greed and selfishness was the hurdle over which idealism about human perfectibility and inevitable progress could not vault. The doctrine of original sin, he once suggested, was the one piece of Christian theology that could be proven simply by reading the daily newspaper. As Chesterton saw it, those who ignored this truth about humanity were destined only to create more injustice in their pursuit of an unrealistic goal. "The modern critics of religious authority," he suggested, "are like those who attack the police without ever having heard of the burglars."[4]

Throughout his writing, Chesterton took aim at such philosophies with great good humor and deadly seriousness. In fact, Chesterton seemed to believe that you could really only be deadly serious when you didn't take yourself too seriously. When he debated famous atheists and agnostics of the day on issues of religion, politics, or culture—men such as George Bernard Shaw and H. G. Wells—he tried to puncture their overblown idealism with such a playful cheerfulness and respect that these debates were as entertaining as they were enlightening. But along with his friendships with these culture-makers, he also was friends with the neighborhood children. He loved their playful outlook on life and would sometimes, at the drop of a hat, abandon his more "serious" pursuits so that he could build a fort with them or engage in war games. Children loved this giant bear of a man whose heart was so full of fun and wonder.

Reading Chesterton's nonfiction requires careful attention, for his arguments move so swiftly that missing a single sentence might mean missing his point. His homey anecdotes, spun so seemingly effortlessly, were used to point to the commonsense truths he was trying to defend or the false notions he was trying to defeat. Among the best of these books are *Heretics* (1905), which shows the intellectual shortcomings of current philosophies, *Orthodoxy* (1908), which shows why Christianity makes better sense of actual human life than these other intellectual systems, and *The Everlasting Man* (1925), an alternative to H. G. Wells's biased account of human history, the bestselling *Outline of History*. In addition to these, he wrote dozens of collections of essays; biographies of famous literary and religious figures such as Dickens, Blake, Browning, Tolstoy, Thomas Aquinas, and Francis of Assisi; travel books about his experiences in Ireland, the United States, Rome, and the Holy Land; a history of England; and a very entertaining autobiography.

His fiction—including *The Man Who Was Thursday* (1908), arguably his best novel—is bursting with wit and invention, and each story features eccentric protagonists who battle (sometimes quite literally) against the encroachments of modern philosophies upon the joys of ordinary life. The novels are sometimes weakened by Chesterton's urgency to make a point, and often the characters are more like allegorical representations of ideas than fully fleshed-out characters; but their high spirits, sense for the adventure of life, and stylish playfulness make for entertaining reads that often evoke a chuckle even as they make their point.

G. K. Chesterton was a larger-than-life figure, a giant among men in so many ways. He stood at an imposing six foot four and weighed about three hundred pounds. He loved good food and drink, hard work, and a rigorous argument. In many ways he seemed like one of the quirky characters he had created in his fantastical novels. Those who knew him recognized him as an intellectual giant but also as a man who might show up at a gathering with the wrong shoe on, or who might forget where he was going and end up some place he never intended. He could cross swords with the greatest intellectuals of his day or be found play-sword-fighting with a child, brandishing his ever-present walking stick. Unlike his Father Brown character, Chesterton rarely failed to attract attention.

44

The Life of Christ

Emil Nolde

(paintings, 1912)

There are few religious paintings—and even fewer religious painters—among the modern artists who emerged as the center of the art world at the turn of the twentieth century, but paintings on spiritual themes were a central focus of Emil Nolde's artistic life. Between 1909 and 1951, he devoted fifty-five paintings to sacred or biblical themes. Perhaps his masterpiece is his altarpiece, *The Life of Christ*, a work that makes use of very traditional imagery but depicts the sacred stories in a thoroughly modern manner.

Modeling his work on the famous altarpieces created by artists such as Jan van Eyck, Emil Nolde fashioned his own personal statement of faith with a collection of nine paintings referred to jointly as *The Life of Christ*. This altarpiece includes eight scenes of the life of Jesus—depicting His birth, preaching, betrayal, and resurrection—arranged around a larger central image of the crucifixion. One of his unmistakable influences was clearly the famous *Isenheim Altarpiece* by Mattais Gruenwald, which Nolde's central painting so stirringly echoes.

Like Gruenwald, Nolde created a harrowing depiction of the horrors of what Christ experienced in His sacrifice for the world. Using exaggerated forms and jarring colors, he captured the unsettling reality of the crucifixion rather than painting it with the calm, serene detachment seen in many religious paintings of the event. The faces of the guards and onlookers are distorted

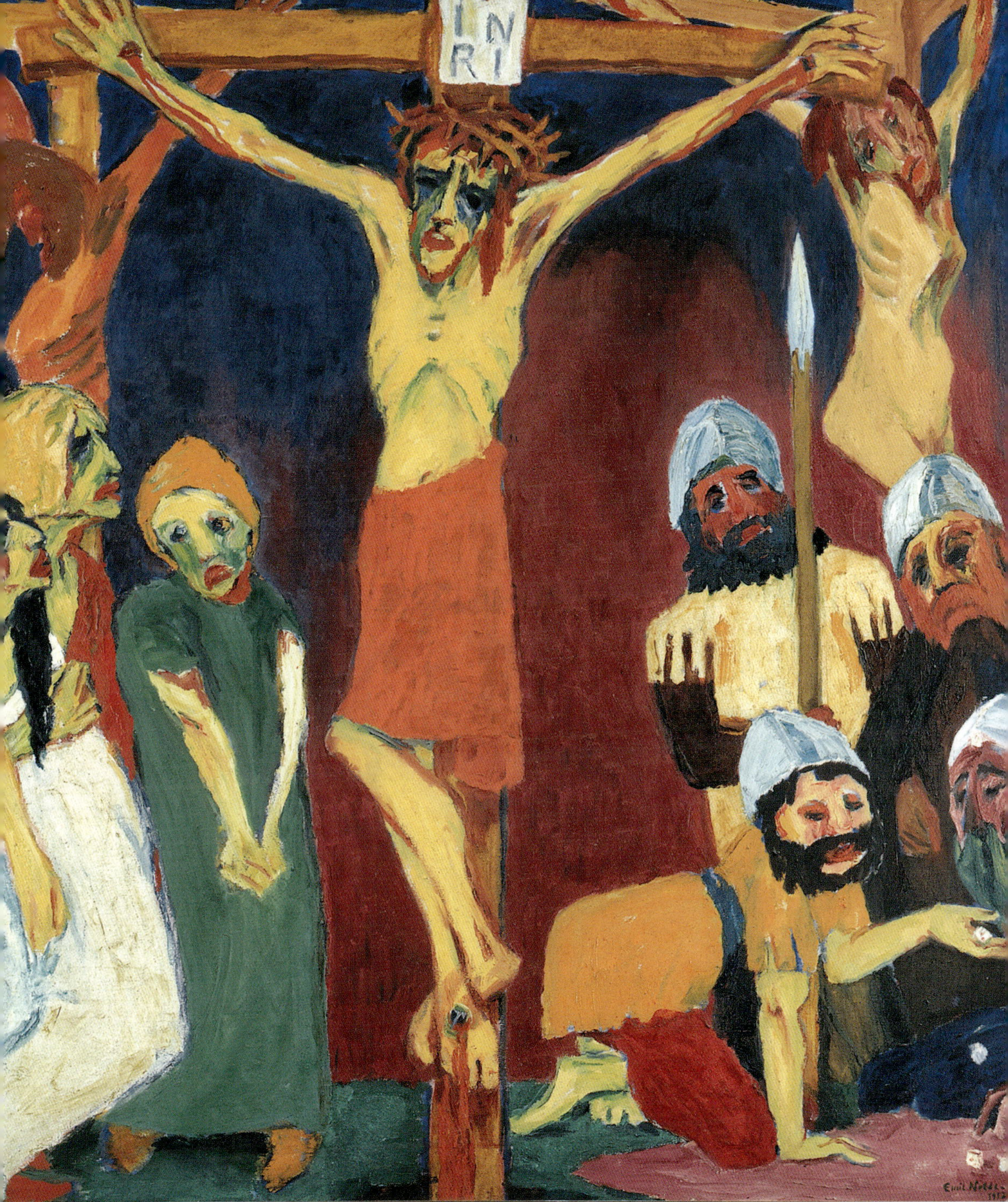

Bridgeman Images

he Life of Christ (center panel) by Emil Nolde,
e Nolde Foundation, Seebüll

and Jesus' body is twisted in pain; His eyes reflect agony and suffering. In keeping with medieval convention, Jesus is larger than any of the other figures in the work, signifying His sacrifice as the central message of the work. Nolde spoke of his goal as "the transformation from optical external charm to an experienced inner value."[1] He wanted the viewer to feel the import of the spiritual realities he was depicting.

Nolde's altarpiece was first conceived when he happened to place three of his already-painted religious works next to one another in his studio and noticed how well they worked together as a unit. So, in 1912, he painted the remaining six paintings and positioned them together to form the finished work. Painted during a time of great stress in his life—he was dealing with his wife's serious illness and grappling with uncertainties about his art and his faith—*The Life of Christ* was a testament to his convictions and a source of strength. He always considered it his greatest artistic achievement, and described it as "drunken with religious feelings and spirituality."[2]

Born Emil Hansen in northern Germany in 1867, near the Danish border, he took on the name of the small village where he was raised—Nolde—when his career began to flourish. Even as a child he loved to draw, sometimes making "paint" from the beets that were grown in the garden when there was no paint to be had. And when the young artist couldn't find paper for his drawings, he would use chalk to cover the barn door with his artistic creations.

Nolde's father and mother were churchgoing Protestants, and as a young boy he took delight in reading the Bible. As an adult he would bring its stories alive in vivid ways. After a series of less-than-satisfying occupations, he found a position as an art teacher, supplementing this income with his own drawings. One of his projects was a series of humorous postcards of famous Swiss mountains that were accented by anthropomorphized faces of a race of mythical giants. These proved so popular—selling one hundred thousand copies in a matter of days—that they brought him immediate notoriety for his talent as well as some financial freedom. Had he chosen to, he could likely have earned a lifelong income from such work.

But around 1900, Nolde began to forge his own individual style, which was more vigorous in its application of paint as well as vivid in its coloration. It was wilder, freer, more instinctive, and more untamed. Often these paintings were more about the violent clash of colors than about representing any object, which is why a contemporary described his paintings as "tempests of color." Considerations of creating spatial illusion or accurate representation were not foremost in his mind; what he really cared about doing was using color to inspire an emotional response. Though he resisted the label, today Nolde is considered one of the key artists of German Expressionism, a movement of artists who were interested in the emotional realities that lurk behind the surface appearance of things. They were more concerned with capturing meanings and feelings than in literal representation, which is why this form of artistic communication was so appealing to the mystically minded Nolde.

Nolde was never afraid to experiment. One day he left some watercolors outside to dry overnight, and in the morning he found that ice crystals had formed on them and then melted, creating unusual streaks and starlike effects. He was so pleased with this happy accident that he sometimes used a wet brush and highly absorbent Japanese paper to achieve similar effects. He enjoyed blurring the forms and colors in his work, though he never moved in the direction of total abstraction, an artistic trend of which he did not approve.

In 1913, Nolde traveled as a kind of ambassador to the German territories in the South Pacific. There he saw firsthand the innocence of the native peoples and the damage that was being done by colonialism. "We live in an evil era," he wrote, "in which the white man brings the whole earth into servitude."[3] Yet despite his views on colonial exploitation, he remained essentially conservative and nationalistic. In fact, after the First World War, he welcomed many aspects of the growing National Socialist movement in Germany and hoped that he would be seen as an artist who could represent his nation. Nolde also thought his work would be applauded by the new government after the Nazis came into power, and that they would resonate with his fierce nationalism. But Hitler was an artistic conservative who thought modern art was repulsive and degenerate, so Nolde's hopes were thwarted when the Nazis gave his work a prominent place in the "Degenerate Art" exhibition in Munich. Nolde's paintings were treated by the Nazi art critics as prime examples of art that signaled the decline of Western culture into barbarism, so his paintings were removed from museums throughout Germany and placed in storage. He was even forbidden to practice as an artist.

Undaunted, Nolde continued to paint despite the prohibition, though secretly and largely for his own enjoyment. During this time he undertook an extensive series of small watercolors he could easily keep hidden away, which he dubbed his "unpainted pictures." After the Second World War his fortunes began to improve again, and by the time of his death he was seen as the Grand Old Man of modern German art.

None of Nolde's religious paintings represent an official commission for church display. He painted them because he cared about expressing his beliefs. "The imaginings of the boy I once was, who sat engrossed in the Bible on long winter evenings, were reawakened. When I read, I saw pictures: the richest Middle Eastern fantasies. They constantly flew around in my mind's eye until much, much later the grown man and artist painted and painted them, as if inspired by a dream."[4]

These biblical paintings were thoroughly modern in their style and in their use of color but traditional in the messages they delivered. He considered them his most important work but found them more difficult to create than his other works. The struggle came because he desperately wanted to get "inside" the stories, to paint the inner emotions they evoked.

In *The Last Supper* (1909), Jesus' face and robe seem to glow, highlighting Him as the focus of the work through the use of light and color. With *Christ Among the Children* (1910), as in so many of his paintings, he made no attempt to hide the marks of the painter at work. The apostles are rendered in weighty, heavy brushstrokes, while the children are painted with lighter strokes and a lighter touch. It is sweet in tone but not maudlin as many pictures of this subject have often been. *Dance Around the Golden Calf* (1910) pictures the scene from Exodus where the children of Israel, in the absence of Moses, have given themselves to idolatry and immorality. Here we see evidence of the ecstatic joy that Nolde took in bright colors, as a barely repressed sensuality and passion burst forth in the tense, frenetic wildness of the figures.

There is a gentler touch to two of his later biblical paintings. *Christ and the Adulteress* (1926) portrays the tenderness of Jesus as He looks with love and forgiveness upon the woman whom He has just rescued from stoning. He cradles the reclining woman in His arms as her judges look on in disapproval, the work a painted meditation on God's grace toward imperfect humanity. *The Great Gardener* (1940) finds God the Father looking down upon His creation as a kindly caretaker, breathing life into the tender foliage that His hand reaches out to touch. The greens and blues are jewel-like, almost as transparent as a stained glass window.

Emil Nolde identified especially with the sufferings of Christ, a mystical connection that he drew upon during the difficult patches in his own life. A visionary and a loner, Nolde had a singular vision that he expressed through wild orgies of violent color as he represented the stories that had nurtured his faith. He did not set out to become a religious painter, but as he painted what interested him, biblical themes came to the fore. "I followed an irresistible desire to represent profound spirituality, religion, and tenderness, without much intention, knowledge, or deliberation."[5] The resulting art shows the power of his intuitions.

45

Poems

Gerard Manley Hopkins

(poems, 1918)

Who would ever have guessed that a quiet, bookish priest who never saw his poems published during his lifetime would be lauded today as one of the great innovators in the history of poetry? At his death in 1889, Gerard Manley Hopkins left behind a collection of poems that celebrate the glory of God in nature, ponder the darkness and confusion of life, and wrestle with his relationship to God. These faith-filled poems were so ahead of their time, their meter so odd and eccentric, that it took many years before his accomplishments were fully appreciated and embraced.

On first reading, many of Hopkins's poems might strike the reader as obscure and obtuse, just a little too erudite for their own good. But when revisited, they reveal profound and universal spiritual insights communicated in a unique off-kilter style, which necessitate a bit of patience and contemplation for their fullness to be grasped. Hopkins unfailingly finds fresh and startling ways of expressing himself as, for example, in this hyphen-laden description of Jesus from one of his poems: "The heaven-flung, heart-fleshed, maiden-furled / Miracle-in-Mary-of-flame, / Mid-numbered He in three of the thunder-throne!"[1] Each rhythmic phrase reveals an important truth about Jesus, as they gather and rise in a Trinitarian crescendo of praise.

Hopkins's poems need to be read aloud to be fully appreciated, for he wrote with his ear, concerned with the way the words rhyme and chime in their breathless building upon each other, and using hyphens to join neighboring thoughts together. Syntax is ruptured, words are inverted and invented, and distinct patterns of sound are created. He called his rhythmic patterns "sprung rhythm."

Hopkins's theological conviction that each and every thing has its own particular qualities that make it unique led him to his conception of "inscape." To understand the "inscape" of an object is to understand the purposes for which God created that particular object, to see the grandeur and splendor within it. So, in many of his poems, he sought to disclose the inscape he perceived in the created world. In "Pied Beauty," for example, he writes with ecstatic joy and urgency:

> Glory be to God for dappled
>   things—
> For skies of couple-colour as a
>   brinded cow;
> For rose-moles all in stipple
>   upon trout that swim;
> Fresh-firecoal chestnut-falls;
>   finches' wings;
> Landscape plotted and pieced—
>   fold, fallow, and plough;
> And all trades, their gear and
>   tackle and trim.
> All things counter, original,
>   spare, strange;
> Whatever is fickle, freckled (who
>   knows how?)
> With swift, slow; sweet, sour;
>   adazzle, dim;
> He fathers-forth whose beauty is
>   past change:
> Praise him.[2]

Gerard Manley Hopkins was born in England in 1844 into an Anglican family that valued music, poetry, and painting. His father was an amateur poet, and Hopkins wrote his first poem at age ten. An excellent student, he won a scholarship to Oxford, where he distinguished himself as an outstanding scholar in the classics. At age twenty-one he underwent a moral and spiritual crisis from which he emerged as a confirmed Catholic, received into the church by the famous theologian John Henry Newman. Two years later he decided to join the Jesuit order, and in a fit of pious self-denial burned all of the poetry he had written up until that point. (He later referred to this impulsive act as "the slaughter of the innocents.") At this point in time he believed that writing poetry would be a distraction from his spiritual focus, and so he determined that he would not write any more poetry unless requested to do so by his superiors in the Jesuit order.

For the next seven years Hopkins did not compose a single poem, surely a painful sacrifice for one who so loved words. Then a tragedy that made news all over the world provided an unexpected opportunity. An ocean liner carrying a group of nuns fleeing religious persecution went down in a storm, and all aboard drowned. The rector of the college where Hopkins was studying asked him to write something about the tragic incident, and the result was a long poem called "The Wreck of the Deutschland." The verse that came spilling out from him perhaps shows the effect of bottling up his talent for so long. The poem was as turbulent as the event he was commemorating—a passionate meditation on the mystery of God's ways, written in a rhythmic style that plunges forward with an unexpected meter that ignores standard grammatical rules while revealing his intense emotional reaction to the event. With this poem, Hopkins had found a poetic voice that was uniquely his own. When submitted for publication it was accepted, though never published. But now that the poetic door had been reopened, he began to compose verse again, and would for the remainder of his life.

After his ordination in 1877, Hopkins served in pastoral and teaching positions for the remainder of his short life in London, Liverpool, Glasgow, Oxford, Lancashire, and finally Dublin. He was never much of a success either as a priest or as a teacher, as his style of communication was too erudite and elliptical for popular consumption, but he was loved and admired for his gentle spirit, his humor, and his holiness. Throughout these assignments, he struggled with persistent health issues and was prone to periods of deep depression, so he used his poems as a way to explore his own spiritual and emotional battles. These poems have been labeled as his "Terrible Sonnets," filled as they are with questions, fears, and an awareness of his own fragility and failure.

When he was assigned to move to Dublin and teach classics, Hopkins again wrestled with the feeling that he was a failure and that no one really understood him. His health was in a fragile state, and the cold, damp climate took its toll; when he contracted typhoid fever it made short work of him. As he lay on his deathbed, though, after receiving the sacraments, he spoke his last words as a final testimony to his life, murmuring, "I am happy, so happy." It was not until twenty-nine years after his death that his poems finally saw the light of day when they were prepared for publication in 1918 by his friend and fellow poet Robert Bridges in a volume titled simply *Poems by Gerard Manley Hopkins*.

Hopkins saw the sacred presence all about him, and in many of his poems he celebrated the ways that nature itself gushed about God's glory. In his poem "God's Grandeur," he wrote of a world that remains fresh and infused with the Spirit, despite its neglect and abuse by generations of human beings:

> The world is charged with the
>   grandeur of God.
> It will flame out, like shining
>   from shook foil;

It gathers to a greatness, like the
    ooze of oil
Crushed. Why do men then now
    not reck his rod?
Generations have trod, have
    trod, have trod;
And all is seared with trade;
    bleared, smeared with toil;
And wears man's smudge and
    shares man's smell; the soil
Is bare now, nor can foot feel,
    being shod.
And for all this nature is never
    spent;
There lives the dearest freshness
    deep down things;
And though the last lights off
    the black West went
Oh, morning, at the brown brink
    eastward, springs—
Because the Holy Ghost over the
    bent world broods
With warm breast and ah! bright
    wings.[3]

In other poems, however, it is his honesty about the seeming absence of God that fuels the verse, especially in his later "Terrible Sonnets." When, in fits of discouragement and depression, Hopkins could not sense God's presence, he explored the terror of being left to his own devices and ached over his failures—including the fact that his poetry largely went unread. "All my undertakings miscarry," he wrote in his journal.[4] In such a state he felt the strong temptation toward despair, but would not ultimately surrender to it, declaring in one poem, "Not, I'll not, carrion comfort, / Despair, not feast on thee."[5] But sometimes, feeling alone and abandoned, and smarting from the perception he had been neglected by God, he wrote poems that reflected the intense lover's quarrel he had with the Lord. Such wrestling brought great pain—agony—but it also earned a hard-won comfort that God loved him enough to purge him of his sin and make him new.

Gerard Manley Hopkins wrote his poems for a small audience—himself and his God. He could never have imagined that he would be so widely read, or that his poetic innovations would influence so many later poets. In his own eyes, he was a failure—as a priest, as a teacher, as a poet, even as a human being. But perhaps he would have agreed that it doesn't really matter how one appears in one's own eyes but only how one appears in the eyes of God. Though we might lose faith in Him, He does not lose faith in us. He will not leave us alone in the deadness of our sin, for as Hopkins reminds us, God is always ready to "easter in us."[6]

46

The Resurrection at Cookham

Stanley Spencer

(painting, 1926)

The Resurrection at Cookham imagines the Day of Judgment occurring not in a biblical Middle Eastern setting but in the churchyard of Holy Trinity Church, a small Methodist chapel in the small English village of Cookham. It is not surprising that Stanley Spencer decided to situate his depiction of the great resurrection of the dead in this humble churchyard, for it was in Cookham that he had first experienced a revelation of the interconnectedness of the physical and the spiritual. Spencer once wrote of the sudden awakening that came over him one day when he perceived that even the most mundane and ordinary objects reflected a divine radiance:

> Quite suddenly I became aware that everything was full of special meaning, and this made everything holy. The instinct of Moses to take his shoes off when he saw the burning bush was very similar to my feelings. I saw many burning bushes in Cookham. I observed the sacred quality in the most unexpected quarters.[1]

The Resurrection at Cookham is a large painting—nine feet high and eighteen feet wide—and it is peopled not only with the Father and the Son but also with friends and family, the people he knew and loved. His first wife, Hilda, is the model for no less than three different figures. Numerous other friends also served as models. There is a flurry of activity as the dead rise out of their graves, but the tone of the picture remains serene. Some lounge about on top of the caskets they have just exited, some struggle out of their coffins or lift up the flowering sod to exit their earthen graves, and some intently study the writing on the tombstones in the churchyard. A group of "prophets"—Moses among them—stands along the wall of the church, rapt in thought, and Spencer painted himself in the bottom right corner, lying on two slabs of a broken tomb as though he is reclining in the pages of a great stone book. "Nobody is in a hurry in this painting," said Spencer of this work. "Those men lying on top of the tombs I like very much, they gave me the feeling that the Resurrection is a peaceful occasion, and very positive. I like the happiness, that's the main idea of the picture."[2] This is not a somber "Last Judgment" picture where the good and bad are being separated but an optimistic celebration of everlasting life. Christ sits under the church porch, surrounded by overhanging roses, holding three babies in His arms. The Father stands behind Him, affectionately tousling His hair.

The local churchyard has become a new garden of Eden, echoing the images of Renaissance painters who imagined heaven as the garden reborn. There are flowers in great abundance, painted with exacting detail and vivid colors. Heaven has come down to Cookham as the bodies rise up, and in a sense Cookham itself has become what Spencer called "a holy suburb of heaven."[3]

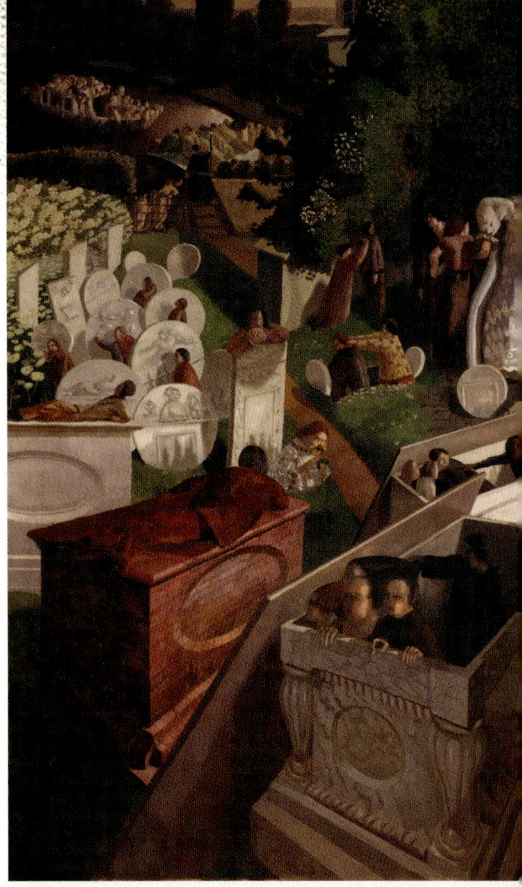

Stanley Spencer was born in 1891 in Cookham, England, where he lived most of his life, and which held a tender place of importance in his memory as well as in his understanding of the world. He grew up in a family who took their faith seriously and whose daily routine included Bible readings by his father. As an adult, he fused his love of the Bible with the simple pleasure he took in ordinary things to

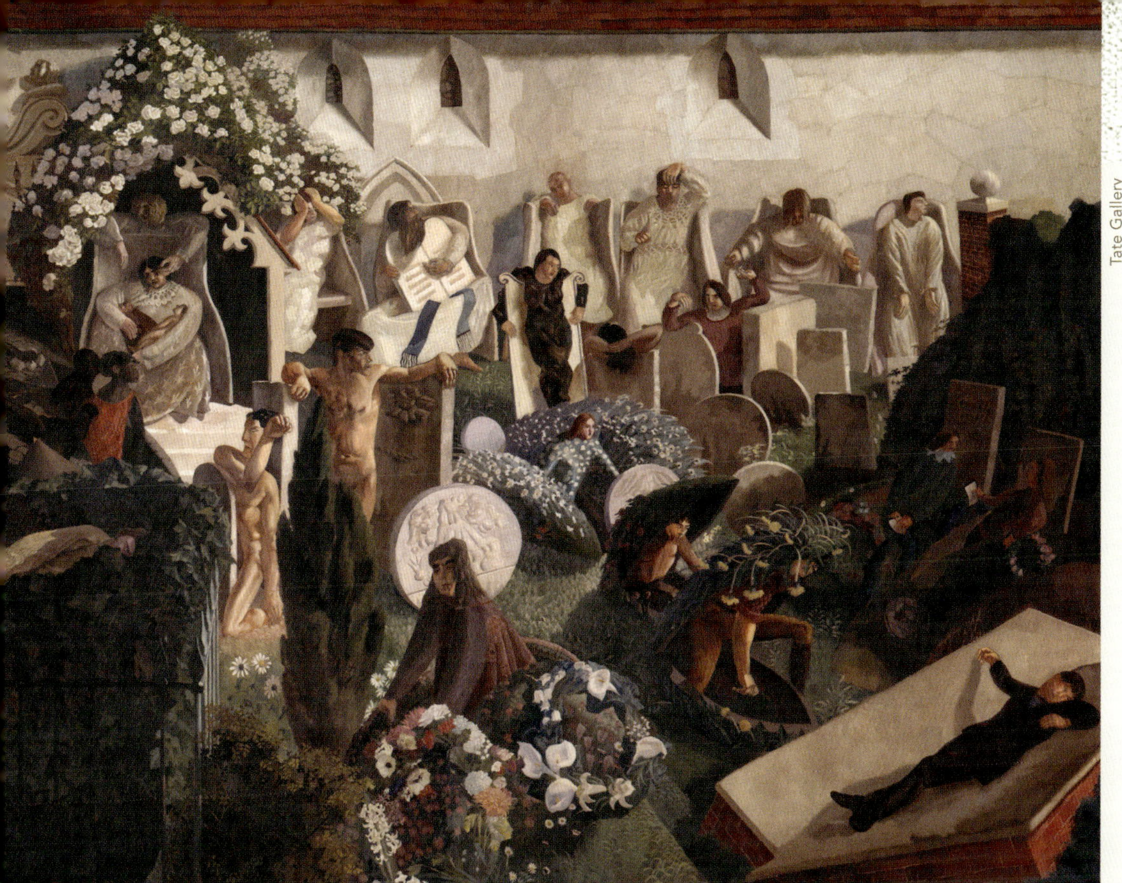

Tate Gallery

The Resurrection at Cookham by Stanley Spencer, Tate Gallery, London

create a unique artistic vision. He sought "the rich religious significance of the place I live in,"[4] and his paintings became his primary way of expressing his sense of the holy ordinary.

A string of early masterworks follow the same format as *The Resurrection at Cookham*—canvases crowded with figures that reenvision stories from the life of Christ as though they took place in his beloved English hometown. *Nativity* (1912) imagines the birth of Christ taking place in a Cookham garden. In *Christ Carrying the Cross* (1920), we are witnesses to a solemn procession toward the crucifixion as it moves through the winding lanes of Cookham. Onlookers peer down from their windows above, and the blowing lace curtains appear almost like angel's wings. An ordinary fence-lined street in Cookham becomes the setting for *Christ's Entry into Jerusalem* (1921), and in *The Betrayal* (1922–1923), Judas's treachery has been relocated to a dark back alley of Spencer's hometown. This relocation of these events invests a sacredness into the environs of his beloved village, and adds a homey familiarity to the biblical stories.

Spencer's most characteristic paintings look as though a pre-Renaissance master such as Giotto or Fra Angelico had consorted with the Cubists. These canvases are usually overcrowded, with lots of action, almost as if the figures can barely be contained within the picture frame; there is little attention given to creating a sense of depth in the paintings, with everything occurring on a pretty shallow and singular plane; and the figures are almost always somewhat distorted. In keeping with his belief that the sacred is best glimpsed through the ordinary, Spencer also embraced the ugliness and ungainliness of the world, using his brush to transfigure objects and illuminate their unnoticed inner beauties. He sought to capture the cozy and homey aspects of normal life and elevate them to a state where they become revelatory about the deepest things.

Spencer always felt a close emotional connection between sexuality and spirituality. He married Hilda Carline in 1925, but over time their differences led to a cooling of affections. In the early 1930s, Spencer became obsessed with a woman named Patricia Preese, to whom he was sexually attracted. She was the subject of several scandalous nudes he painted, often including himself in the pictures. They were honest and unflattering, sagging with all the heaviness of flesh. In them Patricia often has a faraway and uninterested look in her eyes, but that did not keep her from becoming his second wife when Hilda refused to accept the situation of Spencer trying to maintain two love affairs. From what we know it seems unlikely that this second marriage was ever consummated, as Patricia returned to her lesbian lover soon after managing to get ownership of the Spencer home transferred to her name. Spencer was devastated.

In 1939, at the height of his personal problems and a low point in his popularity as an artist, Spencer retreated into a period of relative seclusion. During this time, when he felt like he was undergoing a wilderness experience himself, he turned his efforts to a series of paintings he called *Christ in the Wilderness*. Originally envisioned as forty separate paintings representing the forty days that Christ was tempted in the wilderness, only eight were finished. The period during which he created them was a period of great spiritual renewal for him, a chance to contemplate his own mistakes and the temptations to which he had succumbed. Despite the emotional pain he was experiencing, he found some peace in this time. "I felt there was something wonderful in the life I was living. I loved it all because it was God and me all the time."[5]

The resulting paintings are unlike most of his other work: straightforward, uncluttered compositions that put Jesus at the center of each canvas. Since the Bible only records what happened on the final day of Jesus' wilderness experience, Spencer has imagined the life He might have lived during the other thirty-nine days.

In one, He rises from sleep and kneels with His arms stretched upward, offering Himself to the Father. In another, He gazes fixedly on a dangerous scorpion that crawls about in the palm of His hand. In *Consider the Lilies,* we see Him crouching upon His hands and knees, face down among the flowers, and seeming to drink in the pleasure of their loveliness. Another in the series has Him resting on His side, tenderly watching over a mother hen and her chicks, His body curled protectively around them. Each of these paintings has a Scripture verse attached to it, and Spencer seems to be playfully suggesting that some of the images and illustrations Jesus used in His parables and teachings might have arisen from experiences He had while alone in the desert. As Spencer worked in solitude on these paintings, they were a reflection of the effort he was making to reconstruct his own life.

Toward the very end of his life, Spencer again focused on the biblical themes that had energized his earlier paintings. In a picture filled with much celebration and jollity, Spencer reimagines the passage in Mark 4, where Jesus is preaching to the swelling crowds from a boat, as an event that is taking place at the local boat races (*Christ Preaching at Cookham Regatta,* 1959). For his last major work, Spencer was commissioned to paint a crucifixion for the chapel of a school, but it stirred up controversy because the disturbing violence of the act was being perpetrated by men wearing the distinctive caps of the very brewers' company who had funded the piece. In this final painting we do not witness the peace and celebration of the resurrection, but the horror of the cross, and the wild, evil glint in the eyes of Christ's persecutors. As Spencer tried to explain to his offended patrons, "you are still nailing Christ to the cross."[6]

Throughout the course of his artistic life, Stanley Spencer used ordinary places as the backdrop for extraordinary events—as the "doorstep" upon which is revealed the spiritual significance that can be glimpsed in everyday life. He saw his work of painting as an act of redemption, of recapturing the significance of all things. His life-affirming paintings seem to tell us that the sacred events of the Bible are not just in the past, but are still taking place in ordinary little villages like Cookham, or in yours or mine.

47

Death Comes for the Archbishop

WILLA CATHER

(novel, 1927)

This book, surely a candidate for the best American Catholic novel of modern times, was, interestingly, not written by a Catholic. Although the character and themes are rooted in Catholicism, Willa Cather was herself an Episcopalian, but she evoked the ethos of Catholicism so well in *Death Comes for the Archbishop* that she received countless letters from Catholics who congratulated her that one of their own had produced such a powerful novel. Clearly her respect for Catholicism, and what it represented, helped to make this novel so utterly convincing and so spiritually uplifting.

The impetus for writing this book came from Cather's fascination with the Southwestern region of the United States, where she had frequently spent time.

> "The more I visited in the Southwest," she wrote in an essay about the novel, "the more I felt that the story of the Catholic Church in that country was the most interesting of its stories. The old mission churches, even those which were abandoned and in ruins, had a moving reality about them; the hand-carved beams and joists, the utterly unconventional frescoes, the countless fanciful figures of the saints, not two of them alike, seemed a deeper expression of some very real and lively human feeling."[1]

Cather felt a particular affection for the bronze statue of Archbishop Lamy that stood in front of the cathedral in Santa Fe, and he became for her "a sort of invisible personal friend" in her travels around the Southwest. When she discovered a book about early missions in this region that contained Lamy's letters and those of other missionary priests, she realized that this was a story she wanted to tell—and make come alive.

Death Comes for the Archbishop, like the landscape described in its pages, has a sparse, elegant simplicity. Its pace is languid; the story will not be rushed but rather unfolds quietly in the deserts of New Mexico as it records the life of Father Jean Marie Latour, who comes to these barren lands—a vast territory of red hills, towering mesas, and forbidding heat—to take his place as a missionary to the Mexicans and Native Americans who dwell there. Over a period of forty years, Latour spreads his faith with an inward passion and an outward gentleness, dealing with the harsh conditions, the spiritual confusions of his vast flock, openly rebellious and immoral priests, and his nagging loneliness and longing for his home in Ohio.

Throughout the novel, Cather evokes the strange magnificence and wonder of the Southwest landscape with such precision that the reader can feel the oppressive sun beating down upon the long and dusty roads the archbishop must travel to minister to his widespread flock, yet still revel in the mystery and timelessness of the desolate landscape. Cather, and her archbishop, show great respect for the Native Americans who live on this land and the spiritual relationship they have with it. Though this is not a novel primarily concerned with the ethics of colonialism, the archbishop is aware of the injustices that have been perpetrated upon these people. Near the end of the book he says, "I have lived to see two great wrongs righted; I have seen the end of black slavery, and I have seen the Navajos restored to their land."[2]

Latour is a saintly figure yet believably human; a good man doing his best in difficult circumstances: "His manners, even when he was alone in the desert, were distinguished. He had a kind of courtesy toward himself, toward his beasts, toward the juniper tree before which he knelt, and the God who he was addressing."[3] The novel is, as much as anything, a testament to a life well lived by a man of deep faith and even deeper modesty. As it winds to its close we understand what it means to live a good life: believing deeply, acting with integrity and simple courage, and holding on to the grace of God. As the archbishop says when death finally comes, "I shall not die of a cold, my son. I shall die of having lived."[4]

Willa Cather was born in Virginia in 1873, but her family moved to south central Nebraska when she was very young. The nearly treeless, windswept Great Plains in which they settled was largely populated by immigrants from Europe, whom she would later use as the models for the characters in many of her stories. As she later suggested, "Most of the basic material a writer works with is acquired before the age of fifteen." This is particularly true for Cather, who so often drew upon her past to tell stories that in many ways closely resembled her own. She was also insistent that being a woman would not hold her back from her dreams, saying, "The fact that I was a girl never damaged my ambitions to be a pope or an emperor."[5] By the time she entered college, though, she had already determined that she didn't want to be a pope or an emperor; she wanted to be a writer.

Although she had a very successful stint for several years as an editor for the prestigious *McClure's* magazine, she took the great risk of leaving that position so that she might give her full attention to writing fiction. The novels and short stories she produced afterward were that rare example of books equally embraced by the literary elites and the general reading public. Most were critically acclaimed, many were bestsellers, and *One of Ours* was even awarded a Pulitzer Prize.

Cather's style is distinctive—a quietude and stillness in tone, along with an ability to craft achingly beautiful descriptions of landscape and convincing interior monologues. The stillness the reader finds in her stories, though, is not the stillness of inertia but of a contemplative, nostalgic, and unhurried approach to life and storytelling. Even when the most disturbing or painful things occur in the lives of her characters she does not ratchet up the drama but describes them with serene and measured prose, as though writing from a perspective far above the turmoil of human existence. However, this isn't to say that the stories are without emotion. They are deeply moving and resonant, made more impactful due to the absence of affect.

Cather was raised in a Baptist family, but in her adolescence she became increasingly dissatisfied with an evangelical approach to faith. A deeply private person with quiet convictions and an intense need for solitude, she wrestled with how to integrate faith into her life and art. Though she rarely wrote of her own spiritual convictions, they can perhaps be best glimpsed in her novels and short stories. There are religious themes at work in her early novel *O Pioneers!* (1913), and in *One of Ours* (1922) she records a crisis of faith that may have paralleled her own, as she was confirmed into the Episcopal church in 1922, just after its publication. In *The Professor's House* (1925) and *My Mortal Enemy* (1926), Cather portrays the despair and emptiness of characters who have abandoned faith in the pursuit of other, ultimately less satisfying goals.

These books reflect her growing conservatism, as she became increasingly disenchanted with the trends of modern life and longed for a richer and simpler time—a time that she evoked so well in her books. *Death Comes for the Archbishop* (1927) and *Shadows on the Rock* (1931) are two late novels that are both explicitly religious in theme—historical fiction featuring Catholic characters. Perhaps her evident empathy for Catholicism, while not embracing all its dogmatic tenets, comes from her respect for the Catholic Church as an institution—one that has long stood against the streams of modernity that would seek to sweep away faith and tradition and the other things she held important.

The importance of art was always a central focus for Cather, and she saw a close connection between the way art and faith each move the human soul. As she wrote, "Religion and art spring from the same root and are close kin."[6] Cather was never one to preach about her faith, but she understood its power to transform the human heart and, like great art, to help readers to see their lives differently, and to sense the divine hand that is quietly at work. In a memorable passage from *Death Comes for the Archbishop*, she records this meditation from Father Latour on what really constitutes the miraculous in life:

> "Where there is great love there are always miracles," he said at length. "One might almost say that an apparition is human vision corrected by divine love. I do not see you as you really are, Joseph; I see through my affection for you. The Miracles of the Church seem to me to rest not so much upon faces or voices or healing power coming suddenly near to us from afar off, but upon our perceptions being made finer, so that for a moment our eyes can see and our ears can hear what is there about us always."[7]

Willa Cather would certainly never have identified herself as a "Christian novelist," but she was a Christian who was a novelist, creating art that reflected her beliefs and convictions about life with great subtlety and grace. She steered clear of pious moralizing in her novels, believing that it was off-putting to readers and kept them from appreciating the truth. "Those who make good unattractive," she wrote, "do more harm than those who strive to make evil attractive."[8] Instead, she celebrated the good that could be seen in human life, even as she recoiled at many of the changes that were occurring in mid-twentieth-century American culture. She longed to return to a time of peace and simplicity, and her novels and short stories take us, unforgettably, to just such places and such times.

48

The Passion of Joan of Arc

Carl Theodore Dreyer

(film, 1928)

For many contemporary viewers, silent films are an art form they cannot imagine actually enjoying. In the popular mind, silent films are a repository for overly dramatic gesturing, slapstick pratfalls, and jittery, poorly lit camerawork. While these characteristics might accurately describe some of what was produced in the early years of film, they are not true for the great artistic masterpieces of the era. The finest silent films are triumphs of visual creativity and storytelling, and are as relevant for the contemporary viewer as when they were first made. One such film is Carl Theodore Dreyer's *The Passion of Joan of Arc*, one of the first films to fully explore the possibilities of movies as a serious art form.

The Christian church has always shown a great interest in martyrs, and the early history of the faith is punctuated by the stories of those who gave their life for what they believed. By the Middle Ages, a new kind of martyr began to emerge—one who was persecuted not by unbelievers but by church authorities in response to perceived theological heresies. Joan of Arc, burnt at the stake in 1431, was such a woman. *The Passion of Joan of Arc*, based on careful research of original court documents, chronicles the intense struggle between those Dreyer called "the blind theologians and schooled jurists" and this simple woman of deep faith. Throughout the film, there are many parallels drawn between her own ordeal and that of Christ—she is

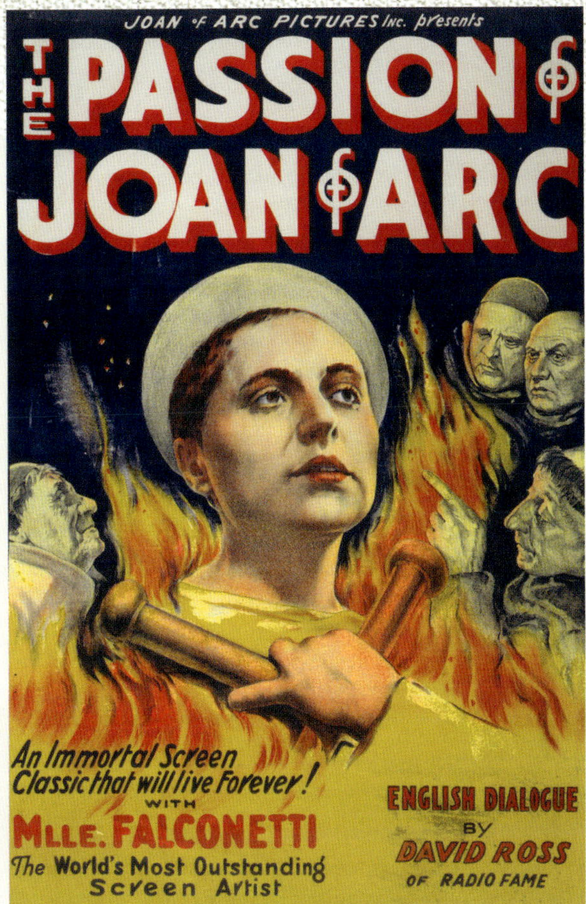

WikiCommons

Poster for *The Passion of Joan of Arc*

mocked and jeered, a "crown" made of rope is placed upon her head, and her hair is sheared like a lamb prepared for the slaughter. When the judges finally force an admission of guilt out of her, it doesn't take, as she recants her confession and willingly goes to her death. Her body, tied to the stake, is consumed by the flames of a roaring fire, but her spirit and soul rise with the smoke, finally set free.

One thing that sets this film apart from its contemporaries is the visual power of its design. Filmed on simple but evocative sets and consisting of carefully composed images, it is masterful in its creation of mood. Never before had a film so effectively exploited the emotional power of the extreme close-up. Dreyer pushed the camera deep into the personal space of his actors as he drew a contrast between the persecuted young woman and her angry, mocking persecutors. Because Dreyer did not allow the actors to wear makeup, we see every pore and imperfection in each face as the camera draws close enough to reveal the interior struggles of the characters, penetrating to the very depths of their souls.

We perceive the intense physical, psychological, and spiritual pain etched into Joan's face as actress Renee Falconetti delivers one of the greatest performances in the history of film. Her large, round, unblinking eyes fill with tears and her lips tremble. Though the only words are those flashed on the screen on the title cards, we clearly understand what she is experiencing: fear, shame, indignation, and finally resignation. Contemporary accounts tell us that when Falconetti wept for the camera, the eyes of the entire crew were filled with tears. Interestingly, this unforgettable feat of acting was both her first and last appearance in a film. But it was a performance that exhibited the possibilities of what film acting could be.

So inspiring and potent is this film that it was banned in occupied Europe during World War II. Nazi authorities feared the impact that this story of French heroism might have in inspiring the populace. Even today, *The Passion of Joan of Arc* is unequalled as a tale of heroic faith in the face of overwhelming odds.

Carl Theodore Dreyer was born in Copenhagen, Denmark, in 1889 to an unwed mother who gave her child up to an orphanage, from which he was adopted at age two. He was raised by his adoptive parents in a Lutheran home. As a young man he was a journalist for a time, and then got a job with Nordisk, the most important Nordic film studio of its day. Initially he was a scriptwriter, but then he began to edit films and eventually got his opportunity to direct. One of his early films was *Leaves from Satan's Book* (1919), the first of several films that dealt with religious and theological concerns. Although Dreyer spoke with great clarity about his style and philosophy of filmmaking, he said little of his personal convictions about faith. We are left to draw our conclusions from his films, which give evidence of a profound understanding of the nature of faith and belief, and which point to a spiritual world that intersects with and interpenetrates our own.

The Passion of Joan of Arc was his last film of the silent era. It was followed by the weird and nightmarish dreamscapes of *Vampyr* (1932), a supernatural thriller with an injection of spirituality. Then, as so often happened in his career, there was a long gap of time when he could not get funding to create another film, despite the fact that his earlier films were so widely esteemed. The wait was finally broken by *Day of Wrath* (1943), a powerful film about religious intolerance and persecution, a common theme in his movies.

In 1954, after another sizeable gap of time, he produced *Ordet* (*The Word*), an undisputed masterpiece and one of the most remarkable religious films ever made. *Ordet* is a portrait of the struggles of faith within a farm family and between two divergent sects of Christianity within their town. One of the family sons wants to marry a woman from another branch of Christendom, a sort of Romeo and Juliet scenario. Another son, Johannes, suffers from delusions that his family thinks have been caused by an excess of theological study. He has come to believe that he is an embodiment of Christ. It is unclear whether he is simply mad or some sort of holy fool—possibly he is both. Following the death of his brother's wife after a miscarriage, Johannes summons the faith of his young niece to pray for her to be resurrected by the power of Christ. The scene where the wife awakens from death and sits up in her coffin is surely one of the most remarkable scenes in all of film, a resurrection filmed in a realistic and understated manner—and all the more powerful for its subtlety. Just as believable is the newfound embrace of faith by her once-skeptical husband, who holds her in his arms as the screen goes dark.

Dreyer once referred to his filmmaking as "realized mysticism."[1] Though some critics have tried to downplay the spiritual content of his films and focus instead on their intense psychological power, it is clear that Dreyer took his faith seriously and portrayed it with dignity and respect. "I would dedicate a hymn to the soul's triumph over life,"[2] he once wrote. It is this very triumph of life over death that fuels so many of his best films. He sought to use his careful observations of reality in the service of spiritual themes, attempting to make the supernatural moments in his films completely believable. Such moments play out without fanfare in his films, as do the moments of great emotional upheaval. In real life great dramas are acted out quietly, so the quiet intensity of his explorations of human passion, together with his openness to spiritual realities that exist alongside physical ones, are what make his work so enduringly powerful.

An indispensable key to creating this kind of realism came in making every element of the film convincing. Dreyer was obsessive about every detail, always wanting to get everything just right. One of his cameramen tells the story of a delay in filming an outdoor scene caused by several days of inclement weather. The day the rain finally stopped, a studio executive visited the set to see if production was on schedule, and enquired of the cameraman if the filming was going smoothly now that there was finally a sunny day. "No," said the cameraman, "Dreyer won't film the scene because the clouds are moving in the wrong direction."

The end result of this emphasis on detail and realism is that the miraculous becomes believable in the context of his films. Dreyer was dead serious about making his audience take even the miraculous events seriously, hoping to make us question the tidy assumption that the only reality is the physical. In his films, the spiritual erupts in the quiet realism of the story, ever so gently but ever so intensely.

One of Dreyer's great dreams was to make a film biography of Jesus, and he got as far as creating a finished script, but he never found the funding to make it a reality. He even indicated that the resurrection scene in *Ordet* was a kind of trial run—an attempt to see if he could make such a miracle believable, knowing the resurrection would be the centerpiece for filming the life of Christ. How unfortunate for all who are moved by the work of this meticulous visionary that Dreyer never had the opportunity to fulfill this dream. Who better to have told Jesus' story in film than a director who had such a gift for making the spiritual visible?

49

Head of Christ

Georges Rouault

(painting, 1937)

Depictions of Christ's face have been attempted again and again throughout the history of art. Many a painter has fixed his or her vision of Jesus on canvas, and most of the resulting paintings have tended toward the saccharine or the sentimental. Although such works may have their decorative or devotional purposes, few can be considered great works of art. Rouault's *Head of Christ* is an exception. Its bright colors shine like panes of stained glass, luminous between the black outlines that separate them. It vibrates with tense energy but also radiates peace. The expression in the eyes of the Savior is particularly affecting. These are eyes that return the viewer's gaze and penetrate into the deep interior of the soul; eyes that speak of love, of gentle compassion, and of forgiveness offered. This face is not the chiseled face of a remote divinity condescending to visit the human realm but rather the face of the God who has entered into our world and experienced firsthand all the pain and agony of the human condition.

When we look at such a painting we are reminded of the prophet Isaiah's words:

> Surely he took up our pain
>   and bore our suffering,
> yet we considered him punished
>   by God,
>   stricken by him, and afflicted.
> But he was pierced for our
>   transgressions,

he was crushed for our
iniquities;
the punishment that brought us
peace was on him,
and by his wounds we are
healed. (Isa. 53:4–5)

Looking at this canvas, one feels understood by the One who looks back. Could anyone who hadn't personally experienced the love of the suffering Savior have painted such a work?

Rouault was one of the greatest painters of sacred subject matter in modern times. Along with religious subjects, Rouault also painted dark and unflattering paintings of prostitutes, melancholy images of circus performers, and searing depictions of human suffering and inhumanity. His paintings and prints cast an unflinching gaze into the depths of human degradation. He was not afraid to tell the truth about the pain of life, especially among the marginalized. But even in his darkest work there is a light of grace that penetrates his depiction of human sinfulness and its consequences. He painted a fallen humanity as well as the One who came to redeem it through His suffering. And his uniquely recognizable style weds relatively traditional subject matter with a thoroughly modern aesthetic.

Georges Rouault was born in France in 1871. As a young man, he served as an apprentice for a stained glass artist, which may account for the high value he placed upon craftsmanship and for his mature style, which stressed thick black outlines and rich, luminous colors. One of Rouault's early paintings, *The Child Christ Among the Doctors* (1894), won a prestigious national award and Rouault seemed set upon a path as a religious painter. However, his much-loved teacher, Gustave Moreau, encouraged his students to find their own individual style, and Rouault followed that advice, in spite of the fact that he could have probably made a very tidy living as a more traditional religious painter.

When Moreau died in 1898, it inaugurated a period of deep personal crisis and reexamination for Rouault, resulting in a strengthening of his faith. It also marked a radical shift away from a style that had already begun to garner positive attention in favor of a new style he called "offensive lyricism."

Interestingly, following the reinvigoration of his faith, Rouault largely left religious subject matter behind—at least for a time. Instead, he began to paint unflinching and unflattering works featuring prostitutes, circus performers, judges, and people of the street. These paintings of the darker and seedier side of French society were fired by his repulsion toward the false ideals of the selfish and spiritually smug bourgeoisie, as well as compassion for their victims on the bottom rungs of society. But his was not a primarily political critique so much as a spiritual one. He saw the suffering of

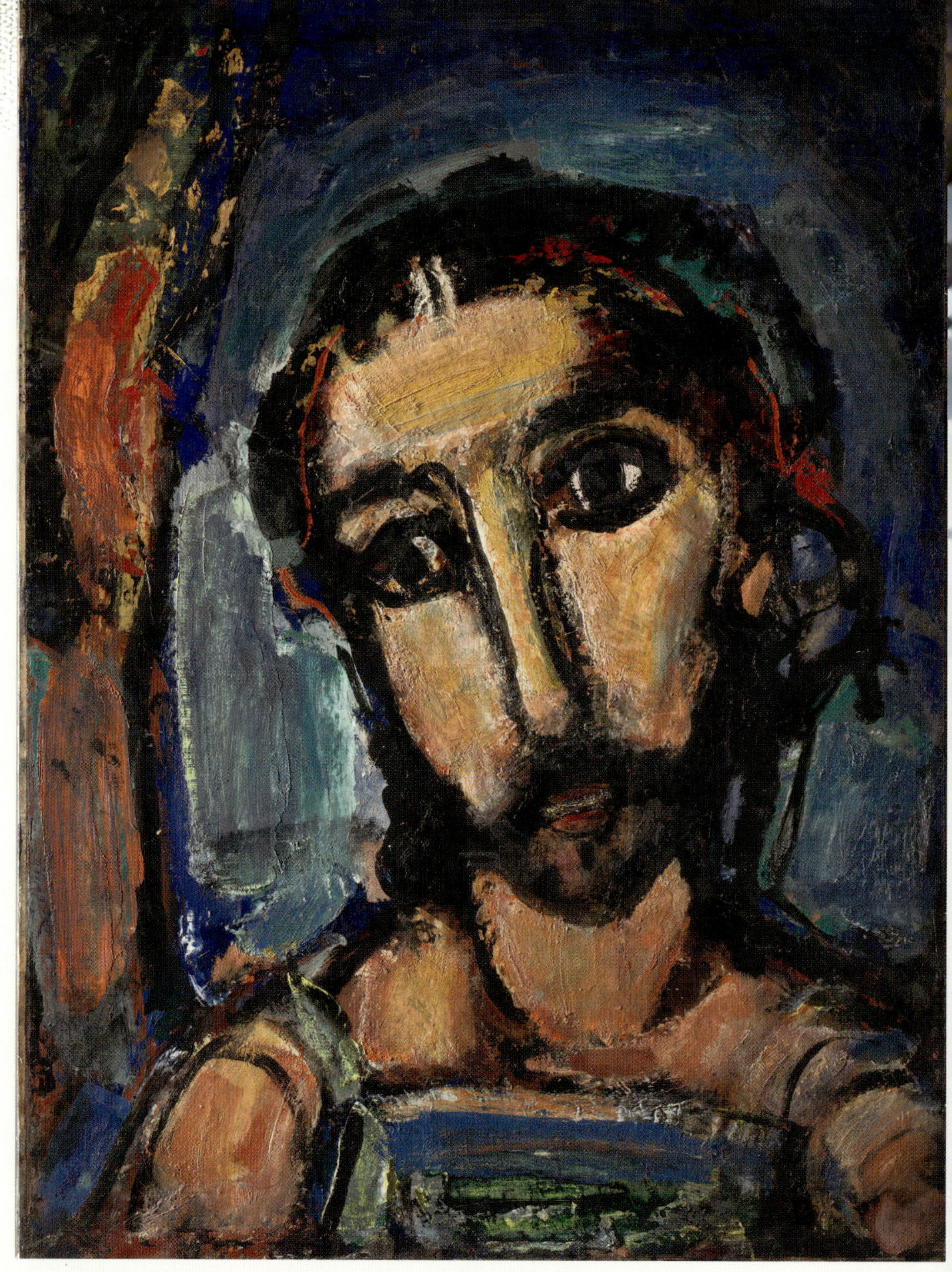

Head of Christ by Georges Rouault, Cleveland Museum of Art

Jesus in the suffering of the downtrodden. He wrote, "Behind the eyes of the most hostile, ungrateful, or impure being dwells Jesus."[1] Rouault did not look upon society's unfortunates with judgment, but with tears. About *The Injured Clown I* (1932), a painting of deep sadness and empathy, he wrote: "In my view it is quite possibly as religious as compositions with a biblical theme."[2] He saw his numerous portraits of circus clowns as a metaphor for human existence. These clowns are clearly suffering even when they appear to be laughing. Just like the clowns, Rouault seems to be saying, we all hide behind our own personal masks, but the greasepaint cannot obscure the truth about our pain.

Rouault's paintings and prints were not pretty in any conventional sense. Nor were they intended to be. He was trying to depict the truth about the human condition. His paintings had a wrenchingly painful effect upon those with the eyes to see them, but his apparently pessimistic vision of humanity did not lead him to hold the human race in disdain for its failures. Instead, his work is suffused with compassion and pity.

Rouault did not see utter hopelessness in the human condition, however, for he saw the suffering of Christ as the answer for human suffering. Between 1917 and 1927, he executed a series of engravings for a book that was published as *Miserere*. The subject matter of these engravings focused largely upon the horrors of death and war, and man's inhumanity to man. Many of the images are dark and disturbing. Taken together, they form a testament to the depths of human suffering comparable to the famous wartime prints by Goya. But unlike the rather hopeless vision of Goya, Rouault's series culminates with a series of engravings of the passion of Christ. All of human suffering, Rouault seems to be saying, is taken up into the redemptive suffering of Jesus. As he wrote, "Christ will be in agony to the end of time."[3]

A humble and reticent man, Rouault did not see himself as a spokesperson for faith. But he painted his vision of a world of suffering that is ultimately redeemed by grace. He knew that such a message was out of step with his time. "I do not feel as if I belong to this modern life," he wrote. "My real life is back in the age of the cathedrals."[4] In contrast to Matisse, who said he would stop painting if he had no audience, Rouault saw his painting almost as a spiritual discipline. He felt no need for a large audience. "Of course I would go on [painting]; I would have need of that spiritual dialogue."[5]

The power of that "spiritual dialogue" can be seen in the best of his paintings. The deep compassion of his vision springs to life through paintings built up of carefully applied layers of textured pigment. The thick black lines and the bright, glowing colors are reminiscent of the structure of a stained glass window, but the light that comes shining through is birthed in the inner light of Rouault's faith.

Rouault's specifically religious paintings, such as *Head of Christ* and *Christ Mocked by the Soldiers* (1932), are among his best-known works. But other, lesser-known paintings provide a glimpse of the peace and tranquility Rouault found in his faith. These canvases are colorful, warm, and timeless, usually bathed in a warm autumnal light with the setting or rising sun, and contain simple architectural forms that could be either ancient or modern. Normally they also contain a cluster of humans in the foreground, and sometimes images of Christ are present, as in *Christ in the Suburbs* (c. 1921), which shows Jesus present with two children on a deserted moonlit street. He called such paintings his "sacred landscapes."

Rouault had a strong distaste for banal and sentimental religious painting, which he saw as superficial. Unlike many modern Christian artists, he was not looking to put his own spin on spiritual matters. "As a Christian in such hazardous times, I believe only in Jesus on the cross. I am a Christian of olden times."[6] His work was orthodox in its approach, while unique in style.

Rouault drew no neat division between his religious and secular subject matter. "All my work," he said, "is religious for those who know how to look at it."[7] The note of grace can be glimpsed even in his paintings of degraded and suffering humanity. "It is not always the subject that inspires the pilgrim, but the accent that he puts there, the tone, the force, the grace, the unction. That is why some so-called 'sacred art' can be profane."[8] The "accent" that Rouault placed in his work was the accent of compassion and love for a fallen and suffering humanity. And the eyes of the Savior in his numerous paintings of Christ are eyes that look with love and mercy upon a broken world.

While not traditionally realistic in its use of perspective and pictorial plane, Rouault's work is definitely not abstract. Instead, it is an art that condenses its subjects to humble forms that speak of human and spiritual essentials, much as the ancient icons his work sometimes resembles. He uses the tools of modernism to reassemble the fragments of a broken world and look back toward a time when humility and mystery were more highly valued. His heart was big enough to hold both the pain of humanity and the serenity of a hope from beyond this dark world. As Jacques Maritain wrote of him, "Tenderness and pity, and a longing for harmony, calm, and serenity, are the true heart of Rouault."[9]

50

The Power and the Glory

Graham Greene

(novel, 1940)

Grace is a theological concept that everyone talks about but few understand in any depth. Perhaps no author did a better job of illustrating what grace involves than a man who knew himself to be in desperate need of such grace, Graham Greene. In *The Power and the Glory*, he tells the story of a priest who is hunted by the authorities during a time of intense religious persecution in Mexico. The priest is morally weak and struggles with alcoholism (Greene calls him the "whiskey priest"), but he is still committed to trying to fulfill his priestly duties for the believers who have had to go into hiding. All the while, his life is in grave danger.

The policeman who tracks the priest through the course of his desperate wanderings is a committed and puritanical atheist, convinced of the rightness of his cause. While the priest is a moral failure, the policeman is an earnest, honest, and morally upright man. But that doesn't mean the priest cannot be used by God in spite of his failings—he is, again and again, an imperfect instrument in the hands of a perfect God, an unexpected saint whose stumbling attempts to follow God produce greater results than he could ever have imagined.

Greene did not originally plan to write a novel when he visited Mexico in 1938 to research the extent of the persecution that was taking place against the Catholic Church. He was going to pen a piece of nonfiction about the violence against the priests and nuns, and about the attempt of the government to systematically eradicate the faith. When he saw what was actually happening, which included the martyrdom of the clergy, he found himself deeply impressed by those who persevered and heroically worked to keep God's message alive. For the first time he began to understand that faith was not simply an idea or a philosophy but a source of unimaginable strength and courage, and he was deeply moved.

This experience also awakened within Greene a desire to side with the underdog, and he spent much of his career speaking out against those who took advantage of the downtrodden and marginalized. He flirted with communism, appreciating its concern for the masses, but became increasingly disillusioned with the way that the communist vision was carried out. Through the years his political ideology was anything but consistent, and it led him at times to support questionable revolutionary leaders. His actions, however wrongheaded they might sometimes have been, were founded upon his desire to challenge the wielders of power and speak out for those who could not speak for themselves.

Graham Greene was born in 1904 in England. His father was a schoolteacher, and Greene suffered much at the hands of fellow students who suspected him of being a snitch for his dad. Greene was likely bipolar, and his sadness and depression became so overwhelming that he was sent to live with a psychiatrist who could teach him how to better cope with life. But despite that intervention, he continued to be stalked by feelings of deep depression and suicidal thoughts.

What began to turn him around was meeting a young woman, Vivien Dayrell-Browning, with whom he was powerfully smitten, but who was a committed Catholic. This was a problem for Greene, who considered himself an atheist. But such was his love for her that he undertook instruction from a priest to see if he could bring himself to believe. If nothing else, he thought, it would be interesting to try to understand how someone could actually believe the tenets of Catholicism. Over time, as he questioned and argued with the priest, he found himself becoming convinced of its truths. He had no great emotional epiphany, but instead a dawning sense of intellectual conviction. "My conversion," he later wrote, "was not in the least an emotional affair. It was purely intellectual."[1]

After his baptism, Greene married Vivien. When he was confirmed, he chose "Thomas the Doubter" as his confirmation name, which seems entirely appropriate. Greene was a doubter par excellence. He doubted God, he doubted others, he doubted himself, and he even doubted his doubts. "The trouble is," he famously said, "I don't believe in my disbelief."[2] Throughout his life he clung desperately and doggedly to a belief in God, and his struggles of living

Alamy

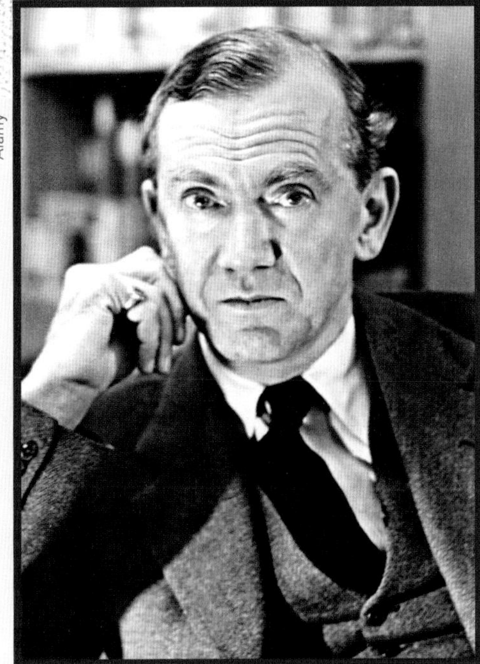

Graham Greene (c.1953) photo by Lida Moser

a life of faith in a world of doubt became the impetus for some of his best novels.

Greene's writing style is almost cinematic in its ability to immerse the reader in environments that feel damp, dark, seedy, and forbidding, yet strangely almost mystical. Perhaps that is why so many of his novels have been made into successful films. Those who have read his books know that there is no other literary experience quite like a sojourn in "Greeneland." Although he also wrote numerous travel books, plays, essays, film reviews, and autobiographical musings, his most memorable work is contained in his novels, which roughly divide into two categories. He wrote what he called "entertainments"—thrillers, spy stories, comedies, and mysterious tales; and he also wrote more serious novels about spiritual crises—what have often been referred to as his "Catholic novels."

These novels, which revolve around characters who agonize about their struggle against evil and temptation, include *The Power and the Glory* and such books as *Brighton Rock* (1938), whose main character, Pinkie Brown, is a young gangster who is utterly and chillingly evil but is convinced of the reality of hell and damnation even as he undertakes his crimes. Pinkie finds his foil in the sweet and loving Rose, whose love is stronger than his evil. *The Heart of the Matter* (1948) unfolds the story of a conflicted Catholic police officer in West Africa who struggles with faithfulness to his marriage and commitment to his faith as he is drawn into a relationship with a young widow. It becomes clear that his feelings for her are as much kindness and pity as they are lust. The controversial conclusion of the novel explores the nature of suicide and the extent of God's grace. *The End of the Affair* (1951) also explores faith and marital unfaithfulness, and ends with a shattering moment of sacrifice and mystical revelation.

One of Greene's last novels, published shortly before his death, is the delightful *Monsignor Quixote* (1982), which plays off the famous book by Cervantes as it tells the story of a road trip between two old friends—one a priest and the other a communist ex-mayor. As they travel they argue and debate about faith and doubt, the meaning of life, the hopes and limits of politics, and the restless sensual urges of human beings. Greene presented these topics with a light, humorous touch, but the novel works toward a powerful and moving conclusion. One cannot help but think that the book is, in a sense, Greene's argument with himself. Though the atheist mayor scores many debate points along the way, it remains clear that Greene's ultimate sympathies were with the kindly old priest and his simple and innocent love for God.

Greene specialized in characters who hold strong convictions about God and faith but find it difficult to live them out. They fight losing battles with their own sensuality and the temptations of drink, sex, and power, but their consciences always exert a largely ineffectual pull toward doing the right thing—until a key moment when their wavering faith is tested and then proves triumphant, even if not in the usually expected ways.

Greene himself was not unlike his flawed characters—a committed Catholic whose conscience was fully active but often ineffectual. Like Paul's dilemma in Romans 7, he knew the right thing to do, but found himself doing the opposite—and then feeling terrible about it. He struggled with drinking too much and with infidelity. As a young man, Greene sometimes even played "Russian roulette." He would load one or two bullets into a revolver, spin the chamber, and then put the gun to his head and pull the trigger. It was a flirtation with the odds, birthed by severe depression and an overwhelming sense of boredom with his life. After his conversion, he no longer played this dangerous game, but he did, with great regularity, place himself in one risky situation after another, clearly not afraid of dying. He was a compulsive traveler and visited out-of-the-way places all over the world; much of his energy throughout his life went toward trying to escape or stave off boredom.

Most specialists believe that if he were alive today, Graham Greene would be diagnosed as bipolar, a diagnosis that certainly fits with the extremes of his mood swings and consistent battles against depression. His own struggles helped make his fiction unique. He had a keen insight into the nature of evil and how it could overtake a life. While other Christian novelists might represent the heroic actions of people of faith, Greene told stories about people who were reluctant heroes or outright failures, people whose beliefs haunted them rather than sustained them. In his novels, one can frequently sense the fiery flames of judgment licking just below the surface of ordinary human lives. But the God we glimpse in his novels is a God who looks beyond our frail and demented humanity and intervenes in unexpected ways, even in ways that sometimes move counter to accepted religious thinking. Perhaps that is what Greene was speaking of when he wrote of "the appalling strangeness of the mercy of God."[3]

51

Quartet for the End of Time

Olivier Messiaen

(classical music, 1941)

It was an unlikely time and place for the debut of a major composition by one of the twentieth century's great composers. But in the middle of the Second World War, on a brutally cold January night in 1941, Olivier Messiaen's *Quartet for the End of Time* was performed for the first time in a Nazi prisoner-of-war camp in Gorlitz, Germany. On that evening, frost covered the windows and the snow piled twenty inches high outside as an audience of several hundred prisoners and guards crowded into an unheated, makeshift performance hall—Barracks 27. They were there to hear a piece that Messiaen had written during his imprisonment in the camp, following his capture as a French soldier during the German invasion the previous year. As the unlikely audience sat transfixed, their cold breath rising in little puffs of steam and their bodies shivering against the cold, few would have guessed that they were being treated to the initial performance of one of the masterpieces of modern concert music.

That such a piece could even be written under these circumstances was partially due to the efforts of Karl-Albert Brull, a music-loving guard who was familiar with some of Messiaen's prewar compositions and went to extraordinary efforts to provide the composer with pencils, erasers, and music paper. He also found a quiet place in an empty barracks where Messiaen could work undisturbed, even posting a guard outside to keep him from being bothered. After the performance, Brull helped forge the documents that made it possible for Messiaen to return to France.

Toarrangethisquartet—borninconditionsofwar,death,famine,andfrost—Messiaen used the only instruments that were available in the camp: a cello with only three strings, a clarinet, a violin, and a dilapidated piano. It was an unusual combination, but around these instruments he fashioned something startling, strangely beautiful, and spiritually evocative.

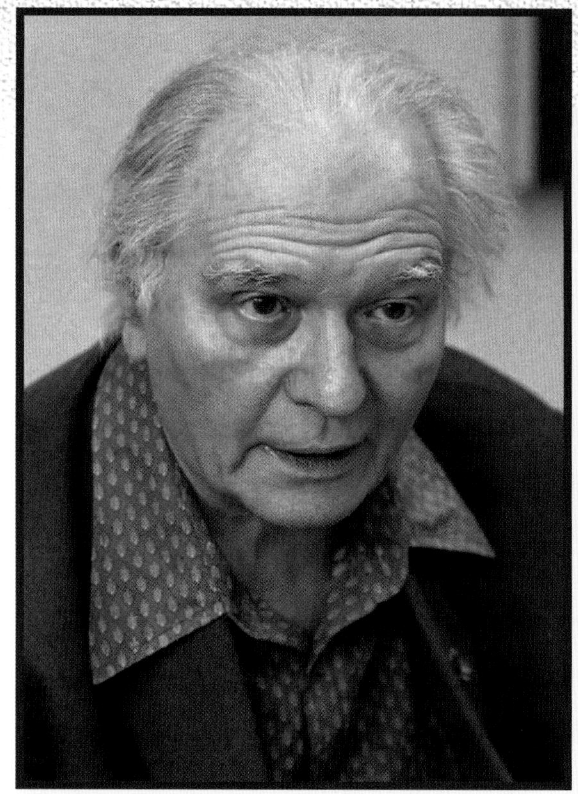

Olivier Messiaen (1986) photo by Rob C. Croes

The title refers to the proclamation of the "seventh angel" from Revelation 10, about the time when all will be made right in eternity—a time beyond time. Messiaen inscribed in his notes to the score, "In homage to the Angel of the Apocalypse, who lifts his hand toward heaven, saying, 'There shall be time no longer.'" Surely it must have felt to many Europeans as though the apocalypse was at hand as Nazi aggressors stormed triumphantly across Europe, set on establishing their Third Reich. But Messiaen's music is not a gloomy meditation on defeat and hardship; it is a musical expression of a hopeful expectation of the future God has promised.

Sometimes, however, hope does not sound like a sweeping romantic wash of strings. Instead, Messiaen's rhythms dance along in intricate patterns without any regular beat to ground them. There are moments of clashing chords jostling against each other as well as long sections of great contemplative serenity called *Louanges*, or "songs of praise." The quartet opens with a movement called "Liturgy of Crystal," highlighting the joyful sounds of birdsong, as transcribed for violin and clarinet. Two later movements celebrate the immortality and eternal life of Christ, and one movement highlights the voice of the archangel with a swirling and cascading piano; it is playfully titled, "A Tangle of Rainbows." There is also a "Dance of Fury" in which all the instruments join together in discordant musical loops of sound. In all, the quartet contains eight movements; seven representing the seven days of creation, and an eighth for the eternal life that follows.

The *Quartet for the End of Time*, like much of Messiaen's work, sets aside many of the musical conventions of Western classical music. He was, like many modern composers, not much concerned with linear progression and development or with harmonic resolution, so his music may initially sound somewhat strange and jarring to the ear of the casual listener. It is a music of contrasts: sometimes funereally slow and contemplative, sometimes nervous and jarring, sometimes voluptuous and grand, sometimes peaceful and spare, and always interesting.

Contemplating the precarious position of humanity deep in the middle of the horrors of the Second World War, Messiaen was not asking the nagging, obvious question of "Why me, Lord?" but instead lifting a voice of praise in the midst of chaos, a musical celebration of a hope beyond this world in a time beyond time.

Born in France in 1908, Messiaen was a musical prodigy who taught himself how to play the piano before he took official lessons and had a special interest in the music of Claude Debussy and Maurice Ravel. Their colorful, impressionistic compositions so fascinated him that he began to compose music himself, and even asked his parents to give him opera scores as Christmas presents. Though neither of his parents were Christians, he embraced Catholicism for himself at an early age.

At age eleven, Messiaen entered the Paris Conservatory, where he became a star pupil. He took a course in the organ from Marcel Dupre, and as his young student had never even seen an organ console, the master organist took an hour to patiently explain the ins and outs of the instrument. When Messiaen returned a week later for his next lesson, he dumbfounded his teacher with a remarkably good performance of a Bach organ fantasia. The year 1931 marked two milestones in Messiaen's life: he saw the first public performance of one of his own compositions, and he was appointed as organist for the Église de la Sainte-Trinité in Paris, where he served faithfully until his death.

After Messiaen's release from the Nazi prison camp, he taught music at the Paris Conservatory, where he was known as a lively and patient teacher. His students included such future luminaries as Karlheinz Stockhausen and Pierre Boulez.

From his childhood, Messiaen had been fascinated by the songs of birds, and he exerted a great deal of effort to study the sounds of different species worldwide, seeking them out and transcribing their songs into music, which he then incorporated into many of his compositions. Often these compositions include a note identifying which birdsong inspired that particular section of the piece. When asked to create a test piece for flutists wishing to enter the conservatory, he offered *Le Merle Noir*, which was based entirely on the song of the blackbird.

Messiaen was forever experimenting with new sounds and techniques that placed him solidly within the world of avant-garde composers. But within that world he was often suspect, as he was a committed Christian who espoused traditional theology against an intellectual and cultural backdrop that was predominantly hostile toward it. Fellow artists recognized his compositional genius but were suspicious of his beliefs, almost as if it were, in their minds, impossible to be so very modern and also be a committed Christian. Despite such criticisms from his musical counterparts, as well as religious critics who found his music odd and incomprehensible, he boldly synthesized ancient and modern elements into his own unique theological and musical vision, combining the musical textures and rhythms of contemporaries such as Stravinsky with resonances borrowed from medieval choral works.

Messiaen's influences were many and varied, including the music of India, Indonesia, Japan, and ancient Greece; medieval chant and polyphonic songs; the impressionism of Debussy and Ravel; and avant-garde modernism. He maintained that music should be interesting, beautiful to listen to, and must touch the heart of the listener. Those who take the time to accustom themselves to his unique palette of sounds, textures, and rhythms will find that his work accomplishes all three goals.

Messiaen was also an amateur theologian and read widely in ancient and modern theological texts, and he often tried to translate those ideas into his musical compositions. "I wished to express the marvelous aspects of the Faith," he said. "I'm not saying that I've succeeded, for in the final analysis they're inexpressible . . . most of the arts are unsuited to the expression of religious truths. Only music, the most immaterial of all, comes close to it."[1] He knew that music could never fully achieve what he wanted it to, but he was trying, through his compositions, to somehow make the invisible just a little bit more visible, and in some manner express what was ultimately inexpressible.

Rather than writing liturgical music for use in churches, Messiaen brought his own brand of sacred music to the concert hall. He "wished to accomplish a liturgical act—that is to say, to transfer a kind of divine office, a kind of communal praise to the concert hall."[2] Therefore, many of his compositions bear religious titles reflective of their inspiration: *Visions of the Amen*, *The Ascension*, *Twenty Gazes Upon the Child Jesus*, *Three Small Liturgies of the Divine Presence*, *The Transfiguration of Our Lord Jesus Christ*, and *Meditations on the Mystery of the Holy Trinity*.

When asked what he wanted to communicate with his music, Messiaen replied that

> the first idea I wanted to express, the most important, is the existence of the truths of the Catholic faith. . . . The illumination of the theological truths of the Catholic faith is the first aspect of my work, the noblest, and no doubt the most useful and most valuable—perhaps the only one I won't regret at the hour of my death.[3]

When esteemed concert pianist Jacqueline Chow first set out to master a set of difficult piano works composed by Messiaen, she was a confirmed atheist. But as she pored over the music and tried to comprehend what Messiaen was trying to say, it had a profound effect. "Little by little," she said, "I started believing." In his attempt to express Christian truths in a fresh, modern idiom, Olivier Messiaen demonstrated—with his transcendent soundscapes—that the old can become new, and that the new is always a product of the past.

52

Four Quartets

T. S. Eliot

(poems, 1943)

Sometimes music can reflect ideas and feelings that words simply cannot express. And sometimes, when poetry reaches its highest level, it can function almost like music—moving the reader with a transcendent force beyond our comprehension. T. S. Eliot's *Four Quartets* borrows its title from a musical form, and it offers up poetry that expresses some of the deepest universal human realities with the musicality of poetic expression. These are poems filled with images drawn from deep wells of the remembered and the half remembered, meditations on the nature of time and memory, and ruminations on human frailty, suffering, and the nature of a living faith. Many readers have found them to be not only resplendent poems but also aids to meditation and prayer, as they seem to find ways to *almost say* the unsayable and provide glimpses of universal spiritual experiences and moments of enlightenment.

Occasionally an ordinary experience—a sight or sound or smell—can trigger a sense of being swept into a timeless moment, a place where time stands still and the breath of eternity rustles through our hearts and minds. Eliot's *Four Quartets* both records and arouses such mystical moments. These are meditative poems that wed the musicality of words with profound spiritual insight to awaken a connection with something—ultimately Someone—who transcends time.

Four Quartets opens with just such an experience in "Burnt Norton," where the poet's stroll through a garden triggers memories that open up and alter the nature of how time is experienced. When we consider how time is experienced, perhaps it might be helpful to think in terms of the difference between the two common Greek words for time, as Eliot seems to be making just such a distinction. *Chronos* is time that unfolds in a linear fashion, moving forward with each tick of the clock, ever new and ever disappearing. *Kairos* is time as something eternal, lasting, and permanent; it is "the appointed time" when an eternal present manifests itself in the now. In Eliot's poems, we experience this present as a *presence*, when God meets us in the moment. This is the "still point" to which Eliot points in the poems, the place where past and future are gathered together and where time merges with the timeless—where there is "a lifetime burning in every moment."

Four Quartets cannot fully be understood without reference to Eliot's Christian convictions. Throughout the poems there are phrases and ideas that are borrowed from traditional Christian mystical writers such as Julian of Norwich, John of the Cross, and the anonymous medieval author of *The Cloud of Unknowing*. These writers stressed the inadequacy of words and images to help us grasp the spiritual realm. They thought it was necessary to move beyond thoughts, feelings, and experiences and reach out to God in "naked faith," detaching the soul from the specific and knowable and traveling onward in faith through experiences of darkness, confusion, and unknowing. Only in this way, they believed, can our illusions be stripped away and we become able to open ourselves to the deepest connection with God.

The paradox, as Eliot saw it, is this: words are always inadequate to the task of speaking about the deepest truths, but they are the sole means to communicate what we have experienced. As Eliot reminds us, "Words strain / Crack and sometimes break, under the burden / Under the tension, slip, slide, perish / Decay with imprecision, will not stay in place."[1] The problem with language is that it is a prisoner of time (*chronos*), so we must understand its limitations when it speaks of the sacred moment (*kairos*).

Eliot puts little trust in human wisdom to help us break the cycles of time. In his earlier poem "The Waste Land," he offers a dreary, chilling portrait of our collective human frailty. In *Four Quartets* he asserts that help must come from outside time, as it did in the incarnation and the atoning work of Jesus. Christ is the "wounded surgeon" whose flesh and blood convey the only true healing for the human condition. For our part, we must detach ourselves from our preoccupations with both past and future and embrace the ways that God comes to us in the present—in the moments of revelation, the "hints and guesses" we occasionally experience when that reality from *outside* time breaks into time.

Since the human condition can only

be healed from outside of time, no social or political strategies can cure the disease from which humanity suffers. We must, instead, realize our own weakness, embrace humility, and practice the discipline of faith in order to receive the offered healing. The church, for Eliot, was the community of those who—however imperfectly—witness to the reality of a Time beyond time. He saw the rituals of the devotional life (prayer, meditation, the Eucharist, worship, and service) as a force for personal and societal transformation, vessels through which the living water was poured out; the timeless becoming part of our experience of time. It is in this that we can hope, and what these poems point toward. As Eliot says, quoting Julian of Norwich, "All shall be well and all manner of things shall be well."

Thomas Stearns Eliot was born in 1888 in St. Louis, Missouri, to a family who was a sort of Midwestern aristocracy. Their brand of Unitarianism was essentially an ethical humanism that stressed hard work, thrift, and public service; it was a religion of high ideals and sacrificial service with little emphasis on personal piety or supernatural belief. Eliot, though, found an example of more traditional Christianity in the much-loved Irish nursemaid who was hired to look after the Eliot children. She was a devout Catholic who took the young Eliot to mass and engaged in conversations with him about matters of faith.

Eliot's exceptional intelligence was apparent early on, and his family encouraged it by introducing him to classic literature and supporting his educational endeavors. He attended Harvard, where he excelled in his studies, and before concluding his graduate work he spent the years 1910–1911 in Paris. Paris had held a fascination for him ever since he had read a book on the Symbolist movement in literature, a movement that called for poets to abandon traditional realism and embrace a more spiritual and symbolic vocabulary. When he returned from Paris, Eliot finished up at Harvard with studies of philosophy and Eastern religious thought. As an avocation, he immersed himself in a study of the Christian mystics. Though he had little religious conviction of his own at this point, he had a strong sense of human imperfection and a desire to find a way to overcome the limitations of human nature. His early poems from this period show him attracted to ideas such as mortification and asceticism.

In 1914, he moved to England, which would become his permanent home, and settled into a life of working as a bank clerk by day and writing poems and hobnobbing with the literary elite by night. His guide to this new life, and also his poetic mentor, was author Ezra Pound, who helped polish Eliot's style and did a major surgical edit on his important early poem "The Waste Land" (1922).

Read in retrospect, the ideas and images of "The Waste Land" seem like a natural

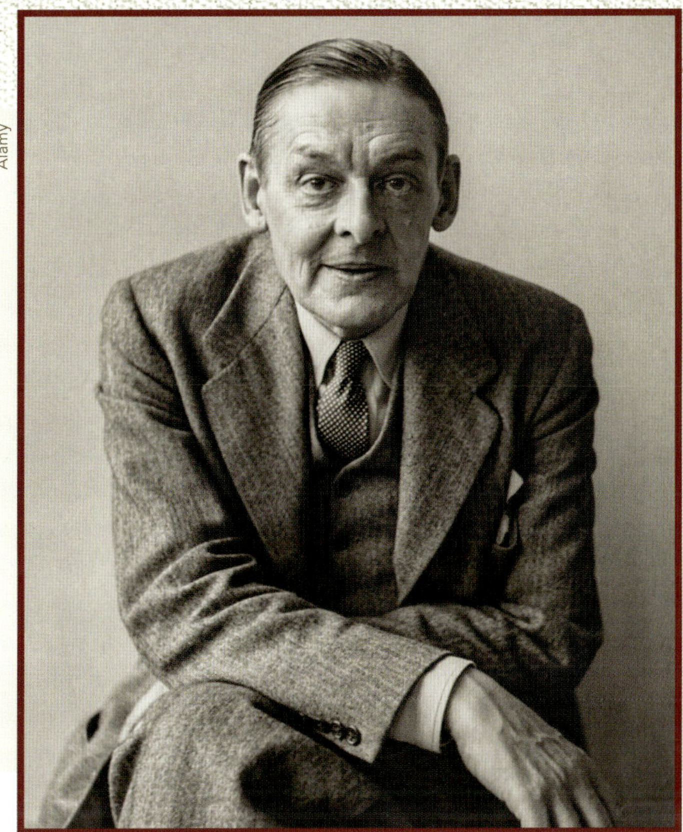

Alamy

T. S. Eliot, photo by Kay Bell Reynal (1955)

step in Eliot's progression toward faith and his growing dissatisfaction with living in a world without God. This poem was widely and enthusiastically embraced as an example of modernism, and made him an overnight literary celebrity. In part a reflection on the fractured state of civilization in post–World War I Europe, it was also a deeply philosophical meditation on a culture that had collapsed in upon itself—a civilization without roots, purpose, meaning, or any of the things that made human beings truly human. It was a Dantean vision of an earthly Inferno, of a culture hopeless and dark and spiritless, characterized by crass materialism, vulgarity, lifelessness, and the desperate search for new sensations to overcome the boredom of life. The poem's fractured form mirrored its content, and its creative expression of these concerns announced that a major poet had arrived on the scene. Its influence on subsequent modern poetry is almost incalculable.

Eliot joined the Anglican Church in 1927. Unfortunately, he left no record of the intellectual and spiritual journey he traveled to reach this conclusion, but we can assume that his perception of original sin and human corruption played a major part. His baptism was performed privately in the presence of a few friends in order not to attract publicity, but in time he saw the need for a public declaration of his decision. He did this not by any autobiographical testimony but by appreciative essays on religious thinkers such as Pascal and Lancelot Andrews, and by poems such as "The Journey of the Magi" (1927), "Ash Wednesday" (1930), and the longer verse drama, *The Rock* (1934).

Eliot also produced a good deal of literary and cultural criticism, which reached a smaller audience but clearly reflected his Christian convictions. What was missing in much of modern literature, he said, was a sense of sin. Instead of the struggle of the soul with sin and guilt on the part of their characters, most modern novelists relied upon experiences of heightened emotionalism as the motivating force in their books. For this reason, Eliot considered much of modern literature to be "spiritually sick," trying to exist outside of any tradition and dependent upon various unreliable forms of "inner light."

T. S. Eliot believed humanity's best hope was in rediscovering the values and traditions upon which we could construct a truly Christian culture, one that was realistic about the flawed nature of humans and the danger of unchecked individualism, and that embraced the hope that could be found in practicing an intellectually responsible Christianity in community with other believers. However insightful such criticisms might be, though, Eliot will be best remembered for the way he was able to bring spiritual experiences alive in his poems, and his gift for using the imprecision of words to arouse something deep and eternal within the souls of his readers—a Time outside of time.

53

The Man Born to Be King

Dorothy L. Sayers

(drama, 1943)

It has become commonplace in our time for the story of Jesus to be staged as a play, a film, or even a television miniseries, but when Dorothy L. Sayers first wrote *The Man Born to Be King*, it was actually against the law in Britain to represent any person of the Holy Trinity on the stage. Technically, since her plays were radio productions rather than stage productions, Sayers was within the law. Nevertheless, she stirred up controversy when *The Man Born to Be King* was first performed. Today we wouldn't think twice about the propriety of such an undertaking, and many have indeed tried to capture the drama and spiritual depth of the Gospels through various mediums. But few, if any, have told their story as successfully as Sayers.

With these radio plays, Sayers was attempting to help modern listeners better understand and identify with the biblical text through making the characters within it more relatable as real people who lived in the real world—not stained glass figures or Sunday school flannel graph cutouts. She believed these biblical stories had become so commonplace and riddled with clichés that people had become dulled to their message and impact. By making her characters more complex, fully rounded, and believable as real human beings, by having them speak in understandable modern language, and by placing them in truly dramatic situations, Sayers hoped to make them come alive in a fresh way. And she wanted to do so as artfully as possible, not creating mere religious propaganda but rather a vivid, dramatic presentation.

Sayers achieved her goal through a respectful reworking of the biblical texts by exploring the interior motivations of characters such as Judas and Lazarus and by adding her poetic touch. These characteristics can be seen in a speech she puts in the mouth of Mary Magdalene. Speaking to Jesus, Mary says:

> You were the only person there that was really alive. The rest of us were going about half-dead—making gestures of life. . . . The life was not in us but with you—intense and shining, like the sun when it rises and turns the flames of our candles to pale smoke. I felt the flame of the sun in my heart. When you spoke to me I came alive for the first time. And I love life all the more since I have learned its meaning.[1]

Forcefully and poetically, Sayers opens up these Bible stories by creating people we can identify with, and then she invites us to experience them with a renewed sense of their mystery, emotion, and spiritual depth.

Not everyone was happy with Sayers's attempt to reinvigorate Jesus' story through drama. When the radio plays were first performed on BBC radio, they set off a firestorm of criticism. Many listeners felt it was sacrilegious and improper to use modern language—much less contemporary slang—to retell the story of Jesus. They found it troubling that she had departed from the text of the Authorized Bible and taken liberties with story details. And they argued that the law prohibiting representation of any person of the Holy Trinity on the stage should also prohibit the presentation of sacred stories in any such down-to-earth manner.

Sayers dismissed these complaints as theologically naïve, as she desired to give her audience something richer than the typical "churchy" art they were used to. She scorned plays written as propaganda, with the primary purpose being evangelizing or edifying.

> If one writes with his eye on the spiritual box-office, he will at once cease to be a dramatist, and decline into a manufacturer of propagandistic tracts. . . . He will lose his professional integrity, and with it all his power, including the power to preach the Gospel.[2]

The often lifeless and unconvincing work that passes for "Christian art" in our own time surely is evidence of the truth of her statement.

Sayers overcame these criticisms by creating a very successful cycle of twelve short plays that were undeniably powerful, both spiritually and artistically. The plays were later gathered together and published as a book. This volume had no less a fan than C. S. Lewis, who wrote to Sayers of his appreciation for it and told her he made a habit of rereading it every year during Holy Week. One cannot but be saddened

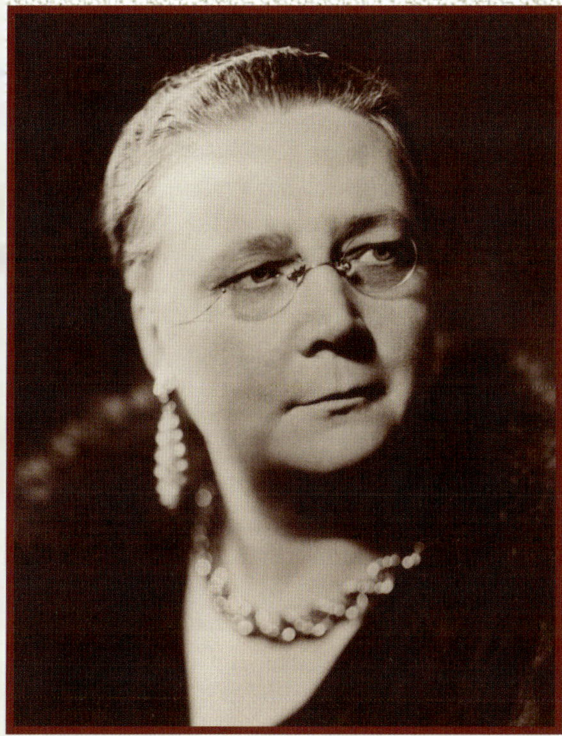
Dorothy Sayers, photo by Howard Coster (1938)

that this dramatic cycle is largely forgotten, and might wistfully ponder the film that could be created using her drama as the shooting script.

The daughter of an Anglican rector, Dorothy L. Sayers was born in Oxford in 1893, and evidenced a precocious ability with languages from childhood. She was learning Latin by age seven, and eventually added French and German. Later in life she also mastered Italian so that she could read Dante's *Divine Comedy* in its original language, and then translated it into English. An excellent student, Sayers won a scholarship to Oxford and became one of the first women to ever graduate from that school with a Master of Arts degree.

Her earliest published writing was poetry, but she made her reputation with a series of mystery novels featuring the eccentric aristocrat and amateur detective Lord Peter Wimsey, who solved crimes for his own amusement. The first Wimsey novel was *Whose Body?* (1922), and the series eventually included eleven novels and a number of short stories. Highlights include *Unnatural Death* (1927), *Strong Poison* (1930), in which he first meets Harriet Vane, whom he will court and eventually marry, *Murder Must Advertise* (1933), *The Nine Tailors* (1934), which revolves around bell-ringing and illustrates the care Sayers took in getting all the details just right, and *Gaudy Night* (1935), which takes place in Oxford and finally brings Wimsey and Vane together. The stories all revolve around puzzling mysteries, are rich in character-driven humor and social satire, and evidence an underlying morality.

By the 1940s, Sayers seemed to tire of detective fiction, and she turned her attention to writing religious drama—including *The Zeal of Thy House* (1937), *He That Should Come* (1938), *The Devil to Pay* (1939), and *The Emperor Constantine* (1951)—as well as a number of influential essays on theology and apologetics, which were gathered together in collections such as *The Mind of the Maker* (1941), a remarkable study of the connection between creativity and the doctrine of the Trinity, *Unpopular Opinions* (1946), and *Creed or Chaos?* (1947). Her keen intelligence, combined with her sharp wit and abundant creativity, made her one of the most able defenders of traditional Christian orthodoxy in the twentieth century.

When Sayers surveyed the landscape of Christianity in her time, she found it intellectually shallow and spiritually stagnant. In contrast to those who thought the problem with the contemporary church was too much emphasis on doctrine and not enough on religious experience, Sayers believed that it was the doctrine—the dogma—that gave faith its substance and its relevance. In her important essay "The Greatest Drama Ever Staged," she asserted that "the Christian faith is the most exciting drama that ever staggered the imagination of man—and the dogma is the drama."[3] Sayers feared that modern Christians had domesticated Jesus in order to make Him more palatable to contemporary sensibilities, thereby blunting the very radical nature of what He said and did.

> The people who hanged Christ never, to do them justice, accused him of being a bore—on the contrary, they thought him too dynamic to be safe. It has been left for later generations to muffle up that shattering personality and surround him with an atmosphere of tedium. We have very efficiently pared the claws of the Lion of Judah, certified him "meek and mild," and recommended him as a fitting household pet for pale curates and pious old ladies.[4]

In *The Man Born to Be King* and other religious plays, Sayers wanted to present the Christian faith in all its scandalous confrontation with our tidy modern pieties. She saw her primary task, though, not as trying to figure out how to illustrate the Christian doctrines but as telling a good story—entertaining and coherent—and letting the theology emerge. As she reminded her readers, "God was executed by people painfully like us, in a society very similar to our own—in the over-ripeness of the most splendid and sophisticated Empire the world has ever seen."[5] If we fail to grasp the shocking reality of that truth, Sayers believed, we have failed to grasp what the story of Jesus is really all about.

A lifelong Anglican, Dorothy L. Sayers never felt drawn toward mysticism or religious enthusiasm. In her own words, she was "quite without the thing known as 'inner light' or 'spiritual experience.'" For her, faith was more about understanding, and she possessed what she called "a passionate intellect." When combined with her creative gifts, her intellect empowered her to communicate the teachings of Christianity in a way that challenged the cynics and skeptics and reminded believers of the faith delivered in the ancient creeds.

Without this connection to its heritage, she believed, Christianity could easily descend into a psychologized secularism, subjectivity, and intellectual chaos. It would be fatal, she wrote, "to suppose that Christianity is only a mode of feeling . . . [it is] hopeless to offer Christianity as a vague, idealistic aspiration: it is a hard, tough, exacting, and complex doctrine steeped in drastic and uncompromising realism."[6] With her gifts, Dorothy L. Sayers could make these traditional teachings not only believable and intellectually respectable but also dramatically compelling.

54

Rome, Open City

Roberto Rossellini

(film, 1945)

Rome, Open City is one of the great masterworks of the Italian neorealist movement in film, of which Roberto Rossellini is perhaps its most famous representative. The neorealists wanted to make movies that were different from normal cinematic fare, replacing Hollywood-style romanticism with the harsh realities of life as their subject. This could be accomplished by dispensing with many of the normal techniques of shooting a film, so they generally shot their films on location, used nonprofessional actors as much as possible, and avoided using cinematic effects to move the audience. They also avoided melodramatic emotion and sought a more impassive tone, trying to capture the way people really acted and spoke.

The title of the film refers to the status of the city of Rome just as WWII was winding down, which is when the film was made. Rome had not yet been liberated by the Allies and still lay tenuously in the hands of the Nazis; its population was demoralized and much of the city was in ruins. In this context, Rossellini tells the stories of some of the members of the resistance who fought against the Germans. Amid the bombed-out buildings, the struggle for daily survival, and all the moral compromises made by characters on both sides of the struggle, there is room for much heroism. One of these heroes is a priest, Don Pietro, who uses the freedom of movement he has as a clergyman to aid the resistance. He is eventually tortured and executed by the Germans when this complicity is discovered. The scene of the kindly priest being shot while neighboring children look on in horror, or of the pregnant Pina being gunned down in the street while running after the truck that is taking away her lover, pack immense emotional power because they feel so utterly real.

Italian filmgoers who had recently emerged into the postwar era recognized the truth that Rossellini was telling about the pain, suffering, privation, and difficult moral decisions that had to be navigated in those dark days. He did not want to allow his audience to avert their eyes but rather to look the grim realities full in the face. Through the character of his heroic priest, though, he offers a hope deeper than any sort of shallow optimism, a hope rooted in the belief that there are realities beyond this life that can be a reservoir for strength and courage.

The making of the film has become almost as legendary as the film itself. Working with virtually no budget, Rossellini scrounged whatever pieces of film stock he could find

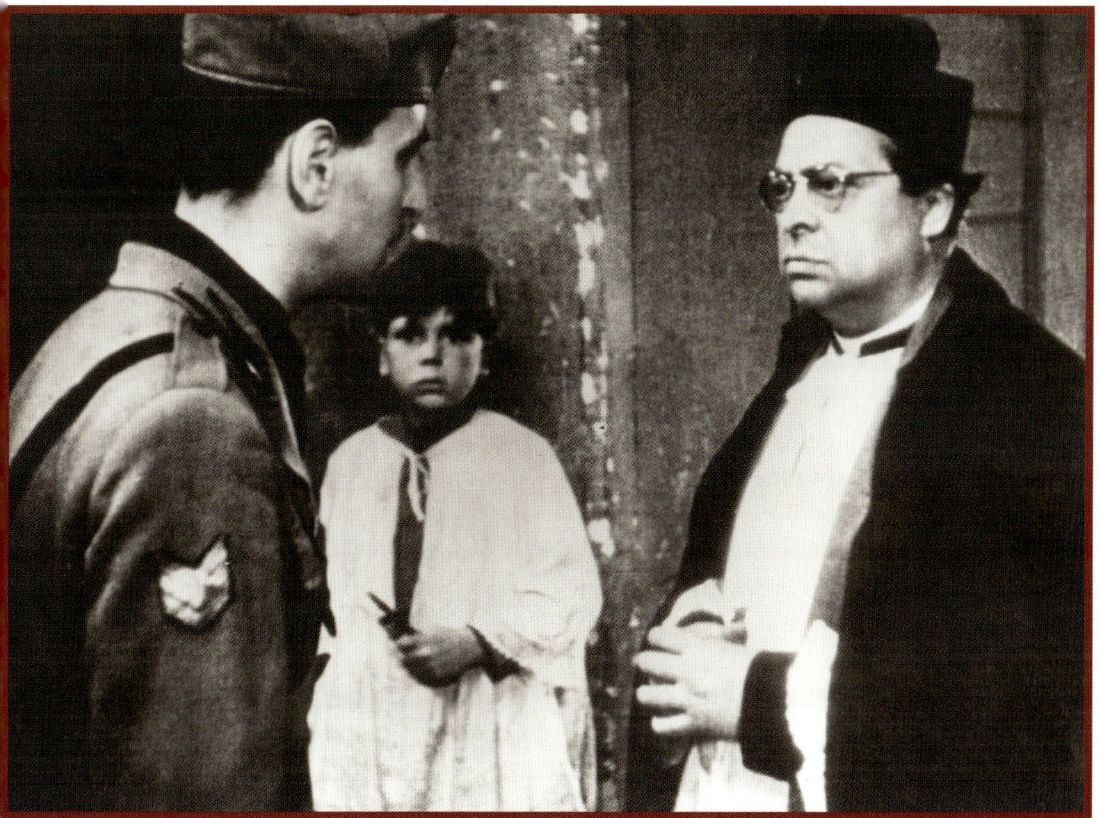

Shutterstock, Kobal Collection

Still from *Rome, Open City*

(often having to buy it on the black market) and shot the film mostly with nonactors in a guerilla "catch as catch can" filmmaking style around locations all over Rome. He had a plan, but he embraced the unplanned and the accidental, which accentuated the film's realism. The resulting film has the rough-hewn look of a homemade documentary but leaves the viewer with no doubt that a powerful controlling intelligence is behind the storytelling. Rossellini's fresh approach to filmmaking inaugurated a new way of making movies that started in Italy but soon spread to filmmakers in France, Britain, and the United States.

Throughout his career, Rossellini generally eschewed camera tricks, unnatural lighting, or studio sets. Whenever possible he filmed on location and used the available light. He sought to get realistic performances out of his actors by either choosing to depend on amateurs rather than professionals or by working in an improvisational style that tried to get realistic performances from them rather than the stagey dramatic deliveries seen in most films. Often his actors were not given their lines until just before the cameras rolled, and he would encourage them to use their own words and natural gestures rather than trying to get them to perform in a preconceived manner. One might argue that this had a tendency to create an emotional flatness in some of his films, but when it worked at its best, it created scenes of searing honesty that rang with truth.

Roberto Rossellini was born in Rome, Italy, in 1906. His father owned a movie theater, so he grew up watching movies. His youthful fascination with cinema led to an interest in how movies were made, and he held a series of jobs in the film industry before finally directing his first film, a documentary, in 1937. This was followed by a series of feature films, culminating in *Rome, Open City*, which used its unorthodox methods to tell a powerful story.

Rossellini's career began to go in a different direction after Ingrid Bergman, one of the most successful actresses in Hollywood, expressed interest in working with him. The films Bergman and Rossellini did together were critical successes but not financial ones. After a string of other mostly unsuccessful films, Rossellini then turned his sights to television and created documentaries and a series of carefully mounted historical dramas that strove for accuracy and realism.

Spirituality was almost always at the center of Rossellini's films, and he was often asking questions about how faith might make a difference in how people lived. *Rome, Open City* features the quietly heroic priest who offers up his life in an attempt to frustrate the evil of the occupying Nazis. *The Flowers of St. Francis* (1950), one of his greatest films, captures the innocence and joy of the great saint, and is filled with humor and pathos as we see Francis of

Assisi and his monks attempt to live a different kind of life, one of detachment from material things and a radical commitment to the needs of others. *Stromboli* (1950) climaxes with a moment of revelation when its protagonist discovers a hope grounded in the Creator of the fearsome beauty that surrounds her. She prays, "O God! What mystery . . . what beauty . . . God, my God. Help me. Give me the strength, the understanding, and the courage."

One of Rossellini's most forthright religious statements came in *Europe '51* (1952), which he made in response to his ponderings on what might happen if someone in our modern times were to, like St. Francis, take seriously the words of Jesus about the kind of love that cares for the poor and marginalized. That Ingrid Bergman's saintly character, having sacrificed her high social standing to suffer with the needy, ends the film by being confined to a mental institution serves as an indictment on the values of modern Western culture. None of the prevailing ideologies and powers represented by the characters in the film (communism, the church, or the legal system) could accommodate such a radically spiritual approach to life without feeling threatened.

When his films are not meditating on the quiet strength of spiritual commitment, they are often unmasking the spiritual despair of the modern age. Films such as *Germany Year Zero* (1948) and *Voyage to Italy* (1954) explore the effects of the vacuum created when faith is no longer central to life. This same pessimism about modernity is seen in the harsh opposition many of his spiritual seekers must face. In many of his films, Rossellini seems not so much involved in making any sort of argument for the truth of faith as in showing what life looks like in its absence, though he is not afraid to portray those moments when faith transformed a life—or a world.

Rossellini's personal stance toward Christianity is frustratingly ambiguous and hard to fathom. He seemed largely uninterested in the dogma of Christianity but was clearly moved and impacted by its moral vision. The films he made during the 1940s and '50s, and some of the statements he made in press interviews of that time, would lead one to assume he was a Catholic believer. In the 1960s, though, he sometimes referred to himself as a "Christian atheist," or a "Christian non-believer," seeming to indicate that though he admired the person and teachings of Jesus, he wanted to distance himself from institutional Christianity and its dogmas. Then, later in life, he made a series of historical films for Italian television that focused on important events and people in the history of the Christian faith: *Augustine* (1972), *Blaise Pascal* (1972), a miniseries *The Acts of the Apostles* (1969), and his last film was a biblically faithful retelling of the life of Christ. We'll probably never really know precisely what personal religious commitments Rossellini might have had, but its influence on his body of work is powerful and undeniable.

Rossellini's film about Jesus, simply named *Messiah* (1976), was the last project he completed before his death and was remarkable in several ways. One is its focus on Jesus' teaching. Rossellini spends more time recording Jesus as a teacher than perhaps any other film ever made about the life of Christ. And one of the interesting ways he does this is to show Jesus teaching as He goes about His life among the disciples. In one scene we see Jesus at work repairing a boat, hammer in hand, while His disciples either assist Him or sit and listen attentively. It is one of several scenes that remind us Jesus grew up working in a carpenter's shop.

With its gritty, earthy believability, *Messiah* shows Rossellini's continuing attempt to achieve realism on film. For scenes where Rossellini would have had to use any sort of special effects to record a supernatural event, he chose instead to have the action occur offscreen. Thus we hear about the miracles Jesus has wrought but we don't actually see them taking place. We know that the Savior has risen, for example, not by seeing a clumsy attempt to portray it literally but through seeing the wonder in the eyes of Mary when she discovers the empty tomb. By avoiding Hollywood-style spectacle, Rossellini produced a film that feels almost like a documentary, a *real* story that *really* happened.

Roberto Rossellini never shied away from making moral statements with his films. He saw his films not as a purely aesthetic experience but as a way of teaching and educating those who viewed them. His distinctiveness as a director, he asserted in a 1954 interview, was in providing "a moral standpoint from which to view the world. Afterwards it becomes an aesthetic standpoint, but the point of departure is definitely moral."[1] Rossellini's "moral statements" were never made in defense of any particular ideology, whether political or religious, but rather in the hope that they would make people into better human beings. He believed that it was not as important to learn to be a filmmaker as to learn to be a human being. Armed with this belief that film had something important to say, he achieved a cinematic output that is unrivaled in its attempt to challenge the viewer to think differently and to act differently.

55

It's a Wonderful Life

Frank Capra

(film, 1946)

Sometimes a work of art is in danger of being so familiar that we can miss the artistry and depth behind it. It can become visual *muzak*—background noise to which we pay only scant attention. *It's a Wonderful Life* is one of these works of art, a film broadcast on television seemingly hundreds of times every Christmas season and a holiday tradition for countless viewers. Many have viewed it numerous times and treasure it as a feel-good classic whose positive message accords well with the season. For them, it simply wouldn't be Christmas without *It's a Wonderful Life*. Though it was a box-office disappointment when it was first released, over time *It's a Wonderful Life* began to be discovered and embraced, until it took up its place as an indisputable film classic.

It's a Wonderful Life has its detractors. For those who are wearied by it, it is another example of what some critics have labeled "Capra corn," a dismissive term suggesting that it is another of the sunny, silly, and sentimental films created by Frank Capra, one of the most successful filmmakers in Hollywood during the late 1930s and early 1940s. Perhaps, however, the cultural divide that opens whenever this film is mentioned is based on an overly simplistic perspective of the film from each side. For Capra's classic film has depths and ambiguities that make it anything but a simplistic purveyor of holiday cheer. Sure, it veers close to the saccharine in a couple of scenes, but its earnest message concerns the dignity and importance of an ordinary human life, as well as how we relate to each other and to God.

Based on a short story by Philip Van Doren Stern, Capra's film tells the story of George Bailey, a kindly everyman unforgettably portrayed by Jimmy Stewart, who spends his life having to put his own dreams aside for the good of others. He wants to travel, to experience life fully, and ultimately to escape his small town of Bedford Falls. "I want to do something *big*, something *important*!" he tells his father.

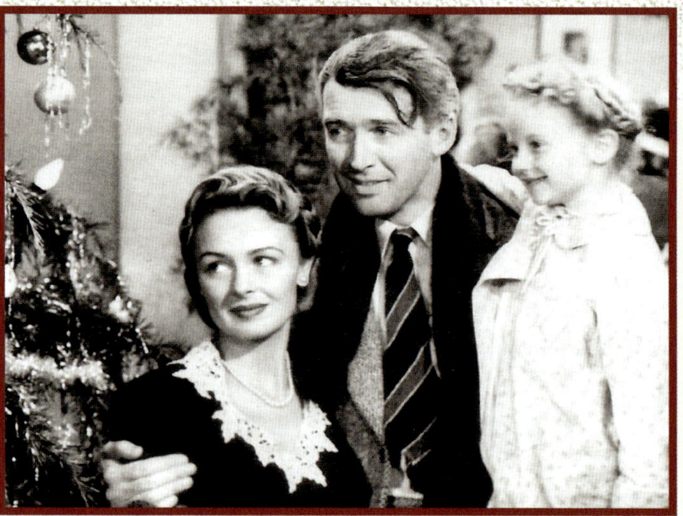
WikiCommons

Still from *It's a Wonderful Life*

But life continually throws obstacles in the path of George's dreams, and he finds himself having to choose between the needs of others and what he really wants from life. He works hard, and settles into operating his father's small-town building and loan business, following the dictates of his heart and investing in the lives of people who are trying to pull themselves up out of poverty, which means taking questionable financial risks on their behalf. His nemesis, the greedy banker Mr. Potter, uses George's reckless goodwill to his own advantage and is finally able to drive him into ruin. When the crusty old man venomously spits out the words, "You are worth more dead than alive!" we see something in George Bailey's eyes that reveals he may believe this to be true. George concludes that the world would have been a better place if he never existed.

George finds himself on a bridge, preparing to jump to his death in the icy waters, when he receives divine intervention in the form of a bumbling guardian angel named Clarence. By giving George glimpses of the dark alternative world that would have existed if he had never been born, Clarence helps him to see that his seemingly small and insignificant life was actually very significant—that the world would be a much poorer place if not for the actions he had taken during the course of his life. These actions sent ripples out for the good, like a stone dropped into a still pond.

Capra once said that he wanted his films to illustrate the truth of the Sermon on the Mount. They are unabashed modern morality tales. He said that making films gave him "a golden opportunity to dramatize 'Love thy neighbor'" and that

"Christ's spiritual law can be the most powerful sustaining force in anyone's life."[1] If these movies are not works of profound theological reflection, they are certainly works of profound human reflection—meditations on how goodness can be a force for making the world a better place. His message is not one of Pollyanna-like cheer, for George Bailey (and other protagonists in other Capra films) must pass through much sacrifice and suffering and injustice and rage in their attempt to stand for what is right and true. There is a theme of revelation and repentance that works its way through many of his films, a dissection of his character's motivations as they come to see themselves more clearly and discover things within themselves that must be overcome if they are to do good.

The youngest of seven children, Frank Capra was born in rural Sicily in 1897. His family immigrated to the United States in 1903 and settled in Los Angeles. Always aware of the limitations placed upon him as an immigrant, Capra worked hard to overcome them and eventually put himself through college, earning a degree in chemical engineering. He bluffed his way into a job in the movie business by pretending to have knowledge that he didn't have—yet—and soon demonstrated great talent, first as a gag writer for Hal Roach and then for Mack Sennett. Before long he was working as a director of silent comedies, showing a skill with visual and physical humor that would add spice to his subsequent films. During the 1930s he directed a string of hits, including *It Happened One Night* (1934), which won the Academy Award in all five major categories, *American Madness* (1932), *Mr. Deeds Goes to Town* (1936), *Mr. Smith Goes to Washington* (1939), and *Meet John Doe* (1941).

During World War II, Capra was commissioned by the US Army to direct a series of documentary films about the war effort, entitled *Why We Fight* (1942–1945). The year after the war ended, he directed *It's a Wonderful Life*, which would be his last undisputed classic. Though he helmed a few other pictures, he never achieved the level of greatness shown in his earlier work. Many critics dismissed his body of work as corny and sentimental. But in more recent decades film historians have revised their opinions and now view him as one of the greatest directors of all time.

The typical Capra hero is an intelligent and compassionate man who has risen from humble beginnings but must be reminded of the deep and abiding values of simple, ordinary people. Such values, he learns, are deeper than those of the upper classes, who are usually portrayed in Capra's films as avaricious—more worried about their financial prosperity than the good of society as a whole. The wealth of the greedy upper crust allows them to buy influence from the government and the media, both of which prove to be eminently corruptible. Capra's grand theme is the individual who takes a stand against injustice and wins the masses of good ordinary folk to his cause, though usually only after much suffering.

His idealism was deeply rooted both in his patriotic convictions about democracy and in his faith, but he was also realistic enough to show that evil is never finally and completely overcome in his films. There was as much pessimism as optimism in Capra's view of human nature. As we see in *Meet John Doe*, the masses may be inherently good but they are also gullible, and they can be easily manipulated and used for the purposes of those who are pulling the strings. Unthinking conformity, therefore, was one of the prime targets of criticism throughout his pictures.

Although raised in a devout Catholic family, Capra initially rejected his heritage, until a midcareer crisis led to a gradual return to his faith. His early sound film *The Miracle Woman* (1931) is one of the few instances where Capra focused directly on a religious theme. This story of the transformation of a woman (the daughter of a minister) who becomes a fraudulent preacher and healer before finally seeing the error of her ways gives evidence of the distrust that Capra seemed to have about organized religion. But while he distrusted the institutional church, he could not ignore his inner urges toward God.

For much of his life Capra was what he called a "Christmas and Easter Catholic," limiting his attendance mostly to the major Christian feast days. When he did show up, however, he wrote of the transcendent effect it sometimes had on him:

> On those holy days I sneaked into a Catholic church to kneel; to smell the incense, hear the angels sing, and be lifted out of my shoes by the passion and resurrection of Christ. It may happen to you only once in a hundred Masses—but it will still happen. You walk back from Communion with the Host on your tongue—a nobody. You kneel, drop your head in your hands. Slowly the wonder of it fills you with joy—the dissolving Host in your mouth is the living Christ.[2]

Although Frank Capra rarely dealt directly with religious issues in his films, his faith was an underlying foundation for his artistic vision. His movies show that the power of goodness can overcome evil and transform human nature. With his character George Bailey in *It's a Wonderful Life*, he showed that it is never too late to offer up a desperate prayer ("Lord, I'm at the end of my rope!") and that we often find God has answered such prayers through the power of a loving community of family, friends, and neighbors. "My films," Capra said, "must let every man, woman, and child know that God loves them, that I love them, and that peace and salvation will become a reality only when they all learn to love each other."[3]

56

"I Will Move On Up a Little Higher"

Mahalia Jackson

(recording, 1947)

On August 28, 1963, tens of thousands of people gathered on the National Mall for the culmination of the March on Washington, a public demonstration calling for civil rights legislation to curb racial inequality and injustice in the United States. Mahalia Jackson, an ardent supporter of the struggle for equality for African Americans, had been asked by Martin Luther King Jr. to sing both before and after his speech at the event. The two shared a similar passion for civil rights and had a supportive friendship. In fact, when King would get discouraged or depressed by the slow pace of change, Jackson would sometimes receive a late-night phone call in which he would ask her to sing to him. She would sing a hymn or gospel song over the phone, which usually brought tears to his eyes and never failed to cheer him up.

At the March on Washington, Jackson took the podium just before King to sing one of his favorite spirituals, "I've Been Rebuked and Scorned," a song recalling the pain of slavery and the hope of emancipation by the power of a righteous God. This was King's chosen theme for his talk, so following her stirring performance he began to read from his prepared notes. Suddenly, midway through his speech, Jackson shouted, "Tell them about the dream, Martin! Tell them about the dream!" Startled, King hesitated only a moment before pushing aside his notes and beginning to speak extemporaneously. With building passion he took on the style of the Baptist preachers whom he had grown up hearing. "I have a dream!" he passionately intoned, and he started winging it, leaving his carefully crafted speech behind, speaking from his soul, and telling his audience of his dream for racial equality under God. The result of Jackson's spontaneous shout of encouragement was spellbinding and historic, one of the most moving speeches in history. She then closed the event with a stirring rendition of another song of emancipation, "How I Got Over."

By the time of this historic event, the name Mahalia Jackson had become synonymous with gospel music, as she was the first artist to bring traditional gospel music to the attention of the masses, to listeners both black and white. Her personal story was one of struggle and false starts, but she finally broke through when she recorded a song with a small record label called Apollo, and it became an overnight sensation.

"I Will Move On Up a Little Higher," a gospel song written by prodigious black composer W. Herbert Brewster, was recorded on September 12, 1947, with a simple piano and organ accompaniment, but Jackson's thrilling vocal stylings overcame the sparse production. She starts near the lowest region of her vocal register and, over the course of the song, she moves to her top register as she celebrates "coming over hills and mountains" on her way to an everlasting life. As the song unfolds, Jackson's voice goes higher and higher. Just when you think she has surely reached the peak of her range and dynamics, she pushes it even further. The result is scintillating, and "I Will Move On Up a Little Higher" became her signature song.

Born in New Orleans in 1911, Mahalia Jackson was raised in a three-room house that was home to thirteen people, suffering together through economic deprivation and racial prejudice. Her mother died when she was very young, and she was largely raised by her aunt. Jackson was a Baptist, but some of the enthusiasm in her singing style was likely influenced by hearing the songs drifting out of the Pentecostal church next door to the family home. The way she invested emotion and passion into the old traditional songs she sang in church was a bit of a shock for the more sedate Baptists she worshiped with, but they were generally supportive. At age fourteen, she had a vision that she interpreted as a call from God to sing for Him, though at that time there was no such thing as a professional gospel singer.

The next year Jackson moved to Chicago to pursue training in nursing and joined the Greater Salem Baptist Church. On the very first Sunday with them, someone heard her singing and asked her to join the church choir. She began to sing for her congregation and also for other congregations in the area. When famous songwriter Thomas Dorsey (his most well-known song was "Precious Lord, Take My Hand")

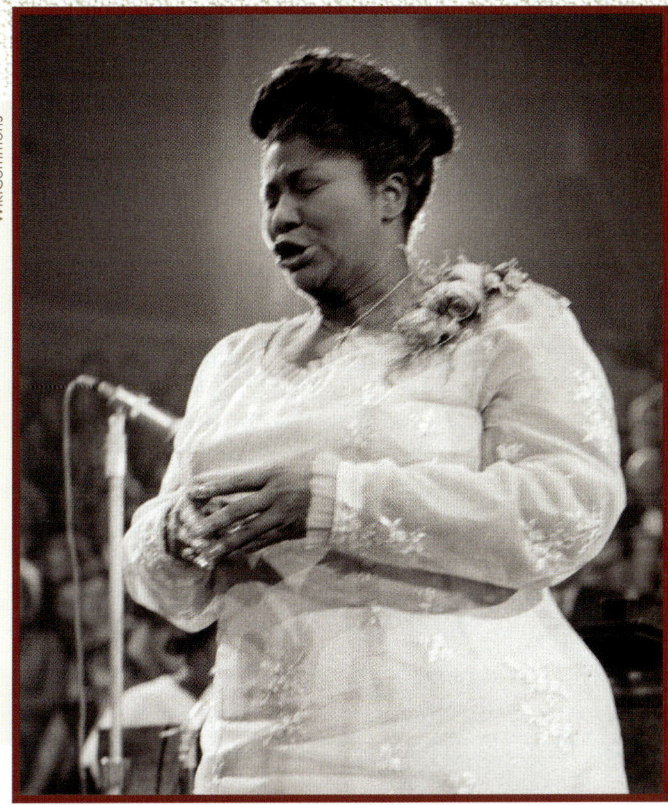

WikiCommons

Mahalia Jackson in concert in the Netherlands (1961)

visited her church and heard her sing, he knew he had found what he was looking for—the perfect person to demonstrate his songs as he traveled around the country. She soon joined him as they traveled all over the United States singing and pitching his songs, and she began her slow climb to becoming "the Queen of Gospel."

Jackson's first attempt at recording for Decca Records was a failure. People who could afford to buy records didn't normally buy gospel, and so the recordings flopped. Music executives tried to get her to record in a more popular genre, knowing that her vocal abilities could make her very successful singing jazz or blues. She refused, feeling it would be a betrayal of her calling. The result was seven years without doing any recording, instead focusing on meeting the growing demand for concerts.

When "I Will Move On Up a Little Higher" was made into a record, the expectations were modest, but it was discovered and played regularly by Chicago DJ Studs Terkel, who actively promoted the song. It sold fifty thousand copies in four weeks, and Apollo Records could not keep up with the orders. It eventually sold over a million copies and got national attention. White audiences discovered her sound and loved it, and as the word about this gospel singer with a voice of unearthly beauty spread, new opportunities began to come her way. She performed at Carnegie Hall (where she broke attendance records), toured the States and Europe, and appeared on the television shows of Dinah Shore and Ed Sullivan. Eventually she even had her own short-lived TV program, which despite its overall popularity was canceled due to the loud complaints of racist viewers.

Throughout her life, Jackson struggled against racial prejudice. When she went for drives in her Cadillac, she was often stopped by police officers who thought a black woman could not possibly own such a car. She was sometimes refused food and lodging in white-only restaurants and hotels. Someone even shot out her front window when she moved into a predominantly white neighborhood. And so, as the civil rights movement began to form around Martin Luther King Jr. and Ralph Abernathy, she joined the fight, singing for free at civil rights events and raising money for the cause. She believed that the same God who had rescued the Israelites from captivity in Egypt would bring emancipation to African Americans. But she knew that emancipation would not come without a battle, and she did not hesitate to throw her influence behind the cause.

The assassination of her friend Martin Luther King Jr. in 1968 was a devastating blow, but Jackson soldiered on, performing her praise to the Lord for audiences around the world and opening the door of acceptance for other singers who wanted to perform gospel music. By the time of her death in 1972, her health had been wrecked—she suffered from chronic pain, heart attacks, and diabetes, probably the result of her intense performance schedule and weight issues she had never addressed. In the end, it was performing for God that kept her going as long as she did.

Jackson's voice was a powerful instrument for proclaiming her love for God. Throughout her career she sang nothing except gospel songs, hymns, and spirituals. Though she was offered a lot of money to record popular music, jazz, or blues, she always declined. But having grown up around such music in New Orleans, she brought a few touches from these genres to her performance of gospel. For that reason she was not always embraced by traditionalists, but most audiences were thrilled by the energy and artistry she brought to the old songs, transforming them into something beyond what they had ever imagined those songs could be. While always exercising impeccable vocal control, Jackson would let her voice wander, stretching the phrasing, modulating between soft and loud, and recasting the techniques of the preachers she had grown up listening to—shouting, chanting, and moaning.

Jackson's contralto voice was big, powerful, and passionate, and when she performed she wore her heart on her sleeve, which showed in her voice. She unfailingly inhabited the songs she sang. The emotion she pulled out of herself and invested in her songs was unquestionably authentic, her eyes often closed in prayer as she sang. She clearly felt every word. Sometimes a tear would trickle down. And when she belted a more energetic song her whole body joined in—moving, swaying, stomping, and clapping. She was not just singing her songs; she was preaching them, lifting her audience to exultation. Responding to an inner rhythm, she spilled out the songs and built them phrase by phrase with her amazing vocal control.

Mahalia Jackson was known for her warmth and generosity, her authenticity, and her unwavering faith in God. She could have been one of the great blues singers, but she chose to sing for God alone. "I sing God's music," she said, "because it makes me feel free. It gives me hope."[1] Jackson used her gift of song to encourage others to find freedom, and she hoped her music would help "break down some of the hate and fear that divide the white and black people in this country."[2] But she would never be completely satisfied with only promoting economic and legal freedom. She also wanted people to find freedom in their souls, and so she sang the songs that continue to lift the hearts of listeners today.

57

The Chronicles of Narnia

C. S. Lewis

(children's stories, 1950–1956)

When C. S. Lewis gave a copy of the rough draft of *The Lion, the Witch, and the Wardrobe* to the wife of one of his good friends, he asked her for any helpful advice she might have to give. She liked the book, she said, but she was worried that children might take the story too literally and might get themselves trapped in a wardrobe. Lewis took her concerns seriously and provided no less than five warnings about this danger in the text of the finished book. But even with all those warnings, Lewis learned from a fan letter about one young reader who was caught by his mother with an axe in his hand, busily chopping the back out of the wardrobe in his parents' room!

Narnia has this kind of profound effect on its readers. They *want* it to be real. One of my friends, now in her fifties, has actually read The Chronicles of Narnia every year since she was a child. Narnia is like a second home to her.

These stories, Lewis tells us, started with images he saw in his imagination.

> All my seven Narnia books began with seeing pictures in my head. . . . *The Lion* began with a picture of a faun carrying an umbrella and parcels in a snowy wood. This picture had been in my mind since I was 16. Then one day, when I was about 40, I said to myself, "Let's try and make a story about it."[1]

But it was only when Lewis envisioned Aslan, the mighty lion who serves as a

Alamy

Early cover of *The Lion, the Witch & the Wardrobe*

Christ-figure in the books, that the stories really took flight.

> Aslan came bounding into it. I think I had been having a good many dreams about lions about that time. Apart from that, I don't know where the Lion came from or why he came. But once he was there, he pulled the whole story together, and soon he pulled the six other Narnian stories in after him.[2]

On initial examination, The Chronicles of Narnia may seem like simple children's tales, with talking animals, witches, and young boys and girls discovering their inner strength and courage. They are that, but they are also much more. In the midst of these stories the reader is always aware that something magical, something supernatural, might just break through at any moment. One can feel the breath of the great lion Aslan rustling through these pages as the story of Lucy, Peter, Susan, and Edmund echoes that of the grand story of redemption.

In speaking of his Narnia tales, Lewis wondered if, by stripping the Christian doctrines of their stained glass and Sunday school associations, he could "steal past the watchful dragons" of religiosity and dogmatism. So the Narnia books are constructed to prepare children for understanding the meaning of the Christian story later, when they are old enough to embrace it, while at the same time resonating with the childlike heart in each of us.

Many Christians tend to think of Lewis primarily as an intellectual communicator. They value the way his writing makes Christianity reasonable and sensible. And Lewis was truly very good at this kind of communication. He used rational argument very effectively, and he knew how to appeal to our common sense with intriguing illustrations. But Lewis also knew that there was another deeper and more mysterious level on which humans needed to be addressed, so he remythologized the gospel, creating new stories that could communicate the truths of the "old, old story." By communicating in this way he could reach all people: the educated and the ignorant, the adult and the child, the scholar and the chimney sweep.

One of Lewis's great gifts was to be able to effectively embody the gospel in story, in myth, in analogy, and in allegory so that we might see the truth with fresh eyes. He does this again and again throughout his writings. He gives flesh to our theological abstractions, and by dressing them in new garb he makes them palatable and strikingly fresh, so that readers don't feel they are being spoon-fed theology as though it were some kind of medicine. And perhaps this allows readers to really hear such truths for the first time.

Lewis had the ability in his writing to capture those transcendent moments that can occur when we come face-to-face with something bigger than ourselves, the hint of a realm beyond our ordinary lives. Through the doorway of his prose, we step from our world into another territory, a realm suffused with a holy mystery. In Lewis's best moments, his reader receives a sense of God breaking into the story—not the tame and tidy God of our creeds but the God of mystery and majesty and holiness.

C. S. Lewis was born in Belfast, Ireland, in 1898 and grew up with his brother, Warren, in a seemingly idyllic world filled with books. But that all vanished when his mother died of cancer and he was sent to England for schooling. In short order he lost his belief in God and became a professing atheist. Part of his education was conducted via a private tutorship with William Kirkpatrick, his father's former tutor, who taught Lewis to be a rigorous thinker and confirmed him in his religious skepticism. In 1916, armed with his estimable intellectual gifts, which had been finely honed by Kirkpatrick, Lewis accepted a scholarship to University College, Oxford, though his academic life was temporarily interrupted by World War I, when he was seriously injured. After convalescence he was able to return to his studies and then begin an academic career that would stretch throughout his life, first at Oxford then later at Cambridge.

Lewis had grown up in a churchgoing family but found that his formal religious experience as a young man seemed superficial compared to the powerful Romantic feelings he drew from nature, literature, and mythology. By age fifteen, he had become an atheist who described himself as "very angry with God for not existing."

Two great writers of the previous generation, George MacDonald and G. K. Chesterton, had an enormous influence upon

Lewis, as reading their work initiated his slow journey toward faith. While waiting for a train on a frosty afternoon at Leatherhead Station, he needed something to read, so he purchased a copy of MacDonald's *Phantastes,* a book he devoured with great joy and later described as having "baptized" his imagination. In MacDonald he found some of the mythic qualities he so valued in Romantic literature, but here they were rooted in MacDonald's Christian convictions. Reading *Phantastes* was, for Lewis, not only a literary experience but a spiritual one as well. He sensed a certain quality that drew him toward the book, though at the time he could not articulate precisely what it was. Reflecting later, he wrote, "I did not know (and I was long in learning) the name of the new quality, the bright shadow . . . I do now. It was holiness."[3]

The glimpses of holiness Lewis saw in MacDonald were complemented by his discovery of the joyous rationality of Chesterton, the engaging author of novels, short stories, poetry, theological musings, and essays on issues of the day. Chesterton's *The Everlasting Man* (a history of the human race written in response to H. G. Wells's wildly popular and antireligious *The Outline of History*) was particularly helpful to Lewis. If MacDonald had moved Lewis's imagination toward faith, the effect of Chesterton was to cause him to begin to question the rational basis of his skepticism and unbelief.

Lewis found himself caught between a love for all things magical and mythological and a philosophic position that reduced existence to chance and ultimate meaninglessness. These two tendencies could exist in tension within him for only so long. Through the intellectual thrust and parry of frequent religious debates with Christian friends such as Owen Barfield and J. R. R. Tolkien, Lewis moved toward theism. The theistic position began to make much more sense out of reality as he experienced it, and drew together the poles of reason and imagination. But he did not want to mindlessly assent to some sort of wish fulfillment for consolation, so his journey to faith was a drawn-out intellectual and spiritual struggle within himself. He later said that he was brought to Christianity like a prodigal, "kicking, struggling, resentful, and darting his eyes in every direction for a chance to escape."[4]

But he could not escape the conclusion to which he was coming—that there was a God.

> You must picture me alone in that room . . . night after night, feeling, whenever my mind lifted for even a second from my work, the steady, unrelenting approach of him whom I so earnestly desired not to meet. That which I greatly feared had at last come upon me. In the Trinity Term of 1929 I gave in, and admitted that God was God, and knelt and prayed: perhaps, that night, the most dejected and reluctant convert in all England.[5]

Two years later Lewis moved from theism to a full embrace of Christianity. His road to faith had been a long and arduous path, taking him through many of the central philosophical systems of the twentieth century, but he emerged as a man thoroughly convinced and willing to use his intellectual and literary gifts to convince others of what he had come to embrace as the truth.

What followed from Lewis's pen was a collection of books that are still widely read, influential, and respected as unusually creative and reasonable expressions of orthodox Christianity. These included *Mere Christianity* (1952), based upon his wartime radio talks on morality and faith, *The Screwtape Letters* (1942), with its profound grasp of the psychology of evil and temptation, *The Abolition of Man* (1943), which warned of the dangers of relativism and subjectivism in modern thought, and *The Problem of Pain* (1940), his meditations on a perennial theological puzzle: the nature of suffering and evil.

In addition to these more apologetic works, Lewis penned an autobiography (*Surprised by Joy*, 1955), science fiction (The Space Trilogy, 1938–1945), children's fantasy (The Chronicles of Narnia, 1950–1956), theological parables (*The Great Divorce*, 1945), literary criticism, and the mythically and psychologically rich novel *Till We Have Faces* (1956).

During his lifetime Lewis became recognized as Britain's foremost defender of Christian faith and values, largely due to his combining a witty and winsome writing style with a rigorous and passionate rationality. For those who were used to only hearing the Christian message expressed with earnest emotional appeal and fiery rhetoric, Lewis was a bracing and persuasive voice of reason. And those who were accustomed to religious writing that was contentious, boring, and ponderous found that Lewis wrote with humor, respect for those with whom he disagreed, and an engaging aura of common sense. He showed little interest in participating in the theological battles that various denominations waged against each other and strove instead to communicate a vision of "mere" Christianity based on the essentials. And he did this all with a creative flourish.

Through both fiction and nonfiction, Lewis was an effective proponent of traditional Christianity. He believed in the truth of the orthodox creeds, and he made these truths come alive for his readers. He managed to communicate with a combination of rationality, imagination, and a sense of the mysterious, holy otherness of God as few writers before or since have managed.

58

The Lord of the Rings

J. R. R. Tolkien

(novels, 1954–1955)

Most novelists would be satisfied with creating a well-written story containing strong characters and an intriguing plot, but J. R. R. Tolkien managed to do something more, something rarely accomplished by any writer: he created an entire alternate universe. And it is a universe that countless readers have embraced and returned to, time and again. Perhaps that is why The Lord of the Rings series has topped several polls for the most popular books of the twentieth century.

The Lord of the Rings series is, in one sense, the ultimate road trip; the story of a journey through perilous lands in search of a ring of unimaginable power that must be destroyed in order to defeat the dark powers of evil and finally restore peace to Middle Earth (Tolkien's name for his alternative world). Its pages are crammed with adventure, humor, moments of heart-stopping terror, and all the little fascinating details that bring the stories to life. As a tale of wonder and heroism, it stands without equal in its genre, and much of its charm comes from the nature of its protagonists. Frodo, and Bilbo before him, are not heroic by nature, but the root of their courage is their love of their friends, their loyalty to their home (the Shire), and their defense of a simple, ordinary life. Theirs is a heroism of mercy, for it is only due to Frodo's compassion toward Gollum at so many junctures along the way that their quest is successful in the end.

The Lord of the Rings series is also a parable about the danger of the misuse of power, with its central object of desire being a ring that can be used to dominate others. Because Tolkien published the books in the postwar era, many readers have tried to connect the ring with the looming threat of atomic warfare. Though this creates an interesting reading, Tolkien himself dismissed such musings by saying that he just wanted to tell a good story. And he did.

Tolkien was a lifelong student of Norse mythology and Arthurian legend. These tales, along with the biblical story of Christ's sacrificial triumph over evil, were the materials he used to shape a mythology all his own in The Lord of the Rings. The resulting vision includes traces of all these influences, but they combine to form a unique invention of his own imagination. The world he created in this trilogy is full of enough intricate details to keep obsessive fans busy debating all its minutiae, including the several languages spoken by the different "races" in the books, each of them with its own vocabulary and grammar. Tolkien even provided maps and invented histories to flesh out his created world. Many years after his death, these books also spawned a tremendously popular series of films that have helped keep interest alive, although most readers of the books find the films only a shadow of the riches contained in Tolkien's originals.

"God is the lord of angels and of men," wrote Tolkien, "and of elves."[1] In his trilogy and its prequels (*The Hobbit* [1939] and *The Silmarillion* [1977]) he has placed these elves, along with sundry wizards, hobbits, dwarves, and other strange creatures, at the center of his storytelling. Yet behind the scenes of his tale there lurks a power of ultimate goodness, a reservoir of strength and courage that gives his unlikely heroes the ability to defeat the darkest powers of evil. Though never mentioned by name, God is very much a character in Tolkien's trilogy. The books, while thoroughly enjoyable as a prime example of the fantasy genre, cannot be fully understood apart from Tolkien's Christian worldview, for this is not a world operating by impersonal fate, as in the Norse myths he so loved, but a world where God's providence assures the eventual victory of good over evil, though not without much struggle and sacrifice.

Tolkien used the world of fantasy to shine an illuminating light on the ultimate questions of life, a light that can awaken readers from their own spiritual slumber. By recasting the ageless theological themes of providence, sacrifice, and virtue into a new and unfamiliar world, Tolkien gave us a fresh perspective from which to view our own lives. As he once wrote, "I would claim . . . to have as one object the elucidation of truth, and the encouragement of good morals in the real world by the ancient device of exemplifying them in unfamiliar embodiments, that tend to 'bring them home.'"[2] All who have made the journey with Frodo and his friends know the reality of this experience. And Tolkien's books are filled with moments of breathtaking mystery and wonder where we see a supernatural reality shining through.

One of the strengths of Tolkien's writing is that he can awaken a sense of spiritual longing without tipping his hand in regard to his personal convictions. Perhaps that is why so many readers who do not share Tolkien's faith can still count The Lord of the Rings series among their favorite books. It does not threaten, it enchants, creating a longing for a better world. It woos us with a story well told and a vision of beauty and true goodness. Instead of relying on allegorical symbols, he chose to create a world constructed around the values of honor, strength, courage, and the existence of a benevolent Creator. Tolkien himself described The Lord of the Rings series as a "fundamentally religious" work. "That is why," he wrote, "I have not put in anything like religion . . . in the imaginary world. For religion is absorbed in the story and the symbolism."[3] The story that Tolkien tells is a mirror of the Christian story of redemption, a story he calls the *euchatastrophe*, the sudden and miraculous incursion of grace into the world that averts a seeming disaster. "The magical," he proposed in an essay on fairy tales, "may be made a vehicle for mystery."[4]

John Ronald Reuel Tolkien was born in South Africa in 1892 when his British father was relocated there by the company he worked for. Two years later his mother, Mabel, moved with her sons back to England because of the serious health issues with which young Ronald was struggling. Their father was to follow them before long, but he died in South Africa.

In 1900, Tolkien's mother was confirmed in the Catholic Church, much to the dismay of her Protestant family, but she died when he was only twelve, and he and his brother were left in the care of a priest, Father Francis Morgan. Morgan was a conservative and unsentimental Catholic whose effect on Tolkien's own growth in faith cannot be underestimated. Morgan helped him with his studies and prepared him for a successful academic career in Oxford, which was interrupted by the outbreak of World War I.

While serving as a soldier (many of the scenes of fighting and devastation in The Lord of the Rings are undoubtedly rooted in horrors he had experienced in WWI), Tolkien carried on his interest in philology. He had been fascinated with languages even as a boy, and he now spent his spare time between battles creating entirely original languages of his own fashioning. Then, in order to give the languages a history (for every language is rooted in its history), he began to create mythical-historical backstories for them. This was the beginning of his lifelong process of fleshing out an entire mythology of his own making. The fruits of this endeavor include *The Fellowship of the Ring, The Two Towers, The Return of the King, The Hobbit, The Silmarillion,* and various other collections of related tales. So vast was the mountain of papers involved in this project that, following Tolkien's death, his son Christopher gathered and edited them into a series of volumes that contained his further inventions concerning Middle Earth.

In an explanatory letter, Tolkien revealed the origins of his mythology, and their connection with his love for England:

> I was from early days grieved by the poverty of my own beloved country: it had no stories of its own (bound up in its tongue and style), not of the quality I sought, and found (as an ingredient) in legends of other lands. . . . I had a mind to make a body of more or less connected legend, ranging from the large and cosmogonic, to the level of romantic fairy story—the lesser in contact with the earth, the lesser drawing splendor from the vast backclothes—which I could dedicate simply: to England: to my country.[5]

The author of these widely imaginative fantasy stories was also an esteemed professor at Oxford and a close friend of C. S. Lewis, participating with Lewis and others in the famous "Inklings" meetings where they read and discussed each other's work over pipes and mugs of ale. Unlike Lewis and other Christian colleagues, Tolkien rarely wrote directly about his Christian faith. But he was known to his friends as a man of prayer, one who took his beliefs very seriously, and one born into the faith who never saw a good reason to look elsewhere for the truth.

J. R. R. Tolkien distinguished what he did in his writing from the act of creation. Any good story, he believed, was not a creation, but a "sub-creation," his term for a story formed by rearranging the elements of the world that God created. To the end of his days he worked on his own Middle Earth sub-creation, continuing to fashion a universe that reflected the one written by the hand of the great Author and Creator of all.

59

A Love Supreme

John Coltrane

(recording, 1964)

Louis Armstrong once remarked of those who wanted to play jazz, the musical style he himself had birthed: "If ya ain't got it in ya, ya can't blow it out." John Coltrane definitely had it in him—the passion, the desire, the skill, and the concentration. In the liner notes to his classic album *A Love Supreme*, Coltrane wrote: "God breathes through us so completely . . . so gently we hardly feel it . . . yet, it is our everything." John Coltrane took his God-given breath and used it to create some of the most challenging, passionate, and emotionally resonant music ever created.

On December 9, 1964, Coltrane gathered his quartet in the studio to record a suite he had written to praise and honor God for the part He had played in his life. With Coltrane on tenor sax, McCoy Tyner on piano, Jimmy Garrison on bass, and Elvin Jones on drums, they knocked out one of the classic albums in the history of jazz in just a few magical hours. His most unified album to date, Coltrane called this suite of four movements *A Love Supreme*.

A famously reticent and humble man, Coltrane rarely gave interviews or offered an explanation of what he sought in his music. For this record, however, for the first and only time he penned liner notes and a poem upon which the final movement of the suite was based. These notes credit God's supreme love as the cause of his praise, and our dependence upon Him as the foundation for life. The album itself, wrote Coltrane, "is a humble offering to

Him," a way of saying, "THANK YOU, GOD." It balances a deep spiritual serenity with a moving emotional outpouring of pure passion.

The first part, "Acknowledgment," opens with the striking of a gong, alerting us that something important is about to be revealed, and then the musical theme for the work is introduced. It builds and then tapers off when, unexpectedly, Coltrane and his group repeatedly chant the phrase, "a love supreme" in time to the main theme. Part two, "Resolution," and part three, "Pursuance," ring changes on this theme and introduce new elements, every member of the quartet getting a chance to solo and each delivering a memorable performance, whether it be Tyner's resonant piano chords, Garrison's gentle and sublime work on the bass, or Jones's turbulent and precise drumming. And the music always returns to the magnificent solo work of John Coltrane expressing the depths of his gratitude and praise through his saxophone.

In the fourth and final section, "Psalm," Coltrane gives an intensely beautiful musical reading of the poem he wrote to accompany the album. This poem, gorgeously simple and loaded with biblical quotations and phrases he probably first heard from the pulpit of his church, is a gushing hymn of praise to the Creator. But rather than just speaking the words, he allows the saxophone to supplant his voice in expressing his passion and emotions, and the voice of the saxophone rises and falls in patterns somewhat similar to those of the black preachers whom he grew up hearing. He plays the words on his instrument rather than speaking them. To experience the fullness of what Coltrane intended, the listener should take the time to read the poem as the music plays, as line by line he interprets the words and expresses the depths of his soul.

Although followed by many more albums, many spiritually themed and some extremely experimental in style, *A Love Supreme* is Coltrane's masterpiece, an example of how an honest exaltation of praise can become art that invites us all into the experience.

Coltrane was searching for the place where music and prayer fuse together and become one. He found his music able to take him places that mere words could not go, capturing the fullness of his spiritual ecstasy. In his later work, this becomes even more apparent. Often the melody is sacrificed in favor of the power of expression. Increasingly, Coltrane saw his art as a form of praying. He once claimed that 90 percent of his playing was prayer.

Coltrane sometimes spoke of his music as "cleansing," a way of opening up to an inner peace that could transcend the worries and struggles of life. And he exemplified this inner peace in his gentleness, patience, and generosity. Yet when he put his lips to his instrument, what gushed forth was passionate and intense but not always beautiful in the normally

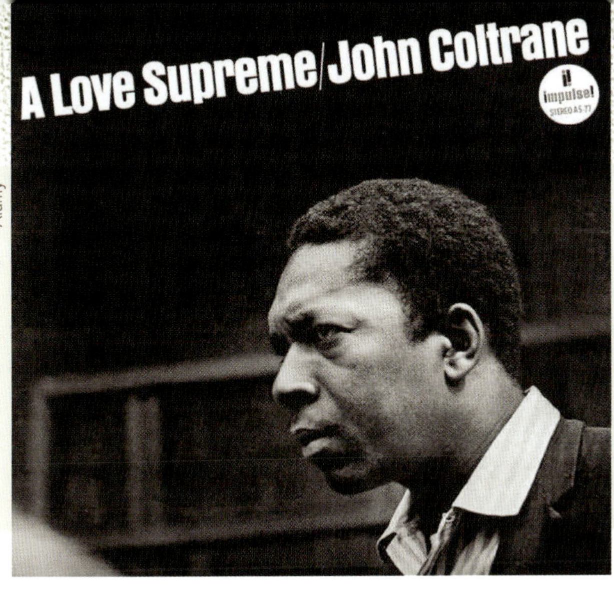

Alamy

A Love Supreme, album cover

accepted sense. The results were often jarring—the primal howl of a soul crying out that sounded to many listeners more like squeaks and shrieks and squawks than music. At times, it seemed as though he was more interested in his divine audience than the response of his human one.

Born in 1926 in North Carolina, Coltrane was raised in a churchgoing family, with a heritage of preachers on both sides of his family. His grandfather, who had a profound influence on him, was a community leader and a powerful preacher as well as a highly educated man. Through his influence, Coltrane was introduced to the writing of Langston Hughes and Paul Laurence Dunbar as well as the Bible. But when, as a teenager, he lost a number of his family members (including his father, his maternal grandparents, and his uncle) in the course of a single year, it was to music that he turned for comfort and solace. It was a spiritual lifeline. His countless hours of dedicated practice with the saxophone gave him strength and focus to weather the trauma of loss.

Coltrane's natural talent was apparent from early on. He played in a variety of jazz and R&B groups, including a stint with the Dizzy Gillespie band, before finally landing his big opportunity in 1955—playing with Miles Davis. By the time he joined Davis's group, he brought with him both a penchant of drinking too much alcohol and an addiction to heroin, a drug favored by many musicians to get them through the taxing late-night gigs and the traveling that was part of the life of a jazz musician. At first he snorted heroin, then began shooting it, finding that it not only helped him deal with his work but also helped alleviate the pain of his chronic toothaches. Before long, his drug and alcohol use began to have a deleterious effect on his playing. Davis found him increasingly undependable and had no choice but to fire him. Devastated, and knowing he might have blown his one big chance, Coltrane realized that his drug addiction would keep him from his spiritual and musical goals. He determined it was time to make a change. And he did, recommitting himself to his faith and his art.

Coltrane's renaissance was twofold, both artistic and spiritual. As he described later, in the liner notes to *A Love Supreme*, "During the year 1957, I experienced, by the grace of God, a spiritual awakening which was to lead me to a richer, fuller, more productive life. At that time, in gratitude, I asked to be given the means and privilege to make others happy through music." Giving up both alcohol and drugs, he went cold turkey and kicked his bad habits. On the artistic front, he recommitted himself to his playing and to a more strenuous regime of practice. His wife at that time, Naima, reported that he worked twenty-four hours a day and usually fell asleep with horn in hand. She said he was "ninety-percent saxophone."[1]

By 1958, Miles Davis was desperate to add a saxophone player to his very successful combo. Despite their past history together, he was willing to give Coltrane another chance. The result of their new partnership was a series of stellar recordings that demonstrated the excellence of their combined styles—Miles muted and intense, creating emotional textures by his combination of sound and silence, Coltrane perfecting the rapid and exuberant style he had developed while playing with jazz legend Thelonious Monk. Jazz critic Ira Gilter coined the phrase "sheets of sound" to describe Coltrane's wildly imaginative playing. In 1959, Coltrane was a part of two landmark projects in the history of jazz, his solo effort *Giant Steps* and an album with Miles Davis that is widely considered the greatest recording in the history of jazz, *Kind of Blue*, where Coltrane's influence is very much in evidence.

By the time he formed his own group the next year, John Coltrane was one of jazz music's superstars. His fame increased with each subsequent release. And always, there was a profound spiritual element to the work he created. As fellow saxophonist Archie Shepp remembers, attending his live concerts "was like being in church . . . he created what became for me a new music. Like Bach and Mozart, Coltrane actually raised this music from the secular to an area of serious, religious world music."[2]

Long a student of the world's religions, Coltrane intensified his study in the latter years of his life, exploring Kabbalah, Sufism, Hinduism, African spirituality, and other traditions for the wisdom they could offer in his spiritual journey. Although he seemed to be firmly rooted in the Christian faith, he felt free to explore. He was not so much interested in dogmas and theologies as in spiritual practices. When a Japanese interviewer asked him, "What would you like to be ten years from now?" his simple answer was, "I would like to be a saint."[3]

60

Au Hasard du Balthasar

ROBERT BRESSON

(film, 1966)

When fabled film producer Dino de Laurentiis wanted to create a series of films based on the Bible, he approached Robert Bresson to direct the initial film on the book of Genesis. After all, Bresson was considered to be one of the greatest living directors and was also a man not afraid to be identified as a Christian. He seemed the perfect fit. But when Bresson, with his usual passion for communicating truth indirectly, said that he wanted to have the dialogue in Hebrew and Aramaic, and that he wouldn't actually show any animals on Noah's Ark, just their footprints, de Laurentiis realized that he had asked the wrong man to helm the rich spectacle that he had in mind. (This movie on Genesis was eventually made as *The Bible: In the Beginning*, with John Huston as director, but was not successful enough to justify further films in the series.)

As a Christian who was a filmmaker, Robert Bresson often dealt with spiritual themes and built his scripts around religious characters, but he did not envision his films as a way to promote his faith. Instead, he used his unique and austere cinematic style to give viewers a glimpse of the realities that lay just beneath the surface of everyday life. Those who have written studies of his work often refer to his style as "spiritual" or "transcendental," as it tries to reveal something deeper than what the viewer initially perceives.

With *Au Hasard du Balthasar*, Bresson

investigates the spiritual impact on life through telling the story of a suffering and saintly donkey. He purposely chose a humble donkey as his lead character because of its resonance with biblical stories and because it was a beast of burden. Jean-Luc Godard once described this film as "the real world in an hour and a half," and Bresson revealed it to be a world filled with pain, suffering, and injustice. Through the experiences of the gentle donkey, we see the cruelty that humans inflict upon animals and upon each other in a heartbreaking story that reveals the depths of human sin while providing a few moments along the way where grace and redemption can be fleetingly glimpsed. Balthasar is a kind of Christ-figure, bearing the sins of man. He is innocent and holy. One woman in the film even speaks of him as "a saint." And at the end of the film it is human selfishness and vice that cause his death. In the unforgettable closing moments, we see the wounded Balthasar stumble and fall in a mountain meadow, and as he brays out his pain he is surrounded by a flock of grazing sheep. We hear the gentle sound of the resonant bells around the necks of the sheep; a strangely moving moment that points to something mystical and sacred.

Robert Bresson was born in France in 1901 and was a painter and a fashion photographer before finally moving into a career in filmmaking. He always believed that films should be more like paintings than filmed theatrical productions. During his forty-year career, Bresson only produced thirteen films, and none of them were popular hits. But his body of work has been an inspiration and guide to countless modern directors who have taken elements of his aesthetic and made them their own.

Among Bresson's thirteen films are several standouts. *Diary of a Country Priest* (1951) adapts the Bernanos novel about an unnamed priest struggling with doubts about God and about his own adequacy for the job, as well as facing outright nastiness from the citizens of his village. The priest becomes sick and dies while still at work trying to bring his parishioners to faith, but not before drawing the conclusion that makes up the final line of the film: "All is grace." *A Man Escaped* (1956), probably his most accessible film, is the story of a member of the French Resistance who manages to escape a Nazi prison by careful and meticulous planning and timely help from the providential intervention of God. *Pickpocket* (1959), reminiscent of Dostoyevsky's *Crime and Punishment*, is the tale of an amoral young man who learns the art of "lifting" wallets and purses. He finally shows signs of repentance and redemption in the closing scene that takes place in the cell block where he is being held. Bresson's later films of the '60s and '70s mostly lack the clarity and power of his earlier works (with the notable exception of *Au Hasard du Balthasar*), and give evidence of

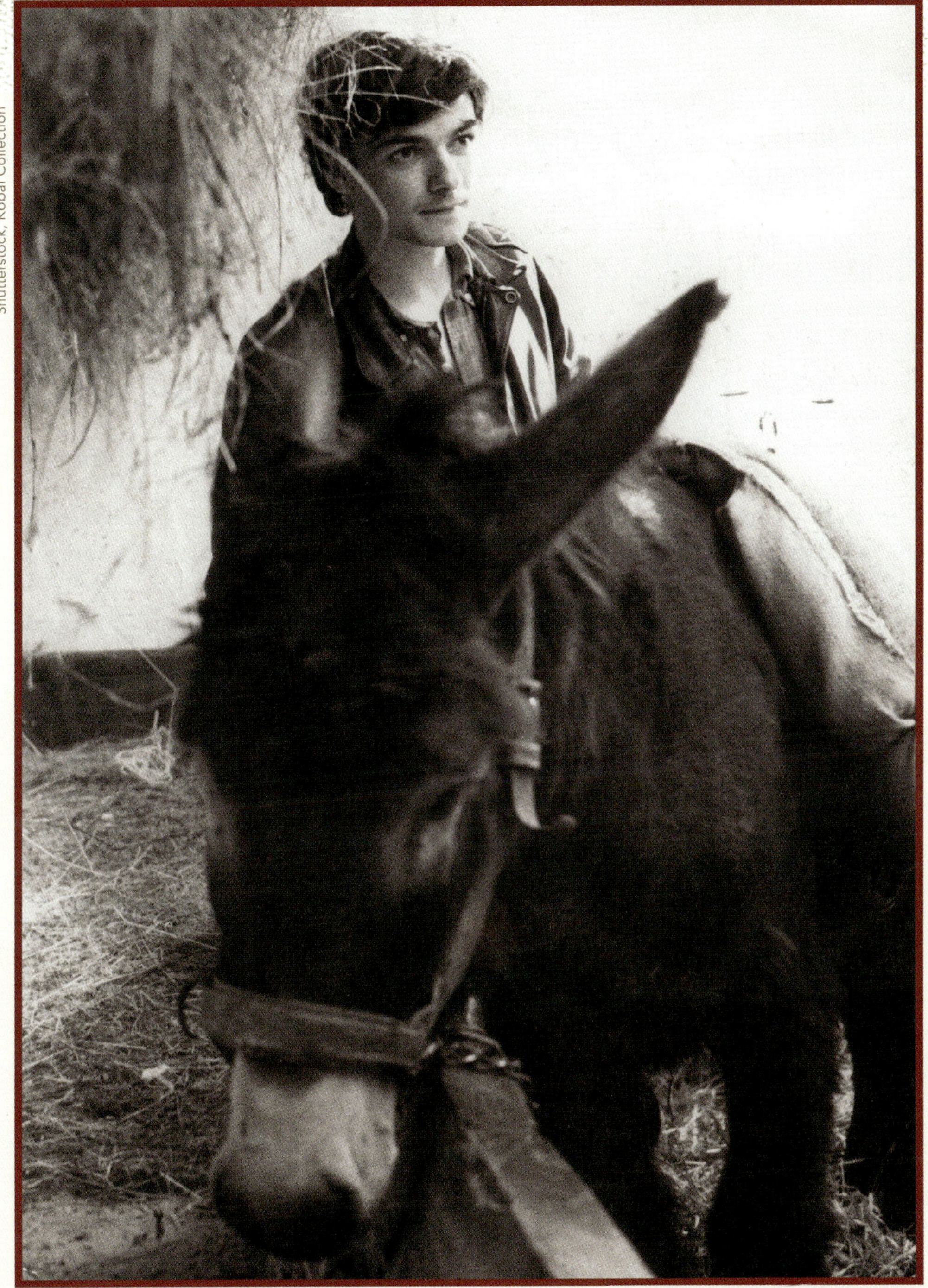

Still from *Au Hasard du Balthasar*

his growing dismay about the nihilism of modern life. "Things are going very badly," he said. "People are becoming more materialist and cruel. . . . They are all interested in money only. Money is becoming their God. God doesn't exist for many."[1]

In creating his films, Bresson believed that form was more important than content. In other words, it was less about what his films said than *how* they said it. And he developed a unique philosophy for filmmaking that guided his productions, which he eventually explained in a small volume of aphorisms he published called *Notes on the Cinematographer* (1975). In this little book he distinguished his own work—*cinematography*—from *cinema*, the traditional way that films are made. He saw most films as being so focused on dramatic acting that they lost their deeper sense of reality and ultimately had less impact on the human soul. Bresson was committed to using a sense of life's mysteriousness to create a place for self-discovery on the part of the viewer. "Hide the ideas," he wrote, "but so that people find them. The most important will be the most hidden."[2] To accomplish this required great focus and economy of means on the part of the director, a rigorous and austere quest for purity of expression. "Everything should not be shown, or there is no art; art lies in suggestion. . . . Mystery should be preserved; since we live in mystery, mystery should be on the screen."[3] He proposes several ways to achieve this end.

First, Bresson was opposed to the normal acting style deployed in most films, a style in which actors used their voice and gestures to communicate the emotional state of the characters they play. Instead, Bresson strove for an emotionally flatter style of acting, where the actor speaks with more restraint, little intonation, and limited facial expression. The actor was coached by Bresson to deliver his or her lines more mechanically, almost in monotone, which Bresson felt would strip away emotional falseness. Basically, he wanted his actors, whom he distinguished from the norm by calling them "models," to quit acting. When this occurred, Bresson believed, the interior life of the character became more evident, as it was not hidden under layers of performance. He was trying to get at something deeper in the portrayal of human beings, and so he quit using professional actors after his first two films, relying on amateurs whom he could train in his own unique acting style. This worked better in some of his films than in others, but when it worked at its best, it could create a performance that felt strangely real and highly revelatory.

Second, Bresson placed great emphasis on the importance of the film's soundtrack. The further he developed in his career, the less he employed the usual kind of background music that tipped viewers off as to how they were supposed to respond, or tried to amplify the emotional impact of a scene through musical cues. There is, of course, no wash of violins that pierce our ears when we feel deeply in real life, so

Bresson didn't want to express that kind of falseness in his films. Instead, he focused on placing the appropriate real sounds into the mix, and sometimes even revealed important actions by sounds offscreen so that the viewer hears rather than sees. "The noises," he wrote, "must become the music."[4] Bresson was also not afraid of stretches of silence in his films, where there is quite literally no sound, something unthinkable in the normal methods of filmmaking. But he believed that silence sometimes best communicated the truths he was filming and created a space for the viewer to respond on his or her own terms.

Third, Bresson limited the movement of the camera to that which was absolutely necessary, and didn't want fancy camera moves to draw attention to themselves. He restricted his use of pans and sweeping shots, instead building up his storytelling through the use of tightly composed scenes, in which he sometimes focused on hands and feet rather than on faces. His camera lingered upon the details. Bresson was fascinated by details, and was meticulous in presenting them—the sleight-of-hand methods of the thieves in *Pickpocket*, the step-by-step procedure by which a prison break was planned in *A Man Escaped*, or the rituals of the daily rounds of a priest in *The Diary of a Country Priest*. Bresson meticulously re-created the mundane repetitiveness of daily life, providing a tension-producing hint that there were deeper forces at work in the midst of that ordinariness, and then creating a moment when something extraordinary erupts from, and breaks through, the placidity. When that happens, the experience is revelatory.

Throughout his films, Robert Bresson was intent on revealing a supernatural order of being that existed behind and beneath the ordinary. As he said in an interview, "I'd like to make perceptible the soul and the superior presence that is omnipresent, this entity which is God." But he didn't want to do this through cinematic preaching or overly dramatic means. "I want to make people who see the films to feel the presence of God in ordinary life. . . . There is a presence of something which I call God, but I don't want to show it too much. I prefer to make people feel it."[5] When his films work at their best, that is what happens—a divine presence makes itself felt in the lives of the struggling and the suffering, which produces a purifying glimpse of the salvation that is ever available.

61

Andrei Rublev

Andrei Tarkovsky

(film, 1966)

One of the early masterpieces explored in this book was an icon painted by Andrei Rublev. This modern masterpiece is a film biography of his life by another Russian master, filmmaker Andrei Tarkovsky. In *Andrei Rublev,* Tarkovsky explores the barbaric medieval world in which this artist/monk lived his life, and highlights his icon paintings as a spiritual testimony of faith in a dark era. He does not idealize the medieval period in which Rublev lived but reveals it to be a time of great violence and spiritual confusion—traits not unlike the times in which he lived—under the shadow of atheistic communism, the threat of atomic warfare, moral cynicism, and spiritual confusion.

To make a film about a religious subject under the repressive system of the Soviet Union was itself an act of great courage, and that Tarkovsky even managed to produce it at all seems something of a miracle. Once *Andrei Rublev* was completed, though, Tarkovsky still had to battle for years with the authorities to get it released. Because he refused to make the changes they demanded, its release was held up until a political thawing in the USSR finally made it possible for the film to be seen.

Andrei Rublev is truly an epic film, both in length and conception. Clocking in at almost three and a half hours in its original version, it has been trimmed by almost an hour in the version usually screened today. It is divided into eight sections, each one focused on a major event in the icon

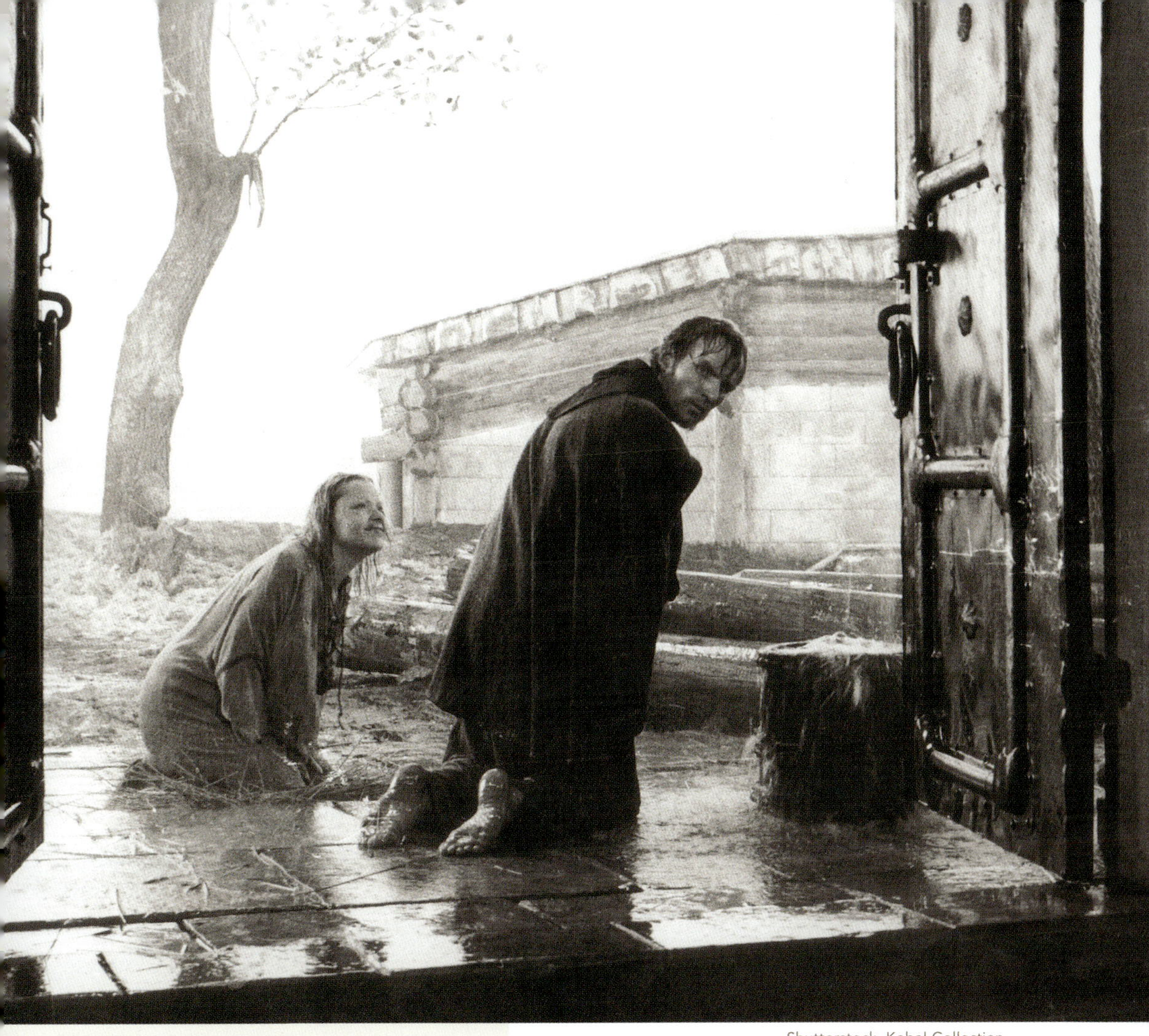

Still from *Andrei Rublev*

Shutterstock, Kobal Collection

painter's life. Though a deeply spiritual story, it is not presented with an air of piety but with gritty realism, captured beautifully in the highly contrasting textures of wide-screen black-and-white film.

During Rublev's journeys through the course of the film, the young monk witnesses the inhumanity and cruelty of the human race, experiencing firsthand the ugliness of war, the horror of rape, and monstrous blasphemy. He experiences pain and poverty and the temptations of the flesh and has a vision in which he witnesses the crucifixion of Christ reenacted on the top of a snowy Russian hill. At one point, in trying to defend a woman being tortured, Rublev even commits murder himself, which leads him to a vow of silence and the decision to forgo his vocation as a painter.

That vow is only renounced late in the picture when he is reminded of the power inherent in the act of creativity and returns to his calling as an icon painter. This decision ushers in the final section of the film, the only portion not filmed in black and white but which gives us, in gloriously vivid color, a close-up look at the icons Rublev has created, a symbol of the ultimate triumph of the spiritual over the darkness of the material world.

Few films so effectively encapsulate a specific moment in history and render it in such stark and unblinking realism, while at the same time offering a deeper spiritual hope that lies beyond this dark and troubling world. This hope shines through in the creation of sacred art. Tarkovsky's film, at its core, is about the spiritual importance of art and is itself a work of art of the highest caliber.

Andrei Tarkovsky was born in Russia in 1932 and studied film at the Moscow State Film School. Even his earliest student films show the promise of his immense talent as a director. Upon graduation, he began to make his own films, often struggling with the limitations set by Soviet censors but finding ways to present his vision regardless. While never a hugely popular filmmaker, as his films place great demands upon their audiences, he was lionized by the likes of Ingmar Bergman, who thought him the best of modern directors. When Tarkovsky found it impossible to continue making the films he wanted under the eyes of the Soviet censors, he chose to go into exile, living for a time in Italy, Germany, and Sweden (where he made his last film). When he was diagnosed with cancer, he moved to Paris for treatment, but died in 1986 at age fifty-four.

Tarkovsky's films, unapologetically emphasizing the spiritual journeys of his protagonists, have caused some critics to label his work as "sacred cinema." The means by which he created his sacred cinema render it somewhat difficult or puzzling to those used to the typical Hollywood film. His plots, usually about some sort of spiritual or intellectual search, do not usually follow a straightforward narrative development. The scenes are often not in chronological order and the viewer is left to put together the pieces that make up the story, which means that it can take more than one viewing to begin to fully comprehend what has happened and why.

Since Tarkovsky viewed cinema primarily as a visual rather than a literary art form, there is much less dialogue in his films than in most motion pictures, and what dialogue does exist is often given to philosophical and theological discussions by his characters. Imbedded in these dialogues are thought-provoking meditations and musings on God's presence or absence from the world, the meaning of human life, the purpose of art, the mystery of human relationships, and a profound critique of where the modern world has gone wrong. When his characters are not speaking to one another, Tarkovsky is not afraid of silence. There are long stretches of silence in his films, a chance for the viewers to meditate on what they are seeing, and which assign primacy to what he felt was most important in film—the images.

What really makes a Tarkovsky film stand out is the way it looks. Perhaps no other director has created so many scenes of such overwhelming and mysterious beauty as he has given us in his films. One could offer countless examples:

- The snowy Bruegel-inspired crucifixion scene in *Andrei Rublev*.
- The moment in *Nostalgia* where a woman is praying in church lit by flickering candles, kneeling before a statue of the Madonna, when suddenly a flock of birds miraculously bursts forth from the breast of the statue.
- The ending of *Nostalgia*, where the camera pans slowly backward, only to reveal that the little cabin before which a man is sitting is in actuality part of the interior of a ruined church.
- The scene of a house deep in the woods that becomes engulfed in roaring flames in *The Mirror*.
- The moment in *Solaris* where it begins to rain *inside* a living room, or the lengthy take of weeds and rushes swaying in a gently flowing stream from that same film.

Such scenes, and they are many, provoke an intake of breath and a deep sense of wonder. They are clearly intended to invite our contemplative gaze; to cause us to see.

One of Tarkovsky's common strategies was to hold a shot for a length to which viewers are not normally accustomed. What happens in such moments, according to Tarkovsky, is that we pretty quickly lose interest in what we are seeing and then boredom begins to set in. But if we are forced by the filmmaker to keep looking as the camera holds the shot, something magical begins to happen—we break through the boredom and we begin to actually *see*, to experience the layers of loveliness that we would normally pass over so quickly. Watching Tarkovsky's films teaches us the patience to see anew; his movies are more objects of contemplation than instruments of entertainment.

His father was an acclaimed poet, and Tarkovsky brings a similar sense of poetry to his films. He does not offer us a primarily rational experience but one that is poetic, mystical, and contemplative. He never wanted his viewers to overthink what they were seeing but rather to share his vision of life; not through arguing for the truths he held dear but by enacting them on film with an ambiguity that makes great demands upon the viewer. This might cause some viewers to become impatient with his films or consider them self-indulgent. But for those willing to sit patiently with a Tarkovsky film, there are luminous truths waiting to be disclosed. He has constructed the conditions in which the sacred and the numinous might be experienced and explored.

Tarkovsky's vision of life was a profoundly spiritual one. His films, therefore, contain much implicit criticism for our contemporary way of life and the materialistic philosophies that undergird it, particularly the Soviet version of scientific atheism. "Our spiritual development," he said, "drags so far behind technical progress that we are in a constant spiritual crisis."[1] He calls us to see that the world is much too mysterious to be explained in scientific terms, and that there is a deeper spirituality at work behind and beyond our present existence, which informs and transforms it. Through his poetic images and explorations, he invites us to experience the invisible through the visible. That's why his films do not steer shy of the unexplained, supernatural occurrences, or miracles.

Though Tarkovsky sometimes made use of Christian symbolism and imagery, he often did not, as his goal seemed less to convince anyone of the Russian Orthodoxy he practiced and more to assert a spiritual reality he left largely open to the viewer to interpret. He was intent upon filming the landscape of the human soul. "Faith is knowledge with the help of love,"[2] he wrote in his diaries. These diaries show him as a man in perpetual quest for the truth, a wrestler with God, an asker of ultimate questions, and a Christian mystic of deep humility.

"The ability to create is our similarity to our Creator," he once said. He defined his art as "an attempt to understand—to find the truth, which is the reason for human existence."[3] Andrei Tarkovsky pointed to the spiritual truths that are often forgotten in our secular age, and his way of exploring such truths was to offer films that were sacred cinema: dense with meaning, teasingly ambiguous, and ultimately revelatory about the nature of human existence and our relationship to God.

62

Cancer Ward

Aleksandr Solzhenitsyn

(novel, 1967)

The instruction often given to young writers is "write what you know." Aleksandr Solzhenitsyn did just that throughout his writing career, taking the events of a life filled with a struggle against political oppression and turning them into a series of books, both fiction and nonfiction, that dealt with universal human issues. *Cancer Ward* is one of his finest achievements, a semiautobiographical novel about a group of cancer patients in a Soviet hospital fighting for their lives and health against the backdrop of the political unrest that occurred after the death of Stalin.

The treatment center in Solzhenitsyn's novel is a sort of representative microcosm of post-Stalin culture in the USSR, and he uses the lives and stories of the patients in the cancer ward to explore various political theories, the reality of human mortality in the face of disease, and how hope might be found in a seemingly hopeless environment. The various patients have different responses to their plight, and the clash of these ways of responding is reminiscent of the ways that people responded to the "cancer" of Stalinist oppression. As the main character, Oleg Kostoglotov (likely based on Solzhenitsyn himself), says at one point in the novel, "A man dies from a tumor, so how can a country survive with growths like labor camps and exiles?"[1]

Oleg has grown to distrust the bureaucracy and its solutions and is looking for love from one of the female doctors with

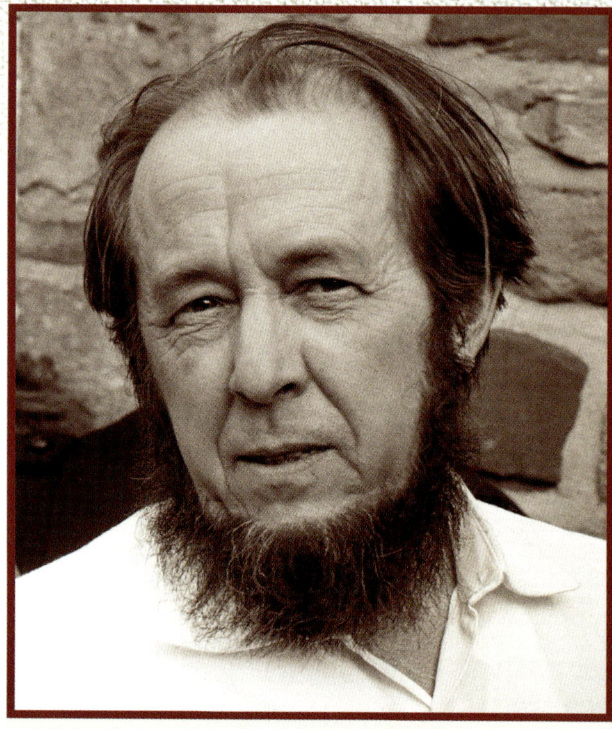

Aleksandr Solzhenitsyn in 1974, after being exiled from the Soviet Union, photo by Bert Verhoeff

whom he imagines the possibility of living a normal life. Another character, Rusanov, is a former bureaucrat and a bully; a true believer in the Soviet state, he fears reprisal from those he has informed upon. Other patients include a former prison guard full of justifications for his actions, a doctor who is herself stricken with the disease but will not acknowledge it, and a quiet librarian who regrets his own silence in the face of injustice.

Each of these characters explores their own mortality in the face of the possibility that they will die from cancer, and struggles to find some meaning in their lives. Finding meaning includes coming to terms with the great evil in the world. In a memorable scene just after his release from the hospital, Oleg visits the local zoo, where he is told the story of a man who, for no reason, threw tobacco into the eyes of a monkey, causing blindness. Oleg's horror mirrors Solzhenitsyn's own:

> Oleg was struck dumb. Up to then he had been strolling along smiling with knowing condescension, but now he felt like yelling and roaring across the whole zoo, as though the tobacco had been thrown into his own eyes. "Why? Thrown into its eyes, just like that! Why? It's senseless! Why?"[2]

Cancer Ward is not poised to provide easy answers to such questions, but with moments of great compassion and tenderness Solzhenitsyn posits love and kindness as partial solutions to the monstrous evil in the world.

Aleksandr Solzhenitsyn was born in Russia in 1918, and was raised by his mother after his father was killed in a hunting accident while she was still pregnant with him. His mother was a devout Orthodox believer and raised her son in the faith, though he drifted away as he came of age. Solzhenitsyn grew up during the years of the Russian Civil War, and his family's property was seized and turned into a collective farm under the Soviets. Though he studied mathematics at Rostov State University, from his early days he knew he wanted to be a writer, and even envisioned someday writing an epic novel about Russia during World War I and the era of the Russian Revolution. This much-delayed dream would eventually see the light of day in the publication of *August 1914* (1971), the first of a series of novels published late in his life that explored this period in Russian history.

During World War II, Solzhenitsyn served as a commander in the Red Army but was arrested for making derogatory remarks about Stalin in a private letter to a friend. Accused of anti-Soviet propaganda, he was arrested, interrogated, and then sentenced in absentia to eight years in a labor camp. His experiences in a series of camps became the inspiration for his first book, *One Day in the Life of Ivan Denisovich*. While serving his time, he continued to write, though he often had to hide his literary labors from the prison authorities. In some cases he even had to write without the benefit of paper, setting the long poems he was composing to memory, only to be written down later.

It was not until he sat in the dark confines of a Soviet prison camp that Solzhenitsyn's own spiritual awakening began, allowing him to later muse, "Bless you prison, bless you for being in my life. For there, lying upon the rotting prison straw, I came to realize that the object of life is not prosperity as we are made to believe, but the maturity of the human soul."[3] When his sentence ended, Solzhenitsyn was released into internal exile in the barren northeastern region of Russia, and a long-undiagnosed cancer nearly ended his life. Because the cancer had spread dramatically, Solzhenitsyn was convinced that his death was fast approaching, but a Christian friend prayed for his recovery and the cancer went into remission. That recovery, which seemed to him a miracle, confirmed the necessity of forging a closer connection with God. Much of what he experienced during this close brush with death made its way into his novel *Cancer Ward* (1968).

In 1956, Solzhenitsyn was freed from exile and began teaching at a secondary school during the day while he secretly worked at night on his writing projects, knowing full well that they might never be published in his lifetime. But in 1962, *One Day in the Life of Ivan Denisovich* was published, albeit in an edited form. The book became a phenomenon, as people were anxious to read about what had happened in the camps. The brief political thaw that allowed this book to be published ended when Krushchev was ousted from power in 1964, but Solzhenitsyn continued to write. It was known by the authorities that he was working on *Cancer Ward*, but he was also secretly penning a searing indictment of the Soviet system and the horrors of *The*

Gulag Archipelago (1973–1978), his name for the system of prison camps.

After the KGB seized his manuscript for *Cancer Ward*, Solzhenitsyn created a network of friends who would help keep his other work secreted away from them, often at great risk to their own personal safety. In 1970, he was awarded the Nobel Prize in Literature for the work that had managed to find its way out of the USSR and into publication in the West, but he could not attend the ceremony for fear that he would not be allowed back into his own country. When *The Gulag Archipelago* was finally published in three volumes, it sold over thirty million copies, and would be universally acclaimed as one of the most important literary works of the twentieth century for its unsparing revelations about the terrors the Soviet system inflicted upon its own people in order to support its ideology.

Because of his popularity in the West, Solzhenitsyn seemed an insoluble problem for the Soviet Union, so in 1974 he was stripped of his citizenship and deported to West Germany. He lived there for a time before settling in the United States, where he continued to work on his fictionalized history of Russia in the modern age. While in the West, he was not only a fiery critic of the ideology of communism but also of what he saw as the vulgar materialism, spiritual stupor, and individualism of the capitalist nations. He pointed toward values deeper than any political ideology, once remarking that "untouched by the breath of God, unrestricted by human conscience, both capitalism and socialism are repulsive."[4] In 1994, he returned in triumph to post-Soviet Russia and settled in Moscow, where he continued to write and speak out for a more traditional Russian way of life. Not long before he died in 2008, a reporter from *The New Yorker* asked him what he thought about dying. He said that it would just be

> a peaceful transition. As a Christian, I believe there is life after death, and so I understand that this is not the end of life. The soul has a continuation, the soul lives on. Death is only a stage, some would even say a liberation. In any case, I have no fear of death.[5]

As a Christian, Solzhenitsyn believed that the evils humans wrought upon one another were not simply the result of trying to defend their corrupt ideologies. No, the problem was deeper; at its root was a spiritual malignancy. In his *Templeton Address*, Solzhenitsyn said:

> If I were asked today to formulate as concisely as possible the main cause of the ruinous revolution that swallowed up some 60 million of our people, I could not put it more accurately than to repeat: "Men have forgotten God; that is why this has happened."[6]

Through his writings, Solzhenitsyn acted as a prophetic voice of conscience, a reminder of the evils of which humans are capable. The human race, he believed, doesn't neatly divide into good and bad people. "If only there were evil people somewhere insidiously committing evil deeds," he wrote, "and it were necessary only to separate them from the rest of us and destroy them. But the line dividing good and evil cuts through the heart of every human being. And who is willing to destroy a piece of his own heart?"[7]

Aleksandr Solzhenitsyn firmly believed in the power of literature to change human hearts and minds—and to change the course of history. "One word of truth shall outweigh the whole world,"[8] he said, and he took it upon himself, despite all the roadblocks placed in his way, to speak truthfully to a world that was often not ready to hear.

> The task of the artist is to sense more keenly than others the harmony of the world, the beauty and the outrage of what man has done to it, and poignantly to let people know. By means of art we are sometimes sent—dimly, briefly—revelations unattainable by reason.[9]

In his books, such revelations are many.

63

At Folsom Prison

Johnny Cash

(recording, 1968)

When Johnny Cash recorded a live album at Folsom Prison, he had a captive audience. Literally. A thousand inmates crowded into the prison dining hall to hear one of country music's legendary characters, a man who had written a hit song about their hated institution and had previously visited prisons to play for the inmates. But no one had ever recorded an album in a prison, and this was a dream that Cash, with deep compassion for these forgotten men, had long nursed. When he was finally able to convince Columbia Records to let him record at Folsom, no one expected the resulting album would become an instant classic, a record that would reinvigorate Cash's faltering career, inspire the prisoners, and bring national attention to the need for prison reform.

As Cash and his backing group arrived at Folsom, there was an almost funereal feeling among them as they heard the iron gates clank shut behind them. No one knew exactly what to expect, and they had been warned that the prison could not guarantee their safety.

Despite some initial technical problems with the sound system, the concert kicked off energetically with Carl Perkins and The Statler Brothers before Johnny Cash finally introduced himself, receiving a roar of approval as he jump-started his classic "Folsom Prison Blues" with a fast and fiery performance. He then sang almost every song he knew about crime and imprisonment. Highlights included a recklessly energetic version of "Cocaine Blues," a tongue-in-cheek song about the anticipation of a hanging, "25 Minutes to Go," and the sentimental ballad "Send a Picture of Mother." June Carter (who would soon become Cash's wife) then joined him on stage for a stomping, steaming rendition of their famous duet "Jackson." The audience embraced Cash with all their raucous energy, sensing that here was a man who understood them.

Then Cash slowed things down a bit with "The Green, Green Grass of Home" before announcing that his closing song had been written by one of the Folsom inmates, who was sitting among them in the audience, unaware his song was about to be performed. Glen Sherley's song "Greystone Chapel" had been passed along to Cash the night before, and the band had little time to learn it. But they performed it with passion and dignity, and the inmates roared their appreciation of this deeply spiritual song about the chapel that stood as a refuge of peace and mercy within the walls of this hellish prison. The chapel, the song promised, was a place where the sinner could meet God and be forgiven.

"Greystone Chapel" was the perfect ending to a concert that showcased both sides of Johnny Cash—the outlaw rebel who identified with the anger and disgust of the prisoners at their subhuman treatment, and the Christian believer who saw God as the only hope for men who had fallen to such a state. He didn't judge; he commiserated. Then he shone the light of truth into the darkness of a prison dining hall. And it was all captured on tape for a record that has become one of the classics of contemporary music.

Johnny Cash was born "J. R. Cash" in rural Arkansas in 1932, and was raised in a family that owned a small farm and struggled to make ends meet. He began working with his family picking cotton at age five, where he would join the family in singing as they worked the fields. He always loved music, especially the gospel music he would hear when the family gathered around the radio. His dream was that he might one day sing gospel songs on the radio, and so he mastered the guitar and wrote songs as early as age twelve. After military service in Germany, he returned to the United States, where he settled in Memphis, married, got a job selling appliances, and met Luther Perkins and Marshall Grant.

Cash, Perkins, and Grant would gather at Grant's home in the evenings after work and fool around with their acoustic guitars. They decided they needed to diversify their instruments, so Perkins got himself an electric guitar and Grant a stand-up bass. Working with instruments that were largely unfamiliar to them, the three experimented with the combination of sounds they could make and stumbled upon a fresh

Alamy

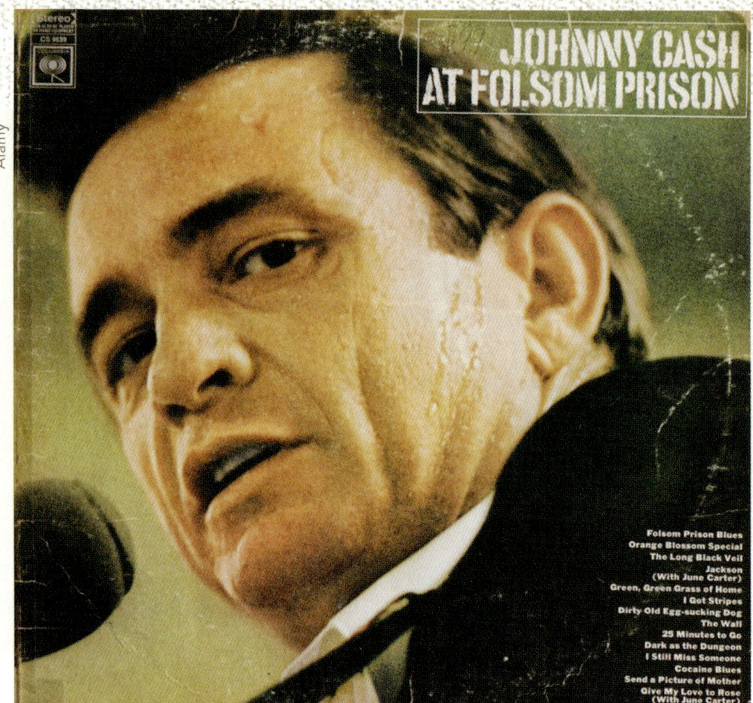

At Folsom Prison album cover

and exciting sound, the rhythmic "chick-a-boom" that would become the characteristic backdrop to so many of Cash's early songs.

Armed with their signature sound and Cash's resonant bass-baritone voice, which had the gravity of rolling thunder, they auditioned for Sam Phillips at Sun Records, hoping to make a gospel record. Phillips had no interest in gospel but liked their sound, so he told them to come back when they had more salable songs. The trio returned with "Hey Porter" and "Cry, Cry, Cry," which became hits, and were followed by such classics as "Folsom Prison Blues" and "I Walk the Line." When Cash, already unhappy with his subpar contract at Sun, found himself getting less attention than labelmate Jerry Lee Lewis, he moved to Columbia Records, where he would record almost sixty albums. Plus, Columbia would let him fulfill his dream of recording a gospel album.

As his career began to take off, Cash started drinking heavily and taking drugs (amphetamines and barbiturates) to cope with the stress. The result was erratic behavior and undependable concert performances, even as his career was kicking into high gear. From the beginning, Cash had cultivated an outlaw image—tough, dangerous, and unpredictable—and now the actions resulting from his drug addiction actually did land him in jail a couple of times (although, despite the popular myth, he never served any time in a prison). In spite of all his troubles, he produced a number of interesting albums during the mid-sixties (such as *Bitter Tears*, a concept album honoring Native Americans, and *Blood, Sweat and Tears*, a tribute to the working man), as well as recording huge hits like "Ring of Fire" and "Jackson," a duet with June Carter, with whom he found himself falling in love.

Near the end of the 1960s, Cash's personal life was a mess, his struggling marriage had ended, and his popularity was ebbing. It was a dark time. One day, under the influence of drugs, he decided to commit suicide by losing himself in Nickajack Cave, where he hoped to "just die." Deep inside the labyrinthine passages of the cave, he collapsed exhausted on the stone floor and decided that this was the end. But then, in the darkness of the cave, Cash felt the presence of God with him, the God from whom he had spent many years running. Suddenly he understood that God still loved him, and he wanted to live. Struggling to his feet, he began to desperately search for the exit to the cave, wondering if he would ever find his way out. He did, and when he emerged back into the light, he determined to change his ways, to kick his drug habit, and to marry the woman who had been a stabilizing force through the darkest of his days, June Carter.

The success of *At Folsom Prison*, and its even more successful follow-up *At San Quentin* (1969), turned his career around almost as quickly as the spiritual odyssey in Nickajack Cave had turned around his personal life. The late sixties and early seventies would see him surpass his earlier notoriety and take his place as a living legend of music. His television series, *The Johnny Cash Show*, his friendship with the likes of Bob Dylan and Neil Young, and the phenomenal popularity of his prison albums earned him fans outside the usual country music scene.

In the seventies Cash became established as "The Man in Black," because he dressed in all-black clothes rather than the rhinestone suits of other country singers. Always a man who looked out for the underdog, he explained in his song "Man in Black" that he wore that color on behalf of the poor and the hungry, the prisoners, the recovering addicts, and the overlooked and neglected. Such concerns were nothing new for Cash. From his earliest days he had sung of the dignity of "the ones who are held back," considering this as part of his duty as a Christian.

It was also his duty as a Christian, he believed, to share his faith with others. He wrote a spiritual autobiography, befriended Billy Graham and appeared on two dozen of his televised crusades, recorded more gospel music, and even wrote, produced, and directed a feature-length movie about the life of Jesus, *The Gospel Road* (1973), which offered his own vision of a Christ who was both ruggedly masculine and deeply compassionate. Cash became an outspoken Christian but steered clear of judging others. "There is a spiritual side to me that goes real deep," he said, "but I confess right up front that I'm the biggest sinner of them all."[1]

Though the years that followed would see their ups and downs, Cash would see a great resurgence of interest in his music in the years just before his death, when he recorded a series of albums (the *American Recordings*) with famous producer Rick Rubin. By that time, Cash's voice had become even more gravelly and world-weary, and it was perfect for the cover songs he recorded, such as "Hurt." But in an interview with Larry King given shortly before his death, Cash spoke of the happiness and beauty he had found in his life.

Johnny Cash was a man of paradoxes: an antiauthoritarian rebel who might offer his middle finger to those in power; a preacher, Bible student, and gospel storyteller; a country singer who sold over fifty million records, many of them to folks who didn't normally listen to country music; a man who struggled with drugs, got clean, but had to fight them off again and again; and a man known to all his friends as a giving, caring, compassionate soul. He never thought of himself as anything other than a redeemed sinner, and because of that, he could gain a hearing from those who would never give the time of day to a saint.

64

The Complete Stories

Flannery O'Connor

(short stories, 1971)

If one expects religious fiction to be sentimental, inspirational, and encouraging, they will be surprised to discover that one of the finest Christian writers of the twentieth century penned unexpectedly dark tales about the murky places in the human heart and the violence that it sometimes takes to awaken it to the motions of grace. Flannery O'Connor was posthumously awarded the National Book Award for *The Complete Stories* in 1971, demonstrating that these strange and fascinating stories, mostly located in the South, resonated with readers and critics alike, whether they were people of faith or those who would never darken the doors of a church. Her stories are marked by unexpected twists and turns, unforeseen moments of violence, profound observation of human motivations, an unmasking of the multiplicity of ways in which we deceive ourselves about ourselves, an earthy and sardonic sense of humor, and a splendid grasp of the rhythms of speech and dialect, particularly those accents one might hear in the Deep South.

O'Connor's stories usually center on the shock of a revelation—a violent and unexpected experience or calamity that causes her characters to have to reevaluate who they are, what they believe, and how they should live. Their vain, artificial sense of self is thoroughly dismantled when they are brought face-to-face with the darker aspects within their own souls. And since it is difficult to get through to the hardened human heart, it sometimes takes the appearance of grace in a violent form to get our attention. "All my stories," she wrote, "are about the action of grace on a character who is not very willing to support it."[1] As the Misfit, a homicidal killer in her story "A Good Man Is Hard to Find," says about another character—the proud, selfish, and self-centered Grandmother, a woman who finally shows a spark of goodness when she is faced with being shot: "She would have been a good woman if it [sic] had been somebody there to shoot her every minute of her life."

In extreme situations we learn a lot about ourselves, and so it is for O'Connor's characters. Moments of death, murder, betrayal, humiliation, and the unveiling of hypocrisy can be moments of searing revelation. O'Connor once explained why her stories were filled with such violence and calamity: "For the hard of hearing you shout, and for the almost-blind you draw large and startling figures."[2] And what startling characters she drew: a Bible salesman who humiliates and steals the wooden artificial leg of a proud young woman, a renegade minister preaching "The Church Without Christ," a hateful woman whose prejudice destroys the livelihood of her family and leads to her own demise, a young man who has a picture of God tattooed on his back to try to please his pious wife, and a 104-year-old ex-general who has lost all sense of reality and connection with life. These are just a few of the freakish people who inhabit the pages she has written. And, because she brought them to life with such humor and believability, the reader is drawn into her strange world and confronted with their own sinful nature.

Who would have expected that such stories, largely centered on Southern Fundamentalist Protestants, would emerge from the pen of a woman of deep conviction and immense intellect? O'Connor was a lifelong Catholic who took her faith very seriously, and to tell her stories she drew on the world she knew so well, a world populated by earnest and simple religious faith, racism, and entrenched social divisions.

Born in Georgia in 1925, Mary Flannery O'Connor was an only child born into a devoutly Catholic family who described herself as a "pigeon-toed child with a receding chin and a you-leave-me-alone-or-I'll-bite-you complex."[3] Her family raised chickens, and the young girl received national notoriety when she was filmed by the Pathe News people with her trained chicken, who had the uncanny ability to walk backward. She later claimed this as the high point of her life. Most of her countless readers might take issue with that, but it did begin a lifelong fascination with birds. Later in life, she raised peacocks, ducks, toucans, emus, chickens, and even a bedraggled one-eyed swan.

O'Connor graduated from Georgia State College for Women, and in 1948 was accepted into the prestigious Iowa Writer's Workshop at the University of Iowa, where

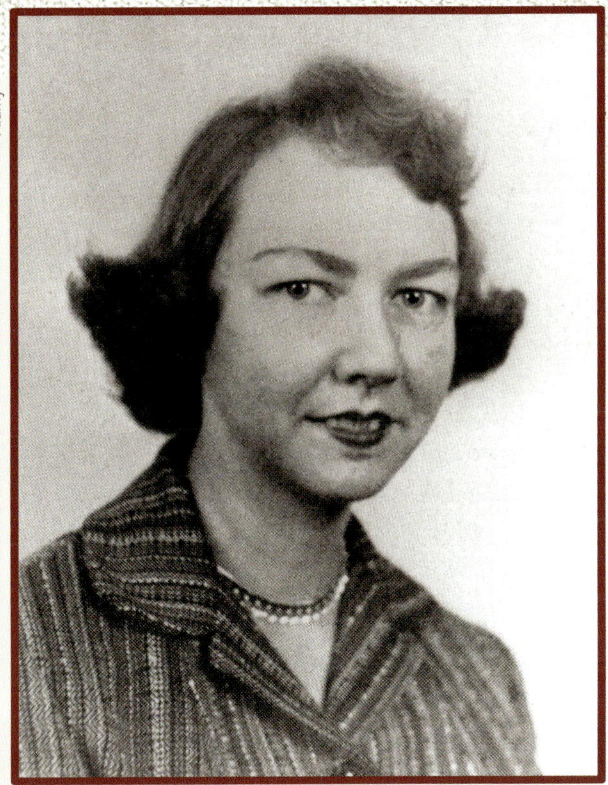

Flannery O'Connor (c. 1950s)

she studied under such important writers as Robert Penn Warren, John Crowe Ransom, and Andrew Lytle. While there, she kept a prayer journal that has only recently been published and shows an intensely serious desire to please God with her life and her writing. "God must be in all my work,"[4] she wrote.

In 1951, O'Connor was diagnosed with lupus, a debilitating disease that had struck down her father at age forty-five, and which began to take a toll on her own life. Following the diagnosis, she moved back to the family dairy farm in Milledgeville, Georgia—not an easy thing to do for a woman so fiercely independent. She was not expected to live long, but managed to survive another fourteen years, spending the remainder of her short life battling the disease, which left her weak and needing crutches to get around. In the midst of her suffering, she found meaning and God's strength, and it might be hard to imagine her work without taking into account the crucible of pain through which she daily passed.

During these years she penned two novels, *Wise Blood* (1952) and *The Violent Bear It Away* (1960), two volumes of short stories, *A Good Man Is Hard to Find* (1955) and *Everything That Rises Must Converge* (1965), numerous essays on writing, collected in *Mystery and Manners* (1962), book reviews, and theological reflections. She died in August 1964, at age thirty-nine, from the complications of lupus.

O'Connor considered herself a "Christian realist," and by that she meant that she thought the doctrines of the Christian faith to be more than symbols. For her, they were realities that shaped the human heart and the human destiny. She had a great interest in theology and read both modern and classic theologians. Her favorite was Thomas Aquinas, whom she read every evening before going to bed. She even laughingly referred to herself as a "Hillbilly Thomist."

Among the things she learned from Aquinas and other theologians was to take evil seriously. It could not be explained away by social forces or psychological malformations, but was a supernatural reality. For O'Connor, the devil was real, and prowling about seeking whom he may devour. She believed that when people were blind to the true nature of evil they were in grave danger of succumbing to its allure. One of the reasons she wrote was to unmask the evil hidden in our customs, our social niceties, and our carefully guarded self-deceptions. She saw her work as "invading territory largely held by the devil," and a weapon in the battle against the nihilism of our age.

"My audience," she wrote in a letter, "is the people who think God is dead."[5] Although a woman of wide reading, she did not trust that the unaided intellect could lead to truth. In fact, the intellect could be a tool of self-deception and create a pride that walled one off from the deepest truths about the world and about themselves. Most of the highly educated characters who appear in her stories, in fact, are prideful and vain; they are smart, but they have little understanding or wisdom about the deep things of existence. Without realizing it, she said, they are "feeling about in all experience for the lost God."[6]

In a biographical essay, Richard Giannone describes the protagonist of one of O'Connor's novels:

> Unlike the liberal, rational, and enlightened persons in the novel who have had the moral and spiritual sense bred out of them, Motes regards sin, Jesus, and redemption as serious matters of life and death. Haunted by his sense of sin and terrified by a pursuing, soul-hungry Jesus, Hazel spends the rest of his life trying to avoid sin in order to avoid Jesus.[7]

When Motes attempts to follow the path of sin and nihilism to prove that sin does not exist, it inevitably leads to a violent collision with the truths he has wanted to avoid.

Flannery O'Connor's stories are unblinking examinations of the mysteries of human existence and the way that God breaks through in unexpected ways. Mystery was, for O'Connor, the great concern of the fiction writer, whose vocation is to record the ways it becomes manifest in human lives. "I am only really interested in a fiction of miracles," she said. But for these outbursts of mystery—these supernatural moments—to be convincing they must occur in the midst of a story that is believable. That is what O'Connor did so very well—use realism to meditate on the mystery of life. And mystery, she reminds us, "isn't something that is gradually evaporating. It grows along with knowledge."[8]

65

Only Visiting This Planet

Larry Norman

(recording, 1972)

Christian music need not be polite.

Such was the conviction that led Larry Norman to wed hard-edged lyrics and contemporary rock music with the message of the gospel, and the result of that conviction was a series of albums that changed the face of Christian music. The second, and arguably the greatest, of these albums was *Only Visiting This Planet*. When the needle dropped into the groove (for these were the days of vinyl LPs), listeners soon realized that they had never heard religious music that sounded quite like this. It was a record that had *attitude*. Sure, these were songs that addressed issues of God and faith and salvation without any hesitation, but they also explored racism, poverty, drug use, sex, and the state of rock-and-roll music.

It was a mixture that some Christians could not stomach. Most of these songs could not be played over the sanitized airwaves of religious radio, as Norman was addressing topics not deemed appropriate for polite, pious conversation. The music had—gasp—a beat, and was performed with electric guitars, drums, and an occasional saxophone, not the normal acoustic guitar and piano sound that passed for contemporary in churches. Then there was that long blond hair and those faded jeans that graced the album cover—couldn't he have at least put on some nice clothes to have his picture taken? Christian bookstores often refused to stock his records, or if they did, kept them under the counter, only available upon request. Even those Christians who liked rock music as a genre (maybe secretly) would not have dreamed of combining it with religious words.

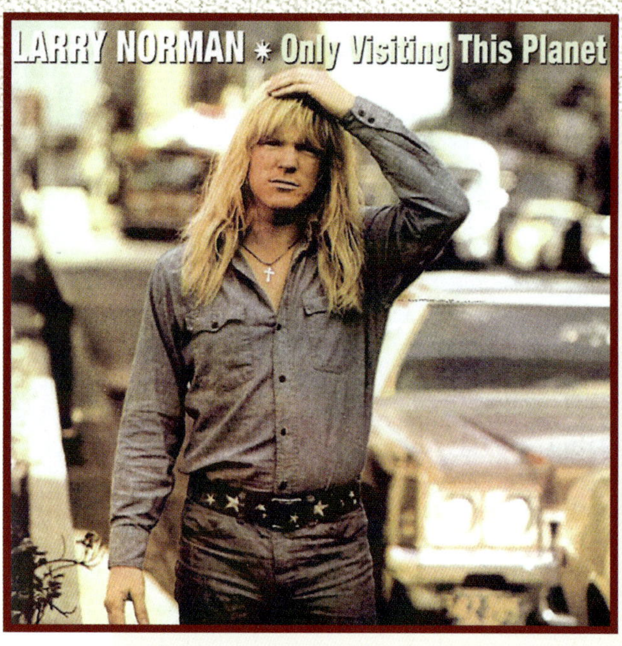

Larry Norman estate

Only Visiting This Planet, album cover

Only Visiting This Planet opens with "I've Got to Learn to Live Without You," a mournful, radio-friendly pop song about lost love without any specifically religious references, making an immediate statement that Norman believed that a Christian could sing about all the issues of life, not just religious ones. But its follow-up, "The Outlaw," leaves no question about where Norman stands. This acoustic guitar–driven ballad celebrates Jesus as one who stands outside and against the system, one who cannot be domesticated and is so often misunderstood. Then Norman gets personal with the listener as he roars into "Why Don't You Look Into Jesus?," a song that is unapologetically evangelistic but also realistic about the struggles people face in their lives that bring them to a point of need. His images evoke the pain of life and wrongheaded attempts to salve it, with phrases such as: "Sipping whiskey from a paper cup / You drown your sorrows till you can't stand up," and "Gonorrhea on Valentine's Day / And you're still looking for the perfect lay." Jesus, says Norman, is the only answer to our searching, which is the theme of the following song, "Righteous Rocker #1." And side one closes with his earnest, apocalyptic, post-rapture ballad, "I Wish We'd All Been Ready," the one song from this album that did get wide distribution among Christian audiences.

With the first side of the record calling his listeners toward faith, the second side engages social injustice as it is seen through his eyes of faith. Norman's superbly imaginative songwriting stands up to comparison with some of the artists from whom he had learned his craft—Bob Dylan, Neil Young, John Lennon, and Paul McCartney. "I'm the Six O'clock News" is an antiwar song as seen through the eyes of a callous television reporter. "The Great American Dream" is a particular highlight of the album, a catalog of the ills confronting modern society, including racism, poverty, loss of privacy and freedom, and misplaced priorities (spending money on NASA missions to space while ignoring the problems next door). "Pardon Me" is a gentler-sounding song that reminds us that free love comes at a great cost, and "Why Should the Devil Have All the Good Music?" is a rollicking, '50s style musical rave-up justifying the use of rock music in the service of God. Its opening lines express the direction of Norman's artistry: "I want the people to know that He saved my soul / But I still like to listen to the radio." What he is hearing on the radio is the theme of the closing song, "Reader's Digest," which skewers the hypocrisy and dead ends (sometimes literally, in the case of deceased artists such as Jimi Hendrix and Janis Joplin) of the musical idols of his era, and closes with these tongue-in-cheek lines, "What a mess this world is in, I wonder who began it / Don't ask me, I'm only visiting this planet."

Only Visiting This Planet came crashing into a Christian subculture that was beginning to feel the effects of the Jesus Movement—a fast-growing revival among hippies, street people, and ex-druggies. The traditionalists, who sought to keep guitars, drums, and any kind of modern sounds out of the church, were fighting a losing battle against a younger generation who wanted to use the music they loved to sing about the God they loved. Norman was at the forefront of this movement, and his songs were an example of how music could be relevant and up-to-date while at the same time espousing a traditional evangelical theology. Clearly, Norman was less interested in inspiring and entertaining the faithful than in sharing the answers he had found with nonbelievers. Sadly, he was never fully embraced by either camp. He was too sacred for sinners and he made the saints squirm uncomfortably. So he forged his own artistic path.

Larry Norman was born in Texas in 1947 and moved with his family to San Francisco at age three, where they settled in the Haight-Ashbury district. He loved the music of Elvis Presley and also the music of the black Pentecostal and Baptist churches where his parents attended. He embraced Christianity at age five and began writing and performing rock-and-roll songs as early as nine. In the mid-60s, he joined a band called People! and became one of their principal songwriters. The band's cover of "I Love You" became a hit single, selling over a million copies, but Norman quit the band on the day their first album was released due to creative and religious differences.

His first solo album, *Upon This Rock*, was released without much fanfare in 1969, but managed to attract criticism from some quarters of Christianity, while being embraced by members of the growing Jesus Movement and getting some limited distribution by a Christian music company after Capitol Records dropped him from their roster. He recorded a couple of independent records that he released himself, then got a contract from MGM for *Only Visiting This Planet*.

Only Visiting This Planet was the first of three albums that Norman referred to as his trilogy. It was followed up by *So Long Ago the Garden* (1973), which took a more oblique and poetic approach to dealing with issues of faith, and was, like its predecessor, very well produced and performed. When neither of these albums sold well in the general market, it effectively ended his recording career in that world.

In 1974, Norman founded Solid Rock Records, which he saw as an outlet not only for his own music but also for talented artists who needed a break. Musicians such as Randy Stonehill, Mark Heard, Tom Howard, and the band Daniel Amos all created exceptional albums for the Solid Rock label. Solid Rock Records were released into the Christian music market through a distribution deal with Word Records, and the third record in Norman's trilogy, *In Another Land* (1976), was the initial release of his new label. It became his bestselling record and stands alongside *Only Visiting This Planet* as his highest artistic achievements. Its impeccable production, creative songs, good humor, and theme about the last days made it more accessible and less controversial to the Christian audience than his previous releases.

These three albums, considered as a conceptual unit (for these were the days of the concept album), are an unparalleled popular music exploration of the sweep of the biblical story, from the fall through the struggles of this life and the hope that lies beyond. The writing, the music, the designs of the covers all sent a message that Christians could produce rock that was as artful and relevant as the best.

Sadly, Norman produced only one more unquestionably great album, a stomping blues-gospel-rock record called *Something New Under the Son* (1981). Clashes with Word Records, and his own tendencies toward sabotaging personal relationships, led to the demise of Solid Rock and the founding of another record company, Phydeaux. But while he recorded some interesting records, none of the subsequent releases had the production values or conceptual vision he had shown in the creation of his trilogy. Norman claimed that this decline in creativity was due to a mild brain injury he had sustained during a rough landing on an airplane, which had damaged his ability to focus on further projects. He also had legal and personal conflicts with some of the artists with whom he had worked, and his marriage ended in divorce. He later testified that his concentration issues were healed during a prayer meeting, after which he settled back into performing, creating some new music, and tinkering with the vast catalog of songs he'd recorded over the years. He died of heart problems in 2008.

Norman's legacy lives on in the world of contemporary Christian music, though few have managed to combine artistry and zeal as effectively as he did. He once complained that most Christian music was crippled by "sloppy thinking, dishonest metaphors, and bad poetry." He wanted to achieve something more than providing "safe" entertainment for those who wanted to avoid secular rock, saying, "If your music is boring, people will reject your message as well as your art."[1]

Larry Norman could never be accused of being boring. In 2013, *Only Visiting This Planet* was chosen as one of twenty-five recordings to be inducted into the Library of Congress National Recording Registry, which represents the richness and diversity of American musical heritage. In their written statement about Norman, those who had given him the award applauded him as one who "commented on the world as he saw it from his position as a passionate, idiosyncratic outsider to mainstream churches."[2] Chris Willman, music writer for *Entertainment Weekly*, wrote that "he really could've been a star if he were singing about something other than Jesus."[3] But with Larry Norman, that is unimaginable.

66

Symphony no. 3, *The Symphony of Sorrowful Songs*

Henryk Górecki

(classical music, 1976)

One afternoon in 1992, a disc jockey at a classical radio station in London played a movement from a symphony by a virtually unknown Polish composer that had been written almost twenty years earlier. The listening audience responded enthusiastically and searched out the record—a performance of the piece featuring the London Sinfonietta and vocal soloist Dawn Upshaw. In a matter of weeks, the recording climbed to the top of the classical music charts, and even landed on the pop music charts, eventually selling in excess of a million copies around the world—not usual numbers for a classical recording. The piece was Henryk Górecki's Third Symphony, which he called *The Symphony of Sorrowful Songs*. It was unlike anything else he had composed, as his early work had been very modern and experimental and anything but crowd pleasing. This symphony, however, was unabashedly emotional, which is likely the reason for its wide popularity and why some music critics were so slow to warm to it.

Along with Estonian composer Arvo Pärt (also a Christian and a composer of sacred music), Górecki has become known as a "holy minimalist," due to a style that often features the human voice and is richly sonorous, often repetitious, and mystical in its overall approach and effect. Many listeners testify to how such music opens up their receptivity toward the transcendent, and find that listening to it often produces both inexplicable tears and a quiet exhilaration.

The first movement of *The Symphony of Sorrowful Songs* opens with a barely perceptible bass melody that repeats slowly and insistently as it grows in volume, evoking a deep well of sadness and grief until, at about the thirteen-minute mark, three piano notes pierce through the growling bass melody almost like the sounding of a bell, and a solo vocalist enters. She sings the text of a fifteenth-century lament of the Virgin Mary over the death of her Son Jesus. The voice is sad and soaring, echoing the emotions Mary must have felt. After the vocal solo, the music slowly fades as the bass melody returns.

The second movement starts with a melody both mysterious and yearning, washing wavelike over the listener as a salve after the intensity of the first movement. But when the solo vocalist enters again, it becomes more passionate and insistent. The gentle, lulling beauty of the second movement is in sharp contrast to the subject of its lyrics, which give voice to a prayer invoking the protection of the Blessed Virgin that was found scrawled upon the wall of a Nazi prison cell, the probable last words of an eighteen-year-old girl. There is a great sobbing tenderness that enters into the music, and the solo vocalist sings her text in a way that is vulnerable, sorrowful, and yet resilient. It evokes a hard-won hopefulness in the midst of mourning as it crescendos and the strings come alongside to carry the weight of the grief.

The third and final movement is built around an orchestration of a traditional Polish folk song, and it once again presents a lament, this time that of a mother mourning her son, who has been killed in an uprising. There are bell-like tones in the midst of the soulfulness of the sound, and when the movement comes to an end quietly and somewhat inconclusively, it is perhaps a reminder that the pain and suffering of life are always with us, no matter how much hope we have to hang on to.

There is a monumental sense of gravity that permeates this symphony. By using these three texts and setting them to music that expresses deep sorrow as well as the unwillingness of the human spirit to be defeated by that sorrow, Górecki seemed to be striving to capture the universality of mourning and loss as an integral part of the human condition, pointing toward a transcendent peace that does not remove the ache but refuses to give suffering the last word. Surprised by the fame the piece brought him, Górecki wondered aloud if "Perhaps people find something they need in this piece of music. . . . Somehow I hit the right note, something they were missing. Something, somewhere, had been lost to them. I felt that I instinctively knew what they needed."[1]

Henryk Górecki was born in 1933 in a bleak industrial town in Poland. As a boy he got little encouragement in music and was forbidden to play the family piano, though he admits that he would often spend time playing whenever others were away and he had the house to himself. As a young man he studied at the local academy of music, where he developed a reputation for fierce individuality. His first works were in a thoroughly modern, avant-garde style, jangly and frenzied and dissonant, very unlike the Third Symphony for which he became so well known.

These early works scandalized audiences who were unprepared for the dissonance and lack of harmonic center that characterized such music. The Communist authorities who then ruled Poland did not approve, but this did not deter Górecki from continuing his musical experiments. He rejected the stifling tenets of Soviet Realism and insisted on following the path of more adventurous composers whose work he admired. But by the 1970s, his music began to be more generally accessible, less aggressive and dissonant, and more introspective and contemplative in nature. He worked for many years as a schoolteacher until his fame reached such a level that in 1975 he became a professor of composition at the State Music School, but once again found himself limited by the interference of Communist Party officials.

In 1978, Górecki was commissioned by Cardinal Karol Wojtya to write a piece to commemorate the nine-hundredth anniversary of the martyrdom of a Polish saint, St. Stanislaus of Krakow, who had become a symbol of the long struggle between church and state in Poland. The piece he composed was a choral work entitled *Beatus Vir*, and when Wojtya unexpectedly became Pope later that year, the piece was set to be premiered at his first appearance in his homeland. When the government refused to allow Wojtya, now known as Pope John Paul II, to visit his hometown, Górecki abruptly resigned his post in protest. However, years later he was able to personally conduct this sacred piece in the presence of the pope.

In 1981, Górecki composed *Miserere* as an unaccompanied vocal piece in response to the violent attacks of Soviet authorities on the growing solidarity movement. But he was not allowed by the censors to perform it until 1987, the same year he composed another choral piece, *Totus Tuus*, an homage to the Virgin Mary written especially for another visit from the pope. While never an outspoken political activist, his compositions certainly played their part in overcoming Soviet dominance in Poland, reminding the people of the strength of a faith that was so often at odds with the atheistic regime.

Growing up in Poland under both the Nazi and Soviet occupations, Górecki always lived in awareness of the pain endured by his beloved native land under a succession of dictatorial leaders. Some of his family had perished in the German concentration camps. He also dealt with pain of his own, including vocational frustrations and disappointments and an ongoing series of health issues, many of them the continuing effects of a serious misdiagnosis and improper treatment he had received as a boy. The gravity and sorrow expressed in his work encapsulate the struggles of his own life and the nightmares experienced by the people of his beloved Poland.

Górecki was a man of deep and sincere faith who, though a bit of a recluse, regularly attended services at his local Catholic church. He was genuinely humble about his accomplishments but also unmoving when it came to approaching music the way he wanted. For him, composing was a way of praying. During his acceptance speech for an honorary doctorate from the University of Warsaw, he spoke with great clarity about the connection between his personal spiritual faith and the music he created:

> Struggling with these twelve notes and musical instruments, it's not so important what I did or how I did it, but what is between and behind the notes . . . that is what matters. Pope John Paul II said at the beatification of Fra Angelico: "His belief became art, which in turn became faith. The art became a prayer."[2]

Górecki never attempted to repeat the success of his astonishingly popular Third Symphony by creating a similar crowd-pleasing work. He moved on, largely focusing on choral and liturgical music that drew on his deep love for the music of the ancient church. He was not interested in playing to the tastes of the public and insisted on writing the music he wanted to write. What he wanted to compose was music that found the greatest beauty in simplicity, and the human voice became increasingly the instrument he was most interested in featuring. The resulting works express a universal pathos that is tinged with penitential sorrow and a mystical hope founded upon his deep faith in God. Through his work, we journey from darkness into light, and grasp both the depths and the limits of human sorrow while being reminded of God's eternal triumph over evil.

67

Dancing in the Dragon's Jaws

Bruce Cockburn

(recording, 1979)

When his record company was promoting the release of *Dancing in the Dragon's Jaws,* they referred to Bruce Cockburn as "Canada's Best-Kept Secret." Although he was a popular, award-winning artist in his own country, he was virtually unknown outside its borders. *Dancing in the Dragon's Jaws* was the album that first caught the attention of the rest of the world, producing his first-ever hit single in the United States and an appearance on the popular *Saturday Night Live* television program. Arguably one of the best songwriters of all time, and one whose lyrics could stand alongside the best of poets, Cockburn has never found the widespread audience he deserves. For those not in on the secret, perhaps *Dancing in the Dragon's Jaws* is as good a place to start exploring as any other.

Dancing in the Dragon's Jaws announced a noticeable shift in Cockburn's work. Up to this time he worked solidly within the folk genre, but this record combined a number of styles to create a sound that was upbeat, joyous, and celebratory. A largely acoustic outing, the album showcased his sparkling guitar work and some of his most poetic and imaginative songwriting. The lyrics show the influence of Charles Williams, whom Cockburn was reading at the time. Williams was a close friend of C. S. Lewis and wrote supernatural thrillers filled with strange and mystically charged moments when the spiritual world burst unexpectedly into an ordinary life. This vision of

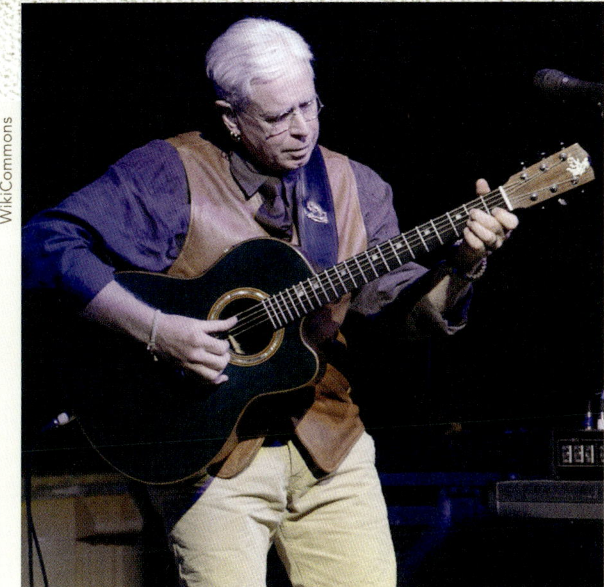

WikiCommons

Bruce Cockburn at Markham Jazz Festival (2014)

the interpenetration between this world and the next fueled Cockburn's imagination and resulted in some of his most vivid songwriting. Cockburn described the theme of the album as "being joyful in the face of everything."

Dancing in the Dragon's Jaws opens with the sound of acoustic guitar and marimba on "Creation Dream," a poetic evocation of the creation and of the God who brings the world into existence with a furious, headlong dance of joy. "Hills of Morning" follows with a tripping, toe-tapping rhythm, offering a prayer of sorts, asking God to "let me be a little of your breath / moving over the face of the deep." While it acknowledges the world's pain and tears, it celebrates the joy of living among all the splendor of nature. So does the largely instrumental "Badlands Flashback," with its gorgeous piano interlude. Then follows "Northern Lights," a meditation of life as seen in the rearview mirror—haunted by memories but comforted by the awe-inspiring beauty of God's world.

"After the Rain" is a song suggesting that the same kind of beauty and revelation found in nature can also be found in the urban world. The centerpiece of the album, and the song that helped introduce Cockburn to a wider audience, is "Wondering Where the Lions Are." It is one of the rare songs in popular music about spiritual ecstasy and transcendence, and celebrates vanquishing the fear of death. Cockburn tells us he is "thinking about eternity" as his song bubbles over with the joy of knowing that darkness will someday be swallowed up by light. In "Incandescent Blue," Cockburn again addresses himself to God and admits his need, especially in the face of the chaos and pain of life. Darkness will not have the last word, for the last word is a word spoken from the eternal realm, a promise celebrated in the slowly building song "No Footprints," as Cockburn returns full circle to the image of the dance, this time the eternal dance that leads us past death into the arms of God. Never denying the pain and struggles of this life, Cockburn reminds us that there are sources of strength and joy that come from beyond this broken world.

Bruce Cockburn was born in Ottawa, Canada, in 1945, and spent his earliest years on the family farm, where he got his first taste for the beauty of the natural world. The young Cockburn discovered a guitar in his grandmother's attic, which he dusted off and adorned with golden stars, and used to play along with his favorite music on the radio. His father would only allow him to take guitar lessons if he promised not to buy a leather jacket, something the elder Cockburn clearly saw as an emblem of rebelliousness. The young Cockburn enthusiastically agreed, but his rebel spirit could not be contained for long. He became a devotee of Allen Ginsberg, Jack Kerouac, and other Beat writers. Although he attended the prestigious Berklee College of Music in Boston, he only lasted about three semesters, as he was more interested in what he was learning about music outside classes than inside them, absorbing the music scene and participating in a succession of bands where he honed his skills with the guitar and with songwriting.

In 1969, Cockburn decided to try his hand as a solo artist and released his self-titled solo album the following year. It showcased his acoustic guitar playing and its breathtakingly complex, intricate gracefulness. It also served notice that a talented songwriter had arrived. *Bruce Cockburn* (1970) and the albums that followed gave evidence of his great love of the natural world and his interest in spirituality. He was, he later said, "a spiritual loner who found truth in nature." But more and more, Christian symbolism began to make its way into his songs, culminating into full expression on *Salt, Sun, and Time* (1974) with the song "All the Diamonds in the World," which he wrote the night he committed his life to Jesus. For Cockburn, who was raised an agnostic, it had been a slow path toward an embrace of Christianity, influenced by reading the books of C. S. Lewis and Thomas Merton and by a mystical experience he had of God's presence with him as he stood before the altar during the exchange of his wedding vows.

Cockburn's faith was very much in evidence in his albums from that time forward. The title track of *Joy Will Find a Way* (1975) was a celebration and anticipation of life after death, and "Lord of the Starfields" from *In the Falling Dark* (1976) was a hymnlike song of praise uncharacteristically straightforward in its lyrical expression of Christian theology. The years that followed his references to faith were generally more oblique, but it was a consistent theme throughout his oeuvre.

After *Dancing in the Dragon's Jaws*, Cockburn went through a difficult divorce, and his subsequent album, *Humans* (1980), which is every bit the masterpiece as its predecessor, has a much darker and more melancholy tone. Here faith is expressed in the context of the struggles of life and its disappointments. There is a sting of pain that accents every song, though a message of hope emerges out of the darkness, especially in "More/Not More," "Fascist Architecture," and "The Rose Above the Sky." This album also contains one of his finest expressions of how the glories of nature and the mysteries of relationships provide us with hints about the ultimate meaning of life in "Rumours of Glory."

Following his divorce, Cockburn moved from the Ottawa countryside to urban Toronto, and his albums began to show his growing concern for social and political causes. These take center stage with *The Trouble with Normal* (1983); the title song reminds the listener that the status quo usually devolves into a system where the rich get richer and the poor get poorer. The trouble with normal, he suggests, "is it always gets worse." Cockburn began to travel widely, often to thirdworld countries. His recent autobiography, *Rumours of Glory*, shows how much his songs have been influenced by what he read, where he traveled, and some of the horrors he witnessed. These experiences began to show themselves in songs that raised a voice against injustices and atrocities. "If I Had a Rocket Launcher," one of his most popular songs, records the depth of his helpless anger on witnessing a Guatemalan refugee camp being strafed by military helicopters. He also penned songs about the plight of Nicaragua, the war in Iraq, the problem of land mines, and environmentalist concerns.

Cockburn's passionate and intense lyrics have an almost prophetic tone of denunciation against purveyors of violence and greed and the human suffering they cause. He distrusted the optimistic modern myths about human progress, as he saw their effect on people—the hardness of heart that allows us to turn our eyes away from the results of our actions. There is an anger in Cockburn's lyrics that sometimes bursts forth in an expletive, which some listeners might find offensive. These occasional outbursts, though, cannot be classified as coarseness for its own sake or an attempt to be cute or hip. They are an articulation of the gut-wrenching realities he has seen, and these provoke an outrage for which there are no polite words. It is the fury that comes from empathizing with the pain of others, and should cause us to engage ourselves with finding solutions. We must, his lyrics remind us, "kick at the darkness till it bleeds daylight." More pronounced than the anger that rises to the surface in his songs is his compassion for the victims and the downtrodden. There is always an accompanying message of hope that a brighter, more just world is possible if we would really follow the path of love.

Cockburn became increasingly reluctant about identifying himself with evangelical Christianity, rejecting outright its conservative politics and moralism. His song "The Gospel of Bondage" is a strong indictment against the wedding of the status quo with a triumphal Christianity. Instead, in songs such as "Shipwrecked at the Stable Door" he reminded listeners that Christ was on the side of the victims, the losers in political gamesmanship, and the morally bankrupt who recognize their need for grace. In a 1999 interview he explained what being a Christian meant to him:

> The word Christian is a little problematic now, I think, because it's so loaded. I'm not sure what I even mean by it anymore, never mind what anybody else means. But I consider myself to be in an ongoing, developing relationship with God. That relationship is central to my life, and I believe it is the most important thing in my life.[1]

Bruce Cockburn's catalog of songs is a kind of musical diary that artistically expresses the complexity of his vision of the world—at once joyful and crowded with "rumors of glory," while also broken and filled with pain and suffering. Above all else, he sees this as a "world of wonders" and continues to offer songs that remind us that the glory of God is all about us, a mystery that should energize us toward love for each other. Ultimately, Cockburn asserts, all of us in this broken world are "waiting for a miracle."

And the best-kept secret is a secret no longer.

68

The Second Coming

Walker Percy

(novel, 1980)

As a novelist who was also a believer, Walker Percy didn't pull his punches. He believed that our modern civilization was in the death grip of despair—despair so deep that few even recognized it for what it was. Through his novels, Percy challenges his readers to see the truth about themselves. He asks the same questions as the great existentialist philosophers and novelists, but his answers are very different. If you are looking for a feel-good celebration of faith, look elsewhere. But if you are trying to understand the underlying spiritual malady of our times, perhaps Percy's books are as good a place as any to begin.

In *The Second Coming*, Percy revisits the main character of his earlier novel, *The Last Gentleman* (1966), and finds him now rich and successful but no less alienated and dissatisfied with his life than when he was a poor, wandering nomad. Will Barrett is a middle-aged lawyer who has retired early, settling into a life of socializing, golf, and mourning his recently deceased wife. The first clue that something is seriously wrong with him occurs on the golf course, where he blacks out and has flashbacks about his childhood. He becomes increasingly ill at ease and grows obsessed with the realization that he is living in a spiritually dead culture. This realization jump-starts a half-crazy search for meaning that ultimately becomes a search for God.

Barrett is looking for some sort of sign. He cannot find answers in the usual places, as he finds believers and nonbelievers equally obnoxious; neither honest about the true state of their selves, their souls, or the culture in which they live. Insistent on finding answers to the questions that haunt him, he concocts a "foolproof" plan to determine once and for all if God is real or just an illusion. The answer he gets—his sign—and the way he gets that answer are not at all what he expected, but make for enlightening and entertaining reading.

For Barrett, finding an answer to his questions is connected with finding love in the form of Allie, a brilliant young woman who just can't cope with existence. As Percy tells it, she "got all As and flunked life." Allie has been placed in a mental hospital and subjected to bouts of shock therapy, which damage her memory and render her unfit to get along in the world. When she finally decides to escape from the hospital, armed with a notebook in which she has written notes to guide herself, Allie begins the long process of reintegration, a virtual blank slate trying to figure out how to navigate in this harsh and confusing world. The intersection of the lives of these two deeply alienated souls suggests that it is only in love—for God and for another person—that we find real meaning in life.

A novel that tackles such existential issues could easily become dry and philosophical, but instead *The Second Coming* is wise, comic, and touching, even as it is cynical about much that passes for wisdom in this post-Christian age. Because Percy is a master at creating wonderfully quirky characters, he can draw readers into his characters' plights and make them feel the struggles as their own. Perhaps that is because Percy's protagonists are all dealing with the same issues with which he personally struggled, and to which he found some answers in the Christian faith.

Walker Percy was born in Alabama in 1916 and raised in a family that was virtual Southern nobility but had some skeletons in its closet. His grandfather had committed suicide, and his father, outwardly successful but inwardly torn, ended his own life when Percy was only thirteen years old by shooting himself in the attic of the family home. A few years later, his mother died in a car accident that looked suspiciously like a suicide. Percy and his brothers went to live with a bachelor uncle, Will Percy, who provided them with much-needed stability and an excellent education. Uncle Will reinforced the stoic humanism that Percy had learned from his parents, and Percy settled into agnosticism.

As a young man, Percy became convinced that science held the needed answers to the basic human questions, and that the scientific method could be deployed to solve the world's mysteries. He graduated with honors from the University of North Carolina with a degree in chemistry, and then studied medicine at Columbia University. Such was his brilliance that he found time to read novels voraciously even in the midst of his demanding medical studies. Following his time at Columbia, he elected to do his residency at Bellevue Hospital in New York City, where his primary duty was to perform autopsies on anonymous corpses discovered along skid row. Because he failed to take proper precautions, he contracted tuberculosis from bacilli still alive in one of the cadavers.

At that time the usual remedy for tuberculosis was extended rest in a peaceful, healthy environment, so Percy was sent to a sanatorium in upstate New York where he spent two years recovering from the illness. While his body healed, he read widely—existentialist philosophers (Sartre, Camus, and Heidegger), novelists (Tolstoy, Kafka, Mann, and Dostoyevsky), and at the urging of a fellow patient, theologians (Augustine, Aquinas, and Kierkegaard). It was particularly the mixture of existentialism and Christianity that he found in Dostoyevsky and Kierkegaard that was to have the most lasting influence on him, and an essay by Kierkegaard entitled "The Difference between a Genius and an Apostle" convinced him of the necessity of fully embracing the faith he had been exploring intellectually. As he wrote:

> When I was thirty, I thought I had things pretty well figured out—or at least I believed that those things which were not already explained by science were in principle explainable. When I was forty, I thought that what was not explainable by science—and that turned out to be a lot—could be explained by bringing God into it.[1]

Upon his release, Percy married and, along with his new wife, joined the Catholic church. From then on, he would be unwavering in his defense of Christianity, though he also was not shy about poking fun at its hypocrisies and idiosyncrasies. Settling in Louisiana, Percy was able, due to an inheritance left him by his uncle Will, to focus on studying and writing. He penned articles about contemporary issues (such as racism in the South), meditations on the existential dilemma of humans in the twentieth century, and technical essays on the science of semiotics (the study of language and signs), which was a special interest.

He considered his first two attempts at writing a novel to be failures, and one of them he even consigned to the flames. But his third, *The Moviegoer* (1961), an entertaining exploration of the Kierkegaardian "stages of existence" through the eyes of Binx Bolling, a compulsive attender of films and a man spiritually adrift, won the prestigious National Book Award. His second, *The Last Gentleman* (1966), was a runner-up for the same award. He continued to write novels that were critically acclaimed, even by those who did not share his faith, for he was never heavy-handed in his storytelling. *Love in the Ruins* (1971) is a very funny apocalyptic send-up of the state of modern culture at a time in the not-too-distant future when wolves howl in the streets of Cleveland, buzzards circle New Orleans, and vines sprout in the cracks of broken-down interstates. In it he posits faith as the only source of sanity for a dying civilization. *Lancelot* (1977) is darker in tone, a bitter critique of the sorry state of modern ethics, and *The Thanatos Syndrome* (1987) continues the theme of cultural collapse and the need for a renaissance of faith. All of them are brilliantly insightful, earthy, irreverent, extremely funny, and beautifully told, as is his quirky nonfiction masterpiece, *Lost in the Cosmos: The Last Self-Help Book* (1983), which deserves a larger audience than it has found. After Percy's death from cancer in 1990, his various essays were published under the title *Signposts in a Strange Land* (1994).

One of his most interesting essays in *Signposts in a Strange Land* is called "Diagnosing the Modern Malaise," and it provides a helpful key to what Percy was trying to do in his novels. As a trained physician, he learned how to diagnose the sickness of a patient, and in this essay he suggests that the novelist might be a diagnostician for the spiritual sickness of our modern world. "Something is indeed wrong, and one of the tasks of the serious novelist is, if not to isolate the bacillus under the microscope, at least to give the sickness a name, to render the unspeakable speakable."[2]

The name he gives to the sickness of our culture is "death in life."[3] We go through the motions, he suggests, but we are not really happy or content. We are the walking dead. We are isolated, lonely, and alienated, and we don't really know how to relate to one another. We are pilgrims and wayfarers wandering and adrift in a strange land. We are in a mess.

> No other time has been more life-affirming in its pronouncements, self-fulfilling, creative, autonomous, and so on—and more death-dealing in its actions. It is the century of the love of death. I am not talking just about Verdun or the Holocaust or Dresden or Hiroshima. I am talking about a subtler form of death, a death in life, of people who seem to be living lives which are good by all sociological standards and yet who somehow seem more dead than alive.[4]

If you don't know what he is talking about, perhaps you just aren't paying attention.

Walker Percy was not one to offer easy answers to the complex task of trying to live an authentic human life. He was no more patient with simplistic religious answers than with simplistic scientific ones, but if we are willing to make the effort of searching, he believed that there was truth and life to be found. But it is hard to find. Part of the problem, he believed, is with the devaluation of our Christian vocabulary.

> The old words, God, grace, sin, redemption . . . now tend to be either exhausted, worn slick as poker chips and

signifying as little, or else are heard as the almost random noise of radio and TV preachers. The very word "Christian" is not good news to most readers.[5]

In the face of this, Percy provides a fresh and quirky vocabulary for the search as he helps us look honestly at the human predicament. He reminds us that we do not have to give in to the despair of our times or keep it at bay by a multitude of distractions. He invites us, instead, to be pilgrims in search of a better way. "The point is that, in a new age when things and people are devalued, when meanings break down, it lies within the province of the novelist to start the search afresh, like Robinson Crusoe on his island."[6] And when we seek, perhaps, like Percy, we will find.

69

The Last Supper

Sadao Watanabe

(print, 1981)

The menu for Sadao Watanabe's version of *The Last Supper* is unlike any other in art history. Jesus is placed at the head of a low table among his kimono-clad disciples as they kneel on a tatami mat and prepare to partake of a traditional Japanese meal. The charming large-eyed fish at the center of the table is the sea bream, or *tai*, a much-prized delicacy that is normally served on ceremonial occasions. It is accompanied by plates of sushi rolls and stylized bottles of *sake*.

As with actors in the Japanese Noh theater tradition, the faces of the figures in this print are masklike and impassive, as is the case in all Watanabe's pictures. The position of the hands of his figures gives more clues to their emotional state than their faces, which is one of the ways that Watanabe creates an aura of reserved quiet and dignity in his work. Following Western art traditions, Jesus, with a halo around His head, is slightly larger than the disciples in order to indicate His importance. The "beloved disciple," John, leans upon Jesus with affection while others gesticulate or fold their hands in an attitude of prayer. Judas can be seen in the foreground, clutching a bag of money behind his back. In a playful commentary, Watanabe adorned Judas's kimono with the symbol of the fox, a traditional Japanese symbol of bedevilment.

Watanabe suggests that this was the kind of meal that would be served to Jesus

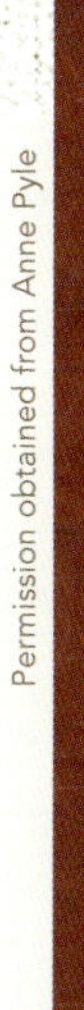

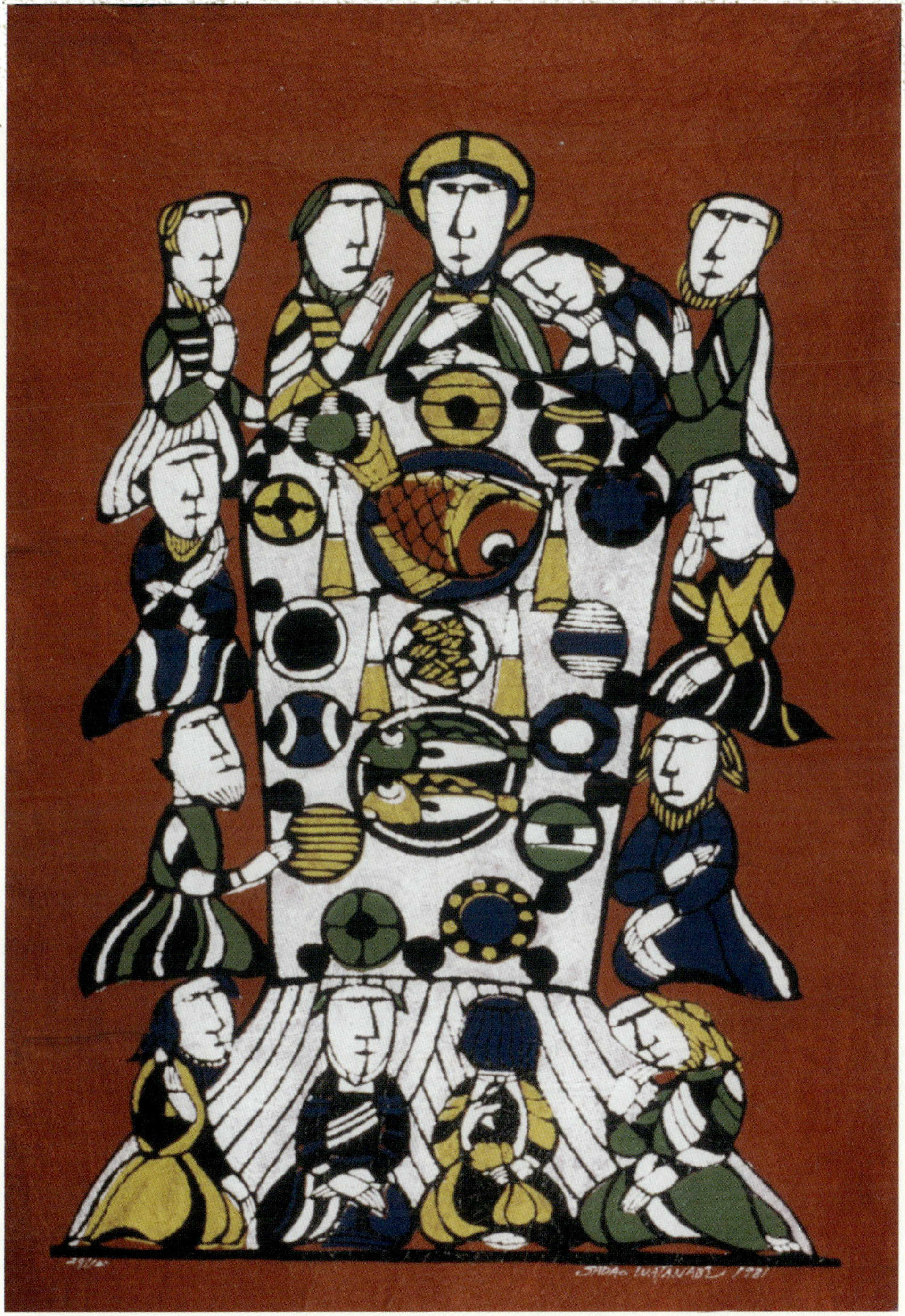

The Last Supper by Sadao Watanabe, collection of Anne Pyle

as an honored guest if he were to visit a Japanese home in our own time. With this fresh vision of the Last Supper, he wedded the East and the West, just as he did in hundreds of other biblical prints he created during his life. He took the familiar stories and symbols of Christianity, sometimes even borrowing poses from medieval and Renaissance masters, and reimagined them as distinctly Japanese, using the traditional Japanese medium of printmaking.

One day, while browsing the shelves in a Christian bookstore in Tokyo, Watanabe was struck by the fact that the covers of most of the books were decorated with European religious art. There seemed to be little art available that represented the Christian faith in the visual language of the Japanese, and he wanted to find a way to communicate the message of Christ to those in his own culture, for whom its stories and teachings were largely unfamiliar. Perhaps, by giving these images a distinctly Japanese flavor, he could overcome some of the stigma toward Christianity. "I wanted to find a way of expressing my Christianity within a Japanese context instead of just adapting the European tradition," he said.[1] And so, Watanabe's prints were created in a style that accords with Japanese ideas of beauty but illustrates people and events of the biblical story.

Watanabe summed up his artistic passions in this way: "I owe my life to Christ and the gospel. My way of expressing my gratitude is to witness to my faith through the medium of biblical scenes. I want to use my ideas and talents for the glory of God."[2]

Sadao Watanabe was born in Tokyo in 1913, the son of a Christian father and Buddhist mother. His father did not attend church with any regularity or speak directly of his faith, but his son would sometimes overhear him quietly singing a hymn as he walked in the family garden: "There is a fountain filled with blood, drawn from Emmanuel's veins." When his father died unexpectedly, the young Watanabe, only ten, was forced to drop out of school to help with the family finances and had to put his dreams of becoming an artist on hold.

A kindly woman from the neighborhood felt sorry for the quiet, artistic boy who had lost his father and invited Watanabe to come to church with her. At first he was not much attracted to Christianity, finding it to have "the smell of butter" (a Japanese expression for something foreign and unpleasant). He moved toward belief slowly, spending considerable time comparing Christian and Buddhist scriptures. It was not primarily this intellectual investigation, however, that ultimately brought him to faith in Christ but rather a miraculous recovery from tuberculosis—which had kept him bedridden for two years. Members of the church prayed for his healing, and following this answer to prayer he decided, at age seventeen, to be baptized. His formerly Buddhist mother was baptized shortly thereafter. In a culture where only about 1 percent of the population practiced Christianity, and where standing out in any way was frowned upon, his decision to publicly identify with Christ was evidence of the seriousness with which he embraced his new faith.

By age twenty-four Watanabe was working as a textile dyer, designing patterns and dyeing cloth for kimonos, doing some occasional drawing, and studying the writings of Soetsu Yanagi, a proponent of *minigei,* the Japanese folk art movement. Yanagi celebrated the traditional arts and crafts of ordinary Japanese people and encouraged the embrace of time-honored techniques. These interests led Watanabe to the work of a textile dye artist named Keisuke Serizawa, who became his teacher and taught him how to use these same techniques with paper to create prints. At first he made some prints of Bible stories solely for his own enjoyment, but eventually came to the realization that this should become his calling.

This method of printmaking, which Watanabe perfected and used throughout his career as an artist, involved a laborious process of drawing, stenciling, and cutting out patterns that could then be printed and accented with colors. All the materials he used were natural, including the paper (made from the bark of mulberry trees), which would be kneaded, crumpled, rolled, and stretched, giving it a wrinkled and weathered appearance almost like a medieval manuscript.

Despite the complexity of his organic method for creating the prints, Watanabe was astonishingly prolific, creating over five hundred large prints and hundreds of smaller ones. The overwhelming majority of these prints were of biblical scenes, encompassing many Old Testament stories as well as almost every major event in the life of Christ. Among his favorite stories, explored in multiple variations, were the Last Supper and the flight into Egypt. He also clearly took great relish in images of animals, as evidenced in his many and varied depictions of Noah's ark, and in the many species of birds that crop up as little accents in so many different prints. When, on rare occasions, he departed from directly biblical subjects, it would be to explore other Christian themes, such as *St. Francis Preaching to the Birds,* or to design a unique portrait of John Calvin.

Watanabe was a diligent student of the Bible, immersing himself in its pages daily and praying that it would provide the inspiration and direction for his creations. He would read the biblical text relating to his subject over and over, pondering its message prayerfully, before he executed the design. For him, the creation of his prints was not only an artistic endeavor but also an act of worship. He would pray during each stage of his creative process.

Watanabe struggled for recognition and acceptance as an artist. In the years following World War II, Japanese art critics began to distinguish between fine art and "applied" art, and there was much disagreement about how to define the differences. Because Watanabe was using traditional folk methods, some critics refused to take his work seriously as fine art. But because it had many of the characteristics of high art, some folk art aficionados didn't feel his work belonged with theirs either. He was often refused entrance into shows that showcased one or the other—his work too much a hybrid for either artistic community to fully embrace.

In 1947, Watanabe finally found some recognition when he entered one of his biblical prints, *The Story of Ruth*, in a contest at the Japanese Folk Art Museum and was awarded a first prize. The next year he received a prize from the Japanese Print Association. Other than that, he gained very little fame in his own country. But slowly, over time, he developed an international following after novelist James Michener discovered Watanabe's work and included some of his art in a published collection of modern Japanese prints. His work was eventually exhibited in the United States at the Museum of Modern Art in New York City, at the Museum of Fine Arts in Boston, at the British Museum in London, and at the Vatican Museum for Modern Religious Art in Rome, where ten of his works are on permanent display. During the Lyndon Johnson administration, one of his prints even adorned a wall in the White House.

The humble Watanabe, though, was less interested in seeing his work hang in these prestigious institutions than in having it understood and embraced by his fellow Japanese. He once said of his prints, "I would like to see them hanging where people ordinarily gather, because Jesus Christ brought the Gospel for the people."[3]

It is perhaps appropriate that in 1996 the hard-working Sadao Watanabe died in the process of creating his art, his heart giving out while in the process of numbering and signing a batch of prints. Those who knew him speak of his gentle humility and passionate faith, a follower of Jesus who wanted to express to his own culture the faith that was central to his life. He wanted to make himself available so that God might use his gifts, which meant that he must himself get out of the way and let God work through him. "As I grow older," he said near the end of his life, "my work becomes less of myself and more of my Lord."[4]

70

Godric

Frederick Buechner

(novel, 1981)

"Five friends I had, and two of them snakes. Tune and Fairweather they were, thick round as a man's arm, my bedmates and playfellows, keepers of my skimped hearth and hermit's heart."[1] So opens Frederick Buechner's novel about the life of a medieval monk, and one might be forgiven for thinking they were reading something from the Middle Ages as its rhythms, cadences, and word choices are so unfamiliar to a twenty-first-century reader. At first the reader may find the book difficult, but with just a little perseverance one can start to appreciate how the unusual writing style adds to the authenticity and beauty of Buechner's storytelling and evokes a sense of the medieval world.

Buechner wrote that the idea for the novel came to him when he discovered a small paperback book about the lives of the saints and accidentally happened upon the entry on Godric. He'd never heard of Godric before, but when he read the entry he "knew he was for me, my saint. Godric came mysteriously alive for me . . . and with him all the people he knew and the whole medieval world he lived in."[2]

Godric, Buechner's first historical novel, was nominated for the Pulitzer Prize and was based upon the life of Godric of Finchale, an eleventh-century English monk whose story is narrated with his own words as he pauses to look back over his own life. When the book opens, Godric is advanced in age and near death, and legends have arisen around him of his spiritual maturity and deep piety. One young monk, Reginald of Durham, has been particularly involved in interpreting his story for others, and his hagiographic writings have portrayed Godric as a great saint. But Godric knows better, and as he unfolds his personal story with honesty and earthiness, we understand that his life includes not only acts of charity and piety but also the most wretched of sins. His journey is the story of the battle between God and "the world, the flesh, and the devil" as it is played out in one man's heart.

Pious folklore is replaced in the novel with psychological realism about a complex and imperfect man—stubborn, fearful, lustful, and deceitful—who nonetheless stands as a witness to the grace of God. Godric scoffs at Reginald's attempts to whitewash his story and tries to correct the record:

> I started out as rough as a peasant's brat and full of cockadoodledoo as any. I worked uncleanness with the best of them or worse. I tumbled all the maids would suffer me and some that scratched and tore like weasels in a net. . . . There's much you're better not to know, but know you this. Know Godric's no true hermit but a gadabout within his mind, a lecher in his dreams. Self-seeking he is and peacock proud . . . All this and worse than this go say of Godric.[3]

But as Godric tells us the truth about himself it begins to dawn on the reader that perhaps, for all his imperfections, he really was something of a saint. His self-effacing honesty, humility, and almost naïve innocence are on view as he tells of his journey to faith from a place of sin and debauchery, through fierce asceticism, and to his ultimate decision to become a hermit who has shut himself off from the temptations of the world. And in the stillness of his chosen solitude he finds the grace of God smack in the middle of a fallen world and his own fallen heart. In one gorgeous passage, Godric speaks of God's grace and of the secrets revealed by the river Wear, a place where he goes to pray and meditate:

> "Praise, praise!" I croak. Praise God for all that's holy, cold, and dark. Praise him for all we lose, for all the river of years bears off. Praise him for stillness in the wake of pain. Praise him for emptiness. And as you race to spill into the sea, praise him yourself, old Wear. Praise him for dying and the peace of death. . . . I kneel down beside him [Wear] till within his depths I see a star.
>
> Sometimes this star is still. Sometimes she dances. She is Mary's star. Within that little pool of Wear she winks at me. I wink at her. The secret that we share I cannot tell in full. But this much I will tell. What's lost is nothing to what's found, and all the death that ever was, set next to life, would scarcely fill a cup.[4]

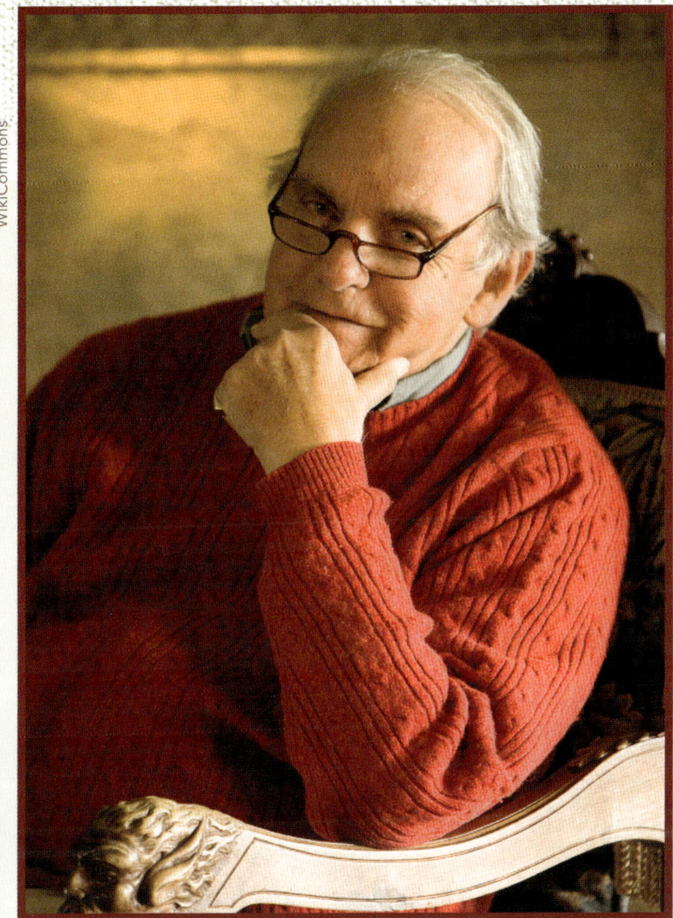

WikiCommons

Frederick Buechner in his home (2008)

Carl Frederick Buechner was born in New York City in 1926. His family moved frequently during the first ten years of his life, as his father carried on a seemingly endless search for lasting employment. When Buechner was ten, his father, judging himself an irredeemable failure, committed suicide by carbon monoxide poisoning. This traumatic event, which had a lasting impact upon Buechner, is reexamined in some of his autobiographical writings and even in his fiction.

Buechner attended Princeton University, and in his last year there began working on a novel, *A Long Day's Dying*, which was released to critical acclaim and commercial success in 1950. His next novel was as significant a failure as the first was a success, but he decided to devote himself to writing anyway and moved to New York City. While there, he began to attend Madison Avenue Presbyterian Church, where George Buttrick was pastor. During one of Buttrick's sermons, Buechner was particularly moved by the description of "the coronation of Christ in the believer's heart," which he described as taking place "among confession, and tears, and great laughter."[5] Buechner decided that Christ deserved to be crowned in his own heart.

Wanting to learn more about the Christian faith, Buechner enrolled at Union Theological Seminary, where he eventually earned a Bachelor of Divinity degree and was ordained as a minister, though he would never serve a local congregation. Instead he took a job as the school minister at Phillips Exeter Academy, a prestigious and academically rigorous preparatory school. Most of the students at this intellectually demanding school were very cynical about religion in general and Christianity in particular, so Buechner learned how to be creative and winsome in presenting the faith—representing it as something intellectually honest, relevant, and appealing. This experience proved invaluable for his future writing, in which he joined his dual callings as a minister and as a writer. He preached, though ever so gently, through the paper pulpit of his books.

Over the course of his career, Buechner published books in a number of genres. Along with *Godric,* he created the unforgettable tetralogy of novels about Leo Bebb, the ex-convict who started a diploma mill in order to ordain all comers to his Church of Holy Love, Inc. This rollicking, irreverent series, gathered into one volume as *The Book of Bebb* (1979), explores the ways that divine truth could sometimes manifest itself through the most imperfect of vessels. Other novels include *The Final Beast* (1965), *Brendan* (1987), and *The Son of Laughter* (1993). The same creativity Buechner brought to his fiction was also evident in his nonfiction, especially in books such as *The Alphabet of Grace* (1970), *Wishful Thinking* (1973), and *Telling the Truth: The Gospel as Tragedy, Comedy, and Fairy Tale* (1977).

In a series of autobiographical books beginning with *The Sacred Journey* (1982), Buechner meditated on the events of his life, searching out meaning in the twists and turns of his own story. There was, he believed, much to be learned even from the ordinary, mundane circumstances of our lives, and he mined this vein with his autobiographical writings. This became one of his great themes—paying attention to what you can learn from your own life.

> Listen to your life. See it for the fathomless mystery that it is. In the boredom and pain of it no less than in the excitement and gladness: touch, taste, smell your way to the holy and hidden heart of it because in the last analysis all moments are key moments, and life itself is grace.[6]

Frederick Buechner saw the motions of grace at work in the most unexpected places and the most unexpected people. He had little patience for religiosity and piousness, and valued honesty about the struggle the life of faith could sometimes be. He wasn't afraid of doubts and questions, or of being a bit irreverent in his search for an honest spirituality. In *Wishful Thinking,* he teasingly defined doubt as the "ants in the pants of faith" that keep it "alive and moving."[7] His own writing is similarly kept "alive and moving" by virtue of its honesty, intelligence, vulnerability, humor, and common sense. Readers can be thankful that Buechner has allowed us to listen in on his life, and perhaps this example will help us listen to our own.

71

Infidels

Bob Dylan

(recording, 1983)

Bob Dylan is an artist famously reticent about discussing the meanings of his complex and sometimes obtuse lyrics. He has always resisted being co-opted by any political or religious philosophy, or for that matter, limited to any particular musical tradition. In the course of his long and distinguished career he has been identified as a bohemian folksinger in the Woody Guthrie tradition, a sixties protest singer, a rock-and-roll surrealist poet, a dissector of his own inner demons, a country music crooner, a fiery Christian evangelist, and always—this is the one consistent trait—a moralist in the tradition of the biblical prophets. Whichever shade the chameleon has sported, he has never been afraid to challenge the cultural status quo.

Perhaps that is why it came as such a surprise to many of Dylan's fans when he publicly embraced Christianity. For the stretch of three albums he wrote with uncharacteristic clarity about what he believed and called on others to see the world in the same way. Even when what has come to be called his "gospel music" stage passed off the scene, he continued to write from a perspective that recognized God as a necessary reality for making sense of the world. Of the albums that followed this period in his musical evolution, *Infidels* is generally considered to be one of the strongest.

At a time when some were convinced that Dylan was through with Christianity and had passed on to other commitments, *Infidels* was a clear sign that he had not abandoned his faith but had simply returned to his original way of expressing his beliefs—with artfulness, ambiguity, and mystery, seen through a very personal lens.

The album opens with one of its best songs, "Jokerman," a poetic jeremiad about the sorry spiritual state of Western culture, enlivened by references to the biblical book of Revelation and propelled by a Caribbean-influenced rhythm track. Other standouts on the album include a haunting critique of nuclear proliferation entitled "License to Kill," a warning against the devil who often comes in disguise as a "Man of Peace," a politically charged defense of the state of Israel in "Neighborhood Bully," and the lovely and mysterious "I and I," which explores the distance between the public persona of Dylan and the inner identity of the man himself. One of the clear themes of the album is the danger of unchecked human pride and greed. Dylan clearly reminds us of the price we pay for our lack of humility, both as individuals and as a nation. All of us are the infidels of the album's title.

Infidels announced to those who were lamenting his turn to gospel songs that the old Dylan was back, but for those listening closely this was a Dylan who continued to embrace a Christian perspective on the world. Interestingly, as great as *Infidels* was, it might have been even better. Some of the songs recorded during these sessions but left off the album were only released some years later on his bootleg collection, and these rank among his finest, especially his haunting song about the dark heritage of slavery, "Blind Willie McTell." But even as released, *Infidels* ranks high among Dylan's many stellar accomplishments.

Born Robert Zimmerman in Duluth, Minnesota, in 1941, Dylan played in various music groups as a young man before becoming part of the burgeoning folk music scene in Minneapolis while attending the university there. He adopted the stage name Bob Dylan and developed a persona similar to that of his musical hero, Woody Guthrie. In the winter of 1961, he moved to New York City to try to break into the Greenwich Village folk music scene. There he played in various coffeehouses and scrambled to make a living before being discovered by influential music critic Robert Shelton. Shelton's laudatory review of a live Dylan performance brought him to the attention of Columbia Records. Dylan's self-titled first album, largely consisting of covers of folk standards, got good reviews but only sold a middling number of copies.

His second album, *The Freewheeling Bob Dylan*, which highlights his own original compositions, was his breakthrough, including such classic songs as "Blowin' in the Wind" and "A Hard Rain's A-Gonna Fall." From there, his fame spread and his reputation soared, each subsequent album offering lyrical poetry unlike anything heard before. For a period of time he was

Alamy

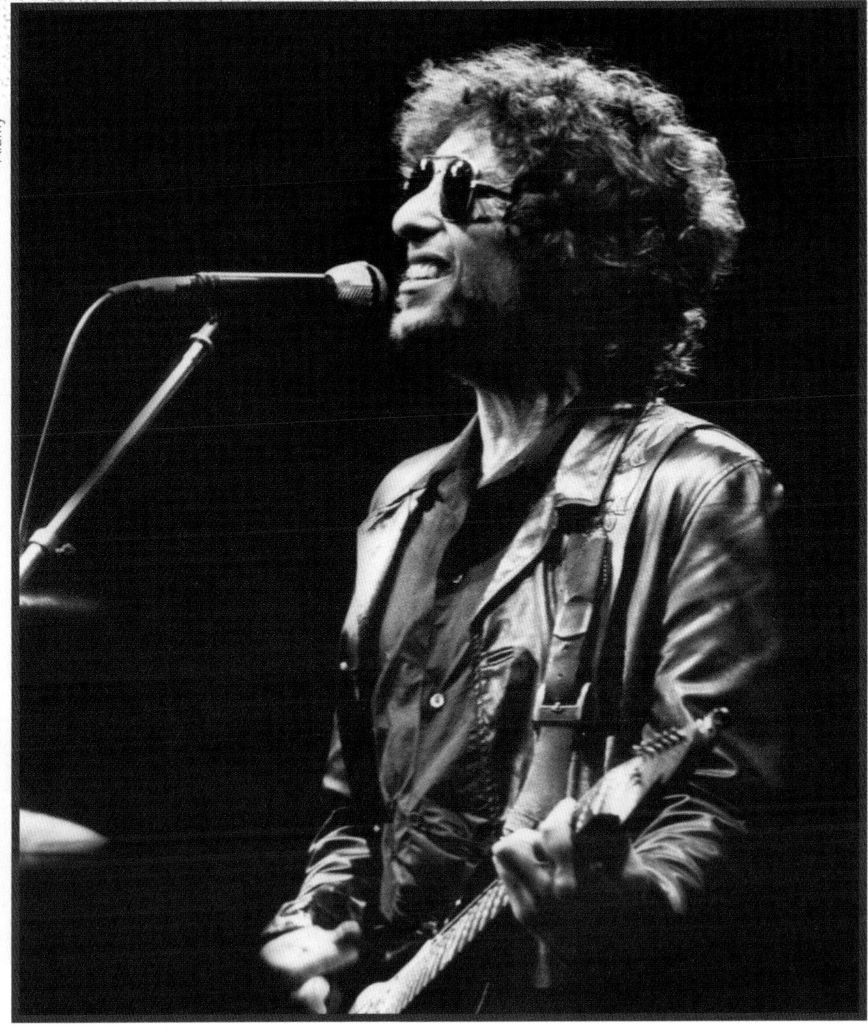

Bob Dylan at Earl's Court, London (1981)

the unofficial poet laureate of the protest singers, addressing issues such as civil rights, the Vietnam War, and the repressive conformity of American culture. In 1965, he changed his sound, adding a hard-driving blues rock to his repertoire. While this alienated some of his folk-loving followers, who thought he had sold out, it gained him an even larger audience in the mainstream music world.

By the late sixties and early seventies Dylan seemed to have grown tired of the adulation and the pressure of being spoken of as "the voice of his generation." He went in the opposite direction—he produced a country album, wrote the music for a Western film, and, for all practical purposes, invented the genre of Americana music, with its combination of country, rock, and folk elements.

Dylan's lyrics have always had a strong moral center, reflecting a generally Judeo-Christian worldview even before his later-in-life embrace of Christianity. His earliest songs of political protest are sprinkled with biblical phrases, allusions, and imagery, empowered by a passion for moral justice and social righteousness. But he was also always concerned about the personal element of morality, not only the desire for a more just society. As the sixties were coming to a close, a new spiritual tone entered his writing, presumably tied to a rediscovery of his Jewish roots. His album *John Wesley Harding* (1967) is highlighted by a series of moral parables and contains countless biblical allusions, featuring songs such as "I Dreamed I Saw St. Augustine" and "The Wicked Messenger." His album *New Morning* (1970) is even more explicit about God in the hymnlike "Father of Night." Though Dylan's output slowed during the 1970s, he produced such classic albums as *Blood on the Tracks* and *Desire*.

In 1979, Dylan shocked the world of rock music by releasing *Slow Train Coming*, an overtly Christian album with a gospel sound and a hard-hitting, unambiguously evangelical message. At a time of personal and artistic confusion, he had been introduced to Christianity by the woman he was dating at the time, and he became involved with the evangelical Calvary Chapel. Dylan's encounter with Jesus Christ influenced both his thinking and his performances. Audiences discovered an unexpected side of Dylan when this usually reticent singer now began to testify of his faith between songs and sing with a passion that had sometimes been lacking in his more recent work.

Slow Train Coming and his next two albums, *Saved* and *Shot of Love*, are filled with evidence of the grace he had found in Christ and a warning of judgment for a world on the wrong course. Some of the songs from this period suffer from a rather strident tone, but he also produced such heartfelt, highly personal gems as "Saving Grace," and the rich spiritual imagery of "Every Grain of Sand."

In the albums that followed, Dylan returned to a more subtle approach to issues of faith and doubt, although his biblical worldview clearly remained intact. As happens with many Christian artists, he passed through an "in your face" proselytizing style in his immediate post-conversion work to a more nuanced and poetic expression. He began once again to explore social and interpersonal relationships and seemed less interested in using his songs to preach a specific message. Some critics, both Christian and not, interpreted this as a signal that he had abandoned his faith, and rumors spread that Dylan was no longer a Christian. This misunderstanding is probably rooted in a narrow and restrictive definition of what a Christian musician should sing about. But for those with ears to hear, there was still plenty of deeply spiritual and biblical content in the songs he wrote.

By the mid-eighties many thought that Dylan's best work was in the past. Then, in the late '90s, when many had written him off as no longer relevant, he produced a series of albums that rank, arguably, among his finest work. The critics raved and a younger audience discovered the artist their parents had cherished. To this day, each new work shows fire and passion, with songs that are dense with poetry and whose riches cannot be mined in a single listening. Plumbing the depths of Dylan's songs takes work, but it is work that rewards those who undertake it.

Dylan is a lyricist without parallel in the history of rock music. When you consider the scope and power of such remarkable songs as "Blowin' in the Wind," "Like a Rolling Stone," "Desolation Row," "Tangled Up in Blue," and "Every Grain of Sand," you'll encounter lovely melodies that are joined to unforgettably poetic phrases, including turns of speech that have become part of our cultural lexicon. Dylan's lyrics are accented by an amazingly wide range of cultural references (both high and low) that demonstrate the depth and breadth of his reading and listening. And there is a playfulness and rich humor even in the midst of his most serious statements.

Then there is that inimitable voice that, while not traditionally beautiful, is filled with an urgency arising from the depths of his inner struggles. It's an honest everyman's voice, with a painterly sense of knowing how to shape and phrase a lyric in unexpected ways for maximum impact. In many ways, Dylan is the Picasso of modern music. He ignores the normal standards of singing and writing, creating from his own inner muse a style uniquely his own—angular, rough-hewn, but soaringly poetic with unforgettable turns of phrase.

Dylan has always been a student and lover of traditional music, and two of the sources for his music have been hymns and gospel songs. He spoke of their importance to him in a 1997 interview with the *New York Times*: "Those old songs are my lexicon and my prayer book. All my beliefs come out of these old songs. . . . I believe in a God of time and space, but if people ask me about that, my impulse is to point them back toward those songs."[1]

Latter-day albums such as *Time Out of Mind* (1997), *Love and Theft* (2001), *Modern Times* (2006), and *Tempest* (2012) have continued to combine a prophetic concern for truth and justice with a world-weary realism about the nature of humanity. Bob Dylan writes knowingly of the battle between good and evil, righteousness and sin, and faith and doubt that is being fought in every human heart. And few have written of these matters so memorably. To the one who listens attentively, Dylan is still singing of a world gone wrong teetering on the precipice of apocalypse, and of a hope that can be found only in the God who holds the master plan.

72

The Joshua Tree

U2

(recording, 1987)

What happens when a famous rock band from Ireland reflects on their love/hate relationship with the United States? You get an album that glories in the beauties of even the harshest of American landscapes (the desert); that celebrates the American musical traditions of rock, folk, and blues; that explores the vicissitudes of the spiritual life; and that raises pointed questions about America's place in the world order. You get U2's *The Joshua Tree*.

In the late 1980s, the Irish rock band U2 decided that they wanted to make an album inspired by their experiences in America: its literature, its landscape, its politics, and its spiritual yearnings. What emerged from their recording sessions was a record that today is widely considered one of the best rock albums of all time, as well as being one of the bestselling with over twenty-five million copies sold worldwide. *The Joshua Tree* also fostered a series of hit singles that helped establish U2 as what magazine covers were calling "the biggest band in the world."

Coming off their previous album, *The Unforgettable Fire*, U2 decided to largely forgo the atmospheric and impressionistic soundscapes of that album and to create something "more straightforward, focused, and concise." From the chiming guitar tones of the opening song, "Where the Streets Have No Name" (likely a reference to heaven), the listener is invited into a muscular, unflinching musical and

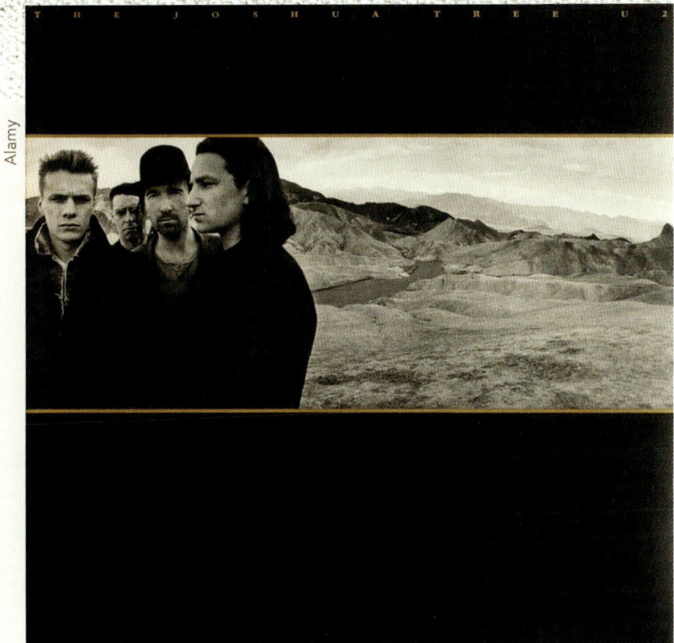

Alamy

The Joshua Tree, album cover

lyrical experience, a place where struggle, exhilaration, and indignation meet and interact. Here lead singer Bono unleashes his full vocal arsenal of sighs, moans, grunts, exhalations, and a voice that cracks with emotion. Such mannerisms are effectively deployed throughout the record. While "Streets" is uplifting, the second song, "I Still Haven't Found What I'm Looking For," strikes a more uncertain tone, and honest reflection bridges clearly expressed belief in "The Kingdom Come" with the nagging sense that even with the comforts of faith there must be more to this life than what the singer has experienced. This theme drives much of the record. "With or Without You," which musically moves from a quiet simmer to a full boil, can be interpreted either as a love song or as an expression of spiritual longing and struggle. "Bullet the Blue Sky" is a scathing (both lyrically and sonically) indictment of an American foreign policy driven more by greed than by idealism, and "In God's Country" explores the myth of America as promised land, a promise many find unfulfilled.

Though America is the big theme of the album, this does not keep U2 from exploring other themes closer to home, as in "Running to Stand Still," which mourns the damage done by an epidemic of heroin use in their hometown of Dublin, "Red Hill Mining Town," a protest song in the cause of a UK miner's strike, and the haunting "Mothers of the Disappeared," written to honor a group of mothers whose children had been victims of the civil war in El Salvador. One of the most moving songs on the album is "One Tree Hill," a memorial to a close friend who had died in a motorcycle accident. The song describes the thoughts that drifted through Bono's mind at the funeral of his lost comrade.

While the music on *The Joshua Tree* has an anthemic energy and punch, it traverses a bleak and harsh landscape of emotions and experiences; it is a record of U2's spiritual pilgrimage through this dark territory. The fact that so many people have so readily embraced the album perhaps speaks to the universality of such a pilgrimage and attests to the way that U2 could bring such beauty and meaning into the bleakness of a fallen world.

U2 grew out of a notice on the Mount Temple High School bulletin board, placed there by Larry Mullen Jr., who was looking for students interested in making music together. A band grew out of those who responded, and went through several changes in personnel and band names before settling on the moniker "U2" and narrowing their membership to Larry Mullen Jr., Paul "Bono" Hewson, David "The Edge" Evans, and Adam Clayton. When the fledgling band won a talent show whose prize included the opportunity to record a demo in a studio, their slow ascent toward fame began. Their debut album, *Boy* (1980), gathered positive reviews and modest sales, and included their first song to chart in the States, "I Will Follow."

The group almost disbanded during the recording of their second album, *October* (1981), due to Bono and The Edge's concerns about whether a rock-and-roll lifestyle could accommodate their seriously held Christian commitments. They had both become members of a church called Shalom Fellowship, which emphasized radical discipleship. After much wrestling with the question, they decided that they could be both Christians and rock musicians, and the songs on *October* reflect their spiritual concerns, as would much of their music thereafter.

Their breakthrough album artistically was *War* (1983), which contains several songs with explicitly Christian lyrical statements, including "40," their paraphrase of Psalm 40: "I waited patiently for the Lord / He inclined and heard my cry." The record's unique sound, driven by an insistent rhythm section and The Edge's chopping guitar work, was different from almost anything else being created by other bands, and the lyrics on the record showed a continued growth in maturity and depth. Its follow-up, *Under a Blood Red Sky* (1983), was a live album and concert film that showed how effectively U2 could engage an audience.

The Unforgettable Fire (1984) finds the band experimenting with a new sound, an arty, atmospheric, ambient vibe that was influenced by Brian Eno and Daniel Lanois. The song, "Pride (In the Name of Love)," which name-checked both Martin Luther King Jr. and Jesus, became their first big hit song in the States. When they performed a mesmerizing fourteen-minute version of their song "Bad" for the televised *Live Aid*, and Bono leapt off the stage to dance with a fan, the world was given notice that U2 had fully arrived.

Subsequent albums explored their

musical roots and a variety of sonic experiments: a tip of the hat to their musical forebearers in *Rattle and Hum* (1988), the highly introspective and musically inventive *Achtung Baby* (1991), which they playfully described as "four men chopping down the Joshua Tree," *Zooropa* (1993), and *Pop* (1997). During this period they specialized in elaborate stage tours that emphasized sensory overload, oversize props (a wall of televisions and a gigantic, glittering mirror-ball lemon), and over-the-top characterizations (Bono as "MacPhisto" and "The Fly"). The music of this period gave evidence of the personal spiritual struggles that Bono and other band members were undergoing at the time.

With *All That You Can't Leave Behind* (2000), *How to Dismantle an Atomic Bomb* (2004), *No Line On the Horizon* (2006), and *Songs of Innocence* (2014), there is a return to the sound that had once made them the world's biggest band. That sound highlights the expressive, deeply emotive vocals of Bono, the chopping, chiming, echoing guitar chords of The Edge, and the often-underappreciated rhythmic backdrop provided by Clayton and Mullen. When fused together, the U2 sound can descend to a place where emotional darkness can be probed, or ascend to musical ecstasy with an exhilaration that echoes the gospel music Bono so dearly loves.

U2's lyrics are often embellished with biblical and spiritual imagery—for example, on songs such as "Sunday Bloody Sunday," "Pride (In the Name of Love)," "Silver and Gold," and "Running to Stand Still." Such songs are often filled with direct references from the Bible. One critic has enumerated more than fifty scriptural quotations in U2's lyrics, sometimes used in songs that are not particularly focused on religious subject matter. They commonly tackle issues like racism, the Irish troubles, war, drug addiction, and social injustice—in the midst of which they posit a hope that arises from a connection to God.

But U2 has not settled for just singing about the problems of the world. The band, especially Bono, has been outspoken about such issues as poverty, AIDS, the third world, and social injustice. Their *A Conspiracy of Hope* tour raised awareness and a great deal of money for Amnesty International. Bono has paid personal visits to Africa in his campaign for the fight against world hunger and the cancelation of crippling thirdworld debt. "There is nothing worse than a rock star with a cause,"[1] admits Bono, but he has spent the currency of his celebrity status to increase awareness for a lot of important issues.

Three of the four members of the band have long self-identified as Christians, and the status of the fourth is at very least that of a passionate spiritual seeker. But all of them evidence a distrust of institutionalized religion. Bono has said:

> I'm not a very religious person. I'm uncomfortable in churches because the

> Christ I love and read about in the Gospels is often not in the churches. Remember, I come from Ireland and I've seen the damage of religious warfare. I am a believer. I don't wear the badge on the outside but on the inside.[2]

However, despite being uncomfortable with religion, and recognizing that he is often "not a very good advertisement for God," Bono understands his personal need for grace. As he told one interviewer: "The thing that keeps me on my knees is the difference between Grace and Karma."[3] He explains,

> At the center of all religions is the idea of Karma. You know, what you put out comes back to you: an eye for an eye, a tooth for a tooth. . . . And yet, along comes this idea called Grace to upend all that. . . . Love interrupts, if you like, the consequences of your actions, which in my case is very good news indeed, because I have done a lot of stupid stuff.[4]

Grace, Bono says, is not an excuse for stupid actions, but he is "holding out for Grace. I'm holding out that Jesus took my sins onto the cross."[5] And Bono also believes that honestly reflecting upon his personal faith struggles is part of his calling as an artist, just as it was for ancient Israel's King David. "What's so powerful about the Psalms are, as well as their being Gospel and songs of praise, they are also the blues. It's very important to be honest with God."[6] The doubt and uncertainty sometimes found in the songs only make their spirituality all the more convincing.

It is this mixture of heartfelt trust in God's grace with honesty about the struggle of living out the spiritual life that has made U2's songs so important to so many listeners. Whether revealing the intensity of their own struggles ("With or Without You," "I Still Haven't Found What I'm Looking For," "Wake Up Dead Man") or celebrating the joy and hope of God's kingdom ("Gloria," "40," "Yahweh"), U2 writes and performs songs that are passionate, authentic, and unforgettable.

73

Paradise Garden

Howard Finster

(artistic assemblage, c. 1990)

One of the most fascinating artistic creations of the twentieth century can be found nestled in the foothills about an hour north of Atlanta, Georgia. It is a four-acre garden designed, constructed, and decorated by Howard Finster, a Baptist preacher and arguably the most important folk artist of modern times. The garden, which came to be called *Paradise Garden*, is a chaotic, crazy-quilt patchwork of ramshackle buildings, odd sculptures and assemblages, rusty automobiles, and hundreds of paintings in his unusual signature style, all nestled among the trees and flowers and shrubbery. All these elements joined together are intended to be the focal point for his urgent spiritual message to modern men and women, a message about ultimate things: heaven and hell, moral admonitions, apocalyptic warnings, and a celebration of God's love. *Paradise Garden* is a place where Finster's mystical visions of faith are made visible through his redemption of the cast-off junk of our society.

Originally begun on a smaller scale, the garden grew over time, and Finster was still working on it at the end of his life. Although it was largely neglected for a number of years, recent attempts have been undertaken to restore it to its original state. Finster sometimes referred to himself as "God's junk man," and he built most of his *Paradise Garden* with discarded material, stuff that most people would think worthless: pieces of broken mirrors, old rusty

Paradise Garden Foundation

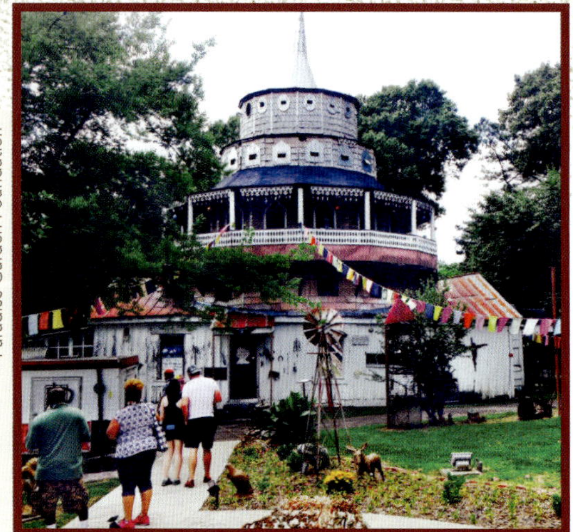

Paradise Garden, Summerville, Georgia

tools, tin cans, random pieces of machinery, children's toys, bus stop signs, Coke bottles, and other materials that were destined for the trash heap. But Finster saw the potential to make something beautiful and interesting from these very ordinary bits and pieces that he rescued from the local dump or from abandoned construction sites. He pieced all this "junk" together to make sculptures, signs, various odd assemblages, and decorative accents.

The defining structures located throughout the garden include the *Bike Tower* (a giant sculptural heap consisting of bicycle parts wired together), a walkway winding through the garden that is embedded with shiny bits of cosmetic jewelry, broken colored glass, and abandoned tools (commemorating his former job as a bicycle repairman, which he gave up to become a full-time artist), and the nearly fifty-foot-tall *World Folk Art Church* (which he designed and built himself) that somewhat resembles a sagging wedding cake and is topped by a spire. There is also a pump house constructed entirely of Coca-Cola bottles and cement, a giant concrete shoe that refers to the "beautiful feet of those who proclaim the Gospel of peace," and the *Bible House*, a small structure covered entirely in Bible verses.

There are also dozens of sculptures and assemblages scattered around the garden, constructed from cement, wire, and all the unexpected little odds and ends that he imbedded in them: a doll's head, broken pieces of mirror, Coke bottles, and so forth. Finster's reclamation and reuse of discarded bits of trash represented, for him, a theological truth: that God is a redemptive God, One who fashions His saints out of the vilest materials, making of them something beautiful and holy. In God's economy, no refuse is refused. A painted banner in the garden proclaims Finster's vision: "I built this park of broken pieces to try to mend a broken world of people who are traveling their last road."[1]

Along with the sheer joyful celebration of the ephemera of life represented by his recycled trash, which he transformed into a tactile wondrousness, are urgent messages calling upon the sinner to repent and turn to God. Finster didn't shy away from calling for moral uprightness or warning of sin's consequences. The garden even contains a wrecked Cadillac upon which he painted various slogans of caution and instruction, such as "This happens to drunk drivers" and "I heard the wreck on the highway, but I didn't hear nobody pray."

And everywhere there are paintings, adorned with Scripture and his own poetic messages, printed in his usual, urgent, all-caps script with often idiosyncratic spelling. There are hundreds of such paintings, usually brushed onto wooden surfaces and ranging in size from two inches to five feet. They mostly proclaim biblical messages, sometimes combining such messages with pop culture references or tributes to his heroes: Elvis Presley, Henry Ford, George Washington, and Shakespeare. Each is painted in Finster's trademark style—simplistic cartoonlike figures crowded into a busy image and accented by an abundance of text that drives the message home. A recurrent theme of these works is the necessity of repentance in order to avoid God's judgment. Finster suggested that the garden had "literally been covered up with Bible verses all over it, where a minister can come in here and bring a sinner and take him round and read him into the Kingdom of God."[2]

At first this backyard garden might seem to some visitors to be the ramshackle construction of a mentally unstable mind, a visual cacophony veering perilously close to insanity. But while it may seem a bit weird and wacky, Finster was deadly serious about his intentions. This strange artistic assemblage, like his astonishing output of paintings, is not the work of a madman but a quirky, eccentric, and incredibly inventive man who wanted to share the gospel through his art. The garden's endlessly fascinating and unexpected elements make it a modern masterpiece that repays close attention. Many who have lingered in its environs have spoken enthusiastically of the sense of peace and spiritual nourishment they have found there.

Born in 1916 in Alabama, Howard Finster was a precocious and unusual child, and had the first of his many lifelong visions at age three when the ghost of his recently departed sister, allegedly, came to him with a message of comfort. Throughout his life, he spoke of the visions that he was given by God, and these visions became the content for much of his art. He claimed that none of his creativity came from his own ingenuity but that he was merely transcribing what God had shown him.

Although Finster was a Baptist, he was converted in a Methodist revival meeting at age thirteen and not long after received what he considered to be a "supernatural call" to the ministry. Although his formal education never proceeded past the sixth grade due to his family's need for him to help out on the family farm, he studied the Bible passionately and wrote his first sermon at age sixteen, which was published in a local paper. Eventually he became an itinerant preacher, sharing the Good News throughout the South and supporting himself by various occupations, including bicycle repair. He was a popular preacher, and people loved the sermonic chalk talks he gave, which were an early indication of his artistic gifts.

Finster always loved making and repairing things, and as a hobby he began to build miniature buildings and whimsical sculptures. Over time, this developed into something that gained a bit of public attention. Then, in 1975, he was repairing a bicycle when he put a dab of paint onto the end of his finger to cover some scratches on the bike. He was startled to see that the paint made a distinct little human face, and he then claimed to have heard a voice speak clearly to him, calling him to make sacred art. Like Moses at the burning bush, he demurred, telling God that he was not an artist. "How do ya know?" the voice insisted. To prove it once and for all, Finster pulled a dollar bill out of his wallet and used the picture of George Washington as a model. He was so pleased with his resulting drawing that he knew the call was genuine. And from that day, his entire focus was upon creating "sermons in paint" to share God's urgent message with humankind. He saw himself as a "second Noah," sent to warn humanity of the need to change their ways and embrace a life of love and moral purity.

As word got around about this eccentric artist/preacher, art students and folk art enthusiasts began to make the pilgrimage to Summerville, Georgia, to meet Howard Finster and see his creations. His work found such a ready market in art galleries that no matter how feverishly he worked, he could not fully meet the demand. His paintings were even featured on albums by popular music groups REM and the Talking Heads, which delighted Finster as it allowed him to imbed Bible verses on album covers that would be seen by millions of people. He was even asked to appear on Johnny Carson's *The Tonight Show*, where Carson was visibly amused and delighted by the straight-talking Southern preacher.

By the time of his death in 2001, Finster had created an astonishing 46,991 original pieces. We know the exact number because he kept track, and usually wrote the appropriate number somewhere on each piece of art. The works by this untrained artist (painted on wood, fiberglass, metal, the sides of buildings, shoes, Spam cans, or whatever might be at hand) have attracted the attention of both art critics and lovers of folk art for their unique stylistic approach and for the way they reveal the heart and passion of a man who found he could do his best preaching with a brush. *Paradise Garden* is the summation of his work and represents both his passion to share God's message and the warm hospitality of the man who delighted in giving personal tours of his creation. A sign at the entrance reads: "Welcome to *Paradise Garden*. God is love."

"I am sure about myself and my work," he said. "I am sure about God and Jesus and the Bible. My responsibility is to get the message out all over the world."[3] In his own unique way, that is what Howard Finster did.

74

The Four Holy Gospels

MAKOTO FUJIMURA

(paintings, 2011)

From the early centuries of the Christian era, manuscript illumination has been an art form that allowed the artistic hand to reflect reverence for the Scriptures while creating beautiful copies of the text. In our own times, with the mass production of Bibles, manuscript illumination has become a largely forgotten creative outlet. But one contemporary Christian artist has reinvented the form for today. Makoto Fujimura, an esteemed modern abstract painter, was commissioned to paint five large-scale images for a volume entitled *The Four Holy Gospels*, which would commemorate the four-hundredth anniversary of the King James Version of the Bible. It was a huge undertaking. In addition to these five major works, Fujimura created abstract doodlings to accompany the pages of text and small paintings to illuminate the initial capital letters for each chapter of the four gospels. The result is a great visual feast, a masterpiece in the form of a sacred book not unlike those created by medieval monks. And just as it was for the manuscript illuminators of old, the project proved to be immensely meaningful for an artist who speaks often of his love for the Scriptures and how he has been personally impacted by the story and person of Jesus Christ.

Fujimura's central theme for the series of five central images was a focus on the tears of Christ, "tears shed for the atrocities of the past century and for our present darkness."[1] Each of the five paintings is unique, though they gain in impact when seen together in an exhibition or within the pages of the published volume. *Charis-Kairos (Tears of Christ)* is the introductory painting, a dark background upon which layers of vivid color have been built. The bright hope represented by these pigments seems to shatter the darkness. *Consider the Lilies* represents the gospel of Matthew and is built up of over sixty layers of colored mineral pigments, including azurite and malachite. The only painting with a representational element, it subtly suggests a trinity of three Easter lilies. *Water Flames* is the painting for the gospel of Mark, and it uses a visual language very similar to the artist Mark Rothko to represent abstracted flames that draw our eyes upward—flames that both consume and sanctify.

Referencing the familiar parable of the Prodigal Son, Luke's gospel is represented by *The Prodigal God*, a painting that Fujimura describes as depicting "my own struggle between the legalism of religion (the elder brother) and the reckless spendthrift nature of the Father's love in the story." The final painting, *In the Beginning* (the gospel of John), is a work that evokes the dawn of creation and makes reference to both Christ as the Creator and to the mystery of His incarnation. Appropriately, it is the most mystical of the five masterful paintings, but all five paintings serve well as objects of contemplation, works that reward patient inspection to allow them to unfold themselves to the gaze of the viewer.

Makoto Fujimura was born in 1960 to Japanese parents living in Boston. Most of his grade school years were spent in Japan, but he returned to the United States at age thirteen. He showed promise as an artist early on and remembers being inspired by a teacher who told him not to "waste God's gift." After being educated in the States, he spent six and a half years in Japan, learning traditional Japanese painting methods. The result of this eclectic artistic education is a style that bridges traditional Japanese art with modern abstract expressionism. He considers his work a hybrid of early Renaissance master Fra Angelico and American expressionist Mark Rothko. The style he has developed is completely unlike the realism of earlier Christian painting: thoroughly contemporary, and yet deeply spiritual in intention.

While studying in Tokyo, Fujimura began to attend church with his wife, who was herself on a spiritual search for greater meaning in her life. At first he was unimpressed, and rejected the teachings of the Bible as outdated and irrelevant. But at the same time he was experiencing a growing need for a sense of meaning and purpose in his life beyond making art. While art was very important to him, it could not answer some of the deeper stirrings in his

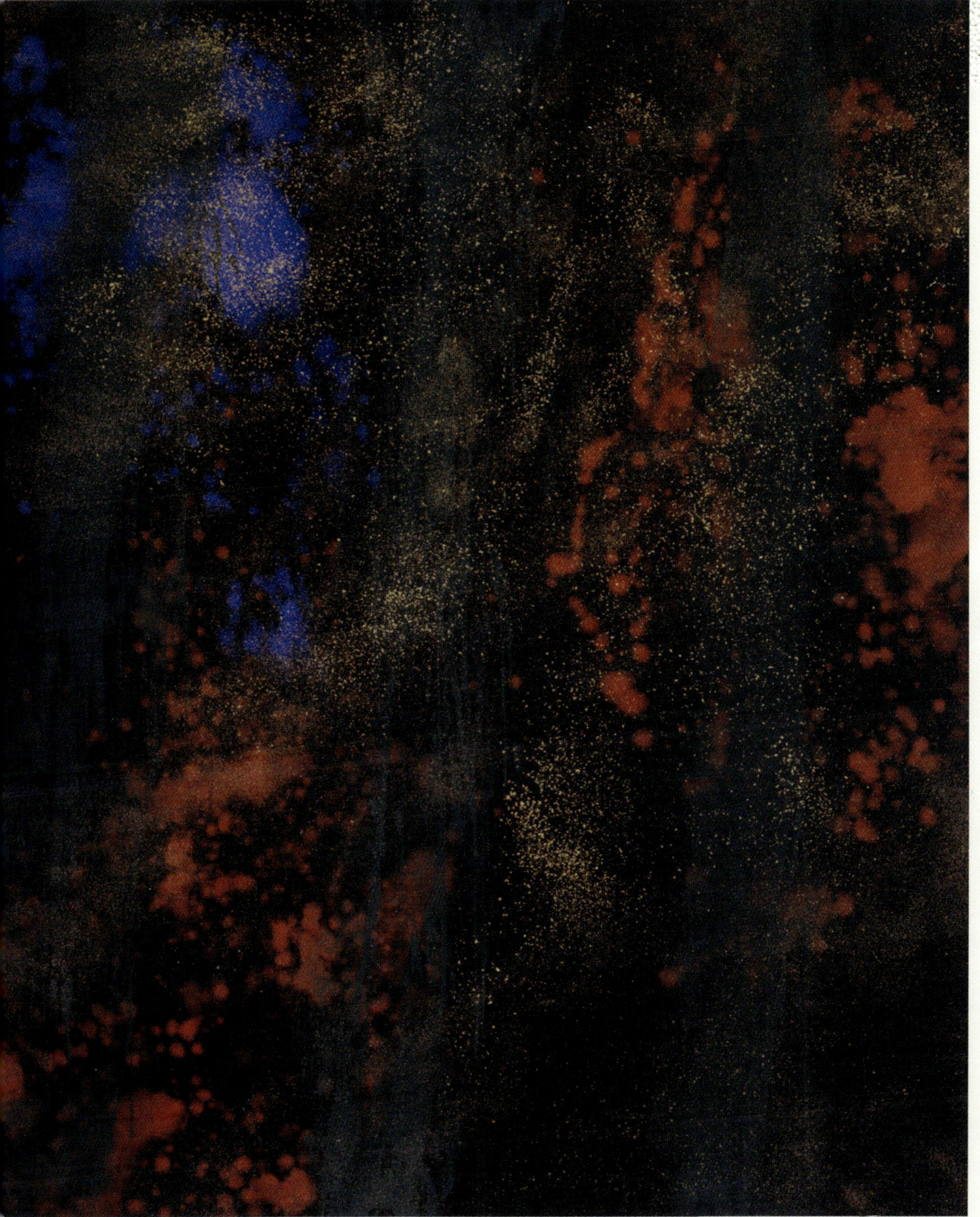

John: In the Beginning by Makoto Fujimura, courtesy of Makoto Fujimura

soul. Ultimately, it was the poetry of William Blake that nudged him toward faith and helped him to begin to make sense of the Christian message. Never one to follow half measures, Fujimura embraced his new faith with passion and with a fervent intellectual desire to understand what it meant to be a Christian in these modern times.

Since that time, Fujimura's Christian commitment has been central to the making of his art. It has been reflected in his paintings and also in his desire to help other artists find a meaningful connection between their faith and their creativity. To that end, he founded the International Arts Movement, an organization dedicated to helping other creative individuals wrestle with issues of art, faith, and living fully as human beings. He also has been a prolific blogger and essayist on such issues and has written a book telling of his personal journey, *River Grace*, published a collection of his blog posts, *Refractions*, and wrote *Silence and Beauty*, his reflection on the novel *Silence* by Shusaku Endo.

On September 11, 2001, Fujimura and his family were living in New York City, in the very shadow of the Twin Towers, and were firsthand witnesses to the devastation of the terrorist attacks that reduced the towers to rubble. He lived only three blocks from Ground Zero, and this shattering experience has shaped his art and his worldview in the years since. A serious artist cannot ignore the pain, suffering, and moral ugliness of the times, but an artist of faith also knows that this is not the end of the story. God is at work in a reclamation project in which the artist can be a participant. "Despite our fallen nature," he writes, "God desires to reflect goodness, beauty, and truth in us. God desires to refract his perfect light via the broken, prismatic shards of our lives. Art and creativity will end up being delivered back to the Creator's hands in that pure light."[2]

Following the ancient Japanese artistic practice of *Nihonga*, Fujimura grinds his own pigments and paints with handmade brushes. He sometimes accents his paintings with touches of gold and silver, applied to the canvas with glue made from animal hides. The process is traditional and very organic, emphasizing the textures, colors, and materials of the natural world. He applies the colors in a "semi-transparent layering effect that traps light in the space created between the pigments and between layers of gold and silver foil."[3] This layering creates depth and ambiguity and brings the surface to life. The finished paintings seem like living organisms, pulsing and breathing under the gaze of the viewer. In his art, Fujimura is constructing a new world from the elements of God's created world. As he describes it, "Coarser mineral pigments, being literally sand, create ripples of color when allowed to cascade down. I stand the painting against the wall, and using broader strokes with abundant water, let the pigments cover the painting. When displayed in a gallery, the pigments reflect the light and shimmer like stars."[4]

Among his other masterworks are a series of paintings that reflect on T. S. Eliot's mystical poems in *Four Quartets*. These poems proved an ideal impetus for creating a series of paintings that are not only beautiful objects of artistic craftsmanship in themselves but also objects for contemplation. The patient eye taking in these paintings is well rewarded by the slow unfolding of all the work has to offer. These are not paintings of any recognizable object but are objects in themselves, ready to be read and experienced on their own terms. As Nicholas Wolsterstorff has said, "Fujimura's paintings invite us to dwell within the painting. When we do, we experience shalom, not in going beyond the painting but in our enchanted dwelling within it."[5]

Fujimura has taken the abstract metaphysical language of such acclaimed artists as Mark Rothko and Barnett Newman and transformed it into something that carries a spiritual resonance. He does not see his own work as abstract, but as "a representational depiction of God's space."[6] In his paintings he takes the elements of the created world, fashions them into something entirely new, and then offers them as an act of adoration to God. That is why he can say, making reference to the gospel story of Mary Magdalene, "The act of painting with precious minerals is like Mary anointing the feet of Jesus."[7] In his beautiful abstractions, the spiritual and the physical come together in an incarnation of God's beauty.

75

The Tree of Life

Terrence Malick

(film, 2011)

Most filmgoers are used to movies that have a clear narrative structure—like a novel—and can be easily accessed and understood. For such viewers Terrence Malick's *The Tree of Life* might seem an impenetrable piece of filmmaking. It is more akin to poetry than it is to prose—visual poetry filled with beautiful and evocative images, a complex structure of storytelling, and a great deal of ambiguity and mystery. If you are looking primarily for a story, you will doubtless be disappointed. But for those willing to approach it more as a work to contemplate than a work to entertain, *The Tree of Life* offers one of the most theologically rich and emotionally moving experiences to be found in any film.

Opening with a quotation from the book of Job, *The Tree of Life* undertakes an exploration of much of the same territory as that biblical book: the problem of suffering, the seeming absence of God, and the glorious way He is revealed in His created universe. All this is explored through the eyes of Jack, an adult on a quest to make some meaning out of his life, who reflects upon some of the events of his childhood, particularly the all-too-early death of his kind and saintly brother, R. L. The scenes of his family life growing up fill the largest part of the running time of the film, as we see the struggles between a father who approaches the harsh realities of life by striving for control and power and a mother who glories in the wonder and

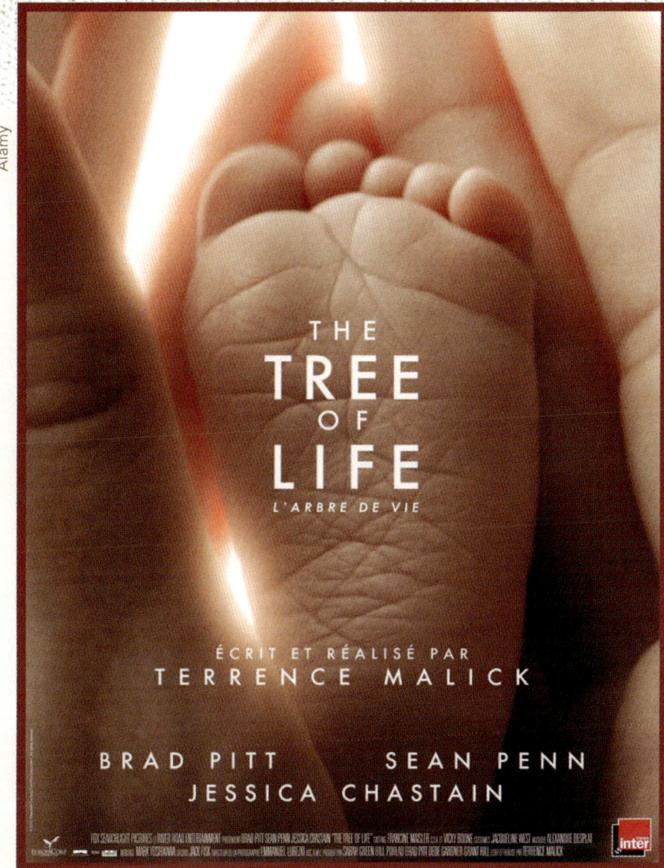

The Tree of Life, movie poster

Alamy

magic of the world. As his mother teaches him, "There are two ways through life, the way of nature and the way of grace." This dichotomy, symbolized by his parents, is at the heart of the film. Jack's father wants to teach his sons to be tough and hardened so they can survive the harshness of this fallen world. Jack's mother wants her sons to see that there is a better path: "The only way to be happy is to love. Unless you love, your life will flash by. Do good. Wonder. Hope. Help each other. Love everyone. Every leaf. Every ray of light. Forgive." Living in a life filled with splendor and with pain, she tells her sons, requires an embrace of the way of grace.

Much of the dialogue in the film consists of the whispered prayers of the main characters: seeking God's help or seeking to understand why He doesn't seem to be helping. The visuals often say more than the words do, and are frequently nothing short of breathtaking. Malick's camera lingers on the powerful rush of water plunging over a waterfall, a father's amazement at studying the feet of his infant son, light filtering down through trees, a spiral of stained glass, sparklers glowing on the front lawn on a warm summer night, and an extended meditation on the creation and evolution of the universe that dares to envisage what it might have been like to be there. There is also powerful imagery representing the course of the spiritual journey Jack travels as he stumbles toward spiritual rebirth, including a doorway in the middle of the desert and a stirring reunion with loved ones past and present on an ocean shore. For this is ultimately a film about redemption. Not about finding all the answers but finding the love that allows some questions to go unanswered.

Born in Texas in 1943, Terrence Malick is a reclusive director who likes to let his films speak for themselves. He gives very few interviews and hence it can be difficult to piece together the full story of his personal life or his own interpretations of his work. He is the son of a geologist and spent much of his early life in Waco, Texas, which is the setting for *The Tree of Life*. He had two younger brothers, one of whom, Larry, was an accomplished guitarist who purposely broke his own hands because he could not master the guitar at the level he desired. Larry later committed suicide, an event that had a lasting effect on Malick and may have been influential in energizing his spiritual search.

Malick studied philosophy at Harvard and Oxford, writing his unfinished thesis on the thought of Martin Heidegger. His translation of one of Heidegger's books remains in print. After college he worked as a journalist for such magazines as *Newsweek*, *The New Yorker*, and *Life*, before finally deciding to pursue his growing interest in film. After achieving some success as a screenwriter, he decided he wanted to direct his own scripts. His first major film, *Badlands* (1973), was a critical success, as was the gorgeously filmed *Days of Heaven* (1978), which earned an Oscar for cinematography and a Best Director prize at Cannes Film Festival.

Then Malick disappeared from the Hollywood radar. He lived for a time in Paris, where he wrote some more screenplays, but he didn't release another film for twenty years. He finally broke the silence with *The Thin Red Line* (1998), a philosophically and spiritually informed picture about the horror and dehumanization of war, which was nominated for seven Academy Awards. Much of the dialogue in this film is done in voice-over, capturing the internal meditations, and sometimes the prayers, of his characters. His next film, *The New World* (2005), told the story of John Smith and Pocahontas with his usual focus on human complexity and the astonishing splendor of the natural world.

When *The Tree of Life* was released in 2011, it was only Malick's fifth feature-length film. It was followed uncharacteristically quickly by *To the Wonder* (2013), which explores the nature of love, both human and divine. Like *The Tree of Life*, it is rich in spiritual musings and constructed around a complicated narrative structure.

Malick is a perfectionist, which is one of the reasons for the lengthy space of time between releases. His working method is to shoot lots of footage and then create the film in the editing room out of the miles of film. Sometimes, much to the dismay of the actors involved, their entire performances end up on the cutting room floor and they are not seen at all in the finished film. But those performances that make the cut are almost always very strong and naturalistic. He manages to get the best out of his actors and also from the cinematographers, who capture the beauty of the natural world that provides the indispensable backdrop to every Malick picture. One of the trademarks of his style is to include frequent pauses in the action of the film that allow the viewer to contemplate for some length the shining grandeur of God's world.

Those who have worked with Malick are often effusive in their praise—not only for the working experience but also for the effect that he has had upon them through his personality and convictions. The great cinematographer Emmanuel Lubezki said that working with Malick changed him as a parent, a spouse, a friend, and a human being. Martin Sheen has spoken of the willingness of Malick to engage in conversation on the deepest and most profound issues of life, and credits Malick's suggestion that he read *The Brothers Karamazov* with being a spiritual turning point in his own life.

Terrence Malick is very protective of his private life, but from the bits and pieces we know of the man, it is clear that there are autobiographical elements to many of his films. He implicitly asks, however, that we make our judgments based upon the films themselves. Films like *The Thin Red Line*, *The Tree of Life*, and *To the Wonder* give clear evidence of a man who takes spiritual realities very seriously and calls upon Christian theology and practice to help us better understand our world and ourselves. Malick uses the medium of film—the most cumbersome and commercially driven of artistic forms—to engage us in a series of questions about beauty, meaning, relationships, and God; an artistic contemplation of the intersection between the human and the divine. For that, he deserves our patient attention, which will be bountifully rewarded.

To explore further works of art and the artists behind them; think about the intersections of creativity, spirituality, theology, and practical faith; and take part in the ongoing conversation, visit **www.terryglaspey.com.**

Acknowledgments

Thanks to the artists, writers, musicians, filmmakers, and other creatives who have so enriched my life by helping me to see the mystery, beauty, and wonder of life. They have also probed the dark corners of suffering and injustice in order to help me experience the world with compassion, a passion for justice, and a clear view of the need for grace. Their works have helped me see a little more clearly, ask better questions, live with the ambiguities, and embrace the mystery of Love.

Thanks to those who read some or all of this book as it was being written and offered encouragement and helpful critiques—and caught some embarrassing errors before they found their way into print. Special appreciation to Carolyn McCready, Steve Miller, Gene Skinner, Hope Lyda, Kim Moore, and Georgia Varozza. Also thanks to the adult Sunday school class at Valley Covenant Church, who allowed me to share with them the content of a number of these chapters before they were even written, and whose insights and questions helped me refine my thinking.

Thanks to my dear friend Jeff Crosby, who saw something in this concept and passed it along to the publisher. You made it possible, dude! And thanks to the team at Baker Publishing for all your efforts in making the concept a reality. You were patient, insightful, and unceasingly kind. Special thanks to Chad Allen, who acquired and championed the book, and Michelle Bardin, who was always so nice and who helped at every phase of the project; to my editors Lindsey Spoolstra and Rebecca Cooper; and to William Overbeeke, Brian

Brunsting, Brian Vos, Heather Brewer, Lauren Carlson, and their team of sales and marketing experts. I so appreciate all of your work!

Thanks to the team at Moody Publishers for this new edition with expanded artwork, and especially to Duane Sherman, Mackenzie Conway, Jeremy Slager, and Erik Peterson. Thanks for your vision in making the book even better!

Thank you to those who offered help and assistance in locating or providing the art displayed in these pages. Of particular note was the generosity of Anne Pyle (possibly the world's greatest authority on Sadao Watanabe), the brilliant Makoto Fujimura, Charles Norman (son of Larry Norman), and Jordan Poole and Kathy Berry of Howard Finster's Paradise Garden Foundation (which really *must* be seen when you are in the vicinity of Summerville, Georgia).

And finally, special heartfelt thanks to my smart and lovely daughters, Emma and Kathryn. I am so proud of the people you have become; and to my mom, Patricia, who never fails to offer love, encouragement, and support. Also thanks to my amazing sister, Debbie.

This book is humbly offered in memory of my father, Larry Glaspey, who died while it was being written. I miss you, Dad.

Notes

Chapter 2 *The Book of Kells*

1. Giraldus Cambrensis, *The Historical Works of Giraldus Cambrensis* (London: George Bells and Sons, 1894), https://openlibrary.org/books/OL7038028M/The_historical_works_of_Giraldus_Cambrensis.
2. As quoted in Ingo Walther and Norbert Wolf, *Masterpieces of Illumination* (Köln: Taschen, 2005), 11.
3. As quoted in Kathryn Bell, *Our Christian Heritage in Art* (Greenville, SC: Bob Jones University Press, 1999), 22.

Chapter 3 Gregorian Chant

1. As quoted in Tim Dowley, *Christian Music: A Global History* (Minneapolis: Fortress Press, 2011), 50.

Chapter 5 *Ordo Virtutum*

1. Hildegard of Bingen, *Mystical Writings* (New York: Crossroad, 1993), 68.
2. Ibid., 33, 28.
3. Ibid., 21.

Chapter 8 *The Divine Comedy*

1. T. S. Eliot, *Selected Prose of T. S. Eliot* (New York: Harcourt Brace Jovanovich, 1975), 227.
2. As quoted in Giovanni Andrea Sbarazzini, *A Handbook to Dante* (Boston: Ginn & Co., 1887), 282.
3. Dante, *Paradiso*, canto 33, translated by John Ciardi (New York: New American Library, 1970).

Chapter 9 *The Holy Trinity* Icon

1. As quoted in Linette Martin, *Sacred Doorways* (Brewster, MA: Paraclete Press, 2002), 233.
2. Ibid.
3. Henri Nouwen, *Behold the Beauty of the Lord* (Notre Dame, IN: Ave Maria Press, 1987), 14.

Chapter 10 *The Adoration of the Lamb*

1. Noah Charney, *Stealing the Mystic Lamb* (New York: Public Affairs, 2010), 3.
2. As quoted in Till-Holger Borchert, *Van Eyck* (Köln: Taschen, 2008), 29.

Chapter 11 *The Four Horsemen of the Apocalypse*

1. As quoted in Hans Rookmaaker, *The Creative Gift: Dürer, Dada, and Desolation Row* (Carlisle, UK: Piquant, 2002), 242–43.

Chapter 13 *The Ceiling of the Sistine Chapel*

1. As quoted in Andrew Graham-Dixon, *Michelangelo and the Sistine Chapel* (New York: Skyhorse, 2009), 3.
2. As quoted in Jim Palmer, ed., *The Pocket Book of Prayers* (Nashville: Thomas Nelson, 2005), 113.
3. As quoted in Gertrude Richardson Brigham, *The Study and Enjoyment of Pictures* (New York: Sully and Kleinteich, 1917), 28.
4. As quoted in J. Patrick Lewis, *Michelangelo's World* (Mankato, MN: Creative Company, 2007), 7.
5. "Celebration of the Unveiling of the Restorations of Michelangelo's Frescos in the Sistine Chapel: Homily of His Holiness John Paul II," *The Holy See*, April 8, 1994, http://w2.vatican.va/content/john-paul-ii/en/homilies/1994/documents/hf_jp-ii_hom_19940408_restauri-sistina.html.

Chapter 14 "A Mighty Fortress Is Our God"

1. As quoted in Kurt J. Eggert, "Martin Luther, God's Music Man," accessed March 20, 2015, http://www.wlsessays.net/node/465.
2. Ibid.
3. Ibid.

Chapter 17 *The Incredulity of Saint Thomas*

1. Francine Prose, *Caravaggio: Painter of Miracles* (New York: HarperCollins, 2005), 3–4.

Chapter 18 *The Holy Sonnets*

1. John Donne, "Sonnet X," in *Holy Sonnets* (DjVu Editions E-books, 2001), http://ebooks.gutenberg.us/DjVu_Collection/DJEDS/DONNE/SONNETS/Download.pdf.
2. Ibid., "Sonnet XIV."
3. Michael Schmidt, *Lives of the Poets* (New York: Random House, 1988), 211.
4. John Booty, "Introduction," in John Donne, *John Donne: Selections from Divine Poems, Sermons, Devotions, and Prayers* (New York: Paulist Press, 1990), 23.

Chapter 19 *The Temple*

1. As quoted in Izaak Walton, *The Life of George Herbert* (Oxford: Oxford University Press, 1973), 314.
2. George Herbert, *The Country Parson, The Temple* (New York: Paulist Press, 1981), 316.

Chapter 21 *St. Teresa in Ecstasy*

1. As quoted in Howard Hibbard, *Bernini* (New York: Penguin, 1990), 137.
2. Joshua Reynolds, *The Discourses of Sir Joshua Reynolds* (London: J. Carpenter, 1842), 176.

Chapter 22 *The Return of the Prodigal Son*

1. Henri Nouwen, *The Return of the Prodigal Son* (New York: Doubleday Image, 1994), 5.
2. Ibid., 15.
3. Bruce Bernard, ed., *Vincent By Himself: A Selection of His Paintings and Drawings Together with Extracts from His Letters* (New York: Barnes & Noble, 2004), 72.

Chapter 23 *The Pilgrim's Progress*

1. John Bunyan, *Grace Abounding to the Chief of Sinners*, Google Books ebook edition, location 7 (Digireads.com,2011),http://books.google.com/books/about/Grace_Abounding_to_the_Chief_of_Sinners.html?id=1TXgjjPi7r4C.
2. As quoted in Michael Schmidt, *The Novel: A Bibliography* (Cambridge, MA: Harvard University Press, 2014), 58.
3. As quoted in Anne Dunan-Page, *The Cambridge Companion to Bunyan* (Cambridge: Cambridge University Press, 2010), 43.

Chapter 24 "When I Survey the Wondrous Cross"

1. As quoted in Douglas Bond, *The Poetic Wonder of Isaac Watts* (Crawfordsville, IN: Reformation Trust, 2013), ebook edition, location 12.
2. George Burder, ed., *The Psalms and Spiritual Songs of Isaac Watts* (London: C. Whittingham, 1806), 221.
3. Isaac Watts, *The Poetical Works of Isaac Watts and Henry Kirke White* (New York: Houghton Mifflin, 1881), lxxvii.

Chapter 25 *St. Matthew Passion*

1. Leonard Bernstein, *The Joy of Music* (New York: Simon and Schuster, 1959), 264.
2. Rick Marschall, *Johann Sebastian Bach* (Nashville: Thomas Nelson, 2011), 78.
3. Ibid., 143.

Chapter 26 *Messiah*

1. As quoted in Jane Stuart Smith and Betty Carlson, *The Gift of Music* (Wheaton: Crossway, 1987), 45.
2. A. E. Bray, *Handel: His Life, Personal and Professional* (London: Ward and Company, 1857), 63.
3. As quoted in Patrick Kavanaugh, *The Spiritual Lives of Great Composers* (Nashville: Sparrow, 1992), 6.
4. Ibid., 7.
5. Smith and Carlson, *Gift of Music*, 47.
6. Louis Kronenberger, *Kings and Desperate Men* (Piscataway, NJ: Transaction Publishers, 2009), 117.

Chapter 28 *Songs of Innocence and Experience*

1. As quoted in Harold Bloom, *William Blake* (New York: Infobase Publishing, 2008), 24.
2. William Blake, *The Marriage of Heaven and Hell* (Oxford: Oxford University Press, 1975), 54.
3. William Blake, "Auguries of Innocence," *The Complete Poems*, edited by Alicia Ostriker (New York: Penguin, 1978), 506.

Chapter 29 *The Creation*

1. As quoted in Jane Stuart Smith and Betty Carlson, *The Gift of Music* (Wheaton: Crossway, 1987), 52.
2. Ibid., 49.
3. As quoted in Patrick Kavanaugh, *The Spiritual Lives of Great Composers* (Nashville: Sparrow, 1992), 23.
4. Ibid.

Chapter 30 *Pride and Prejudice*

1. Jane Austen, *Pride and Prejudice* (Mineola, NY: Dover, 1995), 141.
2. Jane Austen, *The Prayers of Jane Austen*, edited by Terry Glaspey (Eugene, OR: Harvest House, 2015), 51.
3. James Edward Austen-Leigh, *A Memoir of Jane Austen* (Ware, UK: Wordsworth, 2007), 33.

Chapter 31 *The Wanderer above the Sea of Fog*

1. As quoted in Joseph Leo Koemer, *Caspar David Friedrich and the Subject of Landscape* (London: Reaktion Books, 2009), 93.
2. Ibid., 237.
3. As quoted in William Vaughn, *Friedrich* (New York: Phaidon, 2004), 111.
4. As quoted in William Vaughn, *German Romantic Painting* (New Haven: Yale University Press, 1994), 116.

Chapter 32 Symphony no. 5, *The Reformation*

1. As quoted in Jack Alder, *Soulmates from the Pages of History* (New York: Algora Publishing, 2013), 144.
2. As quoted in Patrick Kavanaugh, *The Spiritual Lives of Great Composers* (Nashville: Sparrow, 1992), 53.
3. Ibid., 53–54.
4. Ibid., 55.

Chapter 33 *The Voyage of Life*

1. As quoted in Elwood Parry, *The Art of Thomas Cole* (Newark: University of Delaware Press, 1988), 128.
2. As quoted in Louis Legrand Noble, *The Life and Works of Thomas Cole* (New York: Sheldon, Blakeman, 1856), 289.
3. As quoted in Howard S. Merritt, *Thomas Cole* (Yonkers, NY: Hudson River Museum, 1981), 3.
4. As quoted in Matthew Baigell, *Thomas Cole* (New York: Watson-Guptill, 1985), 25.
5. Noble, *Life and Works of Thomas Cole*, 63.
6. As quoted in Gene Edward Veith, *Painters of Faith* (Washington, D.C.: Regnery, 2001), 72.

Chapter 34 *The Light of the World*

1. As quoted in Helen de Borchgrave, *A Journey into Christian Art* (Minneapolis: Fortress Press, 1999), 176.
2. William Holman Hunt, *A Pre-Raphaelite Friendship* (Ann Arbor: UMI Research Press, 1986), 247.
3. De Borchgrave, *Journey into Christian Art*, 174.
4. William Holman Hunt, *Pre-Raphaelitism and the Pre-Raphaelite Brotherhood* (New York: Macmillan, 1905), 347.

Chapter 35 *The Heart of the Andes*

1. Gene Edward Veith, *Painters of Faith* (Washington, D.C.: Regnery, 2001), 40.

Chapter 36 Fairy Tales

1. As quoted in Roland Hein, *George MacDonald: Victorian Mythmaker* (Eugene, OR: Wipf and Stock, 2014), 388.
2. As quoted in C. S. Lewis, *George MacDonald: An Anthology* (Grand Rapids: Zondervan, 2001), 77.
3. Ibid., xxxv.

Chapter 37 *The Brothers Karamazov*

1. As quoted in Rowan Williams, *Dostoevsky: Language, Faith, and Fiction* (London: A & C Black, 2008), 34.
2. As quoted in Konstanin Mochulsky, *Dostoevsky: His Life and Work* (Princeton, NJ: Princeton University Press, 1971), 141.
3. As quoted in Joseph Frank, *Dostoevsky: The Mantle of the Prophet, 1871–1881* (Princeton, NJ: Princeton University Press, 2003), 712.
4. As quoted in Richard Freeborn, *Dostoevsky* (London: Haus Publishing, 2003), 125.
5. Fyodor Dostoyevsky, *The Brothers Karamazov* (New York: Macmillan, 1922), 339.

Chapter 38 La Sagrada Família Cathedral

1. As quoted in Tom Springer, *Looking for Hickories* (Ann Arbor: University of Michigan Press, 2008), 73.
2. As quoted in Josep Maria Carandell, *El Temple de la Sagrada Família* (Sant Lluis, Spain: Triangle Postals, 1997), 4.
3. Gijs van Hensbergen, *Gaudí: A Biography* (New York: HarperCollins, 2001), 138.
4. Ibid., 250.

Chapter 39 *Starry Night*

1. As quoted in Richard Thomson, *Vincent Van Gogh: The Starry Night* (New York: Museum of Modern Art, 2008), 44.
2. As quoted in Kathleen Powers Erickson, *At Eternity's Gate* (Grand Rapids: Eerdmans, 1998), 40.
3. Ibid., 56.
4. As quoted in Abraham Marie Hammacher, *Van Gogh: A Documentary Biography* (New York: Macmillan, 1982), 32.
5. As quoted in David Sweetman, *Van Gogh: His Life and His Art* (New York: Crown, 1990), 119.
6. As quoted in David Hampton, *Evangelical Disenchantment* (New Haven: Yale University Press, 2008), 129.
7. As quoted in Debora Silverman, *Van Gogh and Gauguin: The Search for Sacred Art* (New York: Macmillan, 2004), 173.
8. As quoted in Jan Greenberg and Sandra Jordan, *Vincent Van Gogh: Portrait of an Artist* (New York: Random House, 2009), 26.

Chapter 40 *The Complete Poems*

1. Emily Dickinson, *The Complete Poems of Emily Dickinson* (New York: Little, Brown, 1976), 433.
2. Ibid., 506.
3. As quoted in Harold Bloom, *Emily Dickinson* (New York: Infobase Publishing, 2008), 11.
4. Dickinson, *Complete Poems*, 100.
5. Ibid., 128.
6. Ibid., 14.
7. Ibid., 211.
8. Ibid., 153.
9. Ibid., 133.

Chapter 41 *The Life of Our Lord Jesus Christ*

1. James Jacques Joseph Tissot, *The Life of Our Savior Jesus Christ: Three Hundred and Sixty-Five Compositions from the Four Gospels with Notes and Explanatory Drawings*, translated by Mrs. Arthur Bell (New York: Werner, 1903), ix.

Chapter 42 *The Annunciation*

1. As quoted in Marcus Bruce,"A New Testament," *Henry Ossawa Tanner: Modern Spirit*, edited by Anna O. Marley (Philadelphia: Pennsylvania Academy of Fine Arts, 2012), 112.
2. Robert Cozzolino,"I Invited the Christ Spirit to Manifest in Me," in Marley, *Henry Ossawa Tanner: Modern Spirit*, 120.

Chapter 43 *The Innocence of Father Brown*

1. As quoted in J. Maurus, *Living Moments of Awareness* (Mumbai: St. Pauls Press, 2011), 45.
2. As quoted in Dale Ahlquist, *G. K. Chesterton: The Apostle of Common Sense* (San Francisco: Ignatius, 2003), 13.

3. G. K. Chesterton, *Orthodoxy* (New York: Dodd, Mead, and Co., 1954), 85.
4. Ibid., 57.

Chapter 44 *The Life of Christ*

1. As quoted in Ashley Bassie, *Expressionism* (New York: Parkstone International, 2014), 30.
2. As quoted in William B. Sieger, "Literary Texts and Formal Strategies in Emil Nolde's Religious Paintings," unpublished paper (Chicago: Northeastern Illinois University, n.d.), https://unomaha.app.box.com/s/m1aihl20an917jyhbeyrrau9ejm7b4z5.
3. As quoted in Peter Howard Selz, *German Expressionist Painting* (Oakland: University of California Press, 1968), 290.
4. As quoted in Jonathan Evens, "Emil Nolde: Inner Religious Feeling," *Between*, March 7, 2012, http://joninbetween.blogspot.com/2012/03/emil-nolde-inner-religious-feeling.html.
5. As quoted in Selz, *German Expressionist Painting*, 121.

Chapter 45 *Poems*

1. Gerard Manley Hopkins, *Mortal Beauty, God's Grace: Major Poems and Spiritual Writings of Gerard Manley Hopkins* (New York: Vintage Books, 2003), 20.
2. Ibid., 25.
3. Ibid., 21.
4. As quoted in Jerome Bump, *Gerard Manley Hopkins* (Woodbridge, CT: Twayne Publishers, 1982), 176.
5. Hopkins, *Mortal Beauty*, 47.
6. Ibid., 20.

Chapter 46 *The Resurrection at Cookham*

1. Adrian Glew, ed., *Stanley Spencer: Letters and Writings* (London: Tate Gallery, 2001), 164.
2. As quoted in Kenneth Pople, "The Cookham Resurrection by English Artist Stanley Spencer," *The Art and Vision of Stanley Spencer*, accessed March 20, 2015, http://www.ikpople.pwp.blueyonder.co.uk/cookres.htm.
3. As quoted in Kenneth Pople, *Stanley Spencer* (New York: HarperCollins, 1991), 309.
4. As quoted in Timothy Hyman and Patricia Wright, *Stanley Spencer* (London: Tate Publishing, 2001), 77.
5. As quoted in Fiona MacCarthy, *Stanley Spencer: An English Vision* (New Haven: Yale University Press, 1997), 47.
6. Ibid., 57.

Chapter 47 *Death Comes for the Archbishop*

1. As quoted in Ralph McInerny, *Some Catholic Writers* (South Bend, IN: St. Augustine's Press, 2007), 25.
2. Willa Cather, *Death Comes for the Archbishop* (New York: Knopf, 2011), 290.
3. Ibid., 19.
4. Ibid., 267.
5. As quoted in Joan Ross Acocella, *Willa Cather and the Politics of Criticism* (Lincoln: University of Nebraska, 2000), 9.
6. Willa Cather, *Willa Cather On Writing* (Lincoln: University of Nebraska, 1988), 27.
7. Cather, *Archbishop*, 50.
8. As quoted in Mildred R. Bennett, *The World of Willa Cather* (Lincoln: University of Nebraska Press, 1995), 135.

Chapter 48 *The Passion of Joan of Arc*

1. Carl Theodore Dreyer, *Dreyer in Double Reflection* (New York: Dutton, 1973), 47.
2. As quoted in Ann Lloyd and David Robinson, *Movies of the Silent Years* (Maryknoll, NY: Orbis, 1984), 122.

Chapter 49 *Head of Christ*

1. As quoted in Jose Maria Faerna, *Rouault* (New York: Cameo-Abrams, 1997), 12.
2. Ibid., 28.
3. As quoted in Frank and Dorothy Getlein, *Christianity in Modern Art* (Milwaukee: Bruce Publishing, 1961), 51.
4. Charlene Spretnak, *The Spiritual Dynamic in Modern Art* (New York: Palgrave Macmillan, 2014), 113.
5. As quoted in William A. Dyrness, *Rouault: A Vision of Suffering and Salvation* (Grand Rapids: Eerdmans, 1971), 53.
6. Ibid., 69.
7. Ibid., 79.
8. Ibid., 63.
9. Jacques Maritain, *Rouault* (New York: Abrams, 1954), 10.

Chapter 50 *The Power and the Glory*

1. As quoted in Adam Schwartz, *The Third Spring* (Washington, D.C.: CUA Press, 2005), 140.
2. As quoted in Norman Sherry, *The Life of Graham Greene*, vol. 3 (London: Jonathan Cape, 2004), 188.
3. Graham Greene, *Brighton Rock* (New York: Penguin, 1991), 246.

Chapter 51 *Quartet for the End of Time*

1. As quoted in Sander van Maas, *The Reinvention of Religious Music* (Bronx, NY: Fordham University, 2009), 26.
2. Charles Philip Dingle, ed., *Oliver Messiaen: Music, Art, and Literature* (London: Ashgate, 2007), 49.
3. Ibid., 14.

Chapter 52 *Four Quartets*

1. T. S. Eliot, *Four Quartets* (New York: Harcourt Brace and Company, 1943), 19.

Chapter 53 *The Man Born to Be King*

1. Dorothy L. Sayers, *The Man Born to Be King* (San Francisco: Ignatius Press, 1990), 180.
2. As quoted in Mary Brian Durkin, "Dorothy L. Sayers: A Christian Humanist for Today," *Religion Online*, accessed March 20, 2015, http://www.religion-online.org/showarticle.asp?title=1267.
3. Dorothy L. Sayers, *Letters to a Diminished Church* (Nashville: Thomas Nelson, 2004), 1.
4. Ibid., 4.
5. Sayers, *Man Born to Be King*, 16.
6. Sayers, *Diminished Church*, 46.

Chapter 54 *Rome, Open City*

1. Isabella Rossellini, *In the Name of the Father, the Daughter, and the Holy Spirits* (New York: Prestell, 2006), 117.

Chapter 55 *It's a Wonderful Life*

1. Frank Capra, *The Name Above the Title* (Boston: Da Capo Press, 1997), 241.
2. Ibid., 130.
3. Ibid., 375.

Chapter 56 "I Will Move On Up a Little Higher"

1. As quoted in Margena A. Christian, "Long Live the Divas," *The New Crisis* 106:1 (January/February 1999): 53.
2. As quoted in Bill Carpenter, *Uncloudy Day: The Gospel Music Encyclopedia* (Milwaukee: Hal Leonard, 2005), 208.

Chapter 57 The Chronicles of Narnia

1. C. S. Lewis, *Of Other Worlds* (New York: Harcourt, 1975), 42.
2. Ibid.
3. C. S. Lewis, *Surprised by Joy* (New York: Harcourt, 1955), 179.
4. Ibid., 229.
5. Ibid., 228–29.

Chapter 58 The Lord of the Rings

1. J. R. R. Tolkien, *The Monsters and the Critics* (New York: Houghton Mifflin, 1984), 156.
2. J. R. R. Tolkien, *The Letters of J. R. R. Tolkien*, edited by Humphrey Carpenter (New York: Houghton Mifflin, 1981), 194.
3. Ibid., 172.
4. J. R. R. Tolkien, *The Tolkien Reader* (New York: Houghton Mifflin, 1965), 5.
5. Tolkien, *Letters*, 144.

Chapter 59 *A Love Supreme*

1. As quoted in Ashley Kahn, *A Love Supreme* (New York: Penguin, 2003), 28.
2. Ibid., 68.
3. As quoted in Ben Ratliff, *Coltrane: The Story of a Sound* (New York: Macmillan, 2007), 109.

Chapter 60 *Au Hasard du Balthasar*

1. As quoted in James Quandt, ed., *Robert Bresson* (Bloomington: Indiana University Press, 1998), 489.
2. Robert Bresson, *Notes on the Cinematographer* (Los Angeles: Green Integer, 1997), 44.
3. Quandt, *Robert Bresson*, 494.
4. Ibid., 321.
5. As quoted in Joseph Cunneen, *Robert Bresson: A Spiritual Style in Film* (New York: Continuum, 2003), 164–65.

Chapter 61 *Andrei Rublev*

1. As quoted in Vadim Moroz, *Andrei Tarkovsky: About His Film Art* (Petersburg, VA: Frost Publishing, 2008), 63.
2. As quoted in Jeremy Mark Robinson, *The Sacred Cinema of Andrei Tarkovsky* (Kent, UK: Crescent Moon, 2007), 183.
3. As quoted in Moroz, *Andrei Tarkovsky*, 83.

Chapter 62 *Cancer Ward*

1. Aleksandr Solzhenitsyn, *Cancer Ward* (New York: Farrar, Straus, and Giroux, 1991), 523.
2. Ibid., 509.
3. As quoted in Edward E. Ericson Jr., *Solzhenitsyn: The Moral Vision* (Grand Rapids: Eerdmans, 1980), 48.
4. Joseph Pearce, "An Interview with Alexander Solzhenitsyn," *Catholic Education Resource Center*, 2003, http://www.catholiceducation.org/en/culture/literature/an-interview-with-alexander-solzhenitsyn.html.
5. As quoted in Ha Jin, *The Writer As Migrant* (Chicago: University of Chicago Press, 2008), 11.
6. Aleksandr Solzhenitsyn, *The Solzhenitsyn Reader: New and Essential Writings, 1947–2005*, edited by Edward Ericson Jr. and Daniel J. Mahoney (Wilmington, DE: ISI Books, 2006), 577.
7. As quoted in Daniel J. Mahoney, *Aleksandr Solzhenitsyn: The Ascent from Ideology* (New York: Rowman & Littlefield, 2001), 50.
8. Ericson, *Solzhenitsyn*, 16.
9. Ibid., 7.

Chapter 63 *At Folsom Prison*

1. As quoted in Leigh H. Edwards, *Johnny Cash and the Paradox of American Identity* (Bloomington: Indiana University Press, 2009), 157.

Chapter 64 *The Complete Stories*

1. Flannery O'Connor, *The Letters of Flannery O'Connor: The Habit of Being*, edited by Sally Fitzgerald (New York: Farrar, Straus, and Giroux, 1979), 275.
2. Flannery O'Connor, *Mystery and Manners* (New York: Farrar, Straus, and Giroux, 1962), 34.
3. Lorine M. Getz, *Flannery O'Connor: Literary Theologian* (Lewiston, NY: Edwin Mellen Press, 1999), 34.
4. Flannery O'Connor, *A Prayer Journal* (New York: Farrar, Straus, and Giroux, 2013), 21.
5. O'Connor, *Letters*, 92.
6. O'Connor, *Mystery and Manners*, 159.
7. Richard Giannone, "Introduction," in *Flannery O'Connor: Spiritual Writings*, edited by Robert Ellsberg (Maryknoll, NY: Orbis, 2003), 26.
8. O'Connor, *Letters*, 489.

Chapter 65 *Only Visiting This Planet*

1. "Larry Norman," Wikipedia.com, accessed March 23, 2015, http://en.wikipedia.org/wiki/Larry_Norman.
2. "Hallelujah, the 2013 National Recording Registry Reaches 400," *News from the Library of Congress*, April 2, 2014, http://www.loc.gov/today/pr/2014/14-052.html.
3. Sarah Pulliam, "Larry Norman, 'Father of Christian Rock,' Dies at 60," *Christianity Today*, February 26, 2008, http://www.christianitytoday.com/ct/2008/februaryweb-only/109-22.0.html.

Chapter 66 Symphony no. 3, *The Symphony of Sorrowful Songs*

1. "Henryk Górecki," Wikipedia.com, accessed March 23, 2015, http://en.wikipedia.org/wiki/Henryk_G%C3%B3recki.
2. "Sacred Music: Gorecki and Pärt," YouTube video, 58:44, posted by Art History Channel on February 9, 2013, https://www.youtube.com/watch?v=w-7C8c7oh1xc.

Chapter 67 *Dancing in the Dragon's Jaws*

1. Susan Adams Kauffman, "Fire in an Open Hand: An Interview with Bruce Cockburn," *The Other Side*, November/December 2009, as quoted by *The Cockburn Project*, http://cockburnproject.net/issues/personal/christianity.html.

Chapter 68 *The Second Coming*

1. Walker Percy, *Signposts in a Strange Land* (New York: Farrar, Straus, and Giroux, 1991), 154.
2. Ibid., 206.
3. Ibid., 162.
4. Ibid.
5. Ibid., 180.
6. Ibid., 221.

Chapter 69 *The Last Supper*

1. As quoted in Anne Pyle, *Printing the Word: The Art of Watanabe Sadao* (New York: American Bible Society, 2000), 25.
2. Ibid., 9.
3. Ibid., 15.
4. Ibid., 26.

Chapter 70 *Godric*

1. Frederick Buechner, *Godric* (New York: Harper and Row, 1980), 3.
2. Frederick Buechner, *Now and Then* (New York: Harper and Row, 1983), 106.
3. Buechner, *Godric*, 20.
4. Ibid., 96.
5. As quoted in Dale Brown, *The Book of Buechner* (Louisville: Westminster John Knox, 2006), 75.
6. Buechner, *Now and Then*, 87.
7. Frederick Buechner, *Wishful Thinking* (New York: Harper and Row, 1973), 20.

Chapter 71 *Infidels*

1. Jonathan Cott, *Bob Dylan: The Essential Interviews* (New York: Wenner Books, 2006), 396.

Chapter 72 *The Joshua Tree*

1. Cathleen Falsani, "Bono's American Prayer," *Christianity Today*, February 21, 2003, http://www.christianitytoday.com/ct/2003/march-web-only/2.38.html.
2. "Band FAQ," U2FAQs.com, accessed March 23, 2015, http://www.u2faqs.com/band/.
3. As quoted in Michka Assayas, *Bono* (New York: Riverhead, 2006), 203.
4. Ibid., 203–4.
5. Ibid., 204.
6. Jeremy Weber, "Six Surprises from Bono's Interview with Focus on the Family," *Christianity Today*, June 21, 3013, http://www.christianitytoday.com/gleanings/2013/june/bono-interview-with-focus-on-family-jim-daly.html?paging=off.

Chapter 73 *Paradise Garden*

1. J. F. Turner, *Howard Finster: Man of Visions* (New York: Knopf, 1989), 101.
2. As quoted in Robert Peacock with Annibel Jenkins, *Paradise Garden* (San Francisco: Chronicle Books, 1996), 31.
3. Turner, *Howard Finster*, 148.

Chapter 74 *The Four Holy Gospels*

1. Makoto Fujimura, "Gallery: The Four Gospels Frontispieces," *Makoto Fujimura*, accessed March 23, 2015, http://www.makotofujimura.com/works/the-four-gospels-frontispieces/.
2. Makoto Fujimura, *Refractions: A Journey of Faith, Art, and Culture* (Colorado Springs: NavPress, 2009), 70.
3. Thomas S. Hibbs, *Roualt/Fujimura: Soliloquies* (Baltimore: Square Halo, 2009), 32.
4. Makoto Fujimura, *River Grace* (New York: Poeima Press, 2007), 3.
5. Makoto Fujimura, *The Splendor of the Medium* (New York: Poiema Press, 2004), 4.
6. Fujimura, *River Grace*,16.
7. Ibid., 6.

For Further Exploration

A Selected Bibliography

General Books on Visual Art

Bell, Kathryn. *Our Christian Heritage in Art*. Greenville, SC: Bob Jones University Press, 1999.

Brown, Michelle P. *The Lion Companion to Christian Art*. Oxford: Lion, 2008.

Burkhardt, Titus. *The Foundations of Christian Art*. Bloomington, IN: World Wisdom Press, 2006.

Couchman, Judith. *The Art of Faith*. Brewster, MA: Paraclete Press, 2012.

de Borchgrave, Helen. *A Journey into Christian Art*. Minneapolis: Fortress Press, 1999.

Dillenberger, Jane. *Style and Content in Christian Art*. New York: Abingdon, 1965.

Getlein, Frank, and Dorothy Getlein. *Christianity in Modern Art*. Milwaukee: Bruce Publishing, 1961.

Morey, C. R. *Christian Art*. New York: W. W. Norton, 1935.

Newton, Eric, and William Neil. *2000 Years of Christian Art*. New York: Harper and Row, 1966.

Romaine, James. *Art as Spiritual Perception*. Wheaton: Crossway, 2012.

Rookmaaker, Hans. *Complete Works of Hans Rookmaaker in Five Volumes*. Carlisle, UK: Piquant, 2002.

General Books on Music

Dowley, Tim. *Christian Music: A Global History*. Minneapolis: Fortress Press, 2011.

Dubal, David. *The Essential Canon of Classical Music*. New York: North Point, 2001.

Kavanaugh, Patrick. *The Music of Angels*. Chicago: Loyola Press, 1999.

———. *The Spiritual Lives of Great Composers*. Nashville: Sparrow, 1992.

Mellers, Wilfrid. *Celestial Music? Some Masterpieces of European Religious Music*. Rochester, NY: Boydell Press, 2002.

Nicholas, Jeremy. *The Great Composers*. London: Quercus, 2007.

Smith, Jane Stuart, and Betty Carlson. *The Gift of Music*. Wheaton: Crossway, 1987.

Wilson-Dickson, Andrew. *The Story of Christian Music*. Minneapolis: Fortress Press, 1992.

General Books on Literature

Cowan, Louise, and Os Guinness. *Invitation to the Classics*. Grand Rapids: Baker, 1998.

Johnson, Paul. *Creators*. New York: Harper and Row, 2006.

Paglia, Camille. *Break, Blow, Burn*. New York: Pantheon, 2005.

Pearce, Joseph. *Literary Converts*. San Francisco: Ignatius Press, 1999.

Rollwer, Julia, ed. *25 Books Every Christian Should Read*. New York: HarperOne, 2011.

Schmidt, Michael. *Lives of the Poets*. New York: Random House, 1998.

———. *The Novel: A Biography*. Cambridge, MA: Harvard University Press, 2014.

General Books on Film

Bandy, Maria Lee, and Antonio Monda, eds. *The Hidden God: Film and Faith*. New York: Metropolitan Museum of Art, 2003.

Cawkwell, Tim. *The New Filmgoer's Guide to God*. Leicestershire, UK: Matador, 2014.

Cousins, Mark. *The Story of Film*. London: Pavillion, 2011.

Johnston, Robert K. *Reel Spirituality*. Grand Rapids: Baker, 2000.

Mast, Gerald. *A Short History of the Movies*. New York: Macmillan, 1992.

Morefield, Kenneth. *Faith and Spirituality in Masters of World Cinema*. Newcastle, UK: Cambridge Scholars Press, 2008.

Schrader, Paul. *Transcendental Style in Film: Ozu, Bresson, Dreyer*. New York: Da Capo Press, 1972.

Thomson, David. *The Big Screen: The Story of the Movies*. New York: Farrar, Straus, and Giroux, 2012.

———. *The New Biographical Dictionary of Film*. New York: Knopf, 2010.

Art of the Roman Catacombs

Johnson, Robin Margaret. *Understanding Early Christian Art*. New York: Routledge, 2000.

Lowden, John. *Early Christian and Byzantine Art*. London: Phaidon, 1997.

Lowrie, Walter. *Art in the Early Church*. New York: W. W. Norton, 1947.

The Book of Kells and Illuminated Manuscripts

The Book of Kells: The Work of Angels? DVD. Directed by Murray Grigor. Forked River, NJ: Kultur Video, 2001.

Brown, Peter, ed. *The Book of Kells*. London: Thames and Hudson, 1980.

de Hamel, Christopher. *A History of Illuminated Manuscripts*. London: Phaidon, 1994.

Walther, Ingo, and Norbert Wolf. *Masterpieces of Illumination*. Köln: Taschen, 2005.

Gregorian Chant

Foil, David. *Gregorian Chant and Polyphony*. New York: Black Dog Music Library, 1995.

Hourlier, Dom Jacques. *Reflections on the Spirituality of Gregorian Chant*. Brewster, MA: Paraclete Press, 1995.

Le Mee, Katharine. *Chant*. New York: Bell Tower, 1994.

Smith, Huston, ed. *Gregorian Chant: Songs of the Spirit*. San Francisco: KQED Books, 1996.

Chartres Cathedral and Gothic Cathedrals

Barron, Robert. *Heaven in Stone and Glass*. New York: Crossroad, 2000.

Branner, Robert. *Chartres Cathedral*. New York: W. W. Norton, 1969.

Ciaga, Graziella Leyla. *Cathedrals of the World*. New York: Metro Books, 2006.

Cook, William. *The Cathedral*. DVD. Chantilly, VA: The Teaching Company, 2010.

Miller, Malcolm. *Chartres Cathedral*. Andover, PA: Pitkin, 1996.

Ordo Virtutum, Hildegard of Bingen

Hildegard of Bingen. *Mystical Writings*. New York: Crossroad, 1993.

Hildegard von Bingen in Portrait: Ordo Virtutum. DVD. Directed by Michael Fields. Forked River, NJ: Kultur Video, 2008.

Jaoudi, Maria. *Medieval and Renaissance Spirituality*. Mahwah, NJ: Paulist Press, 2010.

Sukowa, Barbara. *Vision: From the Life of Hildegard von Bingen*. DVD. Directed by Margarethe von Trotta. New York: Zeitgeist Video, 2011.

Sainte-Chapelle and the Art of Stained Glass

Brown, Sarah. *Stained Glass: An Illustrated History*. London: Bracken Books, 1994.

de Finance, Laurence. *Sainte-Chapelle*. Paris: Itineraires du Patrimoine, 1999.

The Scrovegni Chapel, Giotto

Corrain, Lucia. *Giotto and Medieval Art*. New York: Peter Bedrick Books, 1995.

Stubblebine, James, ed. *Giotto: The Arena Chapel Frescoes*. New York: W. W. Norton, 1969.

Wolf, Norbert. *Giotto*. Köln: Taschen, 2006.

The Divine Comedy, Dante

Dante. *The Divine Comedy*. Translated by John Ciardi. New York: New American Library, 1970.

———. *Vita Nuova*. Translated by Mark Musa. Bloomington: Indiana University Press, 1973.

Holmes, George. *Dante*. Oxford: Oxford University Press, 1980.

The Holy Trinity Icon, Andrei Rublev

Beckett, Sister Wendy. *Real Presence: In Search of the Earliest Icons*. Maryknoll, NY: Orbis, 2010.

Haustein-Bartsch, Eva. *Icons*. Köln: Taschen, 2008.

Martin, Linette. *Sacred Doorways: A Beginner's Guide to Icons*. Brewster, MA: Paraclete Press, 2002.

Nouwen, Henri J. M. *Behold the Beauty of the Lord: Praying With Icons*. Notre Dame, IN: Ave Maria Press, 1987.

The Adoration of the Lamb, Jan van Eyck

Borchert, Till-Holger. *Van Eyck*. Köln: Taschen, 2008.

Charney, Noah. *Stealing the Mystic Lamb*. New York: Public Affairs, 2010.

The Four Horsemen of the Apocalypse, Albrecht Dürer

Forty, Sandra. *Albrecht Dürer*. Surrey, UK: TAJ Press, 2012.

Wolf, Norbert. *Dürer*. Köln: Taschen, 2006.

The Garden of Earthly Delights, Hieronymus Bosch

Belting, Hans. *Hieronymous Bosch: Garden of Earthly Delights*. London: Prestel, 2012.

Bosing, Walter. *Bosch*. Köln: Taschen, 2000.

The Ceiling of the Sistine Chapel, Michelangelo

Buonarrotti, Michaelangelo. *The Poems*. Translated by Christopher Ryan. London: Dent, 1996.

Graham-Dixon, Andrew. *Michelangelo and the Sistine Chapel*. New York: Skyhorse, 2009.

Gromling, Alexandra. *Michelangelo Buonarroti: Life and Work*. Konigswater: Konemann, 2005.

Neret, Giles. *Michelangelo*. Köln: Taschen, 2000.

Richmond, Robin. *Michelangelo and the Creation of the Sistine Chapel*. New York: Crescent Books, 1995.

"A Mighty Fortress Is Our God," Martin Luther

Bainton, Roland. *Here I Stand*. New York: New American Library, 1955.

Eggert, Kurt. "Martin Luther, God's Music Man." Lecture at Wisconsin Lutheran Seminary, November 10, 1983. http://www.wlsessays.net/node/465.

Oberman, Heiko. *Luther: The Man Between God and the Devil*. New York: Image Books, 1992.

The Procession to Calvary, Pieter Bruegel

Hagen, Rose-Marie, and Rainer Hagen. *Bruegel*. Köln: Taschen, 2000.

Hughes, Penelope Le Fanu. *Great Masters: Bruegel*. Edison, NJ: Chartwell, 2003.

Vohringer, Christian. *Pieter Bruegel*. Potsdam: H. F. Ullmann, 2013.

The Burial of the Count of Orgaz, El Greco

Bray, Xavier. *El Greco*. London: National Gallery Books, 2004.

Kasel, Ronda. *Sacred Spain: Art and Belief in the Spanish World*. Indianapolis: Indianapolis Museum of Art, 2009.

Romaine, James. "El Greco's Mystical Vision." *God Spy* (blog). October 22, 2003. http://oldarchive.godspy.com/culture/El-Grecos-Mystical-Vision.cfm.html.

Scholz-Hansel, Michael. *El Greco*. Köln: Taschen, 2004.

The Incredulity of Saint Thomas, Caravaggio

König, Eberhard. *Caravaggio*. Potsdam: H. F. Ullmann, 2013.

Lambert, Giles. *Caravaggio*. Köln: Taschen, 2000.

Prose, Francine. *Caravaggio: Painter of Miracles*. New York: HarperCollins, 2005.

The Holy Sonnets, John Donne

Donne, John. *John Donne: Selections from Divine Poems, Sermons, Devotions, and Prayers*. Edited by John Booty. New York: Paulist Press, 1990.

Kaveney, Roz. *How to Believe: John Donne*. London: Guardian Books, 2013.

The Temple, George Herbert

Herbert, George. *The Country Parson, The Temple*. New York: Paulist Press, 1981.

Piper, John. *Seeing Beauty and Saying Beautifully*. Wheaton: Crossway, 2014.

Agnus Dei, Francisco de Zurbarán

Alcolea, Santiago. *Zurbarán*. Barcelona: Editiones Poligrafa, 2008.

Kasel, Ronda, ed. *Sacred Spain: Art and Belief in the Spanish World*. Indianapolis: Indianapolis Museum of Art, 2009.

Wilson, William. "Zurbarán: The Pain of Spirituality." *Los Angeles Times*. October 4, 1987.

St. Teresa in Ecstasy, Bernini

Hibbard, Howard. *Bernini*. New York: Penguin, 1990.

MacDonnell, Joseph, S.J. "Chapter Two: Artistic Expression of Jesuit Values." http://faculty.fairfield.edu/jmac/sj/cj/cj2art.html. Excerpt from *Companions of Jesuits: A Tradition of Collaboration*. Fairfield, CT: Fairfield University, 1995.

The Return of the Prodigal Son, Rembrandt

Bockemühl, Michael. *Rembrandt*. Köln: Taschen, 2000.

Bonafoux, Pascal. *Rembrandt: Master of the Portrait*. New York: Abrams, 1992.

Dewitt, Lloyd, ed. *Rembrandt and the Face of Jesus*. Philadelphia: Philadelphia Museum of Art, 2011.

Durham, John I. *The Biblical Rembrandt*. Macon, GA: Mercer University Press, 2004.

Housden, Roger. *How Rembrandt Reveals Your Beautiful, Imperfect Self*. New York: Harmony Books, 2005.

Rosenberg, Jakob. *Rembrandt: Life and Work*. New York: Phaidon, 1964.

The Pilgrim's Progress, John Bunyan

Bunyan, John. *Grace Abounding to the Chief of Sinners*. New York: Penguin, 1987.

———. *The Pilgrim's Progress*. New York: Penguin, 2009.

Venables, Edmund. *The Life of John Bunyan*. Public domain eBook, n.d.

"When I Survey the Wondrous Cross," Isaac Watts; "Amazing Grace," John Newton

Bond, Douglas. *The Poetic Wonder of Isaac Watts*. Crawfordsville, IN: Reformation Trust, 2013.

Cook, Faith. *Our Hymn Writers and Their Hymns*. Faverdale North, UK: Evangelical Press, 2005.

Houghton, Elsie. *Classic Christian Hymn Writers*. Fort Washington, PA: CLC Publishing, 1982.

Ryden, Ernest Edwin. *The Story of Our Hymns*. Rock Island, IL: Augustana Book Concern, 1930.

Smith, Jane Stuart, and Betty Carlson. *Great Christian Hymn Writers*. Wheaton: Crossway, 1997.

Turner, Steve. *Amazing Grace: The Story of America's Most Beloved Song*. New York: HarperCollins, 2009.

Watts, Isaac. *A Short Essay Toward the Improvement of Psalmody*, 1707.

St. Matthew Passion, Johann Sebastian Bach

Greenburg, Robert. *Bach and the High Baroque*. DVD. Chantilly, VA: The Teaching Company, 1995.

Koopman, Ton, and the Amsterdam Baroque Orchestra and Choir. *Bach: Matthäus Passion*. DVD. Amersfoort, Netherlands: Challenge Classics, 2006.

Marschall, Rick. *Johann Sebastian Bach*. Nashville: Thomas Nelson, 2011.

Pelikan, Jaraslov. *Bach among the Theologians*. Philadelphia: Fortress Press, 1986.

Messiah, George Frideric Handel

Keates, Jonathan. *Handel: The Man and His Music*. New York: Random House, 2009.

Slover, Tim. *Messiah: The Little-Known Story of Handel's Beloved Oratorio*. Chicago: Silver Leaf Press, 2007.

Songs of Innocence and Experience, William Blake

Blake, William. *William Blake: A Selection of Poems and Letters*. New York: Penguin, 1958.

Langridge, Irene. *William Blake: A Study of His Life and Art Work*. London: Chiswick Press, 1904.

Muggeridge, Malcolm. *A Third Testament*. New York: Little, Brown, 1976.

Sagar, Keith. "William Blake: Songs of Innocence and Experience." http://www.keithsagar.co.uk/Blake/index.html.

The Creation, Franz Joseph Haydn

Greenburg, Robert. *Haydn: His Life and Music*. DVD. Chantilly, VA: The Teaching Company, 2000.

Hogwood, Christopher, Emma Kirby, Anthony Rolfe Johnson, and Michael George. *Haydn—The Creation: Orchestra of the Academy of Ancient Music*. DVD. Directed by Chris Hunt. London: Decca Classics, 2007.

Stapert, Calvin R. *Playing Before the Lord: The Life and Work of Joseph Haydn*. Grand Rapids: Eerdmans, 2014.

Pride and Prejudice, Jane Austen

Collins, Irene. *Jane Austen: The Parson's Daughter*. London: Continuum, 1998.

Giffin, Michael. *Jane Austen's Religious Imagination: A Balance of Reason and Feeling*. Kindle edition. Amazon Digital Services, 2013.

Glaspey, Terry, ed. *The Prayers of Jane Austen*. Eugene, OR: Harvest House, 2015.

Leithart, Peter J. *Jane Austen*. Nashville: Thomas Nelson, 2009.

Stovel, Bruce. "A Nation Improving in Religion." *Persuasions* no. 16. Jane Austen Society of North America, 1994. http://www.jasna.org/persuasions/printed/number16/stovel.htm.

The Wanderer above the Sea of Fog, Caspar David Friedrich

Rewald, Sabine. *The Romantic Vision of Caspar David Friedrich*. New York: Metropolitan Museum of Art, 1990.

Russo, Raffaella. *Friedrich*. London: Dorling Kindersley, 1999.

Vaughan, William. *Friedrich*. New York: Phaidon, 2004.

Wolf, Norbert. *Friedrich*. Köln: Taschen, 2003.

Symphony no. 5, *The Reformation*, Felix Mendelssohn

Lagomarsino, Tom. "Felix Mendelssohn." *Christian Reformed Ink Archives* (blog). March 15, 2011. https://christianreformedink.wordpress.com/2011/03/15/felix-mendelssohn/.

Wenborn, Neil. *Mendelssohn: His Life and Music*. New York: Naxos Books, 2008.

The Voyage of Life, Thomas Cole; *The Heart of the Andes*, Frederic Edwin Church

Baigell, Matthew. *Thomas Cole*. New York: Watson-Guptill, 1985.

Cooper, James F. *Knights of the Brush: The Hudson River School of Painting and the Moral Landscape*. New York: Hudson Hills Press, 1999.

Kelly, Franklin. *Frederic Edwin Church*. Washington, D.C.: National Gallery of Art, 1989.

Millhouse, Barbara Babcock. *American Wilderness: The Story of the Hudson River School of Painting*. Garden City, NY: Doubleday, 1978.

Ryan, James Anthony. *Frederic Church's Olana*. New York: Black Dome Press, 2001.

Veith, Gene Edward. *Painters of Faith: The Spiritual Landscape in Nineteenth Century America*. Washington, D.C.: Regnery, 2001.

The Light of the World, William Holman Hunt

Adams, Steven. *The Art of the Pre-Raphaelites*. London: Quintet, 1988.

des Cars, Laurence. *The Pre-Raphaelites: Romance and Realism*. New York: Abrams, 2000.

Lochnan, Katharine, and Carol Jacobi, eds. *Holman Hunt and the Pre-Raphaelite Vision*. Ontario, Canada: Art Gallery of Ontario, 2008.

Robinson, Michael. *The Pre-Raphaelites: Their Lives and Works in 500 Images*. Leistershire, UK: Lorenz Books, 2012.

Fairy Tales, George MacDonald

Hein, Roland. *The Harmony Within: The Spiritual Vision of George MacDonald*. Grand Rapids: Eerdmans, 1982.

MacDonald, George. *The Complete Fairy Tales*. London: Penguin, 1999.

Manlove, C. N. "George MacDonald's Fairy Tales: Their Roots in MacDonald's Thought," *Studies in Scottish Literature* 8:2. January 10, 1970. http://scholarcommons.sc.edu/ssl/vol8/iss2/12.

Phillips, Michael. *George MacDonald*. Minneapolis: Bethany House, 1987.

The Brothers Karamazov, Fyodor Dostoyevsky

Dostoyevsky, Fyodor. *The Brothers Karamazov*. New York: Farrar, Straus, and Giroux, 2002.

Dostoyevsky, Fyodor, Fritz Eichenberg, and Hutterian Brethren. *The Gospel in Dostoyevsky*. Farmington, PA: Plough Publications, 1988.

Frank, Joseph. *Dostoevsky: A Writer in His Time*. Princeton, NJ: Princeton University Press, 2009.

Gunn, Judith. *Dostoevsky: Dreamer and Prophet*. Oxford: Lion, 1990.

Mochulsky, Konstantin. *Dostoevsky: His Life and Work*. Princeton, NJ: Princeton University Press, 1971.

La Sagrada Família Cathedral, Antoni Gaudí

Boada, Isidro Puig, and Seiji Miyaguchi. *Antonio Gaudi*. DVD. Directed by Hiroshi Teshigahara. New York: Criterion Collection, 2008.

Crippa, Maria Antonietta. *Gaudi*. Köln: Taschen, 2007.

Ivereigh, Austen. "God's Architect." *America*. September 27, 2010.

Kuhl, Isabel. *50 Buildings You Should Know*. Munich: Prestel, 2007.

van Hensbergen, Gijs. *Gaudi: A Biography*. New York: HarperCollins, 2001.

Starry Night, Vincent van Gogh

Bernard, Bruce, ed. *Vincent by Himself: A Selection of His Paintings and Drawings Together with Extracts from His Letters*. New York: Barnes & Noble, 2004.

Bonafoux, Pascal. *Van Gogh: The Passionate Eye*. New York: Abrams, 1992.

Edwards, Cliff. *Van Gogh and God*. Chicago: Loyola University Press, 1989.

Erickson, Kathleen Powers. *At Eternity's Gate: The Spiritual Vision of Vincent van Gogh*. Grand Rapids: Eerdmans, 1998.

Naifeh, Steven, and Gregory White Smith. *Van Gogh: The Life*. New York: Random House, 2011.

Thomson, Richard. *Vincent van Gogh: The Starry Night*. New York: Museum of Modern Art, 2008.

Walther, Ingo F. *Van Gogh*. Köln: Taschen, 2000.

The Complete Poems, Emily Dickinson

Carpini, John Delli. *Emily Dickinson: Poetry as Prayer*. Boston: Pauline Books and Media, 2002.

Dickinson, Emily. *The Complete Poems of Emily Dickinson*. New York: Little, Brown, 1976.

Doyle, Connie. "Experiment in Green: Emily Dickinson's Search for Faith." The Dominican Friars of the Province of St. Albert the Great. http://opcentral.org/resources/2015/01/21/connie-doyle-experiment-in-green-emily-dickinsons-search-for-faith/.

LeMay, Kristin. *I Told My Soul to Sing: Finding God with Emily Dickinson*. Brewster, MA: Paraclete Press, 2013.

The Life of Our Lord Jesus Christ, James Tissot

Dolkart, Judith, ed. *James Tissot: The Life of Jesus*. New York: Brooklyn Museum/Merrill, 2009.

Muffs, Yochanan, and Gert Schiff. *James Tissot: Biblical Paintings*. New York: The Jewish Museum, 1982.

Warner, Malcolm. *Tissot*. London: Medici Society, 1982.

The Annunciation, Henry Ossawa Tanner

Bruce, Marcus. *Henry Ossawa Tanner: A Spiritual Biography*. New York: Crossroad, 2002.

Marley, Anna O., ed. *Henry Ossawa Tanner: Modern Spirit*. Philadelphia: Pennsylvania Academy of Fine Arts, 2012.

The Innocence of Father Brown, G. K. Chesterton

Chesterton, G. K. *The Penguin Complete Father Brown*. New York: Penguin, 1981.

Coren, Michael. *Gilbert: The Man Who Was G. K. Chesterton*. New York: Paragon House, 1990.

Dale, Alzina Stone. *The Outline of Sanity: A Life of G. K. Chesterton*. Grand Rapids: Eerdmans, 1982.

Peters, Thomas C. *Battling for the Modern Mind: A Beginner's Chesterton*. St. Louis, MO: Concordia, 1994.

The Life of Christ, Emil Nolde

Evens, Jonathan. "Emil Nolde: Inner Religious Feeling." *Between* (blog). March 7, 2012. http://joninbetween.blogspot.com/2012/03/emil-nolde-inner-religious-feeling.html.

Juneau-Lafond, Jean-David. "Emile Nolde," *The Art Tribune*. November 11, 2008.

Selz, Peter. *Emil Nolde*. New York: Museum of Modern Art, 1963.

Poems, Gerard Manley Hopkins

Hopkins, Gerard Manley. *Mortal Beauty, God's Grace: Major Poems and Spiritual Writings of Gerard Manley Hopkins*. New York: Vintage Books, 2003.

Lichtmann, Maria. *Gerard Manley Hopkins: Poetry as Prayer*. Boston: Pauline Books and Media, 2002.

Mariani, Paul. *Gerard Manley Hopkins: A Life*. New York: Viking, 2008.

White, Norman. *Hopkins: A Literary Biography*. Oxford: Clarendon Press, 1992.

The Resurrection at Cookham, Stanley Spencer

Cottrell, Stephen. *Christ in the Wilderness*. London: SPCK, 2012.

Harries, Richard. "Understanding Faith Through the Eyes of Stanley Spencer—The Rt Revd Lord Richard Harries." Lecture at Gresham College, March 16, 2011. YouTube video. 1:00:05. Uploaded on August 26, 2011 by GreshamCollege. https://www.youtube.com/watch?v=PhHRFyrEteE.

Hauser, Kitty. *Stanley Spencer*. London: Tate Publishing, 2001.

MacCarthy, Fiona. *Stanley Spencer: An English Vision*. New Haven: Yale University Press, 1997.

Death Comes for the Archbishop, Willa Cather

Birzer, Bradley J. "The Christian Humanism of Willa Cather." *The Imaginative Conservative* (blog). August 27, 2013. http://www.theimaginative-conservative.org/2013/08/the-christian-human-ism-of-willa-cather.html.

Brown, E. K. *Willa Cather*. New York: Avon Books, 1953.

Cather, Willa. *Death Comes for the Archbishop*. New York: Vintage, 1990.

McInerny, Ralph. *Some Catholic Writers*. South Bend, IN: St. Augustine's Press, 2007.

Ryan, James Emmett. *Faithful Passages: American Catholicism in Literary Culture, 1844–1931*. Madison: University of Wisconsin Press, 2013.

The Passion of Joan of Arc, Carl Theodore Dreyer

Carl Th. Dreyer: My Metier. DVD. Directed by Torben Skjødt Jensen. New York: Criterion Collection, 2001.

Dreyer, Carl Theodore. *Jesus: A Great Filmmaker's Final Masterwork*. New York: Dell, 1971.

Falconetti, Renee. *The Passion of Joan of Arc*. DVD. Directed by Carl Theodor Dreyer. New York: Criterion Collection, 1999.

Garrett, Daniel. "The Evidence of Things Not Seen." *Cinetext*. March 28, 2006. http://cinetext.philo.at/magazine/garrett/joanofarc.html.

Hamaker, Christian. "The Spiritual Cinema of Carl Theodor Dreyer." *Crosswalk*. December 5, 2001. http://www.crosswalk.com/1134400/.

Head of Christ, Georges Rouault

Dyrness, William A. *Rouault: A Vision of Suffering and Salvation*. Grand Rapids: Eerdmans, 1971.

Faerna, Jose Maria. *Rouault*. New York: Cameo-Abrams, 1997.

Flora, Holly, and Soo Yun Kang. *Miserere et Guerre: The Anguished World of Shadows*. New York: Museum of Biblical Art, 2006.

Maritain, Jacques. *Rouault*. New York: Abrams, 1954.

The Power and the Glory, Graham Greene

Giffin, Michael. *Graham Greene's Catholic Novels*. Kindle edition. Amazon Digital Services, 2013.

Greene, Graham. *The Power and the Glory*. New York: Penguin, 1978.

Jacobi, Derek, and Bill Nighy. *Dangerous Edge: A Life of Graham Greene*. DVD. Directed by Thomas P. O'Connor. Arlington, VA: PBS Videos, 2013.

Sherry, Norman. *The Life of Graham Greene* (3 vols.). Toronto: Lester and Orpen Denneys, 1989–2004.

Tengo, Alex. *Graham Greene: Bipolar Catholic*. Kindle edition. Amazon Australia Services, 2013.

Quartet for the End of Time, Olivier Messiaen

Bannister, Peter. "Olivier Messiaen—'Plain Old Propaganda'?" *Thinking Faith* (blog). December 10, 2008. http://www.thinkingfaith.org/articles/20081210_1.htm.

Osborne, Steven. "Olivier Messiaen: Beyond Time and Space." *The Guardian*. August 7, 2014.

Shenton, Andrew, ed. *Messiaen the Theologian*. London: Ashgate, 2010.

Four Quartets, T. S. Eliot

Ackroyd, Peter. *T. S. Eliot: A Life*. New York: Simon and Schuster, 1984.

Booty, John. *Meditating on Four Quartets*. Cambridge, MA: Cowley Publications, 1983.

Dale, Alzina Stone. *T. S. Eliot: The Philosopher Poet*. Wheaton: Harold Shaw, 1988.

Eliot, T. S. *Four Quartets*. New York: Harcourt, Brace, and Company, 1943.

———. *Selected Prose of T. S. Eliot*. New York: Harcourt, Brace, Jovanovich, 1975.

Gordon, Lyndall. *Eliot's New Life*. New York: Farrar, Straus, and Giroux, 1988.

The Man Born to Be King, Dorothy L. Sayers

Durkin, Mary Brian. "Dorothy L. Sayers: A Christian Humanist for Today." *Religion Online*. Accessed March 20, 2015. http://www.religion-online.org/showarticle.asp?title=1267.

Godfrey, Monica. "*The Man Born to Be King*: Contextualizing the Kingdom." *Inklings Forever* vol. 7. 2010. http://library.taylor.edu/dotAsset/c95cbdf7-0d3e-497f-9d33-0dd3dde0c4ad.pdf.

Meilander, Gilbert. "The Greatest Drama Ever." *Touchstone*. March/April 2013.

Reynolds, Barbara. *Dorothy L. Sayers: Her Life and Soul*. New York: St. Martin's Press, 1993.

Sayers, Dorothy L. *Letters to a Diminished Church*. Nashville: Thomas Nelson, 2004.

———. *The Man Born to Be King*. San Francisco: Ignatius Press, 1990.

Rome, Open City, Roberto Rossellini

Gallagher, Tag. *The Adventures of Roberto Rossellini*. San Francisco: Da Capo, 1998.

Morefield, Kenneth. "Roberto Rossellini and the Moral Point of View." *Christianity Today*. May 13, 2013. http://www.christianitytoday.com/ct/2013/may-web-only/roberto-rossellini-and-moral-point-of-view.html.

Roberto Rossellini's War Trilogy. DVD. Directed by Roberto Rossellini. New York: Criterion Collection, 2009.

It's a Wonderful Life, Frank Capra

Blake, Richard A. *After Image: The Indelible Catholic Imagination of Six American Filmmakers*. Chicago: Loyola Press, 2000.

Capra, Frank. *The Name Above the Title*. Boston: Da Capo Press, 1997.

de Las Carreras Kuntz, Maria Elena. "The Catholic Vision of Frank Capra." *Crisis Magazine*. February 1, 2002. http://www.crisismagazine.com/2002/the-catholic-vision-of-frank-capra-2.

Schickel, Richard. *Frank Capra: A Life in Film*. New York: New World City, 2011.

Stewart, James, Donna Reed, and Lionel Barrymore. *It's a Wonderful Life*. DVD. Directed by Frank Capra. Hollywood: Paramount Home Entertainment, 2007.

"I Will Move On Up a Little Higher," Mahalia Jackson

Jackson, Mahalia. *Mahalia Jackson: The Power and the Glory*. Directed by Jeff Scheftel. DVD. Santa Monica, CA: Xenon Pictures, 2003.

The Story of Gospel Music: The Power in the Voice. Directed by James Marsh and Andrew Dunne. DVD. London: BBC Warner, 1996.

Willman, Chris. "How Gospel Great Mahalia Jackson Gave Wing to MLK's 'I Have a Dream' Speech." *Yahoo Music*. January 18, 2015. https://www.yahoo.com/music/how-gospel-great-mahalia-jackson-gave-wing-to-108223937471.html.

The Chronicles of Narnia, C. S. Lewis

Glaspey, Terry. *Not a Tame Lion: The Spiritual Legacy of C. S. Lewis*. Elkton, MD: Highland Books, 1996.

Jacobs, Alan. *The Narnian: The Life and Imagination of C. S. Lewis*. New York: HarperOne, 2005.

Lewis, C. S. *Surprised by Joy*. New York: Harcourt, 1955.

McGrath, Alister. *C. S. Lewis: A Life*. Carol Stream, IL: Tyndale, 2013.

Sayer, George. *Jack: C. S. Lewis and His Times*. New York: Harper and Row, 1988.

The Lord of the Rings, J. R. R. Tolkien

Carpenter, Humphrey, ed. *The Letters of J. R. R. Tolkien*. New York: Houghton Mifflin, 1981.

———. *Tolkien: The Authorized Biography*. New York: Houghton Mifflin, 1978.

Duriez, Colin. *The J. R. R. Tolkien Handbook*. Grand Rapids: Baker, 1992.

Purtill, Richard. *J. R. R. Tolkien: Myth, Morality, and Religion*. San Francisco: Harper and Row, 1984.

A Love Supreme, John Coltrane

Bergerot, Frank, and Arnaud Merlin. *The Story of Jazz: Bop and Beyond*. New York: Abrams, 1991.

Kahn, Ashley. *A Love Supreme*. New York: Penguin, 2003.

Au Hasard du Balthasar, Robert Bresson

Bresson, Robert. *Notes on the Cinematographer*. Los Angeles: Green Integer, 1997.

Cunneen, Joseph. *Robert Bresson: A Spiritual Style in Film*. New York: Continuum, 2003.

Pipolo, Tony. *Robert Bresson: A Passion for Film*. New York: Oxford University Press, 2010.

Au Hasard du Balthasar. DVD. Directed by Robert Bresson. New York: Criterion Collection, 2005.

Andrei Rublev, Andrei Tarkovsky

Bird, Robert. *Andrei Rublev*. London: British Film Institute, 2004.

Gianvito, John, ed. *Andrei Tarkovsky: Interviews*. Jackson: University of Mississippi Press, 2006.

Martin, Sean. *Andrei Tarkovsky*. Harpenden, UK: Pocket Essentials, 2005.

Moroz, Vadim. *Andrei Tarkovsky: About His Film Art*. Petersburg, VA: Frost Publishing, 2008.

Robinson, Jeremy. *Andrei Tarkovsky*. Kent, UK: Crescent Moon, 2010.

Solonitsyn, Anatoliy, and Ivan Lapikov. *Andrei Rublev*. DVD. Directed by Andrei Tarkovsky. New York: Criterion Collection, 1999.

Tarkovsky, Andrei. *The Diaries, 1970–1986*. London: Verso, 1993.

———. *Sculpting in Time*. Austin: University of Texas, 1986.

Cancer Ward, Aleksandr Solzhenitsyn

Ericson, Edward E., Jr. *Solzhenitsyn: The Moral Vision*. Grand Rapids: Eerdmans, 1980.

Nielsen, Niels C., Jr. *Solzhenitsyn's Religion*. Nashville: Thomas Nelson, 1975.

Scammell, Michael. *Solzhenitsyn: A Biography*. New York: W. W. Norton, 1984.

Solzhenitsyn, Aleksandr. *Cancer Ward*. New York: Farrar, Straus, and Giroux, 1991.

———. *The Solzhenitsyn Reader: New and Essential Writings, 1947–2005*. Edited by Edward Ericson Jr. and Daniel J. Mahoney. Wilmington, DE: ISI Books, 2006.

At Folsom Prison, Johnny Cash

Cash, Johnny. *Man in Black*. Grand Rapids: Zondervan, 1975.

Hilburn, Robert. *Johnny Cash: The Life*. New York: Little, Brown, 2013.

Rather, Dan. *The Gospel Music of Johnny Cash*. DVD. Nashville: Spring House, 2007.

Streissguth, Michael. *Johnny Cash at Folsom Prison: The Making of a Masterpiece*. San Francisco: Da Capo, 2004.

Urbanski, Dave. *The Man Comes Around: The Spiritual Journey of Johnny Cash*. Lake Mary, FL: Relevant Books, 2003.

The Complete Stories, Flannery O'Connor

Elie, Paul. *The Life You Save May Be Your Own: An American Pilgrimage*. New York: Farrar, Straus, and Giroux, 2003.

Gooch, Brad. *Flannery: A Life of Flannery O'Connor*. New York: Little, Brown, 2009.

O'Connor, Flannery. *The Complete Stories*. New York: Farrar, Straus, and Giroux, 1971.

———. *The Letters of Flannery O'Connor: The Habit of Being*. Edited by Sally Fitzgerald. New York: Farrar, Straus, and Giroux, 1979.

———. *Mystery and Manners*. New York: Farrar, Straus, and Giroux, 1962.

———. *A Prayer Journal*. New York: Farrar, Straus, and Giroux, 2013.

Only Visiting This Planet, Larry Norman

Howard, Jay R., and John M. Streck. *Apostles of Rock*. Lexington: University of Kentucky Press, 1999.

Stowe, David W. *No Sympathy for the Devil*. Chapel Hill: University of North Carolina Press, 2011.

———."Only Visiting This Planet." National Recording Preservation Board of the Library of Congress. 2013. http://www.loc.gov/rr/record/nrpb/registry/essays/only%20visiting.pdf.

Symphony no. 3, *The Symphony of Sorrowful Songs*, Henryk Górecki

Cary, Christopher W. *Henryk Gorecki's Spiritual Awakening and Its Socio-Political Context*. Master's thesis. Gainesville: University of Florida Press, 2005.

Thomas, Adrien. *Gorecki*. Oxford: Clarendon Press, 1997.

London Sinfonietta. *The Symphony of Sorrowful Songs*. DVD. Directed by Tony Palmer. Tyne & Wear, England: Voiceprint Records, 2007.

Dancing in the Dragon's Jaws, Bruce Cockburn

Bruce Cockburn: Pacing the Cage. DVD. Directed by Joel Goldberg. Burlington, Canada: True North, 2013.

Cockburn, Bruce. *Rumours of Glory*. New York: HarperOne, 2014.

Heald, James. *World of Wonders*. Missing Link Records (CreateSpace Independent Publishing Platform), 2012.

Middleton, J. Richard, and Brian J. Walsh."Theology at the Rim of the Broken Wheel," *Grail* no. 9. June 1993.

My Beat: The Life and Times of Bruce Cockburn. DVD. Directed by Nadine Pequeneza. Toronto: Title House, 2001.

Walsh, Brian. *Kicking at the Darkness*. Grand Rapids: Brazos, 2011.

The Second Coming, Walker Percy

Elie, Paul. *The Life You Save May Be Your Own: An American Pilgrimage*. New York: Farrar, Straus, and Giroux, 2003.

Percy, Walker. *Signposts in a Strange Land*. New York: Farrar, Straus, and Giroux, 1991.

———. *The Second Coming*. New York: Picador, 1980.

Tolson, Jay. *Pilgrim in the Ruins: A Life of Walker Percy*. New York: Simon and Schuster, 1992.

Walker Percy: A Documentary Film. DVD. Directed by Win Riley. New Orleans: Winston Riley Productions, 2010.

The Last Supper, Sadao Watanabe

Bowden, Sandra et al. *Beauty Given by Grace: The Biblical Prints of Sadao Watanabe*. Baltimore: Square Halo Press, 2013.

Pyle, Anne. *Printing the Word: The Art of Watanabe Sadao*. New York: American Bible Society, 2000.

Ryan, Antonio."The Art of Sadao Watanabe." *National Catholic Reporter*. December 24, 2004.

Godric, Frederick Buechner

Brown, Dale. *The Book of Buechner*. Louisville: Westminster John Knox, 2006.

Buechner, Frederick. *Buechner*. DVD. Produced by Molly Collins Phelps and Rob Collins. Richmond, VA: New Life Films, 2007.

———. *Godric*. New York: Harper and Row, 1980.

———. *Now and Then*. New York: Harper and Row, 1983.

McCoy, Marjorie Casebrier. *Frederick Buechner: Novelist and Theologian of the Lost and Found*. New York: Harper and Row, 1988.

Infidels, Bob Dylan

Dylan, Bob, and Rubin "Hurricane" Carter. *Bob Dylan 1975–1981: Rolling Thunder and the Gospel Years*. DVD. Directed by Joel Gilbert. Pottstown, PA: MVD Visual, 2006.

Dylan, Bob, and Jerry Wexler. *Inside Bob Dylan's Jesus Years: Busy Being Born… Again!* DVD. Directed by Joel Gilbert. Pottstown, PA: MVD Visual, 2008.

Gilmour, Michael. *The Gospel According to Bob Dylan*. Louisville: Westminster John Knox, 2011.

Heylin, Clifton. *Bob Dylan Behind the Shades*. New York: Summit Books, 1991.

Marshall, Scott. *Restless Pilgrim: The Spiritual Journey of Bob Dylan*. Lake Mary, FL: Relevant Books, 2002.

Sounes, Howard. *Down the Highway: The Life of Bob Dylan*. New York: Grove Press, 2001.

Webb, Stephen H. *Dylan Redeemed*. New York: Continuum, 2006.

The Joshua Tree, U2

Assayas, Michka. *Bono*. New York: Riverhead, 2006.

Editors of Rolling Stone. *U2: The Rolling Stone Files*. New York: Hyperion, 1994.

Rothman, Joshua. "The Church of U2." *The New Yorker*. September 16, 2014.

Scharen, Christian. *One Step Closer: Why U2 Matters to Those Seeking God*. Grand Rapids: Brazos, 2006.

Stockman, Steve. *Walk On: The Spiritual Journey of U2*. Lake Mary, FL: Relevant Books, 2001.

Paradise Garden, Howard Finster

Peacock, Robert, with Annibel Jenkins. *Paradise Garden*. San Francisco: Chronicle Books, 1996.

Riley, Betsy. "Paradise Regained." *Atlanta Monthly*. June 2013.

Turner, J. F. *Howard Finster: Man of Visions*. New York: Knopf, 1989.

The Four Holy Gospels, Makoto Fujimura

Fujimura, Makoto. *Golden Sea*. New York: Dillon Gallery Press, 2013.

———. *Refractions: A Journey of Faith, Art, and Culture*. Colorado Springs: NavPress, 2009.

———. *River Grace*. New York: Poeima Press, 2007.

———. *The Splendor of the Medium*. New York: Poeima Press, 2004.

Hibbs, Thomas S. *Rouault/Fujimura: Soliloquies*. Baltimore: Square Halo, 2009.

The Tree of Life, Terrence Malick

Kierstein, Benjamin. *The Beautiful Light: A Contemplation of Terrence Malick*. Kindle edition. Amazon Digital Services, 2014.

Leithart, Peter J. *Shining Glory: Theological Reflections on Terrence Malick's Tree of Life*. Eugene, OR: Cascade Books, 2013.

Maher, Paul Jr. *One Big Soul: An Oral History of Terrence Malick*, third edition. lulu.com, 2014.

Michaels, Lloyd. *Terrence Malick*. Chicago: University of Illinois Press, 2009.

Pitt, Brad, Sean Penn, and Jessica Chastain. *The Tree of Life*. DVD. Directed by Terrence Malick. Los Angeles: Twentieth Century Fox, 2011

"What comes into our minds when we think about God is the most important thing about us."

—A.W. Tozer

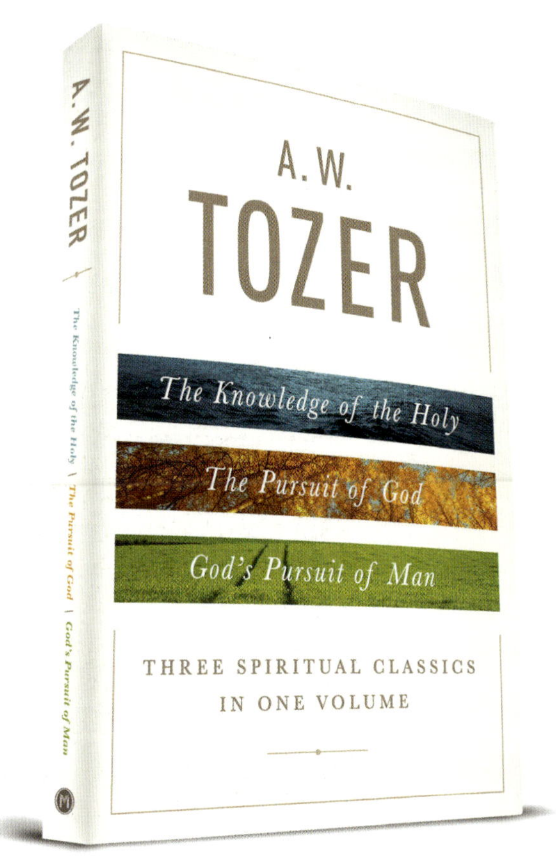

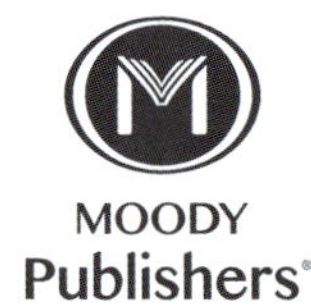

MOODY
Publishers

From the Word ***to Life***

Considered to be Tozer's greatest works, *Knowledge of the Holy*, *The Pursuit of God*, and *God's Pursuit of Man* are now available in a single volume. Discover a God of breathtaking majesty and world-changing love, and find yourself worshipping through every page.

978-0-8024-1861-6 | also available as an eBook